Best Places to Stay in Mexico

The Best Places to Stay Series

Best Places to Stay in America's Cities
Kenneth Hale-Wehmann, Editor

Best Places to Stay in Asia
Jerome E. Klein

Best Places to Stay in California
Anne E. Wright

Best Places to Stay in the Caribbean
Bill Jamison and Cheryl Alters Jamison

Best Places to Stay in Florida
Christine Davidson

Best Places to Stay in Hawaii
Kim Grant

Best Places to Stay in Mexico
Lawrence Foster and Lynn V. Foster

Best Places to Stay in the Mid-Atlantic States
Dana Nadel Foley

Best Places to Stay in the Midwest
John Monaghan

Best Places to Stay in New England
Christina Tree and Kim Grant

Best Places to Stay in the Pacific Northwest
Marilyn McFarlane

Best Places to Stay in the Rockies
Roger Cox

Best Places to Stay in the South
Carol Timblin

Best Places to Stay in the Southwest
Anne E. Wright

Best Places to Stay in Mexico

Lawrence Foster and
Lynn V. Foster

Bruce Shaw, Editorial Director

Fifth Edition

HOUGHTON MIFFLIN COMPANY
BOSTON • NEW YORK

For information about permission to reproduce selections from this book,
write to Permissions, Houghton Mifflin Company, 215 Park Avenue South,
New York, New York 10003.

Fifth Edition

ISSN: 1048-5449
ISBN: 0-618-00536-6

Printed in the United States of America

Maps by Charles Bahne
Design by Robert Overholtzer

This book was prepared in conjunction with Harvard Common Press.

QUM 10 9 8 7 6 5 4 3 2 1

Contents

What's What

Best Places to Stay in Mexico

Making Mexico Magical

Many people who go to Mexico focus on the wrong hazards. They worry about getting sick, about language difficulties, about safety. These are legitimate concerns in almost any foreign country, but usually they can be managed in Mexico in simple ways, as we explain in "Ten Tips to Bliss." A much greater danger is getting seriously shortchanged before leaving home.

The modern tourism industry is not oriented to individual interests and personal styles. It's devoted to a mass-production process that turns out vacations with as much distinctive flavor as a chain supermarket. Unless you have firm ideas about where you want to go and where you want to stay, you may get sent where the computers need to fill a space. When that happens, Mexico is not likely to seem magical, and your vacation may not be much of a value, even if you think you are saving money.

Mexico is a vast and complex country. The many destinations differ enormously from one another. Some will fit your particular needs like a fantasy, and others will flop flatter than a tortilla. Hotels are equally varied. You can stay under a thatched roof and sleep in a hammock or opt for a flashy high-rise that would humiliate the towers of Honolulu. You can have a golf course at your door, a coral reef off your shore, a colonial cathedral framed in the window, or, if you don't plan carefully, nothing outside your room except a tumultuous street filled with buses belching fumes.

As with any popular area in the age of mass tourism, Mexico is magical for you only when you make it so. The key is matching your interests, personality, and budget with your choices of *where to go* and *where to stay*. This book is designed specifically for that purpose. It's a guide to great getaways in Mexico, not a conventional handbook summarizing every spot you might want to see if you had two years to wander. Our focus is deliberately selective so that we can provide the full and relevant information you need to decide on destinations and accommodations that will suit you.

The first step in a memorable trip is a careful consideration of which resort areas or cities to visit. We organize the best options into four broad regions: the "Mayan Riviera" along the Caribbean coast, the "Mexican Riviera" along the Pacific, the heartland in the country's interior, and Baja California. We concentrate on destinations that attract North American travelers and also offer distinctive places to stay, passing over some cities of limited interest and others where none of the hotels stand out as special. Our descriptions avoid an overload of detail on minor matters to make sure we are clear about the things that count, which are the main reasons to consider visiting. Instead of cataloguing all the things you might want to do after you arrive, as the general guidebooks do, we try to help you figure out whether you want to go in the first place.

After choosing your destinations, you should devote equal attention to accommodations. We cover the most distinctive hotels and inns in each city in all price ranges. The reports are as thorough and current as possible, dealing with factors such as location, cost, recreation, services, food, ambience, and, most importantly, the style of experience offered. In each chapter we classify the selected accommodations into the following ten categories based on the crux of their appeal.

Best Romantic Hideaways

Mexico is inherently and passionately romantic. These places capture that spirit in a variety of wonderful ways and offer it to guests with experienced élan. Ranging from exclusive resorts to a "camptel," they vary in price but not in escapist allure. Though each speaks of romance in its own separate tongue, each is sublime when the language is your own.

Best Hotels for Stylish Sophistication

Creating a standard luxury hotel today is simple. Formulas abound. These resort and urban establishments go beyond the formulas, providing frills with deft finesse. Their combination of elegance and overall excellence earns them international distinction.

Best Recreational Resorts and Spas

If you travel for play or pampering, Mexico satisfies in multiple ways. These recommendations vary considerably in style — from polished country club resort hotels to lively Club Meds — but each features extensive sports or spa facilities, and each caters well to its own crowd.

Best Comfort Choices for All-American Abundance

The most popular resort hotels in Mexico are large, luxurious in a familiar fashion, and full of energy. They specialize in the kind of all-American abundance that has a broad appeal for *norteamericano* visitors, from singles to families. Among the multitude of such places, our recommendations stand out in a variety of different ways. Pick your pleasures appropriately and you'll enjoy a spirited getaway.

Best Beachfront Buys

When you want a lot for a little on a beach, these hotels are likely to delight. Usually smaller and more Mexican in character than the pricey all-American resorts that share the shore, they approach a similar level of comfort and fun at a more moderate rate. None of the choices is cheap in any sense of the term, but each provides a combination of beachfront location and value that's hard to top — in Mexico or anywhere else.

Best Intimate and Affordable Inns

For cozy charm and casual elegance, these small hotels and inns are some of the most enchanting places to stay in Mexico. Generally in the interior, they feature polish without pretension at a reasonable price. All offer some qualities that should shame the large resorts.

Best Bargains for Mexican Character

These small hotels and inns hark back to the days before mass tourism. Although they vary in price from dirt cheap to moderate, each is a bargain for authentic Mexican allure. In some cases quaintness may border on eccentricity, but you can always count on a special sense of local character.

Best B&Bs and Budget Inns

B&Bs are less common in Mexico than in the United States, but the ones that exist usually exude charm, personality, and good value. The same is true of the inns we include here, *posadas simpáticas* with a homey feeling. Many of the recommendations sit on or near a fabulous beach, and the others enjoy prime locations in the interior.

Best Adventure Retreats

Mexico brims with natural and archaeological adventures, from hiking in the Copper Canyon to probing Mayan mysteries. These hideaway havens, secluded in splendor, allow you to take full advantage of the opportunities.

Best Places to Combine Business and Pleasure

All major cities and resort areas in Mexico have some hotels that cater equally well to business and pleasure travelers. Our selections offer a range of leisure diversions, a convenient location, and an array of business services, from fax machines to meeting space. Each has a professional and helpful staff, including people who speak English well.

The last part of the book, "What's What," summarizes all our recommendations across the country in each of these various styles, allowing you to compare similar places to stay in different destinations. Additional chapters in this section also identify the top spots nationwide for other special interests, including superior overall quality, the finest beach locations, and the best bargains.

We selected the accommodations for the book on the basis of personal research, but not because they are necessarily personal favorites. Our job, as we see it, is not to tell you what we like but to serve as consumer advocates, helping you make an informed choice for yourself. We try to describe a place's intentions objectively and evaluate the execution instead of the concept.

While we have sought to keep our personal values out of the recommendations, some biases are certainly evident. We have omitted plenty of hotels — including some with well-known names — that strike us as ugly, sloppy in standards, overpriced, too bulky for their surroundings, or otherwise inhospitable. Unlike some guides, *no one paid to be in the book.*

Many of Mexico's millions of visitors last year ended up in places we wouldn't send our local meter maid. Many others went to Cancún looking for Mexican character or to Los Cabos for tropical luxuriance. They tithed their annual income for a getaway that got away from them. Don't let it happen to you. Do your homework before you go.

Mexico can spin more delightful spells than Merlin imagined possible. Despite the peccadilloes of the tourism industry, it's still a land of mythic dreams and exotic realities, a country that makes the Disney empire seem like a dullard's whimsy. The enchantment can be yours with a couple of careful choices about *where to go and where to stay.*

Rack Rates, Packages, and Seasons

Whenever possible, the hotel prices quoted in the book are the 2000 "rack rates." The term derives from days when hotels published their prices to travel agents in brochures that were intended to be displayed on racks in the agent's office. The technology has changed dramatically, but the old term has survived to signify a hotel's official retail charge per day.

What you will actually pay is almost certain to be different from the figures we cite, for several reasons. First, rates are always subject to change. Normally that happens only once or twice a year at most, but new situations can produce unpredictable patterns.

A second variable is the number of people in your party. To keep the rate information as simple and consistent as possible, we quote only the price for double occupancy. If you are traveling alone or with more than two people, usually there will be some adjustment up or down. Children are often an exception, though. Many hotels allow young kids, or even older teenagers, to stay free in the room with their parents, a policy we note when applicable.

Other variables are currency fluctuations and the 12 percent to 17 percent government tax. Some places incorporate the tax into the rack rate, but the majority add it to the bill, especially at the resorts — make sure you ask if it is included or not. Most chain hotels now calculate their charges in U.S. dollars to avoid the impact of shifts in the value of the Mexican peso, but that isn't true of many smaller, less expensive inns.

The good news is that the rack rate, except at small hotels, is usually higher than what you will pay. The official tariff is likely to be flexible in slow periods, subject to a little polite bargaining. Even during the busy winter season, the resorts reduce the official rate for stays longer than one night and urban hotels often have lower corporate rates during the week and special tourist rates on weekends. You can sometimes negotiate a deal in person when there's a vacancy. The opposite may happen around Christmas, however, when many places charge a premium well above the rack rate.

Except in northern Baja California, discounts are most common from April or May until November, when many beach hotels drop prices anywhere from 10 percent to 40 percent, as we indicate in the rate listings. You can't always count on a break, though the chances are far better than during the high season. Small budget hotels vary their rates little, however, whether at the resorts or in highland towns.

Packages are the most popular way of cutting costs, but we think they merit a little caution. Tour operators, airlines, and other wholesalers buy blocks of rooms cheaply to resell to their clients in a package plan that includes airfare and maybe other extras. Hotels participate because they have an occupancy problem, which is sometimes — though not always — a reflection of the quality and value they offer.

The way to approach packages is to identify hotels you want before talking to a travel agent or a wholesaler. It helps to have several options in mind. Most of the large resorts we recommend are solid possibilities; the more rooms, the better the chance of vacancies. Then shop around to see if a package is available for your choices. But don't accept substitutes unless you're certain they're just as suitable as the original selections. That's riskier than lowering your expectations a little to get the same savings at a good, less-expensive place.

There are many tour operators, all with their own groups of hotels. If you approach operators who don't represent your choices, they will try to convert you to theirs. Many travel agents will do something similar. Generally, they have preferred suppliers among the wholesalers, ones they trust and use often enough to get the maximum commission. The agent is likely to suggest alternative hotels handled by the tour operators the firm favors, though a good agent should also be willing to track down package possibilities with other suppliers.

Another option is to go directly to the hotel to inquire about special plans or other discounts available. In the case of many smaller places you'll need to make personal contact anyway just to book a room. Never try it by mail, which takes too long and is sometimes unreliable. Do it by fax in English if we list a fax number for the hotel, or by a regular phone call, though the latter may require a few attempts before you get solid, thorough communication. For more information on phoning and faxing Mexico, see the next chapter, "Ten Tips to Bliss."

Through a package or other means, you may get a discount on the rack rate, but the price specifics we provide should be useful anyway. Even with the fluctuations, they remain the best basis for cost comparisons between different hotels. If one changes tariffs, it's likely similar places are doing the same.

Our data should also help you sort through the various types of rooms offered at a hotel, frequently a key factor in choosing lodging wisely. Don't assume in every case that you want the least expensive or most expensive room your budget allows. As we point out in the hotel descriptions, cost is not always a sufficient guide to the merits of different types of accommodations. A $10 per day upgrade could enhance your vacation enormously, and a $50 saving for equally acceptable quarters could finance an extra stop on your itinerary.

As you trudge through our details about rates and through the hype of wholesalers, just remember that the goal is a getaway tailored to you, an experience to treasure. A good deal is more than a good price.

Perfect Timing

As in all tropical climates, the seasons in Mexico don't vary nearly as much as they do in the States. The coastal lowlands enjoy a perpetual summer, and the interior highlands have a perpetual spring. Winter is the busiest travel period because of the weather north of the border, not south. November through May are the driest months in Mexico, but the increased likelihood of rain the rest of the year is seldom a serious problem.

The only storms that spoil vacations are hurricanes, which occasionally strike coastal areas from mid-August through October. The impact of the rainy season otherwise is usually limited to higher humidity, brief afternoon showers, and evening lightning. The inconvenience is minor to most people and well compensated by reduced hotel rates.

The best time to visit, then, depends more on your budget and schedule than on Mexican weather. The country does offer another advantage, though, at particular times. It's fun to be around when Mexicans are celebrating national holidays or regional fiestas.

Their natural exuberance spills over on such occasions in ways that are delightful to experience. The downside is that many businesses close, and hotels in popular areas can fill with Mexican vacationers.

The most enjoyable national holidays are January 1, May 1 (Labor Day), May 5 (a holiday commemorating the defeat of the French in the Battle of Puebla in 1862), September 15 (when Father Hidalgo's rallying cry for independence from Spain, *El Grito*, is reenacted on every *zócalo* in the country), September 16 (Independence Day), December 12 (the Feast of Our Lady of Guadalupe, honoring the patroness of Mexico), and Christmas.

There are local village fiestas somewhere in Mexico almost every day of the year. Generally, the most colorful are in small towns in the interior that lack good facilities for visitors. The main exception is *Día de los Muertos,* the Day of the Dead, on November 1 and 2. An Indian Catholic variation on traditional observances of All Souls' Day, it's one of the most extraordinary fiestas in Mexico and is particularly dramatic in Pátzcuaro and Oaxaca, both moderately easy to visit. The event pays respect to the dead while mocking death itself in ways that are amusing and amazing. Go a few days early to browse through market stalls brimming with sugar skulls, marigolds, and other ornaments that decorate the elaborate altars carried to cemeteries on the evening of November 1, when an active graveyard is the most fascinating place in the country to spend the night.

Ten Tips to Bliss

As we emphasized earlier, the primary key to a blissful Mexican getaway is making good decisions about destinations and accommodations before you leave home. The tips given here pertain primarily to choices and actions after your arrival, but some require a little planning.

Taming *Turista*

The main fear of *norteamericanos* traveling in Mexico is "Montezuma's revenge," as it is often known in the United States, or *turista,* as it is called in Mexico. Some visitors get it, many don't.

The primary cause is exposure to bacteria not found at home, and it happens to travelers all around the world. There are several simple precautions for avoiding the problem as well as some reliable ways of treating it.

Tap water is the usual source of trouble. In some destinations, particularly in the major resorts, hotels and restaurants purify their supply. The most cautious visitors won't use it even then, and no one should in most of the rest of Mexico. Places with regular tap water almost always provide *agua purificada* in bottles or jugs. You can also purchase it or the tastier *agua mineral* readily anywhere in the country.

Most people make mistakes with the water when they brush their teeth. It's usually easy enough to remember to go to a bottle for a drink, but a habit of running a toothbrush under a faucet is harder to break. Ice can be another sneaky culprit. Anywhere outside an upscale restaurant, you might want to order drinks *sin hielo*, without ice. Also, forgo salads and unpeeled fruit and raw vegetables in the same places, or in any street stand, since they probably have been washed in tap water.

If your stomach isn't accustomed to spicy food or lots of fresh fruit, ease into them. They don't cause real *turista*, but they can send you to the bathroom a few times. Contrary to myth, most Mexican dishes are not very spicy, certainly not compared with some Asian preparations or even such related fare as the traditional cooking of New Mexico.

Take some medication with you in case. Call your doctor for a prescription for something like Lomotil or paregoric, both sold over the counter in Mexican pharmacies if you forget. Milder remedies such as Kaopectate and Pepto-Bismol may be adequate, but the stronger drugs are effective in almost all circumstances. Some people swear by daily doses of Pepto-Bismol tablets as a preventive measure. It's worth a try if you are nervous.

Rest is important when *turista* strikes. People who stay active can make the problem worse. Drink plenty of water to fight dehydration and eat light, easy-to-digest foods to restore strength.

All Mexican hotels have a doctor on call, and many of the larger ones in prime tourist areas have a resident physician. Some are fluent in English, and the vast majority can speak enough to be understood. They know *turista* better than you know your mother. Don't hesitate to use them if symptoms persist, which is rare when you follow the rest of the guidelines.

Speaking Spanish

People who don't know a word of Spanish can get by fine in Mexico's beach resorts and at most of the hotels we recommend in the interior. More employees will know English at the priciest places, but in popular destinations in particular, there's always someone nearby who can communicate in English.

You definitely promote the ugly American stereotype in any country, though, if you don't try to learn at least basic pleasantries in the native tongue. A few hours with a Spanish-language tape, available in most bookstores, plus a little courage in opening conversations in Spanish, pays ample rewards in smiles and goodwill. Rehearse both hearing and speaking the most common words and phrases, such as greetings, numbers, and other expressions taught in the introductory lessons of any tape. When you get to Mexico and a taxi driver or waiter says something in Spanish you don't understand, ask for a repetition and a translation. You'll learn as you go.

If you follow these simple steps, you'll be amazed at how well you manage in Spanish. Just keep using it, and throw in an English word or phrase when necessary. "Spanglish" is even more widely understood than English.

Defensive Traveling

Just as the experts say you should drive defensively, you should also travel defensively, in the United States as well as in foreign countries. It makes no sense to tempt thieves anywhere.

Most of Mexico is safer than Orlando, much less Miami. Despite sensational stories in our media, the overall crime rate is low. The most frequent offense against tourists is simply picking up something that has been left unattended, such as a camera sitting on the beach during a swim or bags lying around an airport unwatched. Common sense is the only protection you need against this. Lock your hotel room and car and don't leave valuables in either. Use your room safe or the hotel's safe deposit box. In crowds, be careful how and where you carry your money.

Violent crime has been increasing. You should exercise the same caution you do at home. Avoid dark beaches and back streets at night. Don't go to remote, isolated areas except in groups, and bypass long, lonely highways if you're driving. In Mexico City, the U.S. State Department (202-647-5225) and Mexican Ministry of Tourism (800-482-9832) advise that you never flag down cabs, but rather take one from a hotel or have a restaurant order one from a taxi stand.

Women traveling alone don't have significantly different problems in Mexico than in the States. When Mexican men flutter and flatter, they are usually trying to impress each other more than you. To keep them at a distance, don't smile or make eye contact, and never go to a neighborhood *cantina.*

Getting Around

In major Mexican destinations, taxis are plentiful and reasonably priced. The only time visitors need a rental car is for touring the interior or for taking excursions from their base. In other situations, rely on the cabs.

Rental cars are moderately expensive and not always in great shape. If you get one, check out the spare tire and make sure everything is in working order before you depart. Roads are generally narrow and bumpy by U.S. standards, though many toll highways throughout Mexico have been constructed in the last decade, making driving conditions much easier, if considerably more costly. (Tolls are higher than in the U.S.) Never, never drive at night in areas that are not well lighted — and that includes the highways.

Deluxe buses have taken advantage of the new highway system, whizzing travelers nonstop from city to city in 24-seat Mercedes Benz comfort. These buses are an affordable way of leaving the driving to others and they often provide viable alternatives to flying. The only drawbacks are the nonstop movies on day trips.

Mexican airlines are a dependable and comfortable way of getting to Mexico and back as well as between cities inside the country. They don't cram as many passengers onto a plane as the fleets north of the border, giving you more sitting space and leg room. Unlike bus travel, however, air travel within Mexico is expensive.

Interesting Itineraries

Anyone going to a Mexican beach should try to take the time to visit the interior too. The coastal areas are increasingly international in character, molded to meet the demands of the mass tourism market. For depth and intensity of Mexican magic, you have to travel inland.

Some combinations of destinations are quite convenient and add relatively little to the cost of a trip. Chichén Itzá and Uxmal are easy overnight jaunts from anywhere on the Caribbean coast. You can visit Oaxaca on a quick flight from Huatulco or Acapulco. There are connections from Puerto Vallarta and Mazatlán to Leon, which is just an hour or so away from San Miguel de Allende and Guanajuato. Any itinerary can be adjusted easily for a stop in Mexico City.

Any of these combinations, or others geared to your personal interests, put a new dimension on a Mexican getaway. At least explore the possibilities.

East vs. West

Too often people decide on a Caribbean or Pacific destination in Mexico on the basis of proximity to their home. They don't seem to realize that going farther doesn't require a great deal more in airfare or time, and they don't take into account the vast differences between the two shores.

The Caribbean has clear, calm, beautiful water. Most water sports — certainly snorkeling and diving — are better here than on the Pacific coast, where the sea is usually rough (except in deep bays). The eastern beaches are also whiter than the western and more tropical in feel, though a recent palm blight has diminished that distinction.

Inland, the Caribbean side is flat and scenically monotonous, while much of the Pacific coast is grandly dramatic. Mountains rise majestically above the water here, and the sun sets in a flare of brilliance just off the shore. The towns are more vibrant and authentically Mexican, too, despite the resort glitz.

The choice you make should depend on your personal inclinations rather than the distance to the destination. If you love the sea, the Caribbean may be the best option. If you love terrestrial beauty and different cultures, you should probably head west.

Service and Tipping

Anyone bothered by service standards in the tropics will appreciate Mexico. Service is often as slow and as untrained as it is in other areas, but it's much friendlier — actually joyful on occasion. Unlike many popular island getaways around the world, the locals don't resent tourists. Mexicans are proud of their country and want people to see and enjoy it.

Two forces do sometimes interfere with service, though. Mexicans relish bureaucracy as much as the French. Customs officials, hotel management personnel, and others who push a lot of paper can get absorbed with the insignificant and act harried. If you have a problem at a hotel, start with the bellman rather than the front desk or the manager. As strange as that may sound, in Mexico the bellmen are usually the local ambassadors for guests, particularly when there isn't a concierge. Often they speak English better than anyone else on the property.

This advice doesn't apply, and service overall is likely to sink, when the second force enters the scene. Mexican labor unions are very powerful, and they take industrial action seriously. If there is a labor-management dispute going on behind the scenes, which is always a possibility, the cracks someone has been filling can become yawning gaps.

When that happens, a little money can make a big difference. The line between tipping and bribing in Mexico is not as distinct as it is in the States. The *mordida* (literally, a "bite") is a payoff common throughout the society as a way of getting something expedited — somewhat like the way tipping originated as a way to improve service. Using the system as necessary does not imply approval.

Regular gratuities will suffice most of the time. In a moderately priced hotel, bellmen expect about a $1 per bag. Go up or down a bit depending on the luxury level; some deluxe hotels have a $3 bellhop fee for checking in and checking out. Leave something extra for the maids as well, but if you are staying in a deluxe hotel, check whether they add a gratuities surcharge to your bill. As at home, waiters get 15 percent for satisfactory service in a fine restaurant. Unlike at home, you don't need to tip taxi drivers unless they do something beyond hauling you, but tour guides will want a dollar or two a person. Anyone else who provides a service, from watching your car to washing its windows, should get a small gratuity appropriate to the value of what was done.

The Steak-and-Lobster Syndrome

In resort areas, too many restaurants — and their patrons — seem obsessed with steak and lobster. One of the two dishes is almost always touted as the house specialty, and the vast majority of *norteamericanos* think of them as the top dining treats. Usually only the chef knows better.

The warm-water lobster of the tropics is a very distant cousin of the Maine crustacean. Dry and rather bland, it's seldom naturally savory, but restaurants try to conceal its shortcomings with lots of butter and seasonings. The problem with steaks is somewhat different. The beef raised in Sonora can be superb. The prime cuts seldom reach tourists' tables, however, and the meat that does usually has the flavor and texture of the scrubby range it once roamed.

The way to eat well in Mexico is to stick with the real specialties, the kind of food the kitchen staff grew up on and know best. In coastal areas that includes many fish and seafood preparations, and in the interior, a variety of local dishes. You won't always have a memorable meal, depending on the skill of the cooks, but you'll probably get the best served that day.

Packing

In Mexican beach areas, dress is always casual. You probably will want long pants or skirts for the evening, but jackets and cocktail attire are seldom necessary, and ties are almost never seen. During the day, most people wear shorts, sandals, and T-shirts.

Dress is more conservative and occasionally formal in interior cities. Avoid resort wear that exposes much skin. Mexicans wear shorts more often than in the past, but you probably don't want to be in the vanguard in this area, especially in high altitudes, where you will not only be out of place, but you might be cold. Fancy urban restaurants sometimes require jackets and ties for men.

Telephoning

It's simple to phone Mexico from the States and not very expensive for short conversations. Don't hesitate to call a recommended hotel for a booking if it doesn't have a reservation agent in the States. When we list a fax number, try it first, if possible. Making a simple request in English is usually not a problem. A regular phone contact probably will demand patience and maybe persistence too, but it's also feasible. To reach Mexico, start with 011-52 and then dial the number given in the hotel description, which includes the area code in parentheses.

Calling home from Mexico is much more expensive, even if you use your long-distance calling card from your U.S. telephone company. Just make sure you carry their Mexican access code with you. If you don't have a calling card, then call collect. Hotels often tack on an exorbitant service charge no matter how you call. If you know you want to be in touch, arrange for people to call you at a specified time when you'll be in your room. Another option is to go to the *Larga Distancia* office that can be found in most towns and have an operator place the call for you. To call the States directly yourself, dial 001 before the area code.

Mexico

Ensenada

Baja California

Los Cabos

The Extraordinary Interior

Copper Canyon

Mazatlán

Guadalajara

Mexico City

The Mayan Riviera

Mérida

Cancún

Cobá

Cozumel

Oaxaca

Bahue'00

The Mexican Riviera

Acapulco

Puerto Angel

The
Mayan
Riviera

Isla Mujeres

Cancún

Puerto Morelos

Playa del Carmen

Akumal

Tulum

Cozumel

The Mayan Riviera

Sian Ka'an Biosphere Reserve

Caribbean Sea

Xcalak

Akumal
Las Casitas Akumal, 58
Vista del Mar, 59
Cancún
Calinda Beach & Spa, 27
Camino Real Cancún, 28
Casa Turquesa, 30
Club Las Velas Cancún, 32
Club Med Cancún, 33
Fiesta Americana Coral Beach, 36
Hilton Cancún Beach & Golf Resort, 37
Hyatt Caribe Cancún, 39
Marriott CasaMagna Cancún, 41
Melia Cancún Beach & Spa, 42
Novotel, 44
Omni Cancún, 45
Ritz-Carlton Cancún, 46
Villas Tacul, 48
Cozumel
La Ceiba, 81
Paradisus Cozumel, 82
Presidente Inter-Continental Cozumel, 84
Scuba Club Dive Resort, 86
Sol Cabañas del Caribe, 87
Isla Mujeres
Na Balam, 50
Playa del Carmen
Chichan Baal Kah, 61
El Faro, 62
La Posada del Capitán Lafitte, 64
Quinta Mija, 65
Rosa Mirador, 66
Shangri-La Caribe, 68
Puerto Morelos
Maroma, 70
Tulum and Sian Ka'an
Cabañas Ana y José, 72
Maya Tulum, 74
Xcalak
Costa de Cocos, 75

Cancún

Best Hotels for Stylish Sophistication

Best Recreational Resorts and Spas

Best Comfort Choices for All-American Abundance

Best Beachfront Buys

Villas Tacul, 48

Best Bargain for Mexican Character

Novotel, 44

Best Places to Combine Business and Pleasure

Marriott CasaMagna Cancún, 41
Omni Cancún, 45

The wildest success story in resort history, Cancún wasn't even on the map as recently as 1970. At that time it was nothing more than a data profile in a government computer programmed to find ideal spots for future resorts. Cancún came out on top because of its superb Caribbean waters and proximity to some of the world's most dramatic ancient ruins. By 1975, the first resort hotel was up and running, and the first American tourists were landing at the spanking new airport.

During the next dozen years, development proceeded at a moderate pace, but increasing popularity resulted in problems with overbooking and led to a massive new construction phase that started in the late 1980s. The room count has now peaked over 22,000, a capacity greater than any other Caribbean destination.

Cancún looks like a Houston suburb on the beach, but its contemporary American style is exactly what has propelled it to superstar status. Don't deceive yourself about this being Mexico. One of the local tourism promoters put it succinctly in describing excursions from Cancún. He suggested that tourists could fly easily to interior Mexican cities such as Mérida and Oaxaca, adding, "it's almost like visiting another country." Cancún is to Mexico what Las Vegas is to the desert Southwest.

That's fine for the majority of visitors. It's the most convenient getaway in Mexico for anyone living east of the Rockies, and the sun, sand, and azure waters are sublime. As long as you aren't looking for native charm and plan to avoid the U.S. college spring break, it's easy to make your own success story in Cancún.

The Main Attractions

Charley and Charlene's Paradise

We figure the computer that chose Cancún for development had to be working from a profile of model visitors. We'll call them Charley and Charlene. They're between 25 and 50 and like to be active, probably both during the day and at night. One of them has traveled out of the States some, but neither has been to Mexico. They're thinking about bringing the kids, if it's safe. Both are nervous about *turista* and encounters with Third World poverty, though they are sufficiently educated to be curious about life beyond the 'burbs. Together they have a good income and they are willing to pay for luxury as long as they aren't being ripped off.

Government tourism officials custom-built Cancún for Charley and Charlene, carefully tailoring the resort to their interests out of whole cloth. Overrun by jungle originally, Cancún was an empty sandbar island, some 14 miles long and about a quarter-mile wide. It had space for scores of high-rise hotels, a golf course or two, a few shopping malls, and plenty of restaurants and night spots. The island was just a few hundred feet off the Yucatán peninsula and could be connected to it easily by causeways, creating a calm lagoon in between.

A tiny village already existed on the mainland near one of the points where the island came close to the shore. That unsuspecting community could be developed into a service base for the resort. Workers with middle-class aspirations would flock to the town from all over southeastern Mexico, and as the village became a city, it would take on a modern, middle-class feel that wouldn't bother the tourists.

It all happened as planned. The island is almost completely rimmed by hotels now, and the little village has a population of a quarter-million. Anyone skeptical about Mexican vision and entrepreneurship should compare Cancún with Miami. Florida would love to have this spot, which has replaced it as the number-one college favorite for spring break.

The Upscale Caribbean Bargain

Cancún has many of the same natural lures as other Caribbean destinations. The multihued sea is actually lovelier here than in most areas, and the conditions are prime for water sports. The surrounding terrain is flat rather than hilly, but Mayan pyramids are more fascinating to climb than hills anyway.

While prices in Cancún are steeper than in the rest of Mexico, they are much lower than in other parts of the Caribbean. You get a lot more for your money, too, in familiar upscale luxury. The construction boom that began in the late 1980s has focused on grand resort hotels. Their regular rates are among the highest in Mexico, but package plans as well as off-season rates can reduce the cost.

Water Sports

All water sports except surfing and deep-sea fishing are better on Mexico's Caribbean coast than on the Pacific, and the fishing isn't bad. Cancún offers the full range of opportunities, though aficionados of underwater sports can find better bases south of the city.

The Nichupte Lagoon, encircled by the island and the mainland, is perfect for water skiing and jet skiing. It's also fine for beginning and intermediate windsurfing, as is the north shore of the island on the Bahía de Mujeres.

Many people fish in the lagoon too, though plenty of charters are available for the heftier challenges in the open waters. Spring and summer are the seasons for the big game.

Day cruises are one of the most popular diversions. A variety of boats, including trimarans and a glass-bottom "submarine," depart the island midmorning and return mid-afternoon. Most stop for lunch on Isla Mujeres at El Garrafón Beach, a national underwater park where snorkeling was better before the tour groups arrived.

Avid snorkelers will also want to travel an hour south of Cancún to Akumal and Xel-Ha. Nichupte Lagoon is okay for beginners but not dramatic. Diving conditions are similar. The shallow reefs off the shore of Cancún are best for learning and practice. Enthusiasts may prefer to stay along the south coast or on Cozumel, other Caribbean destinations covered in the next two chapters.

Cancún's forte is diversity rather than depth. Anyone who wants to sample a range of water sports won't find many better places for it in the world. All the recommended beachfront hotels can arrange any of the activities.

Fabulous Sand

Perhaps the most amazing of Cancún's natural endowments is the quality of the sand on the almost continuous beach. Charley and Charlene may not make this a deciding factor in a getaway, but it could be their most pleasant surprise. The first thing you notice is the blinding whiteness. Then, when you step on the sand, you not only sink into it, you also find that it's as cool as it is deep, however hot the sun may be. The beach is almost pure limestone, so porous that it sheds both water and warmth.

Unfortunately there's less of the sand than there used to be. Hurricane Gilbert in 1988 severely damaged the east shore, the area that directly faces the Caribbean Sea. Some of the sand was displaced to the other developed coast of the island, the north shore on the Bahía de Mujeres, but much of it was washed out into the ocean. Before Gilbert, the east beach was as wide as 50 yards, and you could walk out in the water a similar distance before it got deep. The hurricane scooped up the sandy bottom as well as the beach, bringing the drop-off point closer to the shore and increasing the size of the waves coming in. The surf is rougher now on this side of the island, and the beach is about half its former width.

Natural forces are rapidly restoring the sand, and hotels are helping the process by anchoring the gains with huge rocks. Still, some of the hotels have skimpy beaches, despite the pre-Gilbert photos you may see in their brochures.

Day Trips into Mexico

One of the best things about being in Cancún is leaving it, as that computer knew long ago. Most visitors get away from the resort area at least once, usually in search of Mexican character or Mayan mysteries.

The closest spot for native flavor is the neighboring island of Isla Mujeres. Don't think you've seen the sights if you've gone to El Garrafón on a day cruise. The Mexican personality is concentrated in the town a few miles away. Take the cheap ferry from Puerto Juárez, just outside Cancún. Unfortunately, the ferry doesn't run at night, and that's when the community becomes animated. If you want to stay over, we recommend Na Balam (described at the end of the chapter), one of the scarce hotels on the main beach and a short walk from town.

The Mayan ruins in the region are the most popular day destination. "Chicken Pizza," as Chichén Itzá is often known in Cancún's lingo, is about two and a half hours by rental car or tour bus and worth every minute of the trip. Cobá and Tulum are closer but less majestic. Each of the sites is described briefly in the chapter "Archaeological Treasures."

Cancún

Calinda Beach & Spa

Blvd. Kukulcán
Cancún, Quintana Roo
(98) 83-16-00
Fax: (98) 83-18-57
Reservations:
Quality International
800-228-5151

**A beachfront resort hotel
with somewhat moderate
rates**

Accommodations: 470 rooms. **Rates:** High season $140–$174, low season $112–$140. **Payment:** Major credit cards. **Children:** Under 18, free in room with parents. **Recreation:** Beach, swimming pool, children's pool, 2 tennis courts, water sports center and fitness center with steam bath, Jacuzzi, sauna, and massage.

➤   **The Calinda is just beyond the bridge to Cancún island, making it one of the closest hotels to the shops and restaurants of downtown. Anything you don't find on the grounds is only five minutes away.**

Though far from cheap, the Calinda is still a beachfront bargain for Cancún, a city that can send you looking for second mortgages. At this Quality Inn you will sacrifice very little of the American luxury that drives the local market, but you get your quota at a reasonable price, particularly with package discounts.

It's a huge place, rising nine stories above the shore and sweeping out along the water in two wings that slant toward their base in a hackneyed nod to the Mayan styles. With the potential for over a thousand guests in peak periods, the Calinda tries to oversize everything feasible to meet client needs. The main dining room, though pleasantly decorated, resembles a jumbo coffee shop. The main pool and its deck won't hold a full crowd, but they are spacious, and the big beach absorbs any excess tanners. The music in the lobby bar rocks the whole hotel.

The obsession with amplitude doesn't lead to a neglect of little details, however. A half-dozen hammocks sprawl invitingly over the sand, and the fitness center tempts you away from the pool. The two tennis courts are lighted for night play. Five restaurants, including the sea and poolside restaurants, La Gaviota and La Palapa, and lounges offer everything from a breakfast buffet to pizza snacks. These aren't novel touches, but they mitigate the sense of mass.

The accommodations are colorfully comfortable in a tropical vein, with tile floors, prints on the walls, and polished stone in the baths. Splurge an extra $10 a night if you can for a corner room, which has windows on two sides and a king-size bed instead of a pair of doubles. The basic quarters lack balconies and many face the street and the Nichupte Lagoon rather than the sea. All come with air conditioning, mini-bars, phones, and satellite TVs.

The Calinda is a conventional resort hotel in most respects except rates. That's not a lofty distinction, but you may find it a stellar deal.

Camino Real Cancún

Punta Cancún
Cancún, Quintana Roo
(98) 83-01-00
Fax: (98) 83-17-30
Reservations:
Camino Real Hotels and Resorts
800-7-CAMINO

An established favorite with a prime beachfront perch

Accommodations: 381 rooms and suites. **High-season rates:** Deluxe bay- and ocean-view rooms $235–$280, Camino Real Club rooms $350, junior suites $465. **Low-season rates:** Deluxe bay- and ocean-view rooms $165–$210, Camino Real Club rooms $220, junior suites $335. **Payment:** Major credit cards. **Children:** Under 18, two free in room with parents. **Recreation:** Beach, swimming pool, snorkeling lagoon, 3 tennis courts, water sports center with snorkeling and windsurfing.

➤ **The Camino Real offers one of the best collections of restaurants at any Cancún hotel, but all visitors should dine out occasionally. Our favorite independent restaurant is the very reliable Casa Rolandi (Plaza Caracol, 83-18-17). Try the wild mushrooms with polenta or the black squid pasta with seafood.**

One of the first hotels in Cancún, opened in 1975, the Camino Real established a standard of elegance for the city that went unrivaled for over a decade. Newer places have seized the lead, but not by much. Camino Real remains a distinctive and inviting spot, offering the stunning architecture of Ricardo Legorreta, an experienced staff, 24-hour room service, and the best location in town, on the tranquil central point where the island faces both the Caribbean and the Bahía de Mujeres.

Except for a high-rise luxury tower that was added in the late 1980s, Legorreta's design resembles his master work at the Westin Ixtapa in many ways. In this case the founder of "Mexican minimalism" used his bold, pyramidal lines on an elongated five-story structure that faces the Caribbean on one side and on the other sweeps dramatically toward a small private lagoon. Inside the building, where you enter your room, the layout creates a lovely courtyard brimming with tropical foliage.

The tower, in contrast, is more conventional, however opulent. It houses the Camino Real Club rooms and some deluxe suites with Jacuzzis — all of which come with special concierge services and complimentary Continental breakfasts and cocktail hours — but the original accommodations are just as smart in most respects. All the spacious rooms enjoy water views, lanais, king-size beds or two doubles, marble floors, TVs, phones, and air conditioning.

We prefer the old quarters overlooking the internal lagoon, a saltwater pool rimmed by an ersatz beach. The pond is a good spot for snorkeling, but you may want to do your sunning on the real beach, a few steps beyond, and save your swimming for the nearby freshwater pool or the calm sea. Lounge chairs and *palapa* umbrellas line the sands, competing for your time with a windsurfing operation and a dive shop that together rent enough sports gear to stage a water Olympics. You get a choice of jet skis, boogie boards, small sailboats, sun floats, fishing charters, and catamaran cruises. If you would rather bang a ball around, there are three tennis courts and a pro shop.

The hotel's La Brisa restaurant is a casual seafood café under a thatched roof; it overlooks one of the beaches. In the evening, the boisterous, hokey, and folkloric Maria Bonita, a short distance from the hotel, features a tequila bar and Mexican cuisine in several rooms arranged around a courtyard. A couple of snack bars serve bathers and tanners, and a third major restaurant, Azulejos, serves early risers and late-night revelers. Not to be missed is Cancún's most elegant night spot, Izucar. Adjacent to the hotel, this Caribbean club features live salsa music and dancing.

The Camino Real continues to be one of Cancún's finest. Age and a high-rise horn haven't destroyed the charisma. It maintains a luster few challengers can match.

Casa Turquesa

Blvd. Kukulkán
Cancún, Quintana Roo
(98) 85-29-24, 85-19-74
Fax: (98) 85-29-22
Reservations:
Small Luxury Hotels of the World
800-525-4800

The most exclusive address in Cancún

Accommodations: 32 suites. **Rates:** Garden-view suites $395, ocean-view suites $480, executive suites from $650–$2,500. **Payment:** Major credit cards. **Children:** Under 10, discouraged. **Recreation:** Beach, swimming pool, 1 tennis court, fitness center, spa, sauna.

➤ **Promotional literature calls Casa Turquesa "a favorite hideaway for superstars, celebrities, and royalty from around the world." You may or may not spot any of the above, but the milieu certainly fits the bill.**

Cancún has needed Casa Turquesa for a long time. Despite being one of the most successful resort destinations in the world, the city lacked a distinctive, exclusive small hotel devoted to fine service.

Casa Turquesa filled the void in 1991, providing the kind of hideaway in the hubbub that attracts people who like pampering.

You sense the difference from other Cancún hotels even before you register. Passing a succession of big, flamboyant places, you suddenly come upon a tasteful inn that resembles a private estate. The entrance is understated, particularly for Cancún, and the lobby greets you with an air of refined elegance rather than glitz.

A staff member escorts you to your suite, which is posh in a subdued, soothing style. Most of the accommodations are junior-suite size, featuring a terrace with a Jacuzzi, marble floors and bathrooms, two double beds or a king, satellite TV, VCR, CD player, air conditioning, mini-bar, and two phone lines with three extensions set up for fax and modem transmissions. The bathroom has a double-sink vanity overflowing with amenities. All the quarters face the Caribbean, but only the ones on the upper floors of the four-story mansion provide a good view of the water.

The three master suites are enormous. The one named Prime Minister could house the British Cabinet. The two- or three-bedroom Presidential chamber is a split-level apartment with a pair of terraces and a kitchenette. For the ultimate in opulence, reserve the Royal Suite, a 3-bedroom beachfront beauty with a private entrance and beach access.

A lovely pool separates most of the rooms from the sand, and a tennis court and fitness center provide additional recreation. The staff, which prides itself on filling special requests, will arrange any other sports or diversions you desire, including golf, deep-sea fishing, and diving or snorkeling excursions.

The kitchen at the hotel restaurant has higher aspirations than almost any in Cancún and seems usually to succeed. Primarily Continental in tone, the menu also offers a smattering of Mexican dishes. The dining room is open for breakfast, lunch, and dinner and provides 24-hour room service as well.

Casa Turquesa is a classy sanctuary for Cancún. No other *casa* in the city makes such a heavenly home.

Club Las Velas Cancún

Apartado Postal 1614
Cancún, Quintana Roo
(98) 83-22-22
Fax: (98) 83-24-65

An all-inclusive resort brimming with activity

Accommodations: 285 rooms and suites. **High-season rates:** Garden rooms $140 per person double occupancy, suites $184 per person double occupancy. **Low-season rates:** Garden rooms $120 per person double occupancy, suites $155 per person double occupancy. **Included:** Breakfast, lunch, dinner, all domestic drinks, tax, service charge, all recreation listed below except motorized water sports. **Payment:** Major credit cards. **Children:** 12 years and under, $10 per day in room with parents; Kiddie Club, nursery. **Recreation:** Lagoon beach, 2 swimming pools, 2 tennis courts, fitness center, windsurfing, small-craft sailing, kayaking, water skiing, jet skiing.

➤ **You won't get nickle-and-dimed at Club Las Velas, where virtually everything is included in one price.**

The first of several Club Med clones in Cancún, Las Velas carved a big market for itself almost as soon as it opened in 1989. The real Club Med down the road (see below) has the upstart outclassed in many ways, but the rooms are larger and more luxurious here, and the all-inclusive price covers drinks as well as room and board.

Spread over ten acres on the lagoon side of the city, Las Velas is laid out like a Mexican village, replete with wide cobblestone walkways and low-rise colonial-style buildings with red tile roofs. An expansive beach spreads along most of the shore, affording access to calm waters and a wide range of water sports. Inland you can play tennis, work out in the fitness center, take aerobics classes, learn scuba in a saltwater pool, swim in two freshwater pools, or sign the kids up for special children's activities.

Two principal restaurants feature both buffets and à la carte selections and another offers light meals and snacks all day. Five bars keep your glass full, and strolling musicians and theme parties keep the evenings lively. When you're ready to retire, you can count on a comfortable if conventional chamber with air conditioning, satellite TV, a terrace, red tile floors, and usually a king-size bed.

Club Las Velas is a casual, contemporary alternative to Club Med and, in contrast to the rest of Cancún, a place where you know your costs in advance. If that counts, it could make your vacation add up handsomely.

Club Med Cancún

Cancún, Quintana Roo
(98) 85-23-00
Fax: (98) 85-22-90
Reservations:
888-932-2582

> **A Club Med for athletes and aesthetes alike**

Accommodations: 410 rooms. **High-season rates:** $145–$160 daily or $1,001–$1,101 weekly per person, double occupancy. **Low-season rates:** $125 daily or $875 weekly per person, double occupancy. **Included:** Breakfast, lunch, dinner, beer and wine with meals, all recreation listed below except golf, diving, and deep-sea fishing. **Minimum stay:** 7 nights in high season. **Payment:** Major credit cards. **Recreation:** Beach, swimming pool, golf (18 holes off-property), 8 tennis courts, fitness center with massage, scuba diving, snorkeling, water skiing, small-craft sailing, windsurfing, deep-sea fishing.

➤ **The main attractions at Club Med Cancún are water sports, Maya sightseeing, and ease of access from the States. If those strike a chord, the resort could be your best all-inclusive option in Mexico.**

Like other Club Meds, the one in Cancún has some special characteristics of its own, but much of its appeal is shared with the rest of its clan. When you choose to go to any Club Med, your decision is more about a style of vacation than a particular destination.

Forget any normal notion of a hotel chain. Club Med created the all-inclusive concept years ago and adheres to it with conviction, bundling everything except some drinks, excursions, and other optional expenditures into one package price. Many other resorts now copy that approach and even carry it further, but none of the clones come close to matching Club Med's sense of "club" identification. Rather than a corporate conglomerate, which in fact it is, the organization promotes itself with great success as a fellowship of hedonists. Club Med cultivates zeal more effectively than most religions, both in the intensity of resort exuberance and the devotion of its flock. Nietzsche wasn't quite right. God didn't die; He just went on vacation.

Forget the usual criteria for resort excellence. What counts at Club Meds is communal play and revelry, not accommodations, food, or other conventional considerations. The small air-conditioned rooms — often furnished with twin beds — are more utilitarian than elegant, meant for sleeping rather than private time. The elaborate buffet meals are social occasions as much as dining opportunities. Even when the food is good, as it often is, the family-style seating distracts guests from the fare in favor of meeting and mingling. The chief attraction is always a collective celebration of common interests — in the diverse sports offered, in partying, and in Club Med itself as a shared fraternity.

The creed was founded in France in 1950 on the same basic tenets active today. The only major shift in philosophy has been away from the original singles orientation toward the inclusion of couples and families. The change is more of a marketing emphasis than a new direction, an effort to keep the followers coming as they marry and have kids. The atmosphere remains youthful and yearning even in the Club Meds with mini-clubs for children, such as the ones in Huatulco and Ixtapa. People who come to Club Med alone are assigned a roommate of the same sex unless they are willing to pay more for a single room.

Each of the hundred operations around the world is called a village, which they resemble more in some countries than in others. They are always set apart from the surrounding area by both security gates and an independent identity that doesn't rely much on the country the resort is in. When guests leave the grounds, it's normally in group excursions. Everything is structured to keep your focus on Club Med.

Guests are called G.M.s, *gentils membres,* or "congenial members." Their role is to frolic, and they're in the midst of many role models. When it comes time for the "crazy signs" ritual every evening, shortly before the disco opens, virtually everyone in the village participates. The staff leads the tribal dance, which can last a quarter-hour or more, with Simon Says instructions for various chants and hand gyrations. Outsiders might think they've stumbled into the twentieth reunion of a cheerleader's school, but for committed G.M.s, it's a joyful bonding rite.

The primary staff are known as G.O.s, *gentils organisateurs,* or "congenial organizers," and their role reflects the title. The "passport" issued to new arrivals at one village describes the G.O.s' job succinctly: "These versatile young men and women will be your sports instructors, tour guides, entertainers, and most importantly, your friends." They don't serve you, they play with you. Usually attractive and perky in personality, the G.O.s are dedicated to getting you into the Club Med spirit. They assist you in your choice of recreation, eat with you, drink with you, and do almost anything to make sure you're in the high-energy swing of village life.

Curiously, the G.O.s around the world switch homes each spring and fall. From the chief of a club down through the ranks, they scatter in different directions, changing the character of each place with every semiannual shift. The mood, the food, and the staff's nightly amateur shows all take an unpredictable turn, sometimes small, sometimes big. The only constants are the facilities and activities offered, making them the main factors in choosing one village over another.

As all-American as the destination, the Cancún Club Med is one of the top spots to stay in the city. Some of the regular hotels are more luxurious, but this one has the advantage of being a handsome low-rise complex on the best beach around. The sports programs are extensive and first rate, attracting more jocks than you'll see anywhere in Mexico, and unlike many Club Meds, the village is oriented to its surroundings, sending out excursions daily to the Mayan ruins nearby. No other place in Cancún can top it for overall abundance.

The vast majority of rooms enjoy a water view, either of the Caribbean or a private lagoon on the property, and most have balconies. Moderate in size, the quarters are tastefully decorated with stone sculpture, pottery lamps, and white tile on the floors and in the shower. Some come with king beds, but when they don't, the two twins can be pushed together, which isn't always possible at other Club Meds.

The two restaurants provide more variety in environment than in cuisine. During our last visit the food was international, with an emphasis on American and native dishes, and the cooking was a fair bit better than average for Cancún.

Many guidebooks ignore the Club Meds, as if no one other than members would be interested. You do have to join ($30 per family) and pay an annual membership fee ($50 for each adult for any stay of five nights or more; $20 for children under 12), but that's a meager addition to the cost of a vacation. Everyone is welcome, and almost everyone attracted to the concept enjoys the experience immensely, in Cancún or elsewhere.

Fiesta Americana Coral Beach

Blvd. Kukulkán
Cancún, Quintana Roo
(98) 83-29-00
Fax: (98) 83-31-73
Reservations:
Fiesta Americana
800-FIESTA-1

> **Big, bountiful, bustling, and on the beach**

Accommodations: 602 rooms and suites. **High-season rates:** junior suites $360, master suites $445 with breakfast. **Low-season rates:** junior suites $242, master suites $312 with breakfast. **Payment:** Major credit cards. **Children:** Under 12, free in room with parents. **Recreation:** Beach, swimming pool, 3 tennis courts, fitness center, water sports center.

➤   **Fiesta Americana is near the convention center, a hub for entertainment and shopping as well as business. Don't miss the Ballet Folklorico performances at the Center, the best show in town for our money.**

In a city that likes to gauge quality by quantity, the Fiesta Americana Coral Beach jumped ahead of most of the Cancún pack as soon as it opened in 1990. Not only did it set a megatrend in the number of rooms and the amount of space devoted to meeting facilities, the hotel actually tries to look bigger than it is. A towering porte-cochere arches above the entrance outside and ushers you into a massive atrium covered by stained glass skylights. The scale overwhelms you momentarily, as it's meant to do, encouraging you to believe that you've landed in a realm that's larger than life.

The effect is carried out the back door to an immense playground as stunning as the lobby. A 660-foot free-form swimming pool flows in all directions, through four distinct areas linked by waterfalls, tropical gardens, and swim-up bars. Just beyond, a 900-foot sandy shore is lined with *palapas* and lapped by a gentle surf. An offshore reef helps to keep the water calm, providing fine conditions for the wide range of water sports offered. If you prefer your recreation on land, the Coral Beach excels with its three indoor, air-conditioned tennis courts and fully equipped health spa with steam baths and massage in addition to the usual programs. In 1999 Coral Beach was ranked by *Travel & Leisure* magazine as the fourth best hotel in all of Mexico, Central America, and South America.

A dozen restaurants and bars tend to other needs. You can eat casually by the pool or in an all-day café, or dine in elegant surroundings in two dinner-only restaurants. Our favorite spot is the Coral Reef, with etched glass doors, a blond hardwood floor, conch shell wall sconces, and rosy accents that match the hotel's strikingly pink facade. Though the Continental seafood menu is overpriced, as you have to expect in Cancún, the cooking was better than average in our one experience dining there.

The Fiesta Americana management likes to call all the rooms "suites," but that's only part of the overall pattern of hyperbole. While the so-called junior suites do contain a comfortable sitting area, they are simply spacious quarters rather than true suites. The only real difference between the rooms is the view, which always includes a good perspective on the sea. Each room comes with a balcony, a king bed or two doubles, marble floors, air conditioning, a phone, TV, and mini-bar. The real suites, called master suites, have an extended ocean-view terrace, parlor or conference room, and a Jacuzzi.

Bigger is not always better, but somehow the concept works in Cancún. Fiesta Americana's Coral Beach isn't likely to leave you wishing for more.

Hilton Cancún Beach & Golf Resort

Apartado Postal 1810
Cancún, Quintana Roo
(98) 81-80-00
Fax: (98) 81-80-82
Reservations:
Hilton Reservations Worldwide
800-HILTONS

A luxury resort with its own 18-hole golf course and some of the friendliest service in Cancún

Accommodations: 426 rooms and suites. **High-season rates:** Superior rooms $336, deluxe rooms $370, junior suites $537, master suites $594, Beach Club $420–$1120. **Low-season rates:** Superior rooms $246, deluxe rooms $280, junior suites $448, master suites $504, Beach Club $336–$952. **Payment:** Major credit cards. **Recreation:** Beach, 7 swimming pools, 18-hole golf course, 2 tennis courts, 2 Jacuzzis, sauna, fitness center and water sports center.

➤ **When you decide to pull yourself away from the facilities at the Hilton to go shopping, head for the Plaza Caracol (Blvd. Kukulcan km. 8, near the**

Convention Center), the first and still the best shopping mall in Cancún, filled with quality stores and some fine restaurants.

In November 1999, the popular Caesar Park Cancún was taken over by Hilton and renamed the Hilton Cancún Beach & Golf Resort. This prime property overflows with amenities, such as its own 18-hole, par 72, 6,735-yard golf course set amidst Mayan ruins, a large fitness center with several treadmills as well as bicycles and other quality equipment, seven pools (but only some of them are really used for swimming) that cascade several levels to the sea, a couple of outdoor Jacuzzis that are popular resting spots for sipping piña coladas, and a lovely, large, 700-yard beach perfect for early morning and late evening tranquil walks. In the evening the illuminated outdoor fountains dramatically transform into waterfalls that flow to the beach.

When you have to be indoors at the Hilton you won't be disappointed either. The attractive lobby has soothing colors to complement the marble floors, ivy, potted palms, and rattan shades located in the 9-story open atrium with its glassed-in elevators that provide you with views of the Nichupte Lagoon as they carry you to your room. The comfortable, well-appointed, air-conditioned rooms come with rattan furniture and hand-painted lamps, as well as a phone, cable TV, and a mini-bar. All rooms have sea views but only the deluxe rooms have outdoor terraces and the nice added touches of bathrobes and slippers. In addition to the rooms in the high-rise tower, there are Beach Club rooms and suites in two-and three-story villas. The most desirable ones are beachfront; others are set back on lawns. All Beach Club rooms come with a Continental breakfast and, in the afternoon, complimentary drinks and hors d'oeuvres.

With four restaurants and several bars, the Hilton makes sure that you can eat and drink throughout the day whether you are at the Golf Club, the pool, or the beach. If you prefer to have drinks while you're soaking wet, you have your choice of service at the swim-up bar or one of the outdoor Jacuzzis. Of course, you can eat without losing sight of the sea. La Sirenita restaurant overlooks the turquoise Caribbean. At breakfast time, the Hilton has a particularly nice amenity for light eaters. You can avoid the main breakfast room in favor of the atrium lobby, where you can choose from juices, fruits, pastries, and coffee in a relaxing setting. In the evening, the same atrium lobby transforms into a cocktail lounge with an added treat. In one corner of the lobby, you'll find a gentleman with a pile of tobacco in front of him engaged in making hand-rolled cigars for your evening enjoyment.

Throughout the Hilton you'll be struck by the warm and friendly service. The staff are particularly helpful and well-trained, attentive without being intrusive. They make your stay here all the more pleasurable. No doubt you will be happy that you chose the Hilton.

Hyatt Caribe Cancún

Apartado Postal 353
Cancún, Quintana Roo
(98) 83-00-44
Fax: (98) 83-15-14
Reservations:
Hyatt Hotels and Resorts
800-233-1234

A grande dame with a fresh facelift

Accommodations: 223 rooms and suites. **High-season rates:** Double rooms $235–$250, Regency Club rooms $300, suites $500–$675. **Low-season rates:** Double rooms $170, Regency Club rooms $210, suites $355–$475. **Payment:** Major credit cards. **Children:** Under 18, free in room with parents. **Recreation:** Beach, 3 swimming pools, 3 tennis courts, water sports marina, aerobics.

➤ **Because it has a private marina with direct access to Nichupte Lagoon, the Hyatt can offer golfers express transportation to Cancún's Robert Trent Jones golf course — by speedboat.**

Hyatt closed the Cancún Caribe in 1988 for a thorough renovation, reopening the following winter with a fresh decor and a frisky spirit. The work became a model for the refurbishing of other aging Hyatts in Acapulco and Cancún, but this one was the best of the group from the beginning and the one where the overhaul was most successful. It's now a serious competitor for the flashy new hotels in town — smaller and more personable than they are and just as up to date. A 1997 addition of 31 new beachfront villa suites brought the luxury quotient up as well.

Most of the rooms are in a seven-story tower that overlooks the large central pool and the Caribbean shore. The hotel resisted the Cancún temptation to put additional rooms on the other side, facing the less desirable sight of Nichupte Lagoon. That keeps the Hyatt a manageable size and gives everyone a good ocean view except for the few guests on the first floor, who get spacious patios with lounge chairs in compensation.

About 93 low-rise villas, many housing very private suites with terraces, line the beach on either side of the tower. They place you closer to the sea and the sounds of the surf, but the vistas aren't as broad as from above. The villas to the south, designated for the Regency Club, house the best quarters in the hotel. Though the rooms aren't substantially different from the others, they come with concierge service, private pools, Jacuzzi, and the use of a private lounge where you can have a complimentary Continental breakfast in the morning and free hors d'oeuvres with a cocktail and a sunset view in the afternoon. Wherever you stay, you can count on a king-size or two double beds, contemporary furnishings, a phone, cable TV, and air conditioning.

The Hyatt's premier restaurant, the Blue Bayou, offers a Mexican version of New Orleans food in the evening in a splendid six-level garden setting with a waterfall. Dishes such as Cajun popcorn and blackened redfish may not be exactly like the originals, but they are tasty for Cancún, the service is good, and the mellow jazz wafting in from the Cassis Lobby Bar adds a nice note. Especially delicious are the large coconut beer-battered shrimp and the quite expensive blackened lobster. Lighter dinners are available in the Cocay Café, which opens early in the morning for a buffet or an à la carte breakfast. For lunch, sample the seafood at La Concha, near the oceanfront swimming pool.

The free-form pool wanders inside an expansive sandstone deck in the landscaped courtyard, just above the broad beach. The water sports center is north of this area at a marina in a private lagoon that has direct access to Nichupte for windsurfing, small-craft sailing, and jet skiing. Three lighted tennis courts are on the other side of the tower.

Hyatt has done an admirable job of rejuvenating the Cancún Caribe. The scale is human, the staff are friendly, and the mood is chipper.

Marriott CasaMagna Cancún

Boulevard Kulkucan
Cancún, Quintana Roo
(98) 85-20-00
Fax: (98) 85-17-31
Reservations:
Marriott International
800-223-6388

> **American luxury for those who don't want to venture too far from home**

Accommodations: 488 rooms and suites. **High-season rates:** Standard rooms $200–$220, deluxe ocean-view rooms $275, suites $450–$550. **Low-season rates:** Standard rooms $115–$140, deluxe ocean-view rooms $160, suites $450–$550. **Payment:** Major credit cards. **Children:** Under 15, free in room with parents. **Recreation:** Beach, pool, 2 tennis courts, health club, Jacuzzi, sauna, and access to water sports.

➤   **If you don't get your fill of seafood at the Marriott, head downtown to the casual El Pescador (Tulipanes 5, 84-26-73). The most popular seafood restaurant in the city, it offers fresh fare at half the price of the fancy hotels.**

Designed as an upscale but unintimidating haven for middle-American families, first-time Mexico visitors, and business groups, the Marriott shares the same basic appeal as most Cancún hotels. Its main distinction is a wealth of water, which cascades and splashes through the huge courtyard between the hotel's three mid-rise wings. The casual outdoor La Capilla restaurant seems to float on a pond, and more water tumbles in sheets into an immense pool, lined with regiments of deck chairs. Steps and tiered sunning terraces lead down to a wide beach and the ultimate aqua of the Caribbean.

Most of the time you eat where you swim and sun. La Capilla features local and international dishes at three meals, the poolside La Isla serves light meals and snacks, and the Bahia Club plies beachcombers with drinks and seafood. The only chance to dine inside is in the evening, when Mikado offers teppan-yaki dinners and other popular Japanese fare.

The spacious guest rooms provide all the customary conveniences and more, including a balcony, air conditioning, satellite TV, a mini-bar, phone, and even an iron and ironing board. The standard rooms come with two double beds or a king, and the deluxes have a king and a sofa bed as well as an ocean view.

New in 1990, the Marriott has incorporated all the attractions that have worked at other Cancún hotels. Perhaps it is not unique, but it has sure stacked the odds on success, for both itself and your vacation.

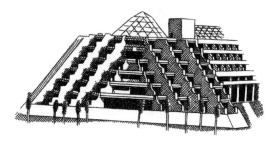

Melia Cancún Beach & Spa

Blvd. Kukulkán
Cancún, Quintana Roo
(98) 85-11-60
Fax: (98) 85-10-85
Reservations:
Melia Hotels
800-336-3542

Perhaps the splashiest resort in Cancún

Accommodations: 450 rooms and suites. **High-season rates:** Double rooms $325, suites $1,350. **Low-season rates:** Double rooms $235, suites $390. **Payment:** Major credit cards. **Children:** Under 12, free in room with parents. **Recreation:** Beach, 2 swimming pools, 2 tennis courts, 2 paddle tennis courts, golf (18-hole executive course), fitness center and spa with massage, mud therapy, and beauty treatments.

➤ **The Melia's gardens provide the setting for an 18-hole executive practice course, but better golf opportunities are nearby at the Robert Trent Jones–designed Pok-Ta-Pok Club de Golf and the Hilton Cancún Beach & Golf Resort. For those who like miniature golf, El Golfito features putting at the pyramids and replicas of Mayan ruins.**

The Melia Cancún is the flagship property of a Spanish chain that swooped into the Mexican market in the late 1980s with seven hotels. This one is quite a beachhead. The staggered structure, rising to a plateau of nine stories, is topped with a series of peaked glass pyramids soaring toward the sky. It's a Mayan motif for the space age, a colossal concept that astounds and dumbfounds the senses.

The lobby of the futuristic temple is a vast atrium garden with streams running beside marble, a wall of pre-Columbian hieroglyphics, and enough potted plants to start a rain forest. Four miles of irrigation systems are required to care for the landscaping.

The water flows even more generously outside. It cascades down a waterfall at the entrance and wraps around the hotel in 900 linear feet of free-form pools. As the sun shifts during the day, guests move with it to whichever swimming site has the best angle on the rays. The more adventuresome head to the sea, sometimes a little rough here since Hurricane Gilbert scooped out some of the sandy bottom and beach. Others find the sea views and massages from the spa *cabañas* all they need to round out the pleasures of the day.

You're seldom out of sight of the water. Each room has some view of either the Caribbean or Nichupte Lagoon, in the direction of the sunset. Spacious and handsomely furnished, the quarters come with private terraces for admiring the view, satellite TV for alternative spectacles, phones, and mini-bars. The junior suites may be worth their extra cost for stylish opulence.

Two of the four restaurants strive for haute cuisine excellence in the evening and always manage at least a good measure of elegance. A less formal beachfront café specializes in seafood, and a casual all-day dining room serves simple dishes at any time, even after the Cancún discos close. The bars include a couple of swim-up options and another with live music nightly.

Opened in 1990, the Melia Cancún is a European hotel in the grand tradition, retooled for a tropical tempo. The new Melia chain is still a toddler subject to stumbles, but there's certainly talent in the family as well as an early eagerness to show off.

Novotel

Apartado Postal 70
Cancún, Quintana Roo
(98) 84-29-99
Fax: (98) 84-31-62

> **A small budget hotel in the center of the city**

Accommodations: 40 rooms. **High-season rates:** $50 with air conditioning, $39 with fan. **Low-season rates:** $41 with air conditioning, $30 with fan. **Payment:** Major credit cards. **Recreation:** Swimming pool.

➤ **The best place to get an authentic Mayan meal in Cancún is downtown. Try Los Almendros (Av. Bonampak at Sayil, 87-13-32), a branch of a famous Mérida restaurant, which serves dishes such as pok-chuc and cochinita pibil in a bright, folkloric setting.**

In downtown Cancún, a bus ride from the beach, the Novotel sparkles with Mexican zest. That's a treat hard to find in this city and possibly worth a lot of commuting time.

The location, right in the heart of the commercial area, actually becomes an asset in the evening, because the lively downtown restaurants and bars are a short walk away. The hotel has a small dining room of its own, but it's primarily for breakfast, which is sometimes included in the rates.

Some of the fan-cooled rooms are in a three-story wood and stucco wing at the back of the property, by the small swimming pool, and others are in the main building with the restaurant and reception desk. When you enter the gaily painted courtyard lobby from busy Avenida Tulum, you sigh in relief at the change in atmosphere. Potted plants reach through the atrium toward the sun and dangle from the hallways above. Carved wood furniture, wrought iron, and tile accent the interior garden and help deliver a hearty welcome that's seconded by the friendly staff.

The Mexican decorative touches extend to the white stucco, somewhat worn rooms, which also feature double beds, small tiled bathrooms with showers, and in the case of superior rooms TV, phones, and, most importantly, air conditioning, a valuable advantage in the sultry, noisy, urban environment. It doesn't cost much extra and could save you from hours of sleeplessness.

The Novotel is a pretty, perky hotel. You can do better in Cancún, but you can also pay much more for little more in comfort and class.

Omni Cancún

Apartado Postal 127
Cancún, Quintana Roo
(98) 85-07-14
Fax: (98) 85-00-59
Reservations:
Omni Hotels
800-THE OMNI

> **A solid choice for families, couples, and singles**

Accommodations: 363 rooms, suites, and villas. **High-season rates:** Lagoon-view rooms $190–$290, ocean-view rooms $200–$325, junior suites $245–$390, villas from $450. **Low-season rates:** Lagoon-view rooms $133–$235, ocean-view rooms $156–$258, junior suites $178–$325, villas from $325. **Payment:** Major credit cards. **Children:** Under 15, free in room with parents. **Recreation:** Beach, 3 swimming pools, 2 tennis courts, fitness center with sauna, steam bath, and massage.

➤ **Like many Cancún hotels, the Omni offers an in-house travel agency that can make all the arrangements for visiting Chichén Itzá and other Mayan ruins. Don't miss the opportunity.**

The Omni Cancún pulls off some wizardry. The reception area — entered from a grand porte-cochere up a circular brick driveway — welcomes you with cultivated elegance. The rich pink marble, the gently trickling waterfall just inside the door, and the formal registration desk all make you wonder whether the hotel is going to be too classy for fun.

Just keep walking toward the Caribbean, into the vast courtyard water park, a fantasy-fulfilling profusion of pools, splashing cascades, and such enticing touches as body-contoured tiled lounge chairs built into the shallow ends of the pools. It's as tasteful in design as the lobby but a contrast in mood. The Omni is both refined and frolicsome, an alchemist's blend bound to please the pickiest hedonist.

If you want to revel in the best the Omni has to offer, avoid the lagoon-view rooms and consider upgrading to the low-rise villa wings that sweep seaward from the main tower like arms embracing the courtyard amusement center. With multiple levels and two bedroom areas, the villas offer the optimum ocean views and the ultimate in spacious sumptuousness. No one suffers much deprivation, though. All the rooms face one body of water or another and have coral marble floors, carved wood furnishings, king-size or two double beds, air conditioning, phones, mini-bars, satellite television, and in most cases balconies.

The five restaurants and lounges provide plenty of variety. You might want to eat breakfast or lunch right on the beach at Piña Colada, a café in an open-air *palapa* that serves seafood and grilled specialties. The café is on a wooden deck adjacent to several hammock-strung sand terraces that supplement the natural beach.

Start the evening with a cocktail and live music in the lobby bar. Dine at colorful La Paloma — where a mural is the focal point and primarily native fare the offerings — noon and night, or try their bountiful buffet in the morning. If necessary, you can work off the calories in the fitness center, on the exercise machines or in the sauna, or outside on two tennis courts.

The Omni has a wealth of ways for you to enjoy yourself. One of the smoothest resort hotels in Cancún, it's a crafty combination of moods and milieus.

Ritz-Carlton Cancún

Blvd. Kukulkán
Cancún, Quintana Roo
(98) 85-08-08
Fax: (98) 85-10-15
Reservations:
Ritz-Carlton Reservations
800-241-3333

> **One of the classiest acts in Cancún**

Accommodations: 370 rooms and suites. **High-season rates:** Ocean-view rooms $349, deluxe oceanfront rooms $389, Ritz-Carlton Club rooms $499, one-bedroom suites $535, with Club Service $600. **Low-season rates:** Ocean-view rooms $169, deluxe oceanfront rooms $189, Ritz-Carlton Club rooms $297, one-bedroom suites $330, with Club Service $409. **Payment:** Major credit cards. **Children:** Under 18, free in room with parents; activities program available. **Recreation:** Beach, 2 swimming pools, 3 tennis courts, fitness center with Nautilus gym, cardiovascular machines and aerobics, massage, and steam bath.

➤ **The Ritz-Carlton restaurants offer an extensive wine list, but the most distinctive list of drinks is in the lobby bar, where the "sommelier" presents a wide-ranging selection of tequilas.**

A little background helps explain what the Ritz-Carlton is trying to achieve at its hotel in Cancún. The elite chain's compound name derives from two grand, historic European hotels, the Ritz of Paris and the Carlton in London. Cesar Ritz, founder of the former, and his chef, the great Escoffier, both of whom had an interest in the Carlton, formed a management firm around the turn of the century with the mission of bringing Ritz-Carlton excellence to other cities.

That company is long gone, but an Atlanta group inherited the name and tradition with the 1983 purchase of the Ritz-Carlton Boston, the last survivor of the initial inspiration. The new owners are expanding steadily to different regions in fresh pursuit of the original goal, providing the kind of timeless elegance away from home that discriminating guests would expect at home. Their hotels strive for an Old World graciousness and refinement, an air usually influenced by local flavors but always aristocratic in bearing.

The Ritz Carlton Cancún is no exception to the chain's tradition. The grand lobby, with its paintings in gilded frames, floral carpets, and armchairs, brings an unusual elegance to the seaside setting, as does the formal attire of the staff. Gracious hallways and spacious, well-proportioned common areas provide a serene architectural setting. Service is excellent and includes 24-hour room service.

The beach is extensive and quite fine. The facilities include two swimming pools, three tennis courts, and an excellent fitness center and spa with views of the sea.

The Ritz-Carlton rooms can be counted on for comfort. All have two double beds or a king, and fresh flowers grace the nightstand. The spacious marble bathrooms contain two showers, plush terry robes, an array of imported toiletries, and one of the room's three telephones. All the rooms enjoy air conditioning, satellite TV, a mini-bar, and a wonderful balcony with a wrought-iron rail and cobalt blue tiles that glisten like the sea just beyond.

As in other Ritz-Carltons, rooms and suites on the Club level can be a great choice. Similar accommodations in other hotels usually provide much more status than value. Here they may be worth the premium price, depending on the special services you use. In addition to a private lounge and concierge staff, the extras include a Continental breakfast buffet, snacks during the day, afternoon tea, and evening cocktails with hors d'oeuvres.

Like the rooms, the principal restaurants are similar to those in Ritz-Carltons elsewhere. The intimate, classy Dining Room, the signature restaurant, features Northern Italian cuisine. The Club Grill offers grilled seafood and prime aged beef in a traditional setting reminiscent of an English club for dinner and dancing. The casual Caribe Bar & Grill, open for three meals a day, serves a bit of everything, from a bountiful buffet breakfast to sandwiches and pasta. The lobby lounge serves excellent Mexican snacks and 70 different tequilas to the accompaniment of live music.

Shortly before its Mexican debut, the Ritz-Carlton company became the first in the travel industry to win the prestigious Malcolm Baldrige National Quality Award. The small chain earned the accolade in the States and has successfully exported its proven commitment to excellence. In 1999, the Ritz-Carlton Cancún was ranked number one by *Travel & Leisure* among all hotels in Mexico, Central America, and South America. The Ritz-Carlton's venerable Old World legacy fits regally in the New World's splashiest resort city.

Villas Tacul

Apartado Postal 290
Cancún, Quintana Roo
(98) 83-00-00
Fax: (98) 83-03-49
Reservations:
Villas Tacul
800-842-0193

Villas for couples, families, and friends traveling together

Accommodations: 23 villas. **High-season rates:** Garden studio $190, 1-bedroom villas $350 for 2 adults, 2-bedroom villas $495 for 4 adults, 3-bedroom villas $675 for 6 adults, 4-bedroom villas $795 for 8 adults. **Low-season rates:** Garden studio $125, 1-bedroom villas $235 for 2 adults, 2-bedroom villas $350 for 4 adults, 3-bedroom villas $495 for 6 adults, 4-bedroom villas $595 for 8 adults. **Payment:** Major credit cards. **Children:** Under 12, free in villa with parents. **Recreation:** Beach, swimming pool, 2 tennis courts.

➤ **Everyone visiting Cancún should rent a car at least one day and drive south to the Mayan ruins at Tulum, about 80 miles away on a good, mainly four-lane road. See the next chapter, "Cancún South," for details.**

Not a conventional hotel or a condominium either, Villas Tacul has been something of an oddball in Cancún since the mid-1970s — and a most welcome one. A couple of dozen white stucco bungalows, Mexican in style, are either along the beach or amid a lush coconut grove in a tranquil setting that is a welcome relief from the hubbub of Cancún. The place can look a bit deserted even when it's full, partly because the accommodations are the reason people come, and the villas are so appealing that guests are often indoors, nesting. For outdoor activities, there's a cozy beach cove.

Entire villas or partial villas, such as a garden studio with kitchen, can be rented. The prices are very good, since they permit families and friends to share the price as well as enjoy spacious accommodations. The air-conditioned villas range in size from some that are ideal for parents with a couple of children up to some that can hold a family reunion. Each has a fully equipped kitchen, a dining area, a comfortable living room, phone, TV, and a terrace. The decor varies some, but all villas are modern and ample, if not luxuriously appointed, and you can depend on native features such as colorful tile, heavy wood furniture, wrought-iron work, and craft pieces. The largest villas get the prime perch along the shore, while the one- and two-bedroom units are back from the water. Personalized cooking arrangements can be made — for example, a maid will come to your villa to prepare breakfast, starting with fresh juice.

A large pool with five palm-shaded islands occupies much of the central lawn, at the opposite end of the grass from the two tennis courts. La Palapa restaurant abuts the pool, allowing you to eat on the stone deck as well as inside under the thatched roof, a space that exudes a tropical aura. Seafood is the specialty.

A congenial, cozy option, Villas Tacul is following a different drummer than the rest of Cancún. It's small enough to personalize the hospitality and big enough to give you a genuine home for enjoying it.

Isla Mujeres

Na Balam

Calle Zazil-Ha 118
Isla Mujeres, Quintana Roo
(987) 7-02-79
Fax: (987)7-04-46
Reservations:
(800) 223-6510

A small beachfront inn with big rooms

Accommodations: 30 junior suites and 1 master suite. **High-season rates:** Junior suites $134, master suite $157. **Low-season rates:** Junior suites $101–$112, master suite $134–$146. **Payment:** MasterCard, Visa. **Recreation:** Beach, swimming pool, yoga classes.

➤ **No one really knows why the early Spanish explorers gave Isla Mujeres its exotic name, "the Isle of Women." Some say the Spaniards found shrines to a goddess of fertility, but a more likely explanation is that all the men were fishing at sea when the Europeans arrived.**

Na Balam squats on the end of the main beach on Isla Mujeres, across the lagoon from the island's largest hotel. It lacks the recreational facilities of its big brother, but it tops the resort property in every other way.

Na Balam's original 18 beachfront junior suites are in plain low-rise structures spread along the sand. They are enormous quarters, exuding the natural essence of wood, tile, and stone. Most of them feature two double beds and a terrace, though a couple come with a king-size bed. Each has an ocean view, a sofa, a dining table with four chairs, a compact refrigerator, a shower, and both a ceiling fan and an air conditioner. They may not be fancy, but they are comfortable and beachy and preferable to the new units surrounding the pool. The master suite has its own Jacuzzi.

The menu is limited at the small restaurant, but the breakfasts at least tend to be bountiful, with homemade breads. The rest of the day you choose between a few sandwiches, seafood, and Mexican and vegetarian specialties. The drink options range more broadly and come with hors d'oeuvres at happy hour in the poolside Palapa Bar.

The sandy grounds retain a wild, untended look characteristic of the long beach. There are a few *palapas* where you can swing in a hammock, a pool, and nearby water sports. For those inclined, there are daily yoga classes. The town is a short, dusty hike or a quick cab ride away. Make the trip in the evening, when the sun-baked streets come alive with local color.

Na Balam isn't a luxury resort, though it does give you some of those trappings in the junior suites. It allows you to dwell in style without spending a fortune.

Cancún South

Best Romantic Hideaway

Best Beachfront Buys

Best B&Bs and Budget Inns

Best Adventure Retreats

We like to call it "Baja Cancún" or "Cancún South," but don't look for either term on a map of Mexico. These are simply our names for an area of idyllic beaches that starts at Puerto Morelos, about 20 miles below Cancún, continues 75 miles farther down to Boca Paila, and then leaps almost 200 miles to the Xcalak Peninsula. More and more frequently, road signs and maps proclaim this beautiful section of the Caribbean coast, along with the greater Cancún area, to be the "Mayan Riviera" (as distinct from the "Mexican Riviera" on the Pacific coast). The Mexican government tentatively decided in the 1970s to leave this coast undeveloped, but condo developments and theme parks are clear signs that the authorities have reneged on the idea. The time to visit is now, before the region is totally overdeveloped.

Hundreds of Cancún tourists pass by the beaches daily on tour buses going to Tulum's Mayan ruins, but the highway is a little too far inland for them to notice the stretches of beach and Caribbean Sea that they're missing. The small *cabañas* and condos around the cove at Akumal and the fast-evolving town of Playa del Carmen are the most notable spots along the shore, except for Tulum itself.

Several of the poorly marked turnoffs lead to splendid sands occupied by small, secluded inns with delightful personalities. And below Tulum, dirt roads and the Sian Ka'an nature preserve keep things the way the Caribbean used to be. The setting and the mood are similar to island hideaways in bygone days, but it's much easier to get here, and the cost of transportation and lodging is substantially lower than in the Antilles. This is paradise as it's never been. For serious diving and uncombed beaches, don't overlook the even less developed Xcalak Peninsula, 250 miles south of Cancún.

The Main Attractions

Greater Playa del Carmen

Playa del Carmen is as urban as it gets in this area, and although it still has somewhat of a small-town beach feel, it is getting more urban every day. The population has grown exponentially over the past several years, and the town bustles as never before, aided by the recent, massive hotel construction. In the south of town, there is a new sterile suburban hotel zone flanking the Playacar Golf Club. To get the flavor of the more authentic Playa del Carmen, you should avoid these hotels in favor of the accommodations found north of the ferry dock in the older, funkier, more charming part of town. Here you will still find Playa del Carmen's long, lovely beach with its eccentric disarray of lodging. And you will also find the best restaurants, bars, and cafés. The ferry dock itself springs to life several times a day when the passenger ferries depart for or return to Cozumel. Nearby, a small airport services the town.

Punta Bete is a few miles north of Playa del Carmen. When you take a rental car from the Cancún airport, you have to watch carefully for a dirt road on the left and a sign for La Posada del Capitán Lafitte. The inn is about a mile down the trail and has a professional water sports center. That's all there is — other than a glorious beach and an ocean with more hues than Crayola.

The sand used to be lined with hundreds of tall palms, but a deadly blight has killed most of them on this Caribbean coast. Like other places to the south, the hotels have reforested the area with seedlings that are believed to be disease-resistant. Scientists say they should survive, but even so, it will take years for them to match the magnificence of their grandparents.

South of Playa del Carmen, shortly before Akumal, you encounter an early example of contemporary resort development in Baja Cancún. Puerto Aventuras is a spanking new city of luxury homes, condos, and hotels replete with a marina, a golf course, a plethora of tennis courts, a private airport, and even an underwater archaeology museum. The massive project seems well designed, but we hope it's the Capitán Lafittes, not the mega-developments that foretell the future for this coast.

Dreamy Days in Akumal

One of the gems of the Cancún area for years, Akumal feels slightly developed itself, particularly since the blight cut down the palms that once screened the three hotels and several dozen villas from each other. The beach is so expansive, however, and the various properties so spread out that the shore continues to radiate a lost-in-the-tropics aura.

Akumal's main advantage over other stops off the highway is its lovely bay, sheltered by reefs that keep the surf calm and provide great snorkeling and diving. Hidden to the north of the bay are newer condos along the shore and the protected snorkeling cove of Yalcu. A number of seaside restaurants and bars, as well as several dive shops, offer ample diversity without producing commercial clutter. It's a languorous hideaway destination, but not so slow that you get restless.

"The Most Beautiful Bay in the World"

It's hard to miss the turnoff a little south of Akumal to Playa Chemuyil, marked with a large sign announcing it as "the most beautiful bay in the world." The claim is characteristic Mexican hyperbole, but Chemuyil is definitely an enchanting spot. After paying a moderate admission fee, you can spend the day swimming, snorkeling, or just lounging on the gorgeous beach in a wooden chair with an umbrella. For an additional fee, you can camp overnight in a screened hut with a hammock.

The restaurant tends to your needs on the beach and serves lunch on the sand as well. Each of the big round tables spread along the shore is sheltered by its own *palapa*. It feels as if you have an open-air dining room to yourself. We once ordered a whole sea bass here, prepared *con ajo* (with garlic), which was excellent, succulent, and perfectly spiced. Even if the kitchen is off, though, the setting is so sublime you won't begrudge paying the bill.

A Perfect Park for Snorkelers

Lunch and libations are also available at Xel-Ha, a little farther south. Pronounced *shell-hah,* the underwater park is the best known of this coast's several *caletas,* or coves, which form a natural aquarium. The alluring lagoons are brimming with tropical fish and, after the Cancún buses arrive, swimmers, snorkelers, and divers. Open from 8:00 A.M. to 5:00 P.M., Xel-Ha is a pretty spot all day but peaceful only in the early morning.

Mayan Magic

The next stop along the highway is Tulum, a Mayan ruin of modest size with a spectacular perch above a beach and the sea. See the chapter "Archaeological Treasures" for additional information.

The End of Civilization

Few visitors venture farther than Tulum, where the coastal road begins to narrow before losing its pavement in an ecological preserve called Sian Ka'an. The name means "where heaven is born," but don't take it literally unless you're looking for wildlife, deserted beaches, and accommodations with dirt-cheap charm. The thin peninsula is an untamed retreat without conventional electricity and plumbing, a place to shuck civilization entirely. Even if the rest of the Mayan Riviera follows in the footsteps of Puerto Aventuras, Sian Ka'an is bound to remain at least a century away from a resort milieu. The main Cancún road also continues south and passes the access road to the majestic ruins of Coba before running past the town of Felipe Carrillo Puerto on its way to the turnoff to Xcalak Peninsula. Here, too, nature has been left to itself except for two tiny villages and a few adventure inns specializing in diving.

Akumal

Las Casitas Akumal

Carretera 307, 65 mi south of Cancún
Akumal, Quintana Roo
(987) 5-90-71
Fax: (987) 5-90-72
Reservations:
Las Casitas Akumal
800-5-AKUMAL

A cottage hotel on an incomparable shore

Accommodations: 18 condominium villas. **High-season rates:** $175–$210 for up to 5 people. **Low-season rates:** $125–$150 for up to 5 people. **Payment:** Major credit cards. **Children:** Free with parents in the same villa. **Recreation:** Beach, expert dive shop for water sports, bike rentals and access to horseback riding, tennis, and golf.

➤ **Divers and snorkelers love Akumal, one of the best places in Mexico for those sports, but you don't have to be devoted to the depths to enjoy Las Casitas. It's a great getaway for anyone, from honeymooners to friends traveling together.**

Las Casitas is a family or friends hideaway in Mexico, a gem we stumbled onto years ago. For younger children, there are preschool and babysitting services. With a brood or without, it's a delightful spot to rediscover each other.

Half of the allure is the sublime sand and the Caribbean water. The beach that starts a few steps from your door sweeps to the horizon in a wide crescent around Akumal Bay. Even when Las Casitas and the other two hotels on the shore are full, every guest gets about an acre of sand. The palm blight along this entire coast killed a magnificent grove of trees that once provided shade and additional scenery, but the beach is still a beauty with its remaining palm trees. The management added a large beachfront *palapa* in 1990 to give guests a break from the intense sun.

A coral reef stretches across the mouth of the bay, attracting thousands of fish and keeping the water calm for swimmers and snorkelers. Scuba diving was the original attraction here, and it's still a thriving sport. Three independent dive shops operate excursions daily and rent the gear for scuba, snorkeling, and windsurfing.

The other half of the allure is your *casita*. It's a two-bedroom, two-bath bungalow with a kitchen, a living room, and a garden patio facing the sea. Each *casita* contains a stove and refrigerator, tile floors, air conditioning, ceiling fans, a wall of windows opening out to the terrace, and usually a combination of king-size and twin beds, or a king and one double with one twin. The four newest villas, at the top of the rate scale, feature a split-level layout with an ocean-view master bedroom and balcony upstairs and an extra half bath on the main floor. Individually owned, mainly by Americans, the *casitas* are furnished differently according to the tastes of the owners. Some are fresh and bright, others more mundane.

There's a grocery store in the tiny village, but if you'd rather not cook for yourself, you can choose among several restaurants on the beach. The *palapa* bar and café in the center of the sand is good for lunch, and in the evening the Lol Ha restaurant offers a broad selection.

After a meal you can wander back to your patio, partially covered by *palapa* thatch, and spread out on a lounge chair for a siesta. Enveloped by the tropical landscaping, listening to the gentle Caribbean surf rolling in a few yards away, you won't have a care in the world. That's a way of life at Las Casitas, and it's likely to tempt you back again and again.

Vista del Mar

Half Moon Bay
North Akumal, Quintana Roo
(987) 5-90-60
Fax: (987) 5-90-58
Reservations:
(800) 925-6325 (#15)

> **Modern, sparkling hotel and condominium apartment accommodations overlooking Half Moon Bay**

Accommodations: 17 hotel rooms and 6 condominium apartments. **High-season rates:** Hotel rooms $75, 2-bedroom condominiums $155–$165, 3-bedroom condominiums $215. **Low-season rates:** Hotel rooms $40–$45, 2-

bedroom condominiums $66–$90, 3-bedroom condominiums $110–$120. **Payment:** Major credit cards. **Recreation:** Beach, pool, water sports including kayaking.

➤   **Just a short walk from the Vista del Mar you'll find La BuenaVista restaurant, wonderfully situated on the beach with views of Half Moon Bay. At lunch dip your feet into the sand at one of the outdoor tables while dining on good soups, seafood, and salad. Dinner is served in the indoor dining room.**

Like Las Casitas Akumal, the Vista del Mar provides very reasonably priced accommodations for several people in its condominiums and quite economical rooms with sea views in its hotel. If you check out the room rates in Cancún, you'll be stunned by the comparatively low prices here for seafront accommodations. And, of course, in Akumal, you'll have the serenity not found in Cancún. While the accommodations at the Vista del Mar are more modern than those at Las Casitas Akumal, the beach isn't as beautiful.

The most desirable accommodations are the contemporary two- and three-bedroom condominiums, housed in two-story buildings, gleaming white in a modern Spanish colonial design, with floor-to-ceiling sliding glass doors opening to the beach and the turquoise sea just a stone's throw away. Light-filled and tastefully designed and decorated, these apartments have such distinctive touches as built-in sofas in the living room and attractive Guatemalan textiles on the walls. There's a full-size dining room to go along with the large kitchen, which even has a microwave oven. The living room, dining room, kitchen, and master bedroom all have sea views. For TV addicts, these condos have cable. The tiled bathroom comes with such features as a double sink. One further delight is the spacious outdoor patio or balcony. The one drawback for some may be the absence of air conditioning. The second floor three-bedroom condominium has the added attraction of a Jacuzzi.

More economical accommodations, suitable for one or two people, can be found in the adjacent modern three-story hotel situated on a pretty cove. Here you'll find small, fresh rooms with tiled bathrooms and small balconies or terraces overlooking the sea. The Guatemalan bedspreads add color and texture to the whitewashed rooms. Unlike the condominiums, the hotel rooms are air-conditioned, and they also come with a coffeemaker and small refrigerator. And, of course, you'll look long and hard along the Mayan Riviera for such modern and well-equipped sea-view rooms at comparable prices.

For recreation there's a pool in addition to the beach and sea. And nearby, the Yalku lagoon offers good snorkeling. For seekers of the sea and serenity with modern comforts, it's hard to beat the Vista del Mar.

Playa del Carmen

Chichan Baal Kah

Calle 16 between Av. 1 and Av. 5
Playa del Carmen, Quintana Roo
(987) 3-12-52
Reservations:
Turquoise Reef Group
303-674-9615
800-538-6802
Fax: 303-674-8735

> **A small, stylish inn that exudes good taste and charm**

Accommodations: 7 one-bedroom apartments. **High-season rates:** $120. **Low-season rates:** $80. **Included:** Tax, Continental breakfast, maid service, use of bicycles. **Payment:** No credit cards. **Children:** No children under 16. **Recreation:** Swimming pool, sun deck.

➤   **Just a few blocks from the Chichan Baal Kah you'll find Hot: The Baking Company (Calle 10, between Av. 5 and Av. 10) serving breakfast and light lunches and featuring tasty sandwiches — turkey, tuna, vegetarian, and more — on fresh, homemade whole wheat bread.**

Looking like a Mediterranean villa, the handsome Chichan Baal Kah ("Small World") offers lovely accommodations in an intimate, romantic setting. Although the villa is quite modern, the scale is small, in keeping with the laid-back style of the old Playa del Carmen. But here you will find amenities, and most welcome ones, not found in old Playa. The seven air-conditioned, white-washed one-bedroom suites feature a queen-size bed in the separate bedroom and a well-designed large area divided into a living room, dining room, and kitchen. Tasteful touches and decorative delights can be found throughout the suites: attractive ceramic lamps in the bedroom, hand-painted Mexican tiles in the bathroom, a comfortable sofa bed and upholstered chair in the cozy living room, and a well-designed, full kitchen with a good-size refrigerator and stove along with Oaxaca-style hand-painted dishes. To enhance the romantic feel of the setting, there are no phones in the suites (although there is cable TV, just in case you can't really bear to be away!), and children are banished. If you decide to venture outdoors, you'll find that each suite features a large, private terrace and surrounds a courtyard with a small pool. For sunbathing, head for the rooftop terrace, and if you have the energy to cook, barbecue facilities are available.

Although the Chichan Baal Kah has a pool, you should try to pull yourself away from this special setting and head for Playa del Carmen's beach, just one and a half blocks away. Unfortunately, the beach area that you immediately come upon borders on a huge ungainly modern hotel development, the Porto Real, looking totally out of place in small-scale Playa. This development, like the ones to the south of Playa's ferry dock, makes you appreciate even more what a special and tasteful place the Chichan Baal Kah is. To avoid this modern eyesore, just walk to the right on the beach and, when the mood hits you, make yourself at home on the sand.

You won't miss not having a restaurant at the Chichan Baal Kah. A Continental breakfast is provided, and a wide variety of eateries, ranging from funky cafés to somewhat upscale Italian and Continental restaurants, are within a short walking distance. The Chichan Baal Kah is a place to relax in style and sophistication, the perfect home base for exploring the many delights of Playa del Carmen.

El Faro

Calle 10 Norte, on the beach
Playa del Carmen, Quintana Roo
(987) 3-09-70
Reservations: (in the U.S.)
888-243-7413
Fax: (987) 3-09-68

The best beachfront hotel in Playa in the midst of all the action

Accommodations: 28 rooms. **High-season rates:** Fan-cooled double rooms $120–$190, air-conditioned ocean-view rooms $215, air-conditioned oceanfront rooms $235. **Low-season rates:** Fan-cooled double rooms $105–$160, air-conditioned ocean-view rooms $185, air-conditioned oceanfront rooms $205. **Payment:** Major credit cards. **Children:** Under 10, free in room with parents. **Recreation:** Beach, swimming pool.

➤ **It's just a short walk from El Faro to Avenida 5, Playa del Carmen's bustling main drag, lined with restaurants, bars, cafés, and shops — the center of action in this once sleepy town.**

Built in 1994, El Faro provides upscale accommodations in a tranquil spot in the heart of Playa del Carmen's busy beach area. The 28 rooms are located in several two- and three-story Mediterranean-style buildings that surround a palm-tree-filled garden area. The contrast between the greenness of the tropical gardens and the whiteness of the buildings is striking. The stone seating areas scattered around the grounds add to the serenity of the setting.

Some of the rooms have sea views, and the most expensive ones are located right on the large, lovely beach just steps from the turquoise Caribbean. Most rooms, however, have garden views. All rooms have either balconies or terraces and are tastefully decorated with white wicker and blond wood furniture, rose marble-tiled floors, and ceramic lamps. Naturally, the air-conditioned rooms are pricier than those with fans only. Whatever price room you choose, when you are at the beach you'll have the comforts of El Faro's cushioned lounge chairs and the shade of its *palapas*. If you ever tire of the soothing Caribbean waters, you can cool off in the kidney-shaped pool. And if you have a car, there's free parking in El Faro's parking lot at the rear of the hotel.

Throughout the day, you can get refreshments at El Faro's attractive thatched-roof bar overlooking the sea or meals in the adjoining restaurant. You'll certainly want, however, to leave your quiet setting to see the hodgepodge of hotels, restaurants, and bars that line the beach as well as the main drag of Avenida 5, to experience some of the music and merriment, and to get a sense of the mixture of people from many lands and backgrounds that are attracted to Playa del Carmen's beaches.

At the end of the day you will be delighted to return to the quiet and tranquillity provided by El Faro, a bit of an oasis in the midst of pulsating Playa.

La Posada del Capitán Lafitte

Carretera 307, 37 miles south of
Cancún
Punta Bete, Quintana Roo
(987) 3-02-14
Reservations:
Turquoise Reef Group
303-674-9615
800-538-6802
Fax: 303-674-8735

A simple but splendid beach hideaway

Accommodations: 60 rooms and suites. **High-season rates:** Double rooms $200, 2-bedroom El Cofre units $380 for up to 4 people. **Low-season rates:** Double rooms $110–$130, El Cofre units $210–$250 for up to 4 people. **Included:** Breakfast, dinner, tax, partial service charge; airport transfer extra. **Minimum stay:** 5 nights in high season. **Payment:** American Express. **Children:** Under 4, free in room with parents; ages 4–10, $40 per night. **Recreation:** Beach, swimming pool, water sports center, horseback riding, massage, playground.

➤   **Just before he disappeared in 1821, Jean Lafitte may have visited Punta Bete to rest up from recent battles in Galveston. Some say he liked the place so well that he married a Mayan woman and retired nearby.**

La Posada del Capitán Lafitte is an embarrassment to the proud villainy of its namesake, the famous Caribbean pirate. Even if the inn leaves your wallet a little thinner when you depart, your body and soul feel enriched. The real Lafitte must be turning over in his grave at that approach to business.

On first glance, the rates seem higher than they are, because they include breakfast and dinner daily. That's done not to hold you hostage, as the old buccaneer would have liked, but because there is no other restaurant nearby. After Hurricane Gilbert blew away the original seaside grill, the *posada* rebuilt its café as part of a bright, fresh hospitality complex that also includes a bar, an attractive free-form swimming pool, and a game room with a pool table and television.

Breakfast is a buffet with fresh fruit, juices, and hot dishes that are mainly American in origin. Dinner is a Mexican or seafood spread some evenings, but usually a four-course set menu. On the day of our last visit, the offerings were carrot salad, seafood soup, fish fillet, and fruit cocktail. Sandwiches and light fare are served at lunch. The cooking isn't exceptional, but the beachfront setting and the congenial Mexican decor add some needed spice to make mealtimes pleasant.

Capitán Lafitte's rooms are in duplex bungalows strung along the sandy shore. Cheerful and spacious, they feature a king bed or two doubles with colorful spreads, terrazzo floors, a tiled shower, a ceiling fan, and louvered windows that provide good cross-ventilation. Each has a porch right on the beach, a few long strides from the lapping surf. An additional 20 rooms, planned for the near future, may vary in some ways.

The El Cofre quarters are in a duplex at the end of the property, near the water sports center that focuses on scuba diving, snorkeling, and fishing. Although the two-story, two-bedroom units work well for families or for couples traveling together, they feel too modern to us for the sandside setting.

Apart from that minor flaw, Capitán Lafitte is a gem of a casual beach hideaway. It's not the kind of treasure the notorious pirate usually sought, but enterprising spirits of today could find it a well-earned reward.

Quinta Mija

Av. 5 at Calle 14
Apartado Postal 54
Playa del Carmen, Quintana Roo
(987) 3-01-11
Reservations:
Turquoise Reef Group
303-674-9615
800-538-6802
Fax: 303-674-8735

A small, serene inn in the heart of Playa del Carmen

Accommodations: 24 rooms and apartments. **High-season rates:** Queen-bed rooms $50, new rooms $72 for up to 4 people, apartments $94. **Low-season rates:** Rooms $39, apartments $78. **Included:** Tax, but extra for airport transfer. **Minimum stay:** 5 nights in high season. **Payment:** No credit cards. **Recreation:** Swimming pool, sun deck.

➤ **Nearby Xcaret, an ancient Mayan *cenote* recently has been turned into an expensive and very commercial nature park. Attractions include the chance to swim with dolphins, ride horseback, and snorkel through an underground river that was created "naturally" by dynamiting a spring.**

The Quinta Mija carries a girl's name, but its source is two boys. American owners Greg and Sally Hrehovcsik christened the inn after their sons Mikah and Jacob, using the first two letters of each name. They call the Quinta the daughter they never had.

She's certainly grown as steadily as a child. The Hrehovcsiks started with a few apartments, gradually added more, and recently completed some smaller and less expensive double rooms, all designed by Greg, who also oversaw the construction. At present there are five buildings, artfully tucked into a lush tropical garden that provides a quiet setting just a short walk from Playa del Carmen's beach.

Although the apartments are beginning to show their age, they are comfortable, especially for families, and are a fine value for the space and the convenience of a full kitchen. Simply furnished with a dining table and chairs, a double bed, and a daybed that serves as a sofa, they contain a living room, a separate bedroom, and a large bathroom gleaming with blue and tan tile. Fans circulate the breezes coming through large screened windows. The original standard rooms with queen-size beds and a private bath are quite simple, but the newer rooms are more spacious, with two double beds and tiled baths. The rooms have no cooking facilities.

If you don't want to bother with the beach or sightseeing, you can laze away a day at the small swimming pool or rooftop sun deck, sipping a drink from the *palapa* bar. That's it for activities on the grounds at the Quinta Mija, but you shouldn't need much more. Though Greg and Sally's daughter may not be overly playful, she's plenty winsome.

Rosa Mirador

1 Privada Norte between Calles 12 and 14
Playa del Carmen, Quintana Roo
(987) 3-07-50
Fax: same as phone

A small budget hotel just steps from the sand and sea

Accommodations: 11 rooms and suites. **High-season rates:** fan-cooled double rooms $38-$45, air-conditioned double rooms $54, air-conditioned suites $60. **Low-season rates:** fan-cooled double rooms $22-$30, air-conditioned double rooms $38, air-conditioned suites $44. **Payment:** No credit cards.

➤ **With the money you are saving by staying at the Rosa Mirador, you might want to treat yourself to a tasty meal of grilled mushrooms and homemade pasta in the romantic setting at Da Gabi (Calle 12, near the beach).**

Not too long ago people came to Playa del Carmen to experience its beautiful beaches and other pleasures, some legal, some not, and to do this on the cheap. The town attracted hippies and other counterculture types, along with straighter folk who enjoyed the beauty of the beaches and simplicity of the setting as well as the bargain prices. Meals were basic, but you could get fresh fish cooked in the standard Mexican ways. Neither *penne all'arabbiata* nor yogurt, whole wheat bread, or edible pizza could be found for miles. Along with the absence of upscale restaurants was the absence of upscale hotels — and with good reason. People did not come to Playa to be pampered or for luxuries. But the challenge was not simply to find inexpensive accommodations, for just about all accommodations were inexpensive. The goal was to find a place that really was a deal, a place where you really were happy, and not simply because it was cheap. Rosa Mirador was our find.

Over the years, Rosa Mirador has changed. The amiable Don Beto, who served as clerk, raconteur, handyman, and friend, has retired. The exterior has a new paint job, and the interior courtyard has been freshened up and even contains a chair or two for relaxing under the trees. Some rooms now are air-conditioned. And the Rosa Mirador even has its own telephone — and fax!

But much has remained the same. The Rosa Mirador is still often not found in Playa del Carmen's list of hotels. And many locals don't know its whereabouts, even though it has a terrific location less than a block from the beach, behind the popular Blue Parrot Inn. In keeping with the ambience of old Playa del Carmen, the Rosa Mirador has remained small. The eleven rooms are still simply and sparsely furnished but clean, and the most desirable ones are those on the top floors, although our favorite, #9, now has its sea view often marred by a nearby tree. The rates remain some of the lowest in Playa, especially for a breezy hotel with a beach flavor that is just a minute's walk to the sparkling sea. For those still yearning for the old Playa — for a basic, comfortable, no-frills hotel with very affordable rates — the Rosa Mirador is still a deal, still a find.

Shangri-La Caribe

Playa del Carmen, Quintana Roo
(987) 2-28-88
Fax: Same as phone
Reservations:
Turquoise Reef Group
303-674-9615
800-538-6802
Fax: 303-674-8735

A Polynesian fantasy on Caribbean waters

Accommodations: 70 rooms. **High-season rates:** Ocean-view rooms $200, beachfront rooms $240, garden-view rooms $180. **Low-season rates:** Ocean-view rooms $150, beachfront rooms $190, garden-view rooms $130. **Included:** Breakfast, dinner, tax, partial service charge; airport transfer extra. **Minimum stay:** 5 nights in high season. **Payment:** No credit cards. **Children:** Under 4, free in room with parents, from 4–12 the charge is $40. **Recreation:** Beach, swimming pool, water sports center.

➤   **When you venture into Playa del Carmen, about a mile from Shangri-La, you can eat very well at Nuestra Señora del Carmen (Avenida 10, near Juárez). Owned by a fisherman, it serves the freshest seafood in town.**

Shangri-La Caribe has a lot in common with Capitán Lafitte. Like the other inn, it's secluded on a long, floury beach with lovely waters a mile north of Playa del Carmen, and because of its location, the hotel includes breakfast and dinner in the rates. The two places are separately owned, but they share a booking service in Evergreen, Colorado, that handles reservations with as much dispatch and personal attention as any U.S. agent. Beyond location and logistics, Shangri-La has a similar ambience, with more of a Robinson Crusoe feel, the same fusion of romantic primitivism and ample comfort that makes Capitán Lafitte such a dreamy escape.

The main difference is the style of lodging. In this case the accommodations are in duplex *cabañas* with handsome *palapa* roofs. Each of the scattered cottages is on the sand, which extends throughout the property, but only five beachfront junior suites directly overlook the sea, and some of the upper duplexes, although not beachfront, have sea views. The regular quarters are moderate in size, sparsely furnished, and a bit worn, with old-fashioned bathrooms, while the suites are spacious rooms with a sunken sitting area containing a *banco* sofa. All feature a languorous patio or balcony draped with a couple of inviting hammocks, and they also have tile floors, ceiling fans, and two double beds. The simple accommodations are comfortable and cool.

The swimming pool occupies the center of the grounds. Nearby on one side is a dive shop offering PADI scuba instruction and rental equipment for snorkeling, fishing, and windsurfing as well as diving. The sea here is good for swimming and near some fine reefs for snokeling. A *palapa* bar and game room sits just beyond the pool, on the opposite side.

There are two restaurants. The more modern one, with sea views, is often used for breakfast, and the older, more atmospheric restaurant, which serves dinner, sits back a good distance from the surf. The meals are not a principal lure, but they provide more options than you get in some M.A.P. situations. Breakfast is a fruit and juice buffet, followed by a choice of entrées. The four-course dinner allows you to select either a hot or cold soup and a fish or meat entrée. There is usually a Mexican buffet one night a week and music on a couple of evenings. If you need more variety, the pleasant walk along the beach into Playa del Carmen will only enhance your appetite.

Shangri-La resembles a South Seas village, a small thatch-topped utopia remote from modern life. Lying in your personal hammock, swayed gently by the breezes, you feel like the monarch of an undiscovered tropical domain. You may wish it were home forever.

Puerto Morelos

Maroma

Apartado Postal 51
Cancún, Quintana Roo 77500
(987) 4-47-29
Fax: (987) 4-47-30

| **A romantic sanctuary less than an hour from Cancún** |

Accommodations: 36 rooms. **High-season rates:** Garden-view rooms $306, ocean-view rooms $360, junior suites $450, one- and two-bedroom suites $576–$720. **Low-season rates:** Garden-view rooms $270, ocean-view rooms $324, junior suites $405, suites $675–$702. **Included:** Breakfast, airport transfers from Cancún, snorkeling equipment, but not tax or service. **Payment:** American Express and Visa. **Recreation:** Swimming pool, Jacuzzi, massage, snorkeling and other water sports, horseback riding. **Children:** Under 16, not encouraged.

➤ **The food at the Maroma shows surprising panache, from pecan pancakes and fresh breads to three-sauce lobster and authentic Mexican dishes.**

Over the past several years José Luis Moreno and his wife, Sally, have overseen the incremental creation of their dream resort from a few rooms to thirty-six guest quarters. Having reached its ultimate size, the resort simply strives for perfection. Located about 32 miles south of Cancún and 11 miles south of the small fishing town of Puerto Morelos, this Caribbean sanctuary has no sign marking its entrance.

The Maroma is truly a romantic hideaway. The feeling of seclusion is enhanced by the bumpy, mile-long entrance road to the hotel. The small stucco buildings housing the guest quarters are protected from the world by more than five hundred acres of tropical vegetation. The pristine, powdery white beach stretches for miles, unblemished by Cancún mega-development. No organized activities need interrupt the rhythm of your days here. No phones disrupt your afternoon naps. It's just you, the breeze rustling in the palms, the soft sand underfoot, and the turquoise sea.

Although there are other isolated retreats along the coast, none provides the comforts of the Maroma. Sculptures adorn the garden pathways, contemporary paintings grace the walls. Teak and mahogany, hand-painted tiles, thatch, bamboo, and terra cotta are the materials that give Mexican touches to an almost Mediterranean sophistication. The air-conditioned and fan-cooled rooms have large terraces or thatch-covered balconies with hammocks and comfortable furnishings; the king-size beds are draped with a royal canopy of mosquito netting; bathtubs are sunken and covered with decorated tiles. The staff is gracious and deserves the ten percent gratuity added to your bill. Room service is available twenty-four hours a day.

During the day you can have meals served on your private terrace, under a *palapa* on the beach, or at the restaurant, if you want to bestir yourself. The Maroma can arrange for fishing and snorkeling trips or visits to nearby ruins, or you can just relax with a massage. In the evening the two-story restaurant is at its most inviting, with candlelight and piano music accompanying a fine meal. The menu offers everything from freshly caught seafood and nouvelle cuisine to local Yucatecan specialties. After dinner, there are books and videos to choose from in the library before your moonlit walk on the beach. What better escape than the Maroma?

Tulum and Sian Ka'an

Cabañas Ana y José

Apartado Postal 15
Tulum, Quintana Roo
(98) 87-54-78
Fax: (98) 87-54-69
Reservations:
80-60-22 in Cancún
Fax: (98) 80-60-21 in Cancún

A friendly roost in the tropical wilds

Accommodations: 14 rooms and 1 suite. **High-season rates:** Standard rooms $75–85, ocean-view rooms $90, oceanfront rooms $100, ocean suite $140. **Minimum stay:** 4 days. **Low-season rates:** Standard rooms $65–$75, ocean-view rooms $80, oceanfront rooms $85, ocean suite $120. **Minimum stay:** 3 days. **Payment:** No credit cards. **Recreation:** Beach, pool, boat excursions, mountain bikes for exploring Sian Ka'an.

➤   **Amigos de Sian Ka'an (98-84-95-83 in Cancún) offers day-long tours of the ecological preserve, bird sanctuaries, Mayan ruins, and remote villages. The organization gets you into places you would never find alone. The tours start at Ana y José.**

Cabañas Ana y José is a couple of kilometers south of the Maya Tulum (see below), just inside the Sian Ka'an ecological preserve. The beach here is broad and beautiful, long enough for hikes and jogs. A little smaller in size and a bit less expensive than Maya Tulum, Ana y José's provides the same basic antidote to civilization.

Ana and José's *cabañas* are spread out among four two-story buildings; the most desirable one sits right on the beach. On the second floor of this beachfront building is the ocean suite, the most sought-after accommodation, with its sitting room, private balcony, CD player, king-size bed, bathtub to soak in — and, of course, great ocean view. The ground floor houses two regular oceanfront rooms. All rooms lack air conditioning, but they contain folkloric touches and hand-carved wooden beds and dressers, tiled floors, and baths. The second-floor rooms have thatched roofs, and a couple of them, while not on the beach, have sea views, and are well worth the slightly higher price. Other rooms have garden and pool views. Ana and José now has a generator that provides electricity 24 hours a day; however, there is one drawback. Some of the rear rooms are noisy for several hours a day because of the operation of the generator.

If you don't have a view of the water from your room, you certainly will from the enticing *palapa* restaurant, right on the big, untamed beach. Though screened against bugs, it's open to the vistas and the breezes. The tables sit on a carpet of the same deep sand that's on the shore, and parrots sass you from a corner. Some evenings there is live Mexican music. Freshly caught seafood, including some of the best lobster we've ever had, is usually available, along with Mexican dishes and sandwiches, french fries, and the like.

The owner and staff are hospitable and helpful, making this spot a most pleasant retreat. Ana and José have created a cheerful little paradise, radiantly rudimentary.

Maya Tulum

Apartado Postal 99
Tulum, Quintana Roo
(987) 4-27-72
Fax: (987) 1-20-94
Reservations:
415-482-8224
Fax: 415-457-3535

> **An alluringly rustic retreat
> from the modern world**

Accommodations: 31 *cabañas*. **Rates:** With shared bath $60–$70, with private bath $70–$85, with private bath and deluxe room $90–$140. **Payment:** No credit cards. **Recreation:** Beach, massage, meditation, yoga.

➤   **Given the limited diversions at the Maya Tulum, it's tempting to head up the highway for a change of pace. Be wary of doing it at night, though; some Mexican drivers navigate by moonlight rather than with headlights, and nocturnal animals often bound out of the jungle thicket along the road.**

Just south of the Tulum ruins, on the road to Boca Paila, you pass several rustic beachfront inns that inspire visions of Robinson Crusoe. Situated on a beautiful beach cove, the Maya Tulum (formerly the Osho Tulum Resort) is the first of these you encounter, five kilometers from the Mayan city, and it's also the first of the group in escapist appeal.

A reproduction of a *chac mool* greets you at the end of a dusty driveway. The reclining stone figure with bent knees holds the traditional receptacle on its stomach, ready in centuries past for a sacrificed heart; today it's more appropriate for any excess baggage you've brought from the 20th century.

The accommodations are a few steps away, spread around the sandy grounds in individual *cabañas* built of rock and thatch. The comely octagonal cabins have stone floors and walls, a conical *palapa* roof, and stick shutters for windows. The standard *cabañas* don't include a private bath, but they are famous for their two hanging double beds suspended from the ceiling and gently swaying under their mosquito nets. The double beds are more conventionally situated on the floor in the newer *cabañas*, which also have private baths, and some even have king-size beds. A few of these are on the wild, deserted beach, but don't be too disappointed if yours is inland. The artfully guileless interiors are even more compelling than the views outside.

All the quarters lacked plumbing and electricity until recently. Now a generator provides low-level power in the evening. Guests staying in a standard *cabaña* share a spotless bathhouse with hot showers that has separate sections for men and women. Torches light the way to the facility at night, though you would do well to carry a flashlight.

The largest rock-and-thatch building contains a restaurant and a makeshift office. The limited, changing menu features international dishes, many vegetarian, but all without red meat. The dinner fare includes fresh fish or seafood several times a week when it's available.

Maya Tulum is an ideal hideaway for a time traveler in search of primordial simplicity. There's yoga and therapeutic massage to add another dimension of well-being. Pretty and primitive at the same time, the accommodations offer a blissful way back to the basics.

Xcalak Peninsula

Costa de Cocos

Xcalak, Quintana Roo
Reservations:
Turquoise Reef Group
303-674-9614
800-538-680
Fax: 303-674-8735

Costa de Cocos provides the best diving and accommodations for adventure travelers to Xcalak.

Accommodations: 10 rooms. **High-season rates:** $120 for a double room. **Low-season rates:** $98 for a double room. **Included:** Breakfast, dinner, and tax; airport transfer extra. **Minimum stay:** 5 nights in high season. **Payment:** No credit cards. **Recreation:** Diving trips and instruction, fishing, snorkeling, birdwatching, kayaking, and sailing.

➤   **The Palancar Reefs of the Chinchorro Banks have made Cozumel an international diving destination. Divers in the know prefer exploring the blue holes, shipwrecks, and reefs of Chinchorro from Xcalak.**

Nearly 250 miles south of Cancún, barely far enough away to avoid the developer's monthly encroachment along this fabulous coast, is Xcalak. Electricity arrived recently in the form of generators and solar panels, but there are no telephones — yet. A paved road threatens, but for the moment this peninsula remains the most unspoiled part of the Mexican Caribbean. A car, or airport pickup arranged by Costa de Cocos, is needed to travel the 200 miles from Cancún to the turnoff for Majahual and the Xcalak Peninsula. Then the car must bump its way along the sand-and-rock road to Xcalak village, 30 more miles along the peninsular coast.

Thirty miles of beachfront wilderness accompany any drive to Xcalak, the Mayan fishing village of 200 people at the tip of the Xcalak Peninsula. Just outside the village on a five-acre stretch of cleared beach is Costa de Cocos. Here octagonal bungalows, built from stone and mahogany, cluster in a shady coconut grove. The accommodations are comfortable for such a remote spot, with fans to cool the rooms in the evening, platform beds with mosquito netting, and private baths with sun-warmed water. An adjacent lodge houses the restaurant, where fresh local seafood and tropical fruits are featured.

Adventurers come to Costa de Cocos. because this small American-run inn offers the most reliable way to become acquainted with the wonders of the region. Lagoons and jungle are here to be explored for their beauty and wildlife. An off-shore island with roseate spoonbills and blue herons' nests, it also has calm reefs, making it a favorite with bird watchers and snorkelers alike. There's great fishing for giant tuna, bonefish, and yellowtail. And then there are the Chinchorro Banks — one of the greatest reef systems in the world. As David Randall, the owner of Costa de Cocos, likes to say, these reefs are a diver's banquet, with walls and blue holes and hundreds of shipwrecks to explore. Costa de Cocos can make all of this available with their excellent dive program, their boats, kayaks, and sailboards There are even longer trips possible to Ambergris Cay in Belize.

With a good fifty miles of beach, the peninsula is not immediately threatened with development. But many have visited here and a surprising number have bought land and started to build. For the traveler this means a few more reliable restaurants and facilities in a remote region. It also means a less pristine environment in the not-too-far future. Come now, before the bulldozers.

Cozumel

Best Hotel for Stylish Sophistication

Presidente Inter-Continental Cozumel, 84

Best Comfort Choice for All-American Abundance

Paradisus Cozumel, 82

Best Beachfront Buys

La Ceiba, 81
Scuba Club Dive Resort, 86
Sol Cabañas del Caribe, 87

Flat and rather featureless above sea level, the Caribbean island of Cozumel teems with marine life and exotic beauty underwater. Jacques Cousteau explored the offshore reefs in the 1950s and declared them one of the world's wonders. Since then, Cozumel has lured divers by the droves.

Like most other premier dive sites in the Caribbean, the island was slow to develop a broader appeal. If you didn't want to visit the depths, there was little reason to visit Cozumel. Hotels were second-rate, and other tourist facilities were minimal. The Cancún boom in the 1980s stimulated some changes that Hurricane Gilbert actually accelerated in 1988. The storm's extensive devastation forced many businesses to rebuild, and some took the opportunity to make major improvements. Then, in the 1990s, new cruise ship facilities made the island a major stopover.

The beneficial effects are most noticeable in the string of small hotels a couple of miles north of San Miguel, the only town on Cozumel. Once tired and mired in mediocrity as a group, several now stand out among the top affordable beach hideaways anywhere in the Caribbean. Cozumel has become the kind of place even a landlubber can love. The less beneficial results come with the crowds in the small town when cruise ships dock.

The Main Attractions

Divine Dives

Cozumel has more than two dozen reef systems off the coast and waters that range in visibility from 100 to 250 feet. Palancar Reef, a name known to all divers, spreads for several miles in length and several thousand feet in depth. Drifting along it with the strong current makes for a sightseeing expedition to rival any on earth.

Other good dive spots include Columbia Reef, which features towering columns and pinnacles, the plunging Santa Rosa Wall, and the area on the north coast, outside the underwater sanctuary, where spearfishing is still permitted. Second to Palancar in popularity, though, may be the shallow sea off Laguna Chankanab, a pleasant park that also has good snorkeling.

Most of the hotels we recommend in Cozumel offer dive packages. If you come on a different plan, there are many dive operators in San Miguel. A three-day resort certification course, costing around $300, will get novices to some of the most spectacular depths.

The Bustling Village

Beachless San Miguel doesn't offer superior accommodations, but it's the center for everything else on the island. An overgrown fishing village increasingly devoted to the pursuit of the dollar, it has absorbed the impact of tourism without completely abandoning its native character. Even the seaside esplanade, the Malecón, long ago sacrificed to visitor interests, comes alive with local color on Sunday evenings, when the town turns out for music on the plaza.

The shops, restaurants, and bars are the usual assortment for a Mexican resort area. They aren't as abundant, glittery, and expensive as in Cancún, but they are similar in the type and quality of their offerings. There's a crafts market, designer boutiques, jewelry stores (note that black coral is banned by the U.S. Wildlife Service and can be confiscated at customs), a Carlos 'n' Charlie's, several discos, and almost anything else a voracious tourist needs.

The Sands of San Francisco

Long and luring Playa San Francisco, about 10 miles south of San Miguel, is easily the grandest beach on Cozumel and one of the top 20 in Mexico. The sand and swimming are glorious at any of the turnoffs from the main road, which seem to divide the extended shore into several different beaches. Restaurants keep the crowds plied with nachos and beer. The best beaches with accommodations are at the Presidente and north of town at Playa San Juan, in front of a couple of our recommended hotels.

Island Touring

Less than 30 miles long and 9 miles wide, Cozumel has paved roads around only the southern half of the isle. Making that circuit in a car or on a rented motorbike is an enjoyable day's adventure. You pass Laguna Chankanab and Playa San Francisco, both worth a break from driving, and turnoffs to some small Mayan ruins, barely worth a detour even for archaeology majors.

If you ever had escapist fantasies, leave the undeveloped windward shore for last. After rounding the southern point of the highway, you swing north along an almost deserted coast punctuated by splendid beaches. The gem of these sands is Punta Chiqueros — white, wild, and sensuously inviting. Try the catch of the day for lunch in the lost-in-the-tropics restaurant, a thatch-roofed complement to the pristine cove.

Playa Chen Río and Punta Morena, farther along the road to San Miguel, are also enticing stops. The former is very private since it has no facilities, and the latter harbors one of the only other places for food and drink on the windward shore. On your return to the western shore, you pass the access road to the largest ruin on the island, San Gervasio.

La Ceiba

Apartado Postal 284
Carr. A Chankanaab Km 4.5
Cozumel, Quintana Roo
(987) 2-08-44
Fax: (987) 2-00-65
Reservations:
800-437-9609
Fax: 800-235-5892

> **A reasonably priced divers'
> hotel that will please
> nondivers as well**

Accommodations: 112 rooms. **High-season rates:** Standard rooms $138, superior rooms $173. **Low-season rates:** Standard rooms $109, superior rooms $138; special package rates for divers and nondivers for 3–7 nights. **Payment:** Major credit cards. **Recreation:** Beach, pools, tennis court, Jacuzzi, sauna, gym, water sports, full-service dive shop.

➤   **Cozumel offers many of the pleasures of the big-time resorts without the frantic atmosphere. But it sometimes seems that Cozumel would really rather be Cancún, an ambition you can see around the cruise ship dock and the surrounding shops where vendors hawk their machine-made goods to gullible travelers.**

La Ceiba is a very reasonably priced beachfront hotel catering to divers, but nondivers will be happy here also. The first thing you'll probably notice after walking through the small lobby to the beach area is a huge cruise ship looming in the Caribbean, just a few hundred yards away. The sight is startling and unsettling—and somewhat surreal—like a scene from a García Márquez short story. Cruise ships regularly are stationed in the sea near La Ceiba, where they unload their eager passengers onto small boats that carry them to shore for shopping sprees in downtown Cozumel. At the tranquil La Ceiba you can enjoy the sight of these intriguing monsters of the sea while avoiding the clamor of their frenzied passengers.

La Ceiba is divided into two parts, a high-rise building of twelve stories and a low-rise of three stories. The large rooms are simply furnished and air-conditioned, with a telephone, satellite TV, and a small balcony with sea views, as well as hooks for drying your water sports paraphernalia. There are two beach areas and two pools, a small one for children and a quite large one for adults that overlooks the sea. The hammocks on the beach add to the serenity of the setting.

Very popular with divers, La Ceiba has a highly respected full-service dive shop, Del Mar Aquatics. Although you can just book a room and enjoy the simple pleasures of La Ceiba, you can also take advantage of its packages for stays of three to seven days. The packages for divers include both boat diving and shore diving. Nondiving packages give you a small discount on the daily room rate.

Although the focus is on divers here, La Ceiba has a surprisingly large number of other facilities for a fairly small hotel—a gym, tennis court, sauna, and outdoor Jacuzzi, as well as La Chopa Loca restaurant located right on the beach, a comfortable lobby/bar area, and several shops.

For divers, La Ceiba is a special place. For nondivers, La Ceiba is hard to beat for its beachfront amenities that don't break the bank.

Paradisus Cozumel

Carr. Costera Norte Km. 5.8
Cozumel, Quintana Roo
(987) 2-04-11
Fax: (987) 2-15-99
Reservations:
Melia Hotels
713-820-9500
800-336-3542
Fax: 713-999-7373

A pretty and perky all-inclusive

Accommodations: 200 rooms. **High-season rates:** Garden-view rooms $370, ocean-view $420–$495 per person. **Low-season rates:** Garden-view rooms $235 per person, ocean-view $275 per person. **Included:** Breakfast, lunch, dinner, all drinks, most recreation, tax, service. **Payment:** Major credit cards. **Children:** Up to 2 children 12 and under, free of charge **Recreation:** Beach, 2 swimming pools, 2 tennis courts, fitness center, water sports center.

➤   **Meals are included in the rate at this Melia hotel, but for a change of pace you may want to visit nearby San Miguel. For authentic Mexican food, try La Choza (Av. 10 Sur and R. Salas 198), and for the best seafood, El Capi Navegante (Avenida 10 Sur #312).**

When it opened as Mayan Cozumel in the late 1970s, the Paradisus almost immediately sank into the doldrums then typical of the Playa San Juan area. Melia, a Spanish chain, took over the property a decade later and wrought wonders, renovating everything from the decor to the vacation verve. Now converted to an all-inclusive resort, it can be a great getaway for divers and landlubbers alike.

The beautiful beach in front of the hotel is supplemented by the hotel's dive and beach club on the southern end of the island, where diving (which is available for an additional fee) and snorkeling arrangements are best. But you can stay at the resort and enjoy Sunfish sailing and windsurfing. If you want to play on the shore, there are two tennis courts and a couple of pools, one a handsome seaside spot with a swim-up bar under a *palapa.* Lazier folks spread out on lounge chairs under the palms lining the sands.

Most guest rooms are on or above the beach in three separate wings. The top-dollar quarters are in a 12-story tower that provides broad ocean views from spacious private balconies. Additional ocean-view rooms sit lower to the sand in the three-story Villas Playa building, secluded at the end of the grounds. Many of the smaller garden-view chambers occupy the similar Villas Plaza wing, set back from the sea behind the second pool. All the rooms boast terraces, contemporary furnishings, air conditioning, satellite TV, phones, mini-bars, and tiled showers.

The restaurants offer an agreeable diversity of fare. La Isla serves breakfast buffets in the morning and theme buffets in the evening. At the handsome La Iguana, a beachfront *palapa,* you can sample local seafood and snacks during the day or just sip a beer in the shade. The Café Paraiso features a more elegant setting for evening dining. One or two nights a week the kitchen prepares a special fiesta dinner to enjoy with music and dancing.

The Paradisus was one of Melia's first ventures in Mexico and may be one of the most successful over the long term. The company is expanding rapidly in other destinations, but the newer hotels are generally larger and more impersonal. This one runs against the grain for the chain in a soothing, satisfying way.

Presidente Inter-Continental Cozumel

Carretera à Chankanaab KM 6.5
Cozumel, Quintana Roo
(987) 2-03-22
Fax: (987) 2-13-60
Reservations:
Inter-Continental Reservations
800-327-0200

A rarity in Cozumel with both a good beach and good shoreline snorkeling

Accommodations: 253 rooms and suites. **High-season rates:** Standard rooms $250, deluxe ocean-view rooms $310, deluxe beachfront rooms $340, reef suites $790. **Low-season rates:** Standard rooms $220, deluxe ocean-view rooms $260, deluxe beachfront rooms $280, reef suites $630. **Payment:** Major credit cards. **Children:** Under 18, free in room with parents. **Recreation:** Beach, swimming pool with Jacuzzi, 2 tennis courts, fitness center, water sports center with dive operation and sailing.

➤ **For a breezy tropical atmosphere in San Miguel, try Las Palmeras (on the Malecón, near the zocalo) for Mexican dishes or Pizza Prima (R. Salas 109 at Calle 5 Sur) for tasty thin-crust or Chicago-thick pizza.**

The Presidente Inter-Continental in Cozumel is one of the chain's most engaging Mexican hotels and one of our favorite beach hotels in the country. Tasteful and unpretentious, it is a luxury hotel with class. Not overwhelmingly massive, but offering the facilities of a large establishment, it spreads over extensive grounds yet maintains an intimate feeling. With several lovely beaches set in coves and a beautiful, calm turquoise sea great for snorkeling, the Presidente allows you to be at one beach area and be totally unaware of the others. One end of the Presidente overlooks a marina, something we didn't discover until about our fifth stay here. The tranquil setting seems to appeal more to couples and families than to the singles crowd found more often at Cancún's bustling beachfront hotels.

As you enter the Presidente, you come upon the handsome thatched lobby, open, airy, and attractively furnished throughout. If you walk through the hotel to the beach area in the rear, you'll find that the beach meanders in both directions. To your right is a five-story tower, and then, following the curve of the coast, there are two rows of single- and double-story rooms, the first hugging the beach. Here you'll find many of the Presidente's suites and at the far end a marina. If you retrace your steps and head back to the left, you'll come upon a pool and a pretty *palapa* restaurant, El Caribeño, on the oceanfront, and then, continuing to the left of the rear exit, you'll find our favorite section, another two-story set of rooms situated right on the beach.

The rooms throughout the Presidente vary in desirability. The least expensive ones have garden views or partial ocean views. More desirable ones are in the deluxe ocean-view category. And our very favorites, the deluxe beachfront rooms in the two-story section on the left side of the hotel as you face the beach, are particularly attractive—and the setting can't be beat. Those on the ground floor (the ones with the best views are numbered 5103–5139) have large patios set directly on the sand. You just stroll out of your room, take a few steps across the patio, and plop on to the beach with the glistening Caribbean in front of you. Delicious. Those on the second floor (the best numbered 5203–5239) have large balconies. The rooms on both floors are quite large and comfortable with marble floors, heavy wooden doors, white cedar furniture, and spacious, modern bathrooms. All of the Presidente's rooms have either patios or balconies and come with air-conditioning, satellite TV, a phone, and a king-size bed or two double beds. Service is quite snappy; there is a concierge, complimentary newspapers at your door, and 24-hour room service. In addition to the beachfront restaurant and several bars, there is El Arrecife, a more formal indoor restaurant with sea views and an adventurous menu featuring dishes such as duck ravioli, rack of lamb, and salmon with fried capers.

Although there are two lighted tennis courts, water sports are the recreational focus here, especially snorkeling and scuba diving. You can also go windsurfing, water-skiing, sailing, and deep-sea fishing. And if you just can't resist your daily treadmill and weights exercises, you can work out in the new gym, which has sea views.

You're likely to love this Presidente Inter-Continental, a very special retreat for relaxation beside a sparkling sea.

Scuba Club Dive Resort

Apartado Postal 289
Cozumel, Quintana Roo
2-06-63
Fax: (987) 2-06-63
Reservations:
Aqua-Sub Tours
713-783-3305
800-847-5708

A dive lodge with local character

Accommodations: 55 rooms. **Rates:** An endless variety of packages offered for high and low seasons; inquire about rates. **Included:** Breakfast, lunch, dinner, and scuba diving for two. **Payment:** Made in advance in U.S. before departure. **Recreation:** Swimming pool, scuba diving.

➤ **Many Cozumel visitors explore the island on motorbikes, which the Scuba Club Dive Resort and many San Miguel agencies rent. They can be fun, but caution is merited on the narrow two-lane roads, where you may encounter speeding taxis and trucks.**

Formerly the Galapago Inn, the inn's new name emphasizes its specialty in scuba diving. The sport is the focus of conversations, activities, package rates, even the all-inclusive meal plan that clutches you to the property with the grip of a diving belt.

What distinguishes this inn from most single-interest operations is the buoyant Mexican Caribbean atmosphere. The entrance to the resort, right on the main road south of San Miguel, announces the inn's personality immediately. The breezeway lobby behind the wrought-iron gates twinkles with bright tile in a fountain and *banco* settee. Just beyond, in a flowery courtyard, the Beachcomber Bar and the Fat Grouper Restaurant beckon. A small swimming pool is adjacent, and along the nearby seawall there are several sandy sunning terraces — a sort of handmade beach — replete with *palapas* and hammocks.

The cheeriness extends into the rooms only partially, particularly in the decorative tile work. Overall, the air-conditioned quarters are plain and cramped. Everyone gets a balcony, but many are tiny and don't offer a view of the sea. The bedding alternatives range from twins to queens, with combinations of doubles and singles being the most common. No phones or TVs distract you from the underwater sights.

Most guests come on a package that includes all meals plus a couple of boat dives a day and unlimited diving close to the shore. The rates we quote are for two people sharing a room for seven nights on this plan. The cost is less if one or both of you aren't submersible, but so is the appeal.

Sol Cabañas del Caribe

Carretera Costera Norte KM 5.8
Cozumel, Quintana Roo
(987) 2-00-17
Fax: (987) 2-15-99
Reservations:
Melia Hotels
713-820-9500
800-336-3542
Fax: 713-999-7373

**A vintage gem for
Caribbean R&R**

Accommodations: 39 rooms and 9 *cabañas.* **High-season rate:** $119. **Low-season rate:** $84. **Payment:** Major credit cards. **Children:** Two children under 12, free in room with parents. **Recreation:** Beach, swimming pool, water sports center.

➤ **While shopping and sightseeing in San Miguel, stop by the Museo de la Isla de Cozumel (Avenida Melgar, near the pier). Small but attractive, the museum features a coral reef diorama and exhibits on island history from the Mayan era to the present.**

A small low-rise inn hugging an expansive beach, the Sol Cabañas del Caribe is reminiscent of the original Caribbean hideaways before jet travel. It used to take days to reach those pioneer lodgings, however, instead of hours, and they were seldom as affordable as this. The Sol Cabañas gives you a timeless sense of sunny ease on Playa San Juan at a very relaxing rate.

It's almost two inns in one. The first section you see, and the largest, is a two-story block of rooms sweeping around the sand to the right of the miniature open-air lobby. Although the wing looks a bit like a motel structure, it loses that air inside. Each pleasant room has a double and a twin bed and a comfortable private terrace.

The second inn is two rows of detached cottages on the opposite end of the beach, near the swimming pool. These are the *cabañas* of the hotel's name, despite the fact they are now known officially as villas. Quaint and cozy compared with the regular rooms, the brick-floor bungalows with queen-size beds possess more of the old-fashioned allure of the property as a whole, but their patios lack privacy. Numbers 6 and 7 are our favorites, close to the sea and away from the pool. All the quarters have ocean views, air conditioning, showers only, and no phones or TVs.

The broad beach starts right outside the reception area and covers most of the grounds. Dotted with *palapas* and lounge chairs, it ends at a rocky shore except in one spot that provides good water access for swimmers and snorkelers. Scuba diving and windsurfing are specialties, and you can also rent masks and fins.

The lovely Las Gaviotas restaurant sits above the shore, well positioned for watching the sun set over the translucent waves. The seafood is fresh and usually flavorful. At one recent dinner we had a delicious *sopa de lima* and a superbly cooked shrimp Oriental with pineapple, cardamom, and honey. During the day, you can buy drinks and cold snacks at a poolside *palapa.*

Unpretentious and easygoing, the inn doesn't try to be flashy or fancy. It has a straightforward appeal aimed at folks who want nothing more, or less, than fine sand, beautiful water, and a congenial atmosphere. That's always been the call of the Caribbean, and it still is at the Sol Cabañas del Caribe.

The
Mexican
Riviera

The
Mexican
Riviera

Mazatlán

Puerto Vallarta
Yelapa

Manzanillo

Pacific Ocean

Ixtapa
Zihuatanejo

Acapulco

Puerto Escondido

Huatulco
Puerto Angel

BiLyne '00

Acapulco
Acapulco Princess, 98
Belmar, 100
Boca Chica, 102
Camino Real Acapulco Diamante, 103
Elcano, 105
Howard Johnson Maralisa, 106
Hyatt Regency Acapulco, 108
Las Brisas, 109
Pierre Marqués, 112
Plaza Las Glorias El Mirador Acapulco, 114
Quinta Real Acapulco, 115
Huatulco
Barcelo Huatulco Beach Resort, 120
Camino Real Zaashila, 122
Casa del Mar, 123
Club Med Huatulco, 125
Ixtapa
Club Med Ixtapa, 132
Double Tree Ixtapa, 133
Krystal Ixtapa, 134
Westin Brisas Resort Ixtapa, 136
Manzanillo and the Gold Coast
The Careyes, 149
El Tamarindo, 151
La Posada, 152
Las Alamandas, 153
Las Hadas, 156
Playa Blanca Club Med, 158
Villa Polinesia, 159
Mazatlán
Camino Real Mazatlán, 164
El Cid Mega Resort, 166
El Quijote Inn, 168
Las Palmas, 170
Pueblo Bonito, 171
Rancho Las Moras, 173

Puerto Ángel
La Posada Cañon Devata, 178
Puerto Escondido
Paraíso Escondido, 180
Santa Fe Hotel, 181
Tabachín del Puerto, 183
Puerto Vallarta
Camino Real Puerto Vallarta, 193
Casa Corazón, 195
Casa Kimberley, 196
Casa Tres Vidas, 198
Condominios Conchas Chinas, 200
Fiesta Americana Puerto Vallarta, 201
Los Cuatro Vientos, 202
Marriott CasaMagna Puerto Vallarta, 203
Playa Los Arcos, 205
Posada de Roger, 206
Presidente Inter-Continental Puerto Vallarta, 207
Quinta María Cortés, 209
Sierra Plaza Golf & Spa, 210
Westin Regina Resort Puerto Vallarta, 212
Yelapa
Lagunita Yelapa, 215
Zihuatanejo
La Casa Que Canta, 138
Las Urracas, 140
Raúl Tres Marías, 141
Sotavento-Catalina, 142
Villa del Sol, 143

Acapulco

Acapulco
Acapulco Princess, 98
Belmar, 100
Boca Chica, 102
Camino Real Acapulco Diamante, 103
Elcano, 105
Howard Johnson Maralisa, 106
Hyatt Regency Acapulco, 108
Las Brisas, 109
Pierre Marqués, 112
Plaza Las Glorias El Mirador Acapulco, 114
Quinta Real Acapulco, 115

Best Romantic Hideaway

Las Brisas, 109

Best Hotels for Stylish Sophistication

Camino Real Acapulco Diamante, 103
Quinta Real Acapulco, 115

Best Recreational Resorts and Spas

Acapulco Princess, 98
Pierre Marqués, 112

Best Comfort Choice for All-American Abundance

Acapulco Princess, 98

Best Beachfront Buys

Boca Chica, 102
Elcano, 105
Howard Johnson Maralisa, 106

Best Bargains for Mexican Character

Belmar, 100
Plaza Las Glorias El Mirador Acapulco, 114

Best Place to Combine Business and Pleasure

Hyatt Regency Acapulco

Acapulco led Mexico and much of the tropics into our modern quest for a sybaritic paradise. The original resort on "the Mexican Riviera," as the Pacific coast has been known since the 1950s, Acapulco was a new kind of adult playground at the time — warmer, wetter, and wilder than anything yet seen on the real Riviera or anywhere else. It redefined Eden for the age and, almost simultaneously, taught us once again about the loss of innocence.

Acapulco did both with Latin gusto, its most characteristic quality. The boom years produced a city of close to two million in population, a tangle of a metropolis full of pollution and poverty. Developers threw up high-rise hotels along the shore as if they were playing Monopoly, establishing a pattern that became the quintessential symbol of resort tackiness. Even by the 1960s Acapulco was acquiring a reputation for being overbuilt, crowded, and garish.

Yet as Acapulco became more chaotic, it thrived on the urban energy. The lights got brighter and the bikinis got slighter. The nights throbbed, first at Tequila à Go-Go and then later at a succession of glitzy discos. Every step backward in the erosion of pristine appeal was a step forward in creating a dynamic, titillating environment for generations brought up on electronic verve. The gusto lives — not even Hurricane Pauline could dampen it in 1997.

The Main Attractions

The First Jet-Set Resort

The jet set began creating the Acapulco legend before jets even existed. Errol Flynn sailed in on his party yacht, *Scirocco,* in the late 1930s for the first of many visits. His boatload of Hollywood bingers spread the word at home about an uninhibited paradise south of the border. As soon as Flynn's colleagues finished fighting the Second World War on film, they were ready to join him on a fling.

The toughest warrior of them all, John Wayne, led the charge. Wayne and such friends as Cary Grant, Richard Widmark, Roy Rogers, and Red Skelton came to be known in Acapulco as "the Hollywood gang." They even banded together to buy a hotel, where Johnny Weissmuller, of Tarzan fame, retired and lived his last years. American celebrities tended to dominate the social scene, but they didn't lack foreign company. Around the same time Brigitte Bardot was introducing the world to Saint-Tropez, she flew to Acapulco for her honeymoon.

There was no more fashionable resort anywhere at the time, but the glamour soon began to dim. The jet setters moved up the thousand-mile shore of the Mexican Riviera in the 1960s and '70s, first to Puerto Vallarta and then to Manzanillo and the Gold Coast. A few went farther north to fish in Mazatlán, and now some head as far south as the brand-new resort of Huatulco. All the Pacific coast shares the popularity today, but Acapulco won its fabled stature first and still thrives on the legacy.

God's Grandest Bay

The air is hazy with traffic fumes these days, and the water is just beginning to recover from decades of dumping, but nothing can diminish the magnificence of Acapulco Bay. The foothills of the Sierra Madres plunge to the sea along the arc of the sweeping shoreline, as if the arms of the mountains were embracing a cherished cove. The contour of the coast undulates gracefully between rocky cliffs and long stretches of fine sand. The verdant hills soar and dip with the dramatic rhythm of Shakespearean verse. Many places in the tropics rival Acapulco in overall natural beauty, but there's not another bay anywhere that matches this one in grandeur.

Dancing Fancy Till Dawn

Acapulco's gusto is most evident in the evening. The nights roar with music and merriment. Many of the most popular haunts are certainly gaudy, but you won't fault them for lack of exuberance.

The nightly dives from La Quebrada cliffs must be the longest-running tourist attraction in any beach area. The only thing comparable in longevity and kitsch is Polynesian fire-eating in Waikiki. Young men jump 156 feet from a bluff into a shallow inlet, timing each dive to catch an incoming wave that prevents them from being crushed on the rocks. It's worth seeing once, if only because everyone does. For the best view, reserve a table for dinner at La Perla (83-11-55) in the old Plaza Las Glorias El Mirador hotel. People who prefer to avoid the bland food can see the show fine from the restaurant's cocktail terrace.

The divers warm you up in the early evening for the late-night action, Acapulco's real specialty. The fashionable mode in the city is to sleep until the early afternoon, lie around on Condesa Beach a few hours, barhop until midnight, and then dance away the darkness.

The number of discos is staggering. Most are right on Costera Alemán, convenient to the beachfront hotels, though two of the flashiest, Palladium and Fantasy, are above the town in the vicinity of Las Brisas, enjoying fabulous views of Acapulco Bay. Virtually all have a cover charge, often hefty. When they are popular enough to be exclusive, they can be snobbish at the door, particularly about single men, shorts, jeans, tennis shoes, and anything else that isn't sufficiently stylish at the moment.

The hot spots on the strip currently are Baby 'O and Le Dome, close together near the south end of the busy Costera. As with Palladium and Fantasy, they set out to stun you with blazing light shows, high-tech sound, and opulent decor. If you don't need to associate with the beautiful people, any door will do.

Acapulco Princess

Playa Revolcadero
Acapulco, Guerrero
(7) 4-69-10-00
Fax: (7) 4-69-10-16
Reservations:
Fairmont Hotels and Resorts
800-866-5577

| **A big, splashy resort on a rough, secluded beach** |

Accommodations: 1,017 rooms. **High-season rates:** Standard rooms $199, superior rooms $219, deluxe rooms $259, junior suites $279–$344, master suites $454 and up. **Low-season rates:** Standard rooms $139, superior rooms $144, deluxe rooms $159, junior suites $229–$289, master suites $304 and up. **Included:** Breakfast and dinner in the high season only. **Payment:** Major credit cards. **Children:** Under 12, free in room with parents. **Recreation:** Beach, 4 swimming pools, golf (36 holes), 11 tennis courts, water sports center, fitness center.

➤ **The Princess and its sister hotel, the Pierre Marqués, are ideal for golfers, with a total of 36 holes between them. Ted Robinson designed the 6,400-yard course at the Princess, and Robert Trent Jones remodeled the course at the Pierre Marqués. To add to this golfing bliss is the nearby 18-hole Tres Vidas course designed by Robert Van Hages.**

You are seriously jaded if your arrival at the Acapulco Princess leaves you yawning. The main building where you alight is a modern version of an Aztec pyramid, one of the most dramatic hotel structures in Mexico. A pond with a waterfall spilling over boulders guards the entrance like a medieval moat. The massive lobby greets you with a 15-story atrium, tons of polished marble, fountains, flowers, and trees stretching toward the sunlight overhead.

As this book goes to press, the Acapulco Princess is undergoing a $14 million renovation of its lobby, guest rooms, restaurants, and meeting facilities. The renovated lobby will also feature a huge "Aztec" marble mask to greet guests. Also on hand will be some old friends — the peacocks and flamingos that regularly stroll the grounds.

Quite understandably, some guests can be overwhelmed by the grandeur and massiveness of the Princess. In a short while, however, most come to appreciate and savor its abundant attractions and endless vistas. Surprisingly, despite its size — 1017 guest rooms spread over three high-rise towers — this is an extremely well run hotel with swift and attentive service throughout. Although it has a somewhat remote location on Revolcadero Beach, about a 20-minute taxi ride to the center to Acapulco, the Princess constitutes a self-contained city, crowded with people and crowing with exuberance. You may find that you have no need to leave.

Although the renovated rooms lack the flamboyance characteristic of the common areas of the hotel, they are tastefully appointed and comfortable — and the suites are particularly spacious and stylish. And although many rooms are without water views and balconies are small, there are lovely views from those rooms with balconies that overlook the bay.

In keeping with the abundance of the Princess, there are numerous restaurants and bars, indoors and outdoors, throughout the vast grounds of the hotel, and you can count on à la carte menus or buffets, garden or seaside settings, and several types of cuisines. Its best-known and most romantic restaurant, the recently renovated La Hacienda, now has a lagoon (!) built into it, while the Beach Club is a new seafront restaurant overlooking Revolcadero Beach. The Chula Vista is our favorite restaurant for its excellent lunchtime salad buffet, one of the great deals in Acapulco. For about $11 you can choose from a large selection of salads, including one made of very fresh seafood, pasta salads, and several vegetable salads as well as ratatouille. To finish off, there is an excellent selection of fruits. Service at the Chula Vista is particularly helpful and attentive.

The bars at the Princess are as varied as the restaurants. You can sip suds or cocktails poolside under a *palapa*, or in a pool, or by a lagoon off the lobby. Throughout the hotel there is live music by first-class groups playing tropical, mariachi, or other traditional Mexican music.

Don't get too hungover to sample the recreational facilities, which are some of the most impressive and memorable features of the Princess. Four freshwater swimming pools, one saltwater lagoon, and one children's wading pool are clustered in an imaginatively designed complex that spreads between the beach and the towers. The hotel's water-sports center will arrange water-skiing, scuba diving, and fishing expeditions. Although the enormous Revolcadero Beach area was formerly forlorn, it now is very lively as locals have taken over, and the sounds and smells of Mexico fill the air. Unfortunately, the surf here is too strong for swimming.

Land sports are the real specialty; this is where the Princess is unrivaled. There are two adjoining 18-hole golf courses, including the one at the Pierre Marqués next door. The nine outdoor tennis courts are lighted, and two additional courts are enclosed and air-conditioned. And there is a fully equipped gym.

The Princess is a hotel in a world of its own. It is big, bustling, visually exciting, and extravagant. If you are coming to Acapulco to play, as most people are, you won't find more opportunities concentrated in a single place.

Belmar

Gran Via Tropical at Av. Cumbres
Acapulco, Guerrero
(7) 4-83-80-98
Fax: Same as phone

A budget hotel with the ambience of old Acapulco, popular with Mexican families

Accommodations: 77 rooms. **High-season rates:** Double rooms $35, $30 for longer stays. **Low-season rates:** Double rooms $30, $25 for longer stays. **Payment:** No credit cards. **Children:** Under 12, free in room with parents. **Recreation:** 2 swimming pools.

➤ **From the Belmar it is a short trip to the Quebrada Cliffs to see, for a fee, one of Acapulco's most famous sights — fearless young men diving off the cliffs into the Pacific some 156 feet below. This spectacle is most dramatic at night, when the divers descend with lighted torches.**

The old Acapulco that first attracted tourists from around the world was centered on the Caleta Beach area, the home of the Belmar hotel. To this day, Caleta Beach has maintained its authentic feel; there is little of the glitz and glamour one finds in other parts of Acapulco. This is where working-class Mexicans come to vacation, so the prices are affordable, the food is authentic, and the beat is unmistakably Mexican. In addition to its attraction for Mexican families, the Caleta Beach area has become popular with Europeans looking for beach bargains and adventurous gringos in search of the soul of Mexico.

Within walking distance of Caleta Beach you'll find the old, reliable Belmar, a tranquil hotel with attractive gardens and grounds, still one of the great bargains in Acapulco. (If you are coming by car into the Caleta Beach area, don't take the first "Gran Via Tropical" sign, but instead keep going straight and then go up a hill for about one and a half blocks until you come upon the Belmar on your left.) Popular with Mexican families, who often take advantage of the even lower prices for longer stays, the Belmar has a good beach feel and a number of facilities for children, like slides and swings — and even a *miniature* miniature golf course. Although the prices are rock bottom, the air-conditioned rooms are surprisingly spacious, comfortable, and light, with whitewashed walls, picture windows, and large balconies. The old-fashioned tiled bathrooms, however, remind you that you are still in old Acapulco and that this is a budget hotel.

The Belmar's two pools are an unexpected luxury for a budget hotel, and its third-floor restaurant with views of the Caleta is yet another special treat. For an authentic Acapulco beach vacation on a budget in a hotel with real Mexican flavor, you won't do better than the Belmar.

Boca Chica

Playa Caletilla
Acapulco, Guerrero
(7) 4-83-63-88
Fax: (7) 4-83-95-13
Reservations:
800-34-MEXICO

> **A budget hotel with its own private pier for water sports**

Accommodations: 45 rooms. **High-season rates:** Double $110, junior suite $130. **Low-season rates:** Double $70, junior suite $90. **Included:** Breakfast year-round, but also dinner in high season. **Payment:** Major credit cards. **Recreation:** Beach, swimming pool, boat for fishing and excursions, windsurfing, and other water sports.

➤ **Overlooking the lively beach favored by Mexican families and lined with little seafood stands and restaurants, Boca Chica is a world apart from the sleek white towers of the Condesa district.**

One of the oldest and smallest hotels in Acapulco, Boca Chica is in the Caleta district, where the city first blossomed into a resort. If this pudgy peninsula had remained the focus of development instead of the modern strip, five miles away, Boca Chica would have the prime location, just above Playa Caletilla on a bluff at the end of the beach. It's probably just as well that didn't happen, because Boca Chica surely would have sprouted high-rise horns by now, and the neighborhood would have lost its lively, sometimes chaotic local character.

The homey, tropical hotel has a lovely setting on a spit of land overlooking the beach in one direction and in the other, a serene rocky cove that's good for snorkeling. The balconies on the rooms and most of the facilities face the pretty cove rather than the sand. The swimming pool overlooks Acapulco Bay on this side of the three-story building, as do several sun terraces and the thatched seafood restaurant. A second restaurant overlooks busy Caletilla Beach.

From January through March, Boca Chica encourages you to take a Modified American Plan rate that includes breakfast and dinner. That's okay if you don't want to leave the grounds, but we prefer the hotel at other times of the year, when you pay a lower price for the room with only breakfast included. The quarters are comfortably plain, with two double beds, white wood furniture, cement floors, a phone, and air conditioning. Their best feature is the close-up ocean view that many have from the balcony, particularly on the upper floors.

Boca Chica lacks the exuberance of the hotels on the Acapulco strip, but it compensates with the native environment of Caleta and splendid scenery along the shore.

Camino Real Acapulco Diamante

Baja Catita 18
Acapulco, Guerrero
(7) 4-66-10-10
Fax: (7) 4-66-11-11
Reservations:
Camino Real Hotels and Resorts
800-7-CAMINO (800-722-6466)

A dazzling new hideaway on a calm, clean shore

Accommodations: 156 rooms and suites. **Rates:** Standard rooms $195, superior rooms $260, Camino Real Club rooms $280, suites $360–$810. **Payment:** Major credit cards. **Children:** Under 12, free in room with parents. **Recreation:** Beach, 3 swimming pools, 1 tennis court, fitness center and massage, water sports center.

➤   **Even if you don't stay at Camino Real, come for a late lunch at La Vela, which offers a delightful buffet set up like a seafood market. You make your own salad and ceviche while you select the daily catch to be cooked to order.**

The Camino Real is easily one of the finest hotels opened in Acapulco in a couple of decades and already the most polished in many ways. On a secluded bay between the airport and the action, the small luxury hideaway strives for a level of tasteful serenity that's in direct counterpoint to the nearby city. You're a short taxi trip from as many thrills as you can bear, and it's an equally quick escape back to comfort and calm.

Your arrival is a bit of a thrill itself, as you descend from the hilltop highway down a steep incline to the shore. You wind through a new luxury residential development until the road dead-ends at a waterfall directly across from the hotel entrance. The bellman ushers you into a small, classy reception area, which opens grandly down marble steps into an elegantly tropical lobby overlooking the ocean.

The rooms are in a series of staggered mid-rise buildings poised on a slight rise above expansive terraced swimming pools, glistening gardens, and a small beach. Each chamber enjoys at least a partial ocean view from a private balcony and features marble baths, handsome light wood furniture, two double beds or a king, and a cozy sitting area. Rooms have air conditioning, ceiling fans, satellite TV, a phone, and a mini-bar. If you want more frills, you can upgrade to a junior or master suite, or to one of the executive Royal Beach Club quarters, which provide upgraded amenities and special services such as a complimentary Continental breakfast and sunset canapés.

A water sports center arranges water skiing, scuba diving, sailing, and fishing, and a fitness center helps keep you in shape for the activities. The calm waters here make it a particularly good spot for swimming and snorkeling. A tennis court is on the property and two 18-hole golf courses are ten minutes away.

The main dining room, Cabo Diamante, features international and regional dishes at three meals daily. La Vela, an outdoor grill on the waterfront, serves some of the freshest seafood in the city in a picturesque setting under a huge sail. The pool bar plies you with drinks and snacks during the day, and the lobby bar opens later with subdued entertainment.

Though Camino Real has offered exemplary accommodations in most major Mexican destinations for a generation, the upscale chain avoided Acapulco until now. With the resort set for a rebound, Camino Real timed its entry perfectly and provides the same opportunity to anyone else who has shunned the city in the past.

Elcano

Costera Alemán 75
Acapulco Guerrero
(7) 4-84-19-50
Fax: (7) 4-84-22-30
Reservations:
800-972-2162

> **A reasonably priced first-class hotel with a tranquil setting**

Accommodations: 180 rooms and suites. **High-season rates:** Standard rooms $155–$200, junior suites $175–$235. **Low-season rates:** Standard rooms $105–$140, junior suites $115–$175. **Payment:** Major credit cards. **Recreation:** Beach, pools, Jacuzzi, fitness center.

➤ **A short taxi ride from the Elcano takes you to Spicey (Carretera Escenica Las Brisas, tel. 4-81-04-70, open dinner only), one of Acapulco's better restaurants, with stunning views of Acapulco Bay from its outdoor tables. The interesting menu has some Asian touches and also includes a very good blackened catfish. This is a good place to try a wine from Monte Xanic, one of Mexico's best vineyards. After a late dinner you might want to sway to tropical music at Salón Q or dance the night away at one of Acapulco's famous discos, like Fantasy or Baby 'O.**

Looking for a very reasonably priced first-class hotel in a relatively tranquil setting, away from the hustle and bustle of the Costera Alemán yet close to the action? Surprisingly, despite its Costera Alemán address, Elcano is set back about one block off this main drag, tucked away on a quiet part of Icacos Beach. The location is convenient. When the mood strikes, it's good to know that you are within walking distance of the action around Condesa Beach. Yet the quieter Elcano setting is appealing, a soothing spot particularly for those who want to avoid the brashness and buzz of some of Acapulco's trendier hotels.

Elcano's breezy blue lobby with white wicker furniture provides a warm welcome to Acapulco. The comfortable, attractive beach has a few *palapas* for escaping the sun, and the sea here is good for swimming. If your preference is for pools, the large pool and Jacuzzi at the beach should please. Children can be found frolicking in the pool reserved especially for them. When hunger strikes, head for the attractive restaurant right on the beach. When guilt strikes, head for the gym with its cardiovascular machines.

All of the recently remodeled air-conditioned rooms at Elcano are a good size, with tiled floors, an airy ambience, and sea views. Most have large balconies for savoring the sea. Cable TV, a mini-bar, and a phone complete the rooms' amenities. Room rates are often negotiable, especially during the low season, when we've sometimes walked in (incognito, of course) without a reservation and have been quoted a price more than 30 percent lower than the official rack rate.

In addition to its beach restaurant, Elcano has an indoor restaurant, a lobby bar, and a beach bar. Several shops and a beauty salon are also housed here. Service throughout the hotel is warm and attentive. Elcano is a terrific choice for a first-class, well-run, very comfortable beach hotel without the glitter or expense of its better-known neighbors.

Howard Johnson Maralisa

Calle Alemania S/N
Acapulco, Guerrero
(7) 4-85-66-77
Fax: (7) 4-85-92-28
Reservations:
800-I-GO-HOJO

An intimate, affordable beachfront hotel with a location in the middle of the action

Accommodations: 89 rooms and suites. **High-season rates:** Standard doubles: $95–$107, superior doubles $112–$127. **Low-season rates:** Standard doubles $68–$80, superior doubles $80–$95. **Payment:** Major credit cards. **Recreation:** Beach, swimming pools, sauna, and water sports.

➤   **Just walk half a block from the Maralisa to the Costera Alemán and you'll be in taco heaven. Here you'll find two of Acapulco's most popular restaurants for tacos and other *antojitos*, El Fogón and El Zorrito — and often there will also be live music to enjoy while you join the many Mexicans consuming some of their favorite foods. A short walk away (near the Acapulco Plaza Hotel) is where Mexicans shop, Acapulco's liveliest shopping mall, the blessedly air-conditioned La Bahia, which contains a cineplex and a bowling alley along with a myriad of shops and eateries.**

Don't be put off by the name. Trust us. The Maralisa is not like the Howard Johnson motels you remember from your youth, found on highways throughout the States. This is a place with charm and a warm, inviting atmosphere. The Maralisa has gone through several management changes, but it seems to have settled down under the Howard Johnson banner.

The location is close to much of the action in Acapulco, yet the Maralisa is set back off the main street of the Costera Alemán on a small, quiet street, Calle Alemania, which can be a bit difficult to find at first. The hotel itself is set on El Morro beach next to the more famous Condesa Beach. The relatively small size of the Maralisa and its inviting setting around a pool and off the Costera are a welcome relief from the seemingly endless string of high-priced high-rise hotels that line the Costera in this area and more and more block the views of beautiful Acapulco Bay. Low-key and without pretensions, the well-run Maralisa provides pleasant accommodations in a relatively quiet setting at affordable rates in one of Acapulco's most popular and populated areas.

The rooms won't knock you out, but they are air-conditioned and ample, if a bit barren. They are equally divided between standard and superior rooms (with a few suites thrown in), but the superiors are worth the extra money for their pool views. A few rooms — very few — have ocean views. The suites have balconies overlooking the pool. Although this intimate hotel is normally laid back, it bursts with life at Mexican vacation time, when families descend and exuberant children frolic in the pools. At any time of the year, guests at the Maralisa seem quite pleased with its ambience, facilities, attentive service, and central location.

Maralisa's large beach area contains *palapas*, a place of refuge from Acapulco's powerful sun. When you decide to leave the beach, you can relax in the hotel's rather spare restaurant/bar, which overlooks the beach and bay, or you can take up residence at one of the two pools. And when your energy returns you can head out to the Costera, just half a block away, and join the throngs of people shopping, bar/restaurant-hopping, or just people-watching. For those who want a beachfront hotel close to Acapulco's action but don't want the prices or pace of this city's luxury high-rise hotels, the Maralisa is a very good choice.

Hyatt Regency Acapulco

Costera Alemán 1
Acapulco, Guerrero
(7) 4-69-12-34
Fax: (7) 4-84-30-87
Reservations:
Hyatt Hotels and Resorts
800-633-7313
Fax: 402-593-9838

> **A high-rise hotel on the quiet end of the main beach**

Accommodations: 690 rooms and suites. **High-season rates:** Deluxe rooms $185, Regency Club rooms $200, suites $540–$1,500. **Low-season rates:** Deluxe rooms $130–$160, Regency Club rooms $170, suites $445–$1,400. **Payment:** Major credit cards. **Children:** Under 18, free in room with parents. **Recreation:** Beach, swimming pool, 5 tennis courts.

➤ **The Hyatt Regency claims to have "the most experienced meeting organizers in Acapulco." We don't doubt the billing, because the hotel is better geared to business travelers than any other in the city.**

The Hyatt Regency Acapulco is at the very beginning of Costera Alemán, close to the convention center and the hottest late-night discos. The location suffers a little from being right next to a naval base, but if you get high enough in the 23-story structure, the armed ships begin to look like bathtub toys.

Don't expect a full measure of the finesse you usually find at Hyatt resorts. The chain's older properties in Mexico are not always as graceful as their cousins in other parts of the world. This one at least offers a fair share of the service you get elsewhere, and it was renovated in 1996.

The expansive lobby, lined with restaurants, bars, and shops, feels closed in for the tropics, but once you get beyond it to the seaside pool, the hotel perks up. The deck around the pool is the center of activity during the day. From there it's just a few steps down to the attractive beach, which the hotel has furnished with *palapas* for shade.

Some of the rooms are in this area in a two-story wing that juts off the lobby toward the sand. The rest of the quarters — and the best ocean views — are in the V-shaped tower that points out to the bay. To get the broadest view of the water, request the side of the building facing the city rather than the one oriented toward the naval base. All the air-conditioned rooms are large enough for families and are well appointed.

The Hyatt provides plentiful opportunities for eating, drinking, and playing. Zapata, Villa, and Compañia serves Mexican food in a fiesta setting, El Pescador specializes in seafood, and the Bar Terraza offers *tapas* with sunset cocktails. The social director organizes bingo, backgammon, and pool volleyball games, or you can round up a match of your own on the tennis courts. The usual water sports are also available.

The Hyatt Regency is a little substandard for its chain, but the hotel is one of the best for beachfront luxury in Acapulco. As long as you're not expecting to be bowled over by elegance, it gives you a choice perch on the main strip.

Las Brisas

Apartado Postal 281
Acapulco, Guerrero
(7) 4-69-69-00
Fax: (7) 4-46-53-28
Reservations:
Westin Hotels and Resorts
800-228-3000

> **One of the world's most romantic hotels**

Accommodations: 263 *casitas* and suites with 210 pools. **High-season rates:** Shared-pool *casitas* $315, private-pool *casitas* $415, Club *casitas* $515, junior suites with private pool $650, 1- to 3-bedroom suites with private pool $415–$1,050. **Low-season rates:** Shared-pool *casitas* $240, private-pool *casitas* $360, Club *casitas* $400, junior suites with private pool $520, 1- to 3-bedroom suites with private pool $465–$1,045. **Included:** Continental breakfast. **Added:** Service charge of $20 daily in lieu of tips. **Payment:** Major credit cards. **Children:** 1 child under 18, free in room with parents in low season; in high season, no children under 12 allowed. **Recreation:** 210 swimming pools, 5 tennis courts, water-sports center, and access to Tres Vidas Golf Club.

➤ **If you need more space than Las Brisas offers, but you want a similar location and attractions, consider a private vacation villa in Las Brisas Estates. Villa Leisure (800-526-4244) is a good source of information. If you want to experience a bit of Las Brisas without staying there, its Saturday night Fiesta Mexicana, with food, fireworks, and music, is open to the public.**

You don't visit Acapulco and decide to spend your nights at Las Brisas. You visit Las Brisas and decide whether you want to bother spending your nights in Acapulco. Perched on a magnificent hill-side high above the city, the hotel is a separate, self-sufficient principality, more detached from the urban hubbub than Monaco is from France.

No place anywhere has been so artfully designed for romance. The *casitas* are truly "little homes," perfectly positioned on five levels up the hill to get optimum privacy and breathtaking views over Acapulco Bay. The vistas from any one of them are a lifetime memory, the kind of experience that puts a notch in the soul.

It's the flowers, though, that transport you from elation into ecstasy. Six thousand hibiscus, gladioli, carnations, and other fresh blooms are spread around the *casitas* and dining rooms daily, an average of almost 100 per guest. They spell "welcome" on your bed when you arrive, they grace your pillow at night, they perfume the soap in the shower, and they float in your private or semiprivate pool like a languorous invitation to love. Easily the most acclaimed honeymoon hotel in the world, as well as the most famous resort in Mexico, Las Brisas earns its repute by giving you a realm of your own that indulges your senses beyond bliss.

Except, perhaps, the sense of taste. Over time the quality of the food hasn't been as elevated as everything else at the romantic aerie, but that may be changing. The management understands the importance of refined cooking today and has been working toward improving their offerings. Our last dinner was superb, with a savory smoked duck appetizer, a salad topped with a tangy vinaigrette, a perfectly cooked sea bass, and a luscious chocolate soufflé with crème Anglaise.

Even if the fare doesn't shine on your visit, you can count on the setting to keep you content. Our favorite locale for breakfast and lunch is the terrace of our *casita*, overlooking the bay alongside the flowering pool. There's a gourmet deli for groceries and beer as well as efficient 24-hour room service. In the morning you don't even need to call room service; Las Brisas has sent buses to pick up the staff at their homes at 4:00 A.M. so they can sneak a complimentary Continental breakfast into your "magic box" before you awake. The ingenious receptacle opens from the outside for the silent delivery and from the inside when you're ready for some hot coffee, fruit, and pastries. You can nibble in bed or, as we prefer, take the snack to one of the patio tables to salute the rising sun.

If you prefer a full breakfast, call the desk. Within minutes, someone will arrive outside the privacy gate of the *casita* to whisk you in a pink and white Jeep to Bellavista restaurant. The beautiful view of the name includes the interior as well as the perspective on the city. On the outside dining terrace in the evening, when the cooking is Continental, starlight shimmers through palm fronds swaying overhead, the lights of Acapulco twinkle in the distance, and the sterling silver beside your plate adds a sparkle of its own.

Las Brisas's second dinner restaurant, El Mexicano, shares the very top of the 1,300-foot hill with five tennis courts. The menu features native dishes, including a broad range of traditional specialties. Saturday is fiesta night at the dining room, when an alfresco buffet is accompanied by *piñata* games, music, folk dancing, and fireworks.

For lunch, in addition to room service, you can pick up a sandwich and some wine in a deli shop or take the hotel shuttle down to the seaside La Concha Beach Club, a recreational complex reserved for guests and a limited number of other members. Next to the open-air café, which specializes in burgers, soups, and salads, there is a freshwater swimming pool and, beyond that, two saltwater pools hewn out of rock. A water sports center offers snorkeling, scuba diving, deep-sea fishing, and water skiing, all extra expenses.

Don't expect a real beach at the club. The closest stretch of sand is about ten minutes by car from Las Brisas. Taxis for the trip are plentiful, or you can rent one of the distinctive hotel Jeeps that are at your summons to haul you around the 100-plus acres of the grounds. The Jeeps are the most solid rental vehicles in Acapulco, but be aware that you are making it plain to everyone on the streets, including the hustlers, that you can afford to stay at the resort.

Personally, we forget all about beaches when we're in our nest at Las Brisas. Getting sand between your toes doesn't feel terribly compelling from your patio, as you float in the pool and gaze across the expansive bay. Inside, the white stucco *casitas* are not opulent, but they are tasteful and pretty. The gray stone on the floors nicely complements the gray marble on the vanity in the bath, on a built-in dressing table, and on end tables by the king-size or two double beds. The pink tone that was so dominant in the 1950s and '60s, when a pink cupid was the hotel's emblem, is now just an accent color. All the quarters have air conditioning, a ceiling fan, a phone, and a mini-bar. And now there is satellite TV in the Royal Beach Club *casitas* and junior suites.

Staying in a *casita* with a private pool is worth the extra cost, both because of the privacy and because those *casitas* tend to be farther up the hill, where the views are better. The quarters with shared pools are concentrated on the first two levels, and the most dramatic panoramas are on the third level and above. The junior and full-size suites, all near the top, are larger than the other rooms, mainly in the baths and on the terraces, which have comfortable covered sitting areas with wet bars. The rates are expensive for Mexico, but the discounts can be substantial from May through mid-December, allowing you in some cases to have a *casita* with a private pool for less than you'd pay for a shared pool in the high season.

No matter where you roost, it will be difficult to leave. You may arrive full of energy, eager to enjoy the bright lights of Acapulco. After one or two forays to the strip, we'll wager the lights begin to look more thrilling from your patio than up close. Las Brisas envelops you in such sensuous seclusion, the titillations of the city quickly lose their lure.

Pierre Marqués

Playa Revolcadero
Acapulco, Guerrero
(7) 4-66-10-00
Fax: (7) 4-66-10-46
Reservations:
Fairmont Hotels and Resorts
800-866-5577

**A golf and convention hotel
on a choppy shore**

Accommodations: 344 rooms and suites. **High-season rates:** Standard rooms $240, superior rooms $267, deluxe rooms $280, junior suites $295–$382, bungalows $540. **Low season:** November–December 15: Standard rooms $105, superior rooms $115, deluxe rooms $125, suites $165 and up. **Included:** Breakfast. **Payment:** Major credit cards. **Children:** Under 12, free in room with parents except for a breakfast charge. **Recreation:** Beach, 3 swimming pools, golf (36 holes), 5 tennis courts, sauna and facilities.

➤ **Together, Pierre Marqués and the Princess offer a total of 16 tennis courts, the most you'll find at any resort property in Mexico.**

The Pierre Marqués is the country cousin of the Acapulco Princess. Owned by the same company and on the same beach, it's a quieter, plainer version of the same golf and convention resort, now usually open only from November to March. The hotel likes to say its elegance is understated, but it's so low-key that you may have trouble finding it.

In contrast to the glittery lobby at the Princess, the Pierre Marqués has a simple reception desk at the entrance. The three pools are pleasant, though they are smaller and less elaborate than the ones down the shore. Similarly, the restaurants and bars, however ample, are more limited in variety and allure. Anything much in the way of nighttime entertainment requires a ride on one of the shuttles that operate regularly to the Princess.

Low-rise tranquillity is the reason to choose the Pierre Marqués over its neighbor. Other than one five-story block of rooms, the accommodations are in two-story wings and a variety of detached bungalows. The multiple-room bungalows occupy about half of the grounds. They are spread nicely to avoid the sense of bulk you get at the Princess, but that requires many of them to be placed well back from the sea. Ocean views are often better from the motel-like wings that run parallel and perpendicular to the beach. All the quarters are comfortable, contemporary, and standard in design.

As at the Princess, the recreational facilities are the main attraction. Everything available at the sister resort is offered here too, including the two golf courses and numerous tennis courts. The difference comes after your game is over. The Pierre Marqués provides a relaxing pace that allows you to unwind in a soothing environment free of glitzy distractions. That may be all the elegance you need.

Plaza Las Glorias El Mirador Acapulco

Quebrada 74
Acapulco, Guerrero
(7) 4-83-11-55
Fax: (7) 4-82-45-64
Reservations: Plaza Las Glorias
800-342-2644

> **The most spectacular dive in Acapulco**

Accommodations: 81 rooms. **High-season rates:** $117. **Low-season rates:** $92.
Payment: Major credit cards. **Children:** Under 12, free in room with parents.
Recreation: 3 swimming pools.

➤   **Acapulco shops specialize in jewelry, but if that's a major interest, you should plan a side trip to Taxco, about three hours inland by rental car or tour bus. Those who just want to admire the artistry can check out Tane at Las Brisas hotel or the chic shops at the Acapulco Princess hotel.**

In one of the best bits of news from Acapulco in recent years, the Plaza Las Glorias chain bought the historic El Mirador and began renovation. Opened in 1933, the hotel was the first major tourist facility in the city and a Hollywood rendezvous. It grew seedy as development moved to other shores, but it continued to draw crowds as the observation site for the La Quebrada cliff divers.

Some of the guest quarters are in the main hilltop building — just inside from a parking lot often filled with hawkers selling tickets to the cliff-diving show — but most of them spill down steep bluffs toward the sea. Originally, the layout insured cool ocean breezes for every room, but now that the accommodations are air-conditioned, fine water views are the main advantage of the spectacular placement. The chief disadvantage is the hike up the hill to the lobby and restaurants when the three funiculars are out of order, which is sometimes the case.

The rooms are attractive for their price but hardly opulent. Red tile floors, dark wood furniture, and pottery lamps provide Mexican flavor, while phones and TVs keep you in contact with the outside world. All the rooms come with a balcony, a small kitchenette, and two double beds or a king. The suites enjoy some of the best ocean views from their balconies, plus a Jacuzzi and a parlor.

The hotel restaurants and bars are the primary spots for watching the nightly dive show, featuring daredevils leaping more than 100 feet into shallow surf. At dinner the entertainment is more exciting than the food, though you can do better at breakfast and lunch with the local fare at El Portal and the international specialties at La Perla. Back down the bluff, two freshwater swimming pools and one with salt water help keep you trim.

El Mirador is once again an alluring hideaway, a short cab ride from most of the Acapulco action and beaches but a time-honored thrill in its own right.

Quinta Real Acapulco

Zona Punta Diamante
Paseo de la Quinta #6
Acapulco, Guerrero
(7) 4-69-15-00
Reservations:
Quinta Real Hotels
800-457-4000

The newest luxury resort to open in Acapulco

Accommodations: 74 suites. **High-season rates:** Master suites $260, Grand Class suites $282, Governor suites $400, Presidential suite $875. **Low-season rates:** Master suites $250, Grand Class suites $270, Governor suites $368, Presidential suite $820. **Payment:** Major credit cards. **Recreation:** Beach, pools, water sports, fitness center, steam bath, sauna, massages, herbal wrap treatment.

➤   **When you decide to have dinner out but don't want poorer quality or less ambience than at the Quinta Real, you should reserve a table at Madeiras (Carretera Escenica No. 33; 4-84-77-76; reservations required), one of Acapulco's most popular restaurants, and deservedly so. It serves a fixed-price Continental dinner in a sophisticated candlelit setting with a breathtaking view of the bay.**

Perched on a rock formation overlooking Revolcadero Beach, between the Acapulco Princess and the airport, the Quinta Real is the latest luxury hotel in Acapulco, having opened in 1999. Part of the Quinta Real chain of quite classy and sometimes stunning hotels, the best known of which is the dramatic Quinta Real in Zacatecas (which is built into the ruins of one of the Americas' oldest bullrings), the Quinta Real in Acapulco starts from scratch with this totally contemporary hotel.

You enter the Quinta Real through a huge, thatched, open-air lobby on what turns out to be the fifth floor of the hotel. (Remember, the hotel is situated on a rock formation overlooking Acapulco Bay.) To get to the accommodations — all suites — as well as the beach, you *descend* in an elevator. The very large beach area contains several pools as well as a beach club, bar, and restaurant. The beach itself, well located on a cove, somewhat surprisingly and disappointingly has dark sand. The fitness center, or spa as it is called, is impressive. Here you'll find stairclimbers, bikes, and treadmills with sea views, and you will be able to enjoy a sauna, steam bath, a variety of massages and facial treatments, and even an herbal wrap treatment. Clearly, this is a place to be pampered.

The suites vary considerably in size, amenities, and price, but all are thoughtfully furnished and have balconies or terraces, some huge, some quite small. If you choose a Master suite you'll have a small balcony, a king-size bed or two double beds with an ornate plaster headboard that is built into the wall, and a small sofa. Soothing natural colors, neutral marble and stone, and stucco work fill the suite, while handsome weavings decorate the walls. If you decide to raise the ante and go for a corner Governor's suite, you will have additional treats. All have separate living rooms (with furniture that is sometimes a bit too heavy for our taste), and one of the Governor's suites (on the third floor) has an enormous terrace with an outdoor Jacuzzi and dramatic views of Acapulco Bay. Bathrobes and slippers are supplied to guests in the Governor's suites. All suites, of course, are air-conditioned and come with satellite TV and mini-bars. The Master suites have the fewest amenities. The Grand Class suites add on a Jacuzzi, and in the Governor's and Presidential suites you'll also have your own private pool. The well-designed hallways leading to all of the suites open to natural rock formations and handsome landscaping.

Quinta Real's Restaurant Gourmet (open for breakfast and dinner), with indoor and outdoor dining, is a show-stopper. With a huge thatched roof, stencil-painted walls, and hand-carved wooden furniture from Michoacan, it is a most inviting setting for its inventive cuisine. If you prefer to eat outdoors, there is lovely terrace dining. For starters try the pumpkin flower (*flor de calabaza*) and mushroom soup. Main dishes include interesting preparations like poached sea bass filled with *huitlacoche* and pumpkin flower sauce, and roast duck with a mango sauce, as well as some of the best dishes from Quinta Real's highly respected restaurants in other Mexican cities. Prices are not outrageously high for Acapulco, and the setting alone is worth the price of the meal.

For the latest in luxury and indulgence, you don't have to look further than the Quinta Real Acapulco.

Huatulco

Best Romantic Hideaway

Best Recreational Resorts and Spas

Best Comfort Choice for All-American Abundance

While Cancún is the established success story among Mexico's planned resorts, Huatulco is struggling. Opened by the government tourism agency in 1989, it's fresh, but all too often its major hotels are in need of an influx of tourists. It's also definitely a work in progress, still in the early stages of development and unspoiled in many ways. If you have ever yearned to see a major resort in its pristine period, Huatulco is the place. You don't want to tarry, but you don't have to rush either. The master plan allows a generous 30 years before the area reaches the size of Cancún and becomes the "ultimate vacationer's paradise," as one official describes the goal.

All the raw materials to fulfill the vision certainly exist. Huatulco encompasses 18 miles of gorgeous Pacific coast southwest of Oaxaca, capital city of the similarly named state, and southeast of Acapulco, its antipode in design. Rugged mountains plunge scenically toward the sea, and nine lovely bays shelter 33 secluded beaches. Each of the bays will be developed differently, with its own mix of lodgings and diversions, presenting travelers with a choice of multiple holiday styles. The only things they will have in common are sun, sand, low-rise buildings, and their own state-of-the-art water treatment and sewage facilities.

Before the bulldozers came, Huatulco was a virgin wilderness, sparsely inhabited for many centuries by Zapotec Indians who farmed and fished contentedly on a subsistence level with little contact with the rest of Mexico, much less the world. The arrival of the first surveyors in 1984 was quite a shock, even if the residents didn't associate the year with Orwellian nightmares. Eventually the authorities gained support, but in the surrounding areas untouched by development, life remains simple and the tropical jungle stays intact. Even 77 percent of the 52,000 acres allotted for the resort itself are set aside as an ecological preserve.

Already roads reach many of the bays, even once remote Playa Entrega. The rustic fishing village on Santa Cruz Bay has suffered a facelift into a modern, commercial marina specializing in boat excursions to the various bays and beaches. Although the Santa Cruz beach is still lined with family-run *palapa* restaurants where you can wiggle your toes in the sand while dining on grilled red snapper, nearby condos and a commercial center surround the marina with a curio market, restaurants, and night spots. Further inland, La Crucecita, a lively Mexican town created from a planner's pen, offers a main square surrounded by a church, sidewalk cafés, and more restaurants and shops.

The sole bay with seaside accommodations so far is Tangolunda, and its golf course and hotels are almost the only first-class tourist attractions of Huatulco for the present. You can have a meal in Santa Cruz or La Crucecita, both a short drive away, or take a day trip to Puerto Ángel and Puerto Escondido, one and two hours respectively by car, or even fly into the colonial city of Oaxaca. Otherwise the hotels, bays, and beaches are it for action. Though Huatulco is destined to glitter by the 21st century, it's a quiet retreat today, a place where natural splendor still holds sway.

Barcelo Huatulco Beach Resort

Bahía de Tangolunda
Huatulco, Oaxaca
(958) 1-00-55
Fax: (958) 1-03-35

A luxury resort hotel with reasonable rates

Accommodations: 337 rooms and 9 suites. **High-season rates:** Pool-view and partial ocean-view rooms $175, ocean-view rooms $185, suites $290–$360. **Low-season rates:** Pool-view and partial ocean-view rooms $150, ocean-view rooms $160, suites $220–$300. **Included:** Breakfast; all-inclusive rates available upon request. **Payment:** Major credit cards. **Children:** Under 18, free in room with parents. **Recreation:** Beach, swimming pool, 4 tennis courts, fitness center with sauna, steam room, and massage.

➤ **The Barcelo provides live entertainment in its lobby lounge and Mexican cantina, but guests can also take in the musical offerings at sidewalk cafés and bars in Huatulco's village, Crucecita.**

Classically graceful in design, the Barcelo Huatulco (formerly the Sheraton Huatulco) was the Sheraton's finest Mexican hotel. It satisfies American tastes for contemporary luxury just as well as most hotels in the country but accomplishes the feat with native ingredients, blending an environment with a broad, auspicious allure.

Oaxacan hardwood adorns the entrance steps, mixes adroitly with marble on the lobby floor, fashions the furniture in guest rooms, and serves as a signature accent throughout the interior. Crafted with superb skill, the polished wood casts a stately glow over the public areas.

The accommodations are equally radiant, from the pink glazed tile on the floors to the lacquer finish on the dressers. The lamps are Oaxacan pottery; so is the ceramic piece in the wall *nicho*. Marble lines the tub shower and forms the vanity. Artful compositions in all respects, the spacious rooms are also modern and functional, with a king bed or two queens, remote control TVs, phones, air conditioning, mini-bars, safes, and balconies facing the water.

A few quarters see little more than the oceanfront pool, but it's an impressive sight, covering — with its sandstone deck — most of a large central courtyard between the hotel's three wings. Near the children's section of the pool, palms wave invitingly from an island, and at the other end adults swim up for libations at a *palapa* café specializing in seafood and pizza. The beach beyond, which slopes heavily toward Tangolunda Bay, offers hammocks, lounge chairs, and thatch umbrellas. The Barcelo's fitness center and four lighted tennis courts and Huatulco's golf course are in the other direction, right out the front door.

In addition to the poolside La Tortuga, there are several other restaurants and bars. Doña Rosa, the all-day dining room, supplies buffet breakfasts in the morning and coffee shop fare the rest of the day. Casa Real offers a fancier alternative for dinner. From the etched glass entrance, you descend a grand stairway to elegantly set tables. The international and Mexican menu is appetizing, even if the cooking doesn't always match the backdrop in finesse.

The hotel resembles recent Hawaiian resorts in style and comfort, but the rates are half of what you would pay in the islands for the same amenities. The Barcelo is as magnanimous as it is magnificent.

Camino Real Zaashila

Bahía de Tangolunda
Huatulco, Oaxaca
(958) 1-04-60
Fax: (958) 1-04-61
Reservations:
800-722-6466

**A sensuously enticing
beachfront resort**

Accommodations: 129 rooms. **High-season rates:** Deluxe rooms $310, deluxe rooms with pools $360, junior suites $460. **Low-season rates:** Deluxe rooms $213, deluxe rooms with pools $263, junior suites $430. **Payment:** Major credit cards. **Children:** Under 18, free with parents. **Recreation:** Beach, swimming pool, 1 tennis court, water sports center.

➤   **Don't miss an opportunity to stop in Oaxaca on the way to or from Huatulco. Many travelers believe the perfect vacation consists of several days imbibing the culture of Oaxaca followed by several more days on Huatulco's beaches. Small regional airlines make the half-hour flight between the cities daily.**

The Camino Real Zaashila is the most stylish place to stay in the budding resort area. It's close to the local golf course and other diversions, yet tucked away by itself on an almost private beach, rising from the secluded shore like a Mediterranean village in a series of white *casas* that climb up a terraced hillside.

The reception lounge, next to the hotel entrance, sits at the top of the property under a conical *palapa* roof. A colorful Mexican mural greets you from the wall behind the antique registration desk, and when you turn to head downhill to your room, the shimmering Pacific extends its own inviting welcome.

Waterfalls and running streams lead you toward the sea and your ocean-view quarters. You step inside onto Italian marble floors to find a king bed or two doubles, an armoire with a TV, a mini-bar, air conditioning, and a spacious, double-vanity bath. If your room is on the ground floor, a small splash pool is directly outside, just beyond a covered patio with a *banco* sofa, table, and chairs. Rooms above get a bigger balcony to compensate for the lack of a private pool.

You may not care about that frill anyway once you've seen the enormous main pool, a flowing, free-form stone and water sculpture longer than a football field. Lined by palms, it sprawls above the wide beach, which is sheltered from the rest of Huatulco by rocky points. A water sports center arranges snorkeling, diving, windsurfing, kayaking, and other ocean activities, and inland you can play golf or tennis.

The open-air, thatched-roof Zaashila Beach Club serves seafood and Oaxacan specialties by the waterfront, and the Bel-La Grill offers simpler selections at poolside. Up the hill, enjoying elevated views, the Bitsa Lounge opens evenings with live music and the Chez Binni Restaurant wraps up the day with Mexican and international dinners in an elegantly casual setting.

The Camino Real represents the potential of Huatulco at its most beautiful and beguiling. Fresh in design and spirit, it sets the standard for the area's bright future.

Casa del Mar

Balcones de Tangolunda 13
Huatulco, Oaxaca
(958) 1-02-03
Fax: (958) 1-02-02
Reservations:
800-262-4500

| **A romantic inn in Huatulco.** |

Accommodations: 25 suites. **High-season rates:** Junior suites $103, suites $140. **Low-season rates:** Junior suites $75, suites $115. **Payment:** MasterCard, Visa. **Recreation:** Swimming pool.

➤ **Undiscovered by travelers, Casa del Mar sits blissfully apart from the resort activity below its hillside location. To retreat from the crowds, take in the mesmerizing views and good food at its Miramar restaurant.**

Even in these early stages of Huatulco's development, the beautiful bay of Tangolunda has witnessed only mega-hotels around its shore. Above the bay, straddling a ridge overlooking the two bays of Conejo and Tangolunda, is an exclusive residential development with an estate belonging to a former president of Mexico. Winding up the narrow streets past the villas, you come to the Casa del Mar, a small inn with barely a sign to lead you into its tranquil setting.

The inn is built around a large open sunning terrace with a sparkling blue swimming pool and views over the hills and sea. Above the pool, the open terrace of the restaurant and cocktail lounge commands a panoramic view. Built into the various levels of the hills around the sunning terrace are gardens and the various *casitas* and duplexes housing the 25 suites of Casa del Mar.

The spacious rooms would cost twice as much at any other Mexican resort. Most have well-furnished terraces with sea views and stark Mediterranean-white architecture with soothing color accents. Headboards for the king-size beds are sculpted from the stucco wall; a separate dressing room leads the way into a sun-filled bathroom with skylights and a small interior garden. All the rooms have VCRs so you can watch movies from the hotel's library; a few of the master suites have a private Jacuzzi. Our favorite junior suites are below the pool area, each with a living-room-size private terrace and unobstructed bay views. These terraces, furnished with lounge chairs and a table and chairs for dining, would be hard to abandon for any serious activity other than dipping in the pool.

Casa del Mar is a romantic retreat. There are few activities to disturb you other than calling for room or poolside service or watching the sunset from the restaurant or bar. The beach club is far below, so far down a path to Tangolunda beach that you would think twice about making the return. Better to take the boat tours to more pristine coastal bays and snorkeling coves or rent a car to explore the many isolated beaches south of Tangolunda. The very accommodating staff can make arrangements for you.

Club Med Huatulco

Bahía de Tangolunda
Huatulco, Oaxaca
(958) 1-00-33
Fax: (958) 1-01-01
Reservations:
Club Med Sales
800-CLUB MED

A sprawling all-inclusive resort for families with teenagers

Accommodations: 482 rooms. **High-season rates:** $630 weekly per adult, $500 weekly per teenager ages 12–17, double occupancy. **Low-season rates:** $600 weekly per adult, $470 per teenager, double occupancy; hotel closed May to early November. **Included:** Breakfast, lunch, dinner, beer and wine with meals, all recreation listed below except golf and deep-sea fishing. **Minimum stay:** 7 nights in high season. **Payment:** Major credit cards. **Children:** Special programs for families with teenagers ages 12–17; otherwise children not accepted except during special holidays when mini-club available for other ages. **Recreation:** 4 beaches, 3 swimming pools, 12 tennis courts, 3 squash courts, fitness center, golf (18 holes, off property), archery, snorkeling, small-craft sailing, windsurfing, kayaking, deep-sea fishing, circus workshops.

➤ **All Club Meds offer excursions for an extra fee, but the choices in Huatulco are particularly varied. You can fly to Oaxaca for the day, take a bus to Puerto Ángel, or tour the gorgeous bays of the resort area by boat.**

As we noted earlier, in the Cancún chapter, a decision to go to any Club Med is first and foremost a choice of a vacation style rather than a choice of a particular place. We described the kind of experience to expect in our report on the Club Med Cancún (see index), which should be consulted as a starting point in considering the Huatulco resort. The general characteristics of a Club Med getaway are similar the world over.

The Huatulco village is the organization's biggest and splashiest in Mexico. It specializes in programs for families with teenage children from 12 to 17 years old. With a beach each for snorkeling, kayaking, and sailing, with five restaurants and four different residential compounds, it is more like a carnival than a hotel.

The rooms are quite a welcome departure from Club Med tradition. They enjoy a hammock-strung, ocean-view terrace large enough for lounging, giving guests much more total space than usual. The interiors are cleverly divided into two identical halves that can be screened off from each other, an ideal arrangement for both singles and families. Instead of the typical twin beds, you get a pair of doubles. There is only one bath, but it has two separate vanities.

The downside of the rooms is their distance from the main dining and activity center. The grounds are so spread out that shuttles are required to get around, particularly when you're staying in the more remote "pueblos." The drivers are usually punctual on their 15-minute schedule, but the need for transportation can be a nuisance in slow periods and a serious irritation when the place is full.

At least the food awaiting you after your ride is worth the bother. The cooking was quite good during a recent visit, and the buffet selection was enormous. Italian, Moroccan, and Tex-Mex victuals are featured in the specialty restaurants.

The international flavor isn't limited to the kitchens. Most of Mexico's Club Meds are heavily *norteamericano* in clientele, but the mix of guests is better balanced in Huatulco. If you don't get the sense of a global village found in some of the foreign Club Meds, at least you don't have flashes of being in Florida.

The sports facilities, as always, are extensive. They don't dominate life, though. There's more to Huatulco, a fuller and grander resort spirit. It's Club Med plus, a successful fusion of the organization's culture and contemporary trends.

Ixtapa and Zihuatanejo

Best Romantic Hideaway

Villa del Sol, 143

Best Hotel for Stylish Sophistication

La Casa Que Canta, 138

Best Recreational Resort or Spa

Westin Brisas Resort Ixtapa, 136

Best Comfort Choices for All-American Abundance

Club Med Ixtapa, 132
Double Tree Ixtapa, 133
Krystal Ixtapa, 134

Best Beachfront Buys

Las Urracas, 140
Sotavento-Catalina, 142

Best B&B or Budget Inn

Raúl Tres Marías, 141

The same computer that chose Cancún for development in the 1970s also selected Ixtapa for a similar fate around the same time. Programming in those days, however, was still a bit primitive and didn't always yield consistent results. Ixtapa has never achieved the size or glamour of its sister resort, remaining less developed and more affordable. It provides the standard international style and recreational amenities that many vacationers seek, but at a modest level of luxury and price.

One of the primary advantages that promoters tout is the proximity of Zihuatanejo, the picturesque village five miles away. The original plan called for preserving the pristine appeal of the town by concentrating mass tourism at the neighboring resort. That element of the design has worked well on the whole, though Zihuatanejo found a new niche for itself in catering to an unusual combination of budget and high-end travelers. The hotels stayed small and Mexican in character, both those at the bottom of the rate scale and a couple of elegant inns at the top.

Together, Ixtapa and Zihuatanejo offer something for almost everyone. Golfers, families, and package tourists congregate at the modern resort of Ixtapa, visiting the village of Zihuatanejo for local color, and a range of young and experienced travelers head directly for the native charm, going occasionally to Ixtapa for all-American diversions. As long as you pick the right stop for you, either place should please.

The Main Attractions

Downtown Zihuatanejo

The foothills of the Sierra Madre line the shores of Zihuatanejo Bay, dangling their tropical foliage over the sea. It's an intimate bay compared with the ones in Acapulco and Puerto Vallarta, but it shares much of their natural grandeur.

Downtown Zihuatanejo is on the waterfront, built inland from Playa Principal, a colorful beach busy with community activity much of the day. A dozen short streets constitute the central area, walkable in an hour or so without stops. Cobblestones now cover the old dirt surfaces of the streets, but the architecture remains plain and traditional, with few concessions to cute trends except in the growing number of T-shirt shops.

Tourist and local businesses mingle in a pleasant montage with an authentic Mexican feel. Children play on the beach after school, and their parents come in from nearby residential sections for the market, the post office, the bus station, and the current gossip. The town is real and vital though small and relaxed, easy for visitors to explore and enjoy.

In the scattered shops the proportion of distinctive handmade wares to tourist schlock is as high as it gets in a beach destination. Start your browsing at Coco Cabaña, on Vincente Guerrero behind Coconuts restaurant. The store's "collectibles for the home" include exquisite folk art. Galería Maya (Nicolas Bravo 33) displays equally fine taste in crafts, though the selection is slightly smaller.

Several interesting stores are clustered near Playa Principal. In the same building at Paseo del Pescador 9, El Jumil sells masks and silver jewelry and La Zapoteca features weaving and hammocks from the southern regions of the country. Next door on Juan Alvaréz, El Embarcadero offers imaginative Mexican designs in clothing. For casual beachwear and sandals, roam the half-dozen blocks of Calle Cuauhtemoc. We always find something we need, often in the plainest places.

Most of Zihuatanejo's hotels are on two adjoining beaches, Playa La Madera and Playa La Ropa, a few miles by car and just 15 minutes along the scenic coastal walkway. There are a handful of low-rise inns on each beach, scattered haphazardly around the sand. La Ropa is easily the more alluring of the pair, a wide white beach that sweeps along the bay for more than a mile past hillside hotels, thatch-roofed restaurants, and gently splashing surf.

The Ixtapa Strip

For all practical purposes a one-street resort, Ixtapa consists of little more than a row of seaside hotels and a sprawling shopping center separated from each other by a broad boulevard. The boulevard ends at a marina complex with outdoor restaurants. Since nothing was here before the government chose the spot for development, everything is contemporary and international in character. The mid-rise hotels, rather standard except for the Westin, feature elaborate swimming pools where guests congregate to avoid the rough water surging onto Playa del Palmar, a long, comely beach that seldom gets crowded or busy.

An 18-hole public golf course, designed by the Robert Trent Jones clan, spreads inland alongside the mall. It's one of the top resort courses in Mexico, though not superior by U.S. standards. A second course opened recently at the other end of the strip, near the marina.

Secluded Sands

Though La Ropa is one of the finest beaches in Mexico, and Playa del Palmar is even more expansive, you should rouse yourself occasionally for excursions to some hidden sands, generally reached by boat. The closest and most convenient to Zihuatanejo is Las Gatas, a 15-minute walk around a rocky point from La Ropa, but basically inaccessible by road; the unspoiled shore with a few simple restaurants was a favorite of Tarascan royalty before the Spanish arrived. One of the Indian monarchies built a breakwater to protect the cove from unruly waves, creating a superb site for modern snorkelers. Most people catch a boat at the municipal pier in town for the reasonably priced 10-minute trip to Las Gatas.

Along the coast between Zihuatanejo and Ixtapa, La Manzanilla and Majahua beaches had long been accessible only by boat, but a recently constructed road has ended their isolation.

In Ixtapa, a road right off the main boulevard continues north from the strip a few miles to Playa Quieta, home of a Club Med. Boats depart regularly from a pier at the south end of the sand to Isla Ixtapa, a wildlife preserve that is a popular day-trip destination. The island shelters the coast in front of the Club Med from the Pacific surf, giving it the name that translates as "quiet beach."

Isla Ixtapa is a trove of sandy shores. The one where the boats land, lined with seafood eateries, is the spot for lunch. The farther you wander from there, the more attractive and deserted the beaches become. Make it at least to Playa Baradero, a short walk from the arrival area. Snorkeling and diving are good around Isla Ixtapa, and birding is also popular in the sanctuary.

Farther north (about 30 miles) is long and beautiful Playa Troncones, a favorite spot for horseback riding and bird-watching. A number of small inns and restaurants have opened along the beach, making for a pleasant and easy day trip.

Ixtapa

Club Med Ixtapa

Playa Quieta
Ixtapa, Guerrero
(7) 55-2-00-44
Fax: (7) 55-2-00-40
Reservations:
Club Med Sales
800-CLUB MED

> **A Club Med for family and tennis getaways**

Accommodations: 375 rooms. **High-season rates:** $960–$1,295 weekly per person, $686–$910 ages 1–11, double occupancy. **Low-season rates:** Approximately $840 weekly per person, $590 ages 1–11, double occupancy; hotel closed September–October. **Included:** Breakfast, lunch, dinner, beer and wine with meals, all recreation listed below except golf and horseback riding. **Minimum stay:** 7 nights given preference in high season. **Payment:** Major credit cards. **Children:** Accepted over 12 months; under 12 years, reduced rates. **Recreation:** Beach, swimming pool, 12 tennis courts, golf (18 holes, off property), riding, aerobics, archery, snorkeling, small-craft sailing, windsurfing, kayaking, circus workshops.

➤ **Club Med's tennis center offers a dozen composition courts, four lighted for night play, plus a clubhouse, ball machine, competitions, and two and a half hours of instruction daily.**

As we noted earlier, in the Cancún chapter, a decision to go to any Club Med is first and foremost a choice of a vacation style rather than a choice of a particular place. We described the kind of experience to expect in our report on the Club Med Cancún (see index), which should be consulted as a starting point in considering the Ixtapa resort. The general characteristics of a Club Med getaway are similar the world over.

Located on long Playa Quieta, the "quiet beach," the Ixtapa Club Med specializes in family getaways. Its Baby Club tends to toddlers 12 to 23 months old, and the Petit, Mini, and Kids clubs take children from that age up to 12 years. Parents can play with their kids if they wish or leave them in supervised activities while they play with each other.

The youngsters are introduced to juggling in the circus workshop, go on picnics and excursions, learn arts and crafts, and perhaps try archery. An intensive tennis program provides several hours of instruction and practice daily for children between 8 and 14 as well as for adults.

The pleasant Mexican village atmosphere, the rooms, and the meals are all geared to suit families. Little is too flashy or too spicy for children, and the comfort level is moderately high for their elders. Parents who want to travel with young children won't find many better resort environments anywhere in Mexico.

Double Tree Ixtapa

Blvd. Ixtapa
Ixtapa, Guerrero
(7) 55-3-00-03
Fax: (7) 55-3-15-55
Reservations:
Double Tree Ixtapa
800-222-TREE

**One of the prettier hotels
on the Ixtapa beach**

Accommodations: 255 rooms and 26 suites. **High-season rates:** Oceanfront rooms $200, junior and executive suites $280–$285. **Low-season rates:** Oceanfront rooms $120, junior and executive suites $185–$190. **Payment:** Major credit cards. **Children:** Under 17, free in room with parents. **Recreation:** Beach, swimming pool, tennis, water sports center, fitness center.

➤ **To eat out in style, head to Beccofino, an Italian restaurant in the marina area, or Villa del la Selva, up the hill near the Westin. Once the home**

of former President Luis Echeverria, the Villa serves expensive Continental dinners in the loveliest setting in the area.

The Double Tree is easily the finest hotel on the resort's main strip, not in the class of the secluded Westin nearby but a real blockbuster for this busy beach.

You enter a lobby that fuses high-tech decor with flamboyant Mexican colors and accents, a potential disaster that succeeds artfully. One of the hotel's bars is here, set up for the nightly live music, and La Gran Tapa, a Spanish café and cantina, adds an air of international flair.

A splashy free-form pool occupies the seaside just beyond the lobby. A bridge over the water takes you to the beach, a wide, sandy section of the long shore that's dotted with thatch umbrellas and lounge chairs. The Palapa Restaurant and Bar sits beside the pool, providing swim-up service and convivial dining under its thatched roof. La Terraza restaurant handles the breakfast buffets and regional cuisine.

Although the rooms are rather less than opulent, they are fresh and fashionable. Each room has a satellite television, a mini-bar, a phone, and a balcony with a good if somewhat distant ocean view. True spaciousness and the optimum vistas are reserved for the junior and executive suites, some of the choicest accommodations in Ixtapa.

The Omni is tasteful, a claim few of its competitors can make. It won't stun you with the spectacular but it will give you an environment that's stylishly soothing.

Krystal Ixtapa

Blvd. Ixtapa
Ixtapa, Guerrero
(7) 55-3-03-33
Fax: (7) 55-3-02-16
Reservations:
Krystal Hotels
800-231-9860
Fax: 713-952-9941

**A beachfront hotel
brimming with activity**

Accommodations: 256 rooms and suites. **High-season rates:** Standard rooms $190, junior suites $240, master suites $270. **Low-season rates:** Standard rooms $150, junior suites $160, master suites $235. **Payment:** Major credit cards. **Children:** Under 12, free in room with parents. **Recreation:** Beach, swimming pool, 2 tennis courts, exercise room.

➤ **The most elegant disco in Ixtapa is the Krystal's Christine, with tables tiered around the dance floor and a show at 11:30 P.M. nightly. For a more boisterous night of dancing, check out the beachfront location of Carlos 'n' Charlie's, near the Posada Real.**

The Krystal hotels in Mexico are similar in many ways. The one in Ixtapa is not substantially better than the rest, but the competition is weaker here than in other cities. It wins honors on a popular beach more by default than by its success.

The principal virtue for vacationers is the Krystal's constant attention to fun. Activity centers around the sprawling free-form pool, replete with a short water slide, a contrived waterfall, a concrete island, and a swim-up bar. The social director keeps the scene jumping with organized events, perhaps free scuba lessons, an egg toss, volleyball, a tug of war game, a balloon race, or a wine-tasting contest. Part of the pool deck overlooks the beach, a quieter spot with *palapa* umbrellas and lounge chairs.

For the children there's a petting zoo; for the adults, a trio of bars in addition to Christine, the rollicking disco. The restaurants contribute more to the playful atmosphere than to haute cuisine. The all-day Aquamarina promises to get you back to the games simply and rapidly. Bogart's and Rarotonga both specialize in beef and seafood, one in the midst of the poolside animation and the other in a Casablanca setting intended to make you feel like Bogie himself at home in Rick's Café.

The rooms in the ten-story tower are not notable for luxury, but every one enjoys an ocean view from a balcony. They come with a king-size or two double beds, a phone, satellite TV, a mini-bar, and air conditioning. The suites may merit consideration for the extra elbow room.

Like most Ixtapa hotels, the Krystal is basically a package tourist property, slightly gaudy and slightly silly, as the wholesalers seem to like. What's above average for the destination is the level of enthusiasm. In some places, a commitment to good times is as good as it gets.

Westin Brisas Resort Ixtapa

Playa Vista Hermosa
Ixtapa, Guerrero
(7) 55-3-21-21
Fax: (7) 55-3-07-51
Reservations:
Westin Hotels and Resorts
800-228-3000

A masterpiece of Mexican resort architecture

Accommodations: 428 rooms and suites. **High-season rates:** Ocean-view rooms $155–$185, Royal Beach Club rooms $215, junior suites $385, master suites from $510. **Low-season rates:** Ocean-view rooms $130, Royal Beach Club rooms $160, junior suites $300, master suites from $425. **Payment:** Major credit cards. **Children:** 1 child under 18, free in room with parents. **Recreation:** Beach, 4 swimming pools, water sports center, 4 tennis courts, health club with massage.

➤ **Just down the hill from the Westin, the Ixtapa Golf Club, designed by Robert Trent Jones, wanders along palm-lined fairways past three blue lakes. It's also a game preserve, home to alligators and a trove of tropical birds.**

Renowned architect Ricardo Legorreta had already designed impressive Camino Real hotels in Mexico City and Cancún when he was asked to work on the Westin resort in Ixtapa. He started in the sea, surveying the coast for a site, and ultimately selected a dramatic hillside on a secluded beach. In his emphatic minimalist style, Legorreta set out to create a structure that matched both the personality of the land and the character of modern Mexico as he saw it, "Strong, colorful, spacious, romantic, and spiritually in harmony with its environment." The result makes other hotels, including his own, look like cookie cutter copies of each other.

Unless you're coming in by boat, little of the building is visible as you approach. You enter a lobby you don't expect, stark and angular rather than plush, accented with hot pink and glossy yellow instead of trendy mauves and aquas. A little dazed, perhaps, you descend from there to your room, on one of 12 levels cascading from the hilltop in a geometric sweep that would have made Euclid swoon.

Your room is the pièce de résistance. Each room has three distinct realms, not counting the tile-filled bath. The sleeping area is the least interesting, though it contains a bright bedspread and rugs as well as all the modern conveniences — air conditioning, a ceiling fan, a phone, a TV, a mini-bar, and adequate storage. Don't worry that it's less than exquisite because you'll spend very few waking moments inside.

The two other areas are on the large ocean-view terrace. The portion just outside the sliding glass door is covered on the top and sheltered by walls on the sides, making it a totally private, shady space for relaxing and dining. A few steps farther is the open, sun-drenched part of the patio, ample for lounging in a hammock that's perfectly positioned for the sunset. If you upgrade to a junior suite, there's a Jacuzzi on the balcony, and the master suites have their own pools.

The four pools next to the four-court tennis and health club complex and the Solarium restaurant are more than adequate for most people. They can be reached by the hotel shuttles or by taking an elevator down to the tenth floor (the lowest level and the only one to avoid for lodging) and following a flagstone pathway through a lush, bird-filled swath of jungle. Spread over three tiers dotted with blue umbrellas, the pools cascade into each other, creating one of the most enticing sites in Mexico for sunning and swimming. Another woodland trail leads from here to the wide crescent of sand at the bottom of the hill, an uncrowded beach that feels pristine and wild because of the landscaping above.

The Westin's seven restaurants and lounges offer substantial variety in venues and menus. The drinks are sometimes prepared with more care than the dishes, but in the two fancy dinner-only establishments — one Mexican, one Italian — the cooking excels as often as any place in town. The other principal dining rooms feature water views, at poolside and on a terrace overlooking the sea. The Lobby Bar, which also has a grand Pacific vista, swings in the early evening with live music. There is also a small deli where you can purchase items for your room or for picnics (which aren't available through room service).

There are more polished hotels in Mexico, but few are prettier than the Westin. It's a stunning spot for stirring the juices, built with passion for the passionate.

Zihuatanejo

La Casa Que Canta

Camino Escénico a la Playa la Ropa
Zihuatanejo, Guerrero
(7) 55-4-70-30
Fax: (7) 55-4-70-40
Reservations:
Small Luxury Hotels of the World
800-525-4800

> **A serene, sensuous hideaway overlooking the Pacific**

Accommodations: 24 suites. **High-season rates:** Terrace rooms $315, grand suites $355, private pool suites $550, 2-night minimum. **Low-season rates:** Terrace rooms $250–$270, grand suites $290–$320, private pool suites $435–$485. **Included:** Continental breakfast. **Added:** 10% service and 17% tax. **Payment:** Major credit cards. **Children:** Under 16, not permitted. **Recreation:** Beach, 2 swimming pools, Jacuzzi, fitness center.

➤ **If the fashionable crowd at La Casa Que Canta gives you a notion to go jewelry shopping, Zihuatanejo offers some good options. Don't miss Alberto's and Ruby's, about a block apart on Cuauhtemoc in the center of town.**

Perched handsomely on a cliff above the bay, peering out to the Pacific over Playa La Ropa and Playa La Madera, La Casa Que Canta is an elegantly enchanting addition to Zihuatanejo's small hotels. Personally designed by Jacques and Yvonne Baldassari, the French-Mexican owners, "The House that Sings" offers a lyrical escape from the mundane into the magnificent.

The inn flows organically up and around the hillside in a trio of low-slung, adobe-colored buildings. Thatched roofs and awnings enhance the Mexican flavor, which extends exquisitely inside with native tile and woodwork. Each of the 24 rooms is individually decorated in tribute to a different song. Though details vary considerably, all have an expansive terrace and a range of delightful accents, from folk art to hammocks.

Even the smallest quarters, a moderate size, enjoy a double-vanity marble bath, a mini-bar stocked with complimentary drinks, an elaborate floral welcome covering the beautiful bedspread, and an ample lounging area on the balcony overlooking the bay and town. Ask for number 9 for particularly grand views. For extra space in the air-conditioned interior, upgrade to a grand suite, which features a parlor, king beds, and an oversize bathroom. For the ultimate indulgence, the chambers at the top of the rate scale come with private pools.

If you don't splurge for your own pool, you have a choice of two others, a freshwater option on the bluff and a languorous saltwater alternative right above the rocky shore. The hotel's small beach club on La Ropa, a quick walk downhill, will arrange water sports, and the hospitable reception staff can organize an outing for golf, tennis, fishing, or horseback riding, all available nearby.

La Casa serves breakfast and lunch in an alfresco café by the freshwater pool. Nearby, an intimate dinner restaurant occupies the same *palapa*-style structure as the classy, cozy lobby. Combining tastes of Mexico and the Mediterranean, the menu sings with a sophistication rare in beach resorts. We started our dinner with a delightful tuna carpaccio, followed by a hearty seafood fettuccine and succulently tender *arracheras* (skirt steak), all accompanied by excellent house wines. The dessert was a perfect climax, fresh cherries soaked in tequila and vanilla.

La Casa Que Canta is a smart and snug retreat, truly Mexican but also worldly in its ways. You'll love making La Casa *su casa*.

Las Urracas

Apartado Postal 141
Zihuatanejo, Guerrero
(7) 55-4-20-49

A low-key cottage hotel on the sand

Accommodations: 16 bungalows. **Rates:** $70. **Payment:** No credit cards. **Recreation:** Beach.

➤ **In the winter in particular, downtown Zihuatanejo becomes a lively village in the late afternoon. The favorite spot for a drink is Coconuts (Ramirez 1, near Guerrero at Alvarez), a colorful restaurant and bar in a historic abode.**

Las Urracas is an unlikely place, perhaps doomed in the future by the pressures of modern development. Near the center of one of Mexico's finest beaches, Playa La Ropa, the dozen-plus cottages of the small inn are spread around a serene, shady garden just off the sand. Each of the old-style brick bungalows has a kitchen and a big front porch, making it an ideal — and affordable — winter home.

As you might expect, the high season is booked far in advance by repeat guests, many of whom stay a good spell. Try Las Urracas first at other times of the year, when it's equally desirable. The value peaks between Easter and Thanksgiving, and there's a much better chance of getting in.

Most of the cottages face a landscaped courtyard rather than the sea. Only two of the original buildings have direct ocean views from the beachfront, but the management has added a new two-story structure on the sand, sadly out of character with the rest of the property. We would opt for the garden bungalows ahead of the contemporary rooms, for their spaciousness and rustic Mexican aura. In addition to the kitchen and patio, each contains a bath with a shower, at least one bedroom, and occasionally a second bantam bedroom for children.

Las Urracas has some thatch umbrellas and wood lounge chairs on Playa La Ropa, but no recreational or dining facilities. They aren't needed. This is less a hotel than a *casa* away from home, a place to settle in for the leisurely life on a splendid shore.

Raúl Tres Marías

Juan Alvarez 52
Zihuatanejo, Guerrero
(755) 4-29-77
Reservations: Contact Raúl Lara
Juárez at the hotel

**A friendly, family-run inn
for budget travelers**

Accommodations: 17 rooms. **Rate:** $35–$45. **Payment:** MasterCard, Visa.

➤ **A short walk away is the Playa Principal and the open-air restaurant La Sirena Gorda ("The Fat Mermaid"), next to the pier (Paseo del Pescador, 554-31-36), a local favorite for its unusual variety of tacos. Come anytime but Wednesday, and when you come, try the smoked fish tacos.**

Raúl Tres Marías actually has two branches in what its business card used to call "dawn town" Zihuatanejo. The one whose address is given above is our preference of the pair because of its central location and the presence of the Restaurante Garrobos, one of the best places to eat in the area. If this branch is full, Raúl Lara Juárez, the English-speaking manager, may be able to accommodate you at the other one, which is nearby and similar in all respects.

The rooms to request are numbers 11, 12, 14, and 15, on the third floor, facing the bay. These chambers have a good view of the water — over electrical wires and roofs — and each has a small balcony for enjoying the scene. Otherwise they're like the rest of the rooms — clean, somewhat worn, and furnished with an air conditioner, a double and a twin bed usually, and a tiled shower.

Plenty of cafés, bars, and shops are a stroll away, and the Playa Principal is within a block. Diversions and services are limited at the hotel itself, but you're in the middle of one of Mexico's most winsome villages. A cot in the corridor would be worth the cost.

Sotavento-Catalina

Apartado Postal 2
Zihuatanejo, Guerrero
(7) 55-4-20-32
Fax: (7) 55-4-29-75

> **Two older hotels joined
> above Playa La Ropa**

Accommodations: 124 rooms. **Rates :** Standard rooms or *casitas* $95, *terraza* rooms and deluxe bungalows $120. **Payment:** Major credit cards. **Children:** Under 12, free. **Recreation:** Beach.

➤ **Rossy, a short surfside walk from the Sotavento-Catalina, offers some of the best seafood on La Ropa. Convivial and moderately priced, the popular hangout attracts scores of beachcombers all day.**

The Catalina and the Sotavento hotels are as inseparably linked as Siamese twins. The only remaining vestiges of their independent identities are the two names used as one in their odd-sounding modern moniker. They share a hillside above Playa La Ropa, a lobby, restaurants, bars, and a playful, budget-friendly atmosphere.

The rooms are a maze, both in their configuration on the steep grounds and in their rate categories. The standard rooms include four different types of quarters that command the same price. Most are a moderate size, but they feature a balcony with an ocean view. For the difference in price, the *terraza* rooms and deluxe bungalows offer the best value. These rooms are quite large, with huge terraces. Our favorites are the corner ones that overlook the long stretch of La Ropa Beach. Even more desirable are the Catalina deluxe bungalows, completed in 1989. They come with two double beds, a built-in sofa in a sitting area, screened windows with wrought-iron grillwork, attractive tile in the shower and on the floors, and a private terrace with a hammock, a lounge chair, and a fine perspective on the beach and sea.

The hotel used to require a Modified American Plan, meaning you had to pay for breakfast and dinner whether you ate them or not. That policy has been dropped now, making the two restaurants and bars seem more captivating since guests no longer feel like captives. The kitchen claims expertise with French, Italian, and Mexican dishes, but the menus don't go far beyond spaghetti and seafood.

The Sotavento-Catalina puts you on a great beach at a modest price. The first hotel on the Playa La Ropa, it shows its age in many areas, but it has managed to maintain a youthful vigor. Given that resilience, the rates, and the setting, the shortcomings lose some of their significance.

Villa del Sol

Apartado Postal 84
Zihuatanejo, Guerrero
(7) 55-4-22-39
Fax: (7) 55-4-27-58
Reservations:
Small Luxury Hotels of the World:
800-525-4800

A Relais & Châteaux inn on a grand beach

Accommodations: 55 rooms, mini-suites, and suites; 18 villas (contact the inn directly for villa rates and availability). **High-season rates:** Standard rooms $230, superior suites $275, deluxe suites $300, lagoon suites $450, garden suites $550, beach suites $700–$800, presidential suite $900. **Low-season rates:** Standard rooms $160, superior suites $220, deluxe suites $250, lagoon suites $350, garden suites $400, beach suites $500–$600, presidential suite

$750. **Added:** MAP (breakfast and dinner meal plan) required in high season at an additional cost of $60 per person daily; 10% staff gratuity suggested, 17% tax. **Payment:** Major credit cards. **Children:** With a few exceptions, no children under 14 accepted. **Recreation:** Beach, 4 swimming pools, 2 tennis courts, water sports including sailing and windsurfing, massage.

➤ **You won't want to leave Villa del Sol for many meals, but when you go shopping downtown, try Los Garrobos (in the Raúl Tres Marías Hotel, 55-4-29-77) for a paella brimming with shellfish.**

In his student days in Germany, Helmut Leins wanted to pursue a career as an inspector for the Michelin red guides. He still has the necessary dedication to excellence and consistency, but fate landed him instead on the opposite side of the same business, providing the food and hospitality rather than evaluating it. Michelin's loss was clearly our gain. Helmut has crafted his Villa del Sol into one of the finest beachfront hotels in Mexico — and certainly one of the most expensive.

The most notable difference is the careful attention to cooking. In the low season you can save a little by declining the breakfast and dinner meal plan (MAP) — required in the winter. Helmut and his cooks rely mainly on the simpler dishes and ingredients of Mexico, preparing them with skill. The quality is considered so high that the prestigious Relais & Châteaux organization recognized Villa del Sol for membership in 1992, making it the only beach resort so honored in all of Latin America.

Breakfast begins with a buffet of fruit, juice, and bread, followed by an à la carte entrée selection. Try the beef *puntas* for a hearty way to start the day. The lunch menu changes daily but always focuses on a limited number of items that thrive on freshness.

A casual dinner can be had at the hotel's La Cantina Bar & Grill, but for a more romantic setting you should dine at the oceanfront Restaurant at Villa del Sol. Start perhaps with a fine green salad with salsa vinaigrette or a superb red ceviche, perfectly balanced in its robust spicing. The entrée selections always include meat and seafood options, such as succulent Baja shrimp in a diablo sauce or a pepper steak made from Sonora beef. The formal restaurant menu is replaced once a week by a beach barbecue and Mexican buffet with live entertainment.

Until 1990, meals were served in a small, open-air seaside café. The new, larger dining room, several steps along the beach, sits under three handsome *palapas* built with log beams to support the thatch. A pool with a swim-up bar and a waterfall has been added behind the restaurant, and in front a terrace stretches out to glorious Playa La Ropa for casual daytime snacking.

Villa del Sol has been expanding even more up the hill beyond the small inn, building condominium villas and a second tennis court. Ranging in size from studio to two-bedroom and two-bath apartments, they are available through the hotel for accommodations when the owners are absent. Helmut is supervising the construction, as you might imagine, insuring that the villas are some of the top rental condos in Mexico by designing them in the same style as the inn's mini-suites and suites.

The originals are a splendid model, the kind of quarters that make you want to move in forever. The one- and two-story stucco buildings gracefully frame several courtyards, one accented with a palm-crowned fountain, another embracing the *palapa* bar and a pool. Although few of the chambers have an ocean view, all the patios and balconies enjoy a scenic setting. Some of the deluxe mini-suites even come with a private plunge pool or whirlpool, as well as a phone and TV, lacking in the more traditional rooms. Three enormous beachfront suites, added recently, have marble floors with pebble designs and an open-air living area or private plunge pool.

The interiors differ slightly, but all are in good taste. We stayed recently in one of the least expensive mini-suites, entered through a long, narrow terrace equipped with a hammock and *equipale* furniture. The screened wood doors slid open into a sunken *banco* sitting area, nicely trimmed with colorful tile that contrasted smartly with the glazed natural tile on the floor. The king-size bed was covered with a fine gauze mosquito net, tied at the corners with strands of bright fabric. Other fiberwork, principally embroidery, hung on the walls. The overall effect of the room was delightful, from the layout of the spacious bathroom to the ingenious use of baskets rather than drawers to keep clothes fresher.

Even if you're as tough to please as a Michelin inspector, you'll be reaching for the stars as you leave the Villa del Sol.

Manzanillo and the Gold Coast

Manzanillo and the Gold Coast

Best Romantic Hideaway

Best Hotel for Stylish Sophistication

Best Recreational Resorts and Spas

Best Adventure Retreat

Best Beachfront Buys

Forget the city itself. A busy commercial port, Manzanillo has little more vacation appeal than Detroit. Everything of interest to visitors is north of town, starting a half hour or less from the center and stretching another couple of hours farther along the Costa de Oro (Gold Coast) toward Puerto Vallarta to the Careyes and Chamela areas. The Manzanillo airport serves all of the extended region from a convenient location well north of the city.

The hotels we recommend are self-contained hideaways, isolated from each other and not close to much else that's truly tempting in the way of recreation, restaurants, shops, or night spots. Except for Las Hadas, what you get is what your hotel has got, which is extraordinary in most cases. We encourage you to rent a car and explore, but we wouldn't make that a high priority either. The main attraction of Manzanillo and the Gold Coast is roosting and playing on your own sandy shore.

The Careyes

Carretera Barra de Navidad KM 53
San Patricio, Jalisco
(335) 1-00-00
Fax: (335) 1-01-00
Reservations:
Small Luxury Hotels of the World
800-525-4800

A beachfront resort built on an old dream

Accommodations: 51 rooms and suites. **High-season rates:** Deluxe rooms $240, 1-bedroom suites $340, junior suites $375, garden suites $400, oceanfront junior suites $425, 2-bedroom suites $475, Careyes suite $675. **Low-season rates:** Deluxe rooms $210, 1-bedroom suites $240, junior suites $335, garden suites $335, oceanfront junior suites $360, 2-bedroom suites $350, Careyes suite $530. **Payment:** Major credit cards. **Children:** Under 12, free in room with parents. **Recreation:** Beach; swimming pool; 2 tennis courts; fitness center and spa with massage therapies, facials, and yoga; horseback riding; polo; non-waterized water sports.

➤ **On a secluded beach next to the Careyes, Playa Rosa Restaurant (1-04-62) serves seafood dishes prepared with French aplomb.**

Now that the masses have moved into Mexico, what are the jet setters to do? The crowds have driven them from Acapulco, Puerto Vallarta, and then Las Hadas, leaving them without a home in a country they have always called their own. It almost makes you want to scrap the plane.

Gian Franco Brignone, a wealthy, flamboyant Italian, set out to find an answer. In the late 1960s, flying along the shore between Vallarta and Manzanillo, he spotted some "sacred and forgotten beaches" populated only by sea turtles in egg-laying season. Brignone bought ten miles of the Turtle Coast, Costa Careyes, and began fantasizing a future for the estate. As ultimately revealed, his plans called for the creation of an exclusive international community centered around a special resort with a landing strip, golf course, marina, spa, hundreds of beautiful homes, and of course, a good Italian restaurant.

Brignone worked on his utopia for two decades, building a small beach hotel, two polo fields, a pair of tennis courts, and a collection of seaside villas and hilltop *casitas* that belong mainly to nonresident "town and country" types. Beyond that, the grand project slumbered in a dreamlike trance until recently, when a well-heeled Mexican company took over the development, scaled back the concept to a manageable level, and focused professional attention for the first time on the hotel. The resort is now beginning to fulfill much of its original promise.

The new owners gave up the notion of a full airfield, though you can still fly in from Manzanillo via helicopter if you wish. Most guests come by car or pre-arranged taxi, which takes one and a half hours from the port city. However you arrive, the reception staff greets you with a cooling drink, registers you while you sit comfortably at a desk, and then escorts you to your quarters.

Virtually every room is different, in price as well as size, features, and views. The minimum requirements for us would be a good ocean view and a terrace large enough for lounging. That eliminates most of the deluxe rooms and suites, because the views are usually partial. Upgrade if possible to an oceanfront junior suite.

We loved our night in 101, a one-bedroom deluxe suite. You enter a living room with *banco* sofas, bright yellow and pink cushions, a TV and VCR, and a full bath. The bedroom is up a winding stairway with a second, similar bath, king bed, ceiling fan, air conditioning, and a big balcony with a big ocean view. On the third floor, on top of everything, sits a rooftop deck for serious sunning in private.

The original *casitas*, tucked away on their own cliffs, now are managed separately (contact 395-1-00-54); the remaining quarters wrap around a luscious palm-fringed courtyard in a horseshoe-shaped building. A large pool skirts the sea; a secluded beach is off to the side. The water is good for snorkeling, windsurfing, and sailing, and the hotel rents all the equipment. You sign up for the sports in the intimate spa, home to a seaside fitness center and facilities for various health and beauty treatments. Farther inland, The Careyes maintains Brignone's tennis courts and even his polo field, now part of a broad-ranging equestrian program.

It's too bad about the Italian restaurant, though. The old owner's attempts never quite succeeded, and the restaurant was also struggling with quality when we last ate there, early in the management company's tenure. We suspect the food has improved by now, but you'll certainly enjoy the beachfront setting in any case, featuring a bar terrace with huge cushions that invite you to sprawl Roman-style while toasting the descending sun. If the dining room does disappoint, just head over to Playa Rosa, an adjoining beach where a French expatriate serves wonderful fresh seafood dishes in an enchanting *palapa* restaurant.

In most respects the resort is finally ready to receive the jet set, but The Careyes may have left them behind with other delusions in the old dream. This is a place for pristine natural beauty, not prissy beautiful people. It's the great escape that was always promised, but the lucky ones are finding romantic solitude rather than runways.

El Tamarindo

Carretera MEX 200 Km 7.5
Apartado Postal 24
Cihuatlán, Jalisco
(335) 1-50-32 or 1-50-31
Fax: (335) 1-50-32

> **El Tamarindo is in a unique category: Best Place for a Golf Adventure**

Accommodations: 29 villas. **High-season rates:** Forest bungalows $300, garden bungalows $400, beachfront bungalows $475, 1-bedroom palm tree bungalows $375, 2-bedroom palm tree bungalows $550. **Low-season rates:** Forest bungalows $230, garden bungalows $320, beachfront bungalows $360, 1-bedroom palm tree bungalows $320, 2-bedroom palm tree bungalows $460. **Payment:** Major credit cards. **Children:** Under 12, free in room with parents. **Recreation:** 3 beaches, golf (18 holes), 2 clay tennis courts, mountain bikes, hiking trails, polo and horseback riding, speedboats, and Sailfish.

➤ **El Tamarindo is a 2,000-acre-resort with three beaches and jungle nature trails. It is full of promise and is slowly fulfilling it.**

El Tamarindo began as the Bel-Air's ultimate luxury hideaway in Mexico. It was to be an "exclusive resort village nestled in tropical palm groves and surrounded by more than 2,000 acres of ecological reserve and jungle" with three sequestered beaches. But the Mexican peso crisis shattered these ambitious plans, forcing Bel-Air to bail out, and leaving the Tamarindo with an ownership crisis as well.

Several years later, El Tamarindo has made some progress. There are 18-holes of golf open to the public. The 2,000 acres remain mostly pristine jungle except for the scenic roads to the various beaches, the golf club, and the reception area for the hotel, the tennis courts, swimming pool, and the dock on Playa Majahua. There are hiking, biking, and nature trails. The restaurant and bar are now open, and spa facilities are projected to be completed soon.

When we first visited El Tamarindo in 1997, there were only nine villas (or bungalows, as they are called here), and they certainly fulfilled every promise made by Bel-Air. Now the count is up to 29, and they range from beachfront bungalows to those scattered among the palm trees. Some of the latter have partial views of the sea. All of these spacious bungalows have been constructed with tropical materials and are elegantly furnished. There are finely thatched roofs, wooden floors in the bathrooms, and sliding doors to provide more privacy for bedrooms in the open villa design. Each air-conditioned and fan-cooled villa has one or two bedrooms, a living room with dining alcove, a private plunge pool and terrace, and an immense bathroom with double sinks. The beachfront bungalows even have Jacuzzis.

The hotel is truly secluded, a half-hour drive through the forest from the main road. Still pretty much a secret, El Tamarindo makes for a great escape.

La Posada

Apartado Postal 135
Manzanillo, Colima
(333) 3-18-99
Fax: Same as phone

| **A popular budget inn on the beach** |

Accommodations: 24 rooms. **High-season rate:** $85. **Low-season rate:** $60. **Included:** Breakfast. **Payment:** Major credit cards. Recreation: Beach, swimming pool.

➤   **Manzanillo has been an important port since the Spanish arrived in Mexico. Cortés himself named the city after an abundant tree, and a few decades later the harbor served as the launching point for the naval conquest of the Philippines. Today Manzanillo is a bustling commercial port**

with lots of shops for bric-a-brac from Hong Kong and other parts of the world.

La Posada calls itself "the passionate pink hotel by the tropical sea." It's definitely pink. The passion, on the other hand, seemed a little constrained during our last visit, and the sea had more cargo ships than coral.

A Manzanillo fixture since 1957, the hotel sits on a sand-fringed peninsula facing the city's busy port. It's away from the commercial clutter of the town, but not altogether out of sight of it. The many repeat guests simply focus on the close-up views, which are much more attractive. The beach is a beauty, the oceanfront pool is playfully pretty, and the pinkness gets rosier the longer you stay.

Proprietor Bart Varelmann is particularly proud of the *sala*, the communal living room that serves as a restaurant and bar. Furnished with *equipale* tables and chairs, the beamed, brick-and-tile lounge has a casual ambience that reminds Bart of scenes from the old Bogart film *Key Largo*. Cocktails are served from a cart in the evening, followed by a dinner limited to a few specials. You help yourself to beer and soft drinks at any hour on an honor system.

The guest quarters don't match the *sala* in magnetism. They are clean, functional sleeping spaces and not intended to be much more. Most come with two or three twin beds, and all have ceiling fans, showers, and tile floors. Some enjoy a balcony and an ocean view, some don't.

Hotel La Posada is a cozy, convivial hideaway with a location that keeps the rates low. The nearsighted could love it.

Las Alamandas

Carretera MEX 200 Km 85
Quémaro, Jalisco
(328) 5-55-00
Fax: (328) 5-50-27
Reservations: Robert Reid Associates
800-223-6510

> **An intimate, chic inn meant for a select few**

Accommodations: 10 suites in 6 villas. **High-season rates:** Casita San Miguel $490, junior and king suites $390–$699, master suites $950, presidential suite $1,200, villas $1,649–$2,598 for 4–6 people. **Low-season rates:** Casita San Miguel $390, junior and king suites $290–$520, master suites $690, presidential suite $780, villas $1,210–$1,820 for 4–6 people. **Included:** Breakfast and all sports facilities. **Added:** 15% service charge; 17% tax; optional full meal plan, $100 per person daily. **Payment:** Major credit cards. **Children:** Under 6, $100 plus $20 per meal. **Recreation:** Beach, swimming pool, tennis court, fitness center, horseback riding, mountain bikes, hiking trails, boats, and boogie boards.

➤ **Las Alamandas is several miles off the coast highway, down a bouncy dirt road, through the rustic village of Quémaro, and beyond an armed security post, where the guard carefully verifies that you're on the guest list. If you're among the Hollywood guests, you'll land on the private airstrip and rent the entire resort. This is serious seclusion.**

The founder of Las Hadas, Antenor Patiño, intended Las Alamandas to be his second shot at immortality in the hotel trade. He envisioned a grand resort on the 1,500-acre estate, an elite jet-set enclave with 200 luxury condominiums lining the long, surf-slapped beach, a private airfield, and a golf course. Before Patiño got much farther than the landing strip, however, his granddaughter Isabel Goldsmith inherited the property and threw the project in reverse. She created a place different from the original vision, even more exclusive perhaps but far more intimate, sensuous, and tranquil.

Instead of a row of boxy condos, Goldsmith erected a handful of artful villas. She let weeds overtake the beginnings of the golf course and limited the recreation to a languorous swimming pool, a single tennis court, a fitness center, a boat for river and lagoon tours and fishing, and a stable of horses for riding. She left most of the estate untouched, several pristine beaches for picnics and swims, a bird-filled scrub jungle for riding, biking and hiking. Near the *casitas* she groomed the grounds luxuriantly, with large expanses of grass bordered by bougainvillea, jasmine, palms, and the yellow-flowered alamandas for which the inn is named.

On a remote stretch of the Gold Coast, about two hours from both Manzanillo and Puerto Vallarta, the inn makes an absolute virtue of serene seclusion. The only thing approaching nightlife is the adeptly concealed television and VCR in the bar, complemented by the well hidden movie library. The isolation means the food preparations are relatively simple and straightforward, but it insures that all the ingredients are fresh. Local fishermen are the only source for the catch of the day, which is exactly that, and the staff grow most vegetables and fruits in an ample garden. You can dine privately on your terrace or eat with others at El Oasis, but meat eaters will not have much to choose from in either place.

All the accommodations are suites within villas or entire villas. One of the most expensive is Casa Rosa, bound to spoil any four people, its maximum number of guests. Rented only as a complete villa, it contains a beachfront verandah, living room with a TV and VCR, a rooftop terrace, and a fully equipped kitchen where the hotel staff will prepare food for private parties. Casa del Sol and Casa del Domo enjoy an equally good location — just back from the ungroomed beach, behind a broad lawn — and they are similar in most other respects, but they can be split into two separate suites when not booked as entire villas. Casa Azul and Casita San Miguel sit on a plaza behind the other buildings, largely out of sight of the sea.

For a couple who don't need an ocean view, the best value is the *casita*, a cozy one-bedroom villa. The junior suites in two of the larger *casas* come with a pair of queen beds and the king suites with a single king, but they are comparable in size and amenities. The master and presidential quarters are immense, with spacious living rooms and huge terraces.

The suites are exquisitely decorated. The fine *equipale* furniture and the *bancos* on the terraces are colorfully covered and accented by embroidered pillows. Hand-hewn wood pieces from Michocán cradle pottery from Guadalajara and animal carvings from Oaxaca. Many of the accents in the large, luxurious baths — from the tiles to the robes — are custom-made to display the inn's logo of alamandas and a dolphin.

Goldsmith runs Las Alamandas more like an exclusive guest house than a standard hotel. The staff outnumber guests about three to one, and they approach their work in the style of house servants rather than resort employees. The inn is a personalized business, and Goldsmith's staff makes you feel like a personal guest. It's a rare experience, unmatched in Mexico for aristocratic graciousness.

Las Hadas

Apartado Postal 158
Manzanillo, Colima
(333) 4-00-00
Fax: (333) 4-19-50
Reservations:
Camino Real Hotels and Resorts
800-7-CAMINO (800-722-6466)

A legendary resort on the rebound

Accommodations: 233 rooms and suites. **High-season rates:** Resort rooms $265, Ocean-view rooms $300, Camino Real Club rooms $330, club rooms with private pool $395, Fantasia suites with pool $425, other suites $355–$900. **Low-season rates:** Resort rooms $175, Ocean-view rooms $190, Camino Real Club rooms $250, Fantasia suites with pool $370, other suites $515–$875. **Payment:** Major credit cards. **Children:** Under 18, free in room with parents. **Recreation:** Beach, 2 swimming pools, golf (18 holes), 10 tennis courts, marina, water sports center, small gym and massage.

➤ **One of the finest vacation rental homes in Mexico, Villa Playita, perches above the Pacific in a secluded spot near Las Hadas. For information on the staffed three-bedroom villa or others in the area, call Villa Leisure at 800-526-4244.**

Las Hadas was the dream of Bolivian tin magnate Antenor Patiño, who searched the world for a fabulous hideaway location before choosing this spot in 1964. He hired an architect known for bold, whimsical designs and spent ten years building a fantasy village of domes and turrets, of cobblestone streets and fountains, a utopian city that's part Moorish, part Mexican, and part mythological. The "Gala in White" opening in 1974 was the jet-set event of the year, virtually a command performance for the glitter gang.

The hotel lost its cachet after new owners bought it for prestige purposes in the 1980s. They maintained the airs of an exclusive estate while draining the substance with additional construction, overcrowding, and neglect of details. Then Camino Real moved in and began bringing the resort back, not to the glamour days but to a solid version of a golf and tennis resort.

The rooms needed attention and generally got it. They still vary substantially, though all the air-conditioned quarters are contemporary in appointments and most enjoy pleasant views; if a vista is important to you, ocean-view rooms have reliably better views and have either larger quarters or a larger balcony than the resort rooms. Any of the Camino Real Club rooms or the suites should please the pickiest of patrons. Found in the original part of Patino's resort, these turreted and very private quarters can be quite romantic and even stunning with their marble floors, pristine white walls, and terraces with full sea views. Even the complimentary toiletries encourage the romantic with bubble baths and body scrubs. Consider a splurge on an enormous and well-designed deluxe Fantasia suite with an arched ceiling in the sitting area and a large terrace with private pool.

Camino Real enhanced the cooking as well as the accommodations. Among the half-dozen restaurants, our favorite is Terral, which features a sophisticated approach to Mexican cuisine and wonderful views. Los Delfines, with the sea lapping outside its windows, lets you select your dinner from a display of the day's seafood catch. The other top option for dinner is Legazpi, an elegant dining room and terrace with bay views that strives for international finesse.

Las Hadas's salt-and-pepper beach isn't one of the most beautiful in Mexico, but the large free-form pool is, making it a superb spot for sunning and swimming. Most guests spend at least part of the day on Pete Dye's admirable 18-hole golf course, on one of the eight tennis courts, or at the 70-vessel marina, where you can satisfy urges for fishing, sailing, and water skiing.

If that range of recreation matters, you won't do much better than Las Hadas. Now that Camino Real has rejuvenated the spirit, the hotel is once again a legend worth living and perhaps more than ever a paradise for players.

Playa Blanca Club Med

Carretera MEX 200 Km. 53
Cihuatlán, Jalisco
(335) 1-00-01
Fax: (335) 1-00-04
Reservations:
Club Med Sales
800-CLUB MED

**A comely all-inclusive
beach hideaway for singles
and couples**

Accommodations: 295 rooms. **Rates:** $616 weekly per person, double occupancy. Closed May to mid-November. **Included:** Breakfast, lunch, dinner, beer and wine with meals, all recreation listed below except deep-sea fishing, horseback riding, and massage. **Payment:** Major credit cards. **Children:** Under 17, not accepted. **Recreation:** Beach, swimming pool, 6 tennis courts, circus workshop, fitness center, archery, horseback riding, snorkeling, scuba diving, small-craft sailing, kayaking, deep-sea fishing, rock climbing, massage.

➤   **Playa Blanca operates a scuba school for beginners that, for an extra fee, provides PADI and NAUI certification.**

As we noted earlier, in the Cancún chapter, a decision to go to any Club Med is first and foremost a choice of a vacation style rather than a choice of a particular place. We described the kind of experience to expect in our report on the Club Med Cancún (see index), which should be consulted as a starting point in considering the Playa Blanca resort. The general characteristics of a Club Med getaway are similar the world over.

Among the distinctive features at Playa Blanca, natural beauty ranks high. It's the prettiest Club Med anywhere near the States, including the Caribbean. Set on a secluded cove on Costa Careyes, an hour and a half from the Manzanillo airport, the brick and bougainvillea village wanders over artfully landscaped hills down to a fluffy, palm-lined beach. Off the shore, huge boulders form islands that are lapped by the surf, creating a romantically scenic backdrop for the property. Intimate for a Club Med, it's a delightful spot for lovers or for singles in search of companionship.

You may have to be skinny, though, if you want to share a bed. Playa Blanca has added some king beds, but many of the rooms come with a pair of oversize twins, each capable of holding a couple of dieters or a lonesome linebacker. The rest of the room is cramped but comfortable and attractive, a place where you could spend private time. Some of the accommodations afford good ocean views, though none has balconies for enjoying the sights.

The recreation program includes some unusual options. The stables, in addition to daily trail rides, offer an intensive one-week English riding course. The circus workshop teaches high trapeze, trampoline, juggling, and clowning. Archery, kayaking, and rock climbing are also available, plus a full range of customary resort sports from tennis to snorkeling.

Don't expect the same diversity in food. The isolated environment presents challenges in getting prime ingredients, forcing the kitchen to focus on staples. There are two specialty restaurants in addition to the main dining room, but they serve little beyond steak and local lobster.

Playa Blanca is a splendid hideaway, far more playful than most, yet still escapist in its aura and captivating in its lusciousness.

Villa Polinesia

Carretera MEX 200 Km. 72
Chamela, Jalisco
(328) 5-52-47

> **One of the best beach
> bargains in Mexico**

Accommodations: 2 *casas* with 4 bedrooms each, 11 *cabanas,* RV sites. **Rates:** Entire house $220, room $60, *cabanas* $12 per person, RV sites with hookups $6 per person. **Payment:** No credit cards. **Recreation:** Beach, swimming pool.

➤ **Highway signs a few miles away offer land for sale, but for the moment the gorgeous crescent bay of Chamela is blissfully undeveloped. Unless you hop in a car to visit a restaurant or bar at Costa Careyes some 15 miles away, there are few restaurants. Just a short walk to the highway from Villa Polinesia, a simple but clean, nameless restaurant serves fresh juices, good eggs *a la mexicana,* and decent chiles rellenos. It is very difficult to contact the Villa Polinesia to make a reservation; the phone is rarely answered. The best policy is simply to drop in.**

We last visited the Villa Polinesia on a weekend in January during the height of the resort season on the Pacific coast. For as far as we could see up and down the very long Playa Chamela, there was only one other person. He told us that during school holidays (Christmas, Easter, and July and August), the Villa Polinesia is enlivened by Mexican families. The rest of the year it is a Robinson Crusoe–style paradise.

The Villa Polinesia couldn't be more magnificently situated. A wide and empty swath of inviting beach makes its sweep around the blue-green waters of the Bay of Chamela for more than a thousand feet in either direction. At the northern tip of the bay is the fishing village of Perula. Otherwise, Chamela has been left to its original sandy and pristine state. Two rocky islands rise from the bay, calming the waters for delicious swims. Fishermen can be hired to make an excursion to the islands; one, Isla La Pajarena, is an ecological preserve for tropical and aquatic birds.

The Villa Polinesia itself barely intrudes on the setting. The campgrounds and RV sites, with hookups and communal bathrooms, are found among the tall stands of palm trees. The *cabañas,* nothing more than thatched huts on stilts with double beds and a mini-fridge above and a bathroom below, are screened but primitive affairs requiring an occasional fumigation. Most have a beachfront location.

The beautiful *casas* rise to an entirely different level of accommodation from the rest. They provide a degree of comfort and style rarely seen for the price. Nestled off to the side of the beach, both beach houses have thatched roofs and their white stucco facades open to the sea. One comes with the only swimming pool at the Villa Polinesia and the other has a glass-enclosed penthouse with private kitchen. Each of the other rooms has a handsome, private, tiled bathroom but shares the large living and dining area and well-appointed kitchen.

There are small grocery stores in the villages of Perula and Chamela, a half-mile away, to supply your beach house or RV kitchen. There are barbecue pits to grill fish you've caught or bought right off the boats. When the Villa Polinesia has lots of guests, the restaurant opens, otherwise you can sometimes arrange for the resident manager's wife to prepare meals for you.

Villa Polinesia is a magnificent budget retreat. Life here is simplified and serene. Walk the beach. Watch the birds. Swim. Snorkel around the islands. Fish. Watch the sunset. And sleep well.

Mazatlán

Mazatlán

Best Hotel for Stylish Sophistication

Best Comfort Choices for All-American Abundance

Best Beachfront Buy

Best Bargain for Mexican Character

Best Place to Combine Business and Pleasure

At the northern end of the Mexican Riviera, just below the Tropic of Cancer, Mazatlán is better known for its superb fishing than for its beaches. Local leaders are striving to expand the tourism appeal and have succeeded in some ways, but the economy continues to depend far more on the city's busy commercial port than on vacation dollars. That makes Mazatlán more real in some ways than rival destinations to the south, though the reality is less riveting than prosaic.

A big natural harbor has always been the primary asset, used by the Spanish as early as the 17th century to ship Mexico's wealth of gold and silver out of the country. Over the years, Mazatlán grew into a bustling city of almost 500,000 people and became the biggest port between Los Angeles and the Panama Canal. Home to an enormous shrimp-fishing fleet, its 800 boats catch and ship over 37 million tons of the succulent crustaceans each year.

The beaches and the main tourist hotels are west of the harbor, a short drive from the downtown business district. Sand extends for ten miles along this shore, but it is sometimes gravelly, and the water often attracts more surfers than swimmers. Most of our recommendations for places to stay are in this area, near the crowded Zona Dorada, though the best spot of all enjoys a secluded setting in the countryside outside the city.

The Main Attractions

A Sportsman's Paradise

Sitting on the Sea of Cortés, due east of the southern tip of the Baja peninsula, Mazatlán is the best deep-sea fishing port on the Pacific coast and one of the finest in the world. Marlins are the prime catch from November to May, sailfish from May through September. The record marlin caught here weighed nearly half a ton. If you're not up for that kind of challenge, you'll find plenty of smaller fish, including sea bass, tuna, and snapper.

Wild game is almost as abundant. While migration patterns have changed since the time the Nahuatl Indians named Mazatlán "place of the deer," hunters don't have to travel too far into the hills in search of deer, wild boar, and more. Dove, pheasant, quail, and many species of duck nest close to the city. English-speaking guides and outfitters can arrange hunting licenses and equipment.

Proximity to the States

Because of its northern location — just over 700 miles from the Arizona border — and dependably good winter weather, Mazatlán attracts more motorists from the States than other Pacific coast cities in Mexico. Some "snowbirds" stay for months, often in the town's RV camps and condominiums, but other drivers come for shorter, regular vacations made affordable by car travel. Get advice from AAA or another reliable source before attempting the trip, but the sunny skies and mild temperatures should be ample reward for any potential difficulties.

The proximity to the border can be a boon for air travelers too. Though most flights to Mazatlán are not significantly cheaper than to Puerto Vallarta and some other beach areas, you can find bargains on occasion.

Carnival Capers

Mazatlán's carnival is one of the most joyous in Mexico. Similar in some ways to Mardi Gras in New Orleans, the festivities start about a week before Ash Wednesday. If you're interested, book a room at least six months in advance and be prepared to pay rates much higher than at other times.

Camino Real Mazatlán

Playa Sabalo
Mazatlán, Sinoloa
(69) 13-11-11
Fax: (69) 14-03-11
Reservations:
Camino Real Hotels and Resorts
800-7-CAMINO (800-722-6466)

An old favorite built into a bluff above the beach

Accommodations: 169 rooms and suites. **High-season rates:** Lagoon-view rooms $120, ocean-view rooms $140, junior suites $220, suites $340. **Low-season rates:** Lagoon-view rooms $95, ocean-view rooms $120, junior suites $200, suites $330. **Payment:** Major credit cards. **Children:** Under 1 year, free in room with parents. **Recreation:** Beach, swimming pool, 2 tennis courts, water sports center.

➤ **Mazatlán's restaurants specialize in parrillada, a mixed seafood grill. Shrimp, oysters, calamari, fish, lobster, and sometimes frogs' legs sit atop an enormous ceramic vessel resembling Noah's ark.**

Dominating the rugged Punta del Sabalo on the west end of Mazatlán, the Camino Real has the best location of the city's hotels, sitting on a rocky promontory above its own virtually private beach. It isn't one of the luxury chain's most glamorous resorts, but it fits intimately into the fine setting and provides a genially apropos atmosphere.

A lengthy cobblestone driveway off the main road passes palms, shrubbery, and grassy lawns to arrive at the simple porte-cochere and understated lobby. From the hilltop reception area the mid-rise hotel tumbles toward the beach. Two areas of hard-packed sand are divided by rocky points that offer some protection from the open surf. *Palapas,* lounge chairs, and food and drink service are available for tanners, and there is minimal distraction from vendors peddling wares on this secluded shore. The water sports center offers surfing, snorkeling, scuba diving, and, of course, the justly famous deep-sea fishing.

The deliberately rustic Chiquita Banana restaurant and bar hangs over the beach, trying to convince you that you're lost in the South Seas. The fresh seafood is good, the drinks are better, and the sunset views are superb.

Up the steep walkway from the sand, a free-form pool is perched a few steps below the lobby, commanding a broad ocean view. Las Terrazas restaurant is nearby, for casual all-day dining designed to please any palate. It's popular with city residents on important business and out for social occasions.

The rooms feature a few Mexican touches along with the familiar comforts. All come with phones, color TV, air conditioning, and a mini-bar. Most have king beds and a private balcony. The ocean-view rooms are definitely worth their premium over the lagoon-view quarters for the vista alone. Unfortunately, Camino Real no longer offers Club service at this branch.

Although it's not destined to dazzle, the Camino Real is well established as one of the top hotels in Mazatlán. You won't find fault with much, particularly the enviable location.

El Cid Mega Resort

Apartado Postal 813
Mazatlán, Sinoloa
(69) 13-33-33
Fax: (69) 14-13-11
Reservations:
El Cid Mega Resort
310-810-0772
800-525-1925
Fax: 310-815-0776

> **A massive hotel, sports, and entertainment complex**

Accommodations: 1,320 rooms and suites. **Rates:** Economy and standard rooms $72, superior rooms and studios $89–$100, junior suites $143–$231, suites $235–$440. **Payment:** Major credit cards. **Children:** Under 12, free in room with parents; playground and special programs available. **Recreation:** Beach, 6 swimming pools, golf (18 holes), 14 tennis courts, 2 squash courts, fitness center with aerobics, sauna, steam (men only), water sports center with Jet Ski and kayaks, marina and fishing fleet.

➤ **La Carreta offers one of Mazatlán's best selections of Mexican crafts, folk art, and other products. One of three locations is in El Cid.**

El Cid deserves the "mega" in its name. With a private golf and country club, a wealth of other sports and entertainment facilities, a half mile of beach, a marina, 14 restaurants and lounges, 1,100 rooms, and almost as many acres, the hotel is the biggest independent resort in the country and Mazatlán's largest employer.

To fill all the rooms El Cid has to do a lot of discount wholesale and convention business, and it also offers packages for independent travelers that can be a sound value, reducing the reasonable rates even further. Be sure to ask about special offers that may be available at the time of your trip.

The room choices are almost endless, scattered among four hotels-within-a-hotel that share a common reception area. The oceanfront Castilla Beach was the original building, a sprawling combination of mid- and high-rise blocks overlooking lagoon swimming pools and the Pacific. The 25-story El Moro, just north of Castilla on the beach, has some of the most luxurious accommodations, including handsome junior suites with kitchens. A marble quarry must have given its life for the tower's construction. The more tranquil low-rise, Granada, mainly a time-share operation, is across a highway from the water, near the golf and tennis facilities. The newest hotel, the Marina, is styled like a cluster of townhouses. Wherever you lodge, your room will have a private balcony, a king or two double beds, air conditioning, satellite TV, a marble tub-shower bathroom, and standard upscale furnishings, contemporary in style.

The resort faces a lengthy stretch of good sand. A section of it is roped off to restrict vendors and to supply guests with lounge chairs, refreshments, and *palapas* for shade. A beachside activities center arranges a full array of water sports, including windsurfing, snorkeling, sailing, scuba diving, kayaking and superb deep-sea fishing. For freshwater fans, the main pools meander around two courtyards formed by the wings of the Castilla. The body count on the expansive decks can rival Fort Lauderdale at spring break.

The par-72 golf course designed by Lee Trevino (another nine holes are planned) and the 14 clay and Laykold courts of the tennis center both come with pro services and they share a gym and saunas. If you would rather gamble than play, limited sports betting is available. A fitness facility overlooks one of the main pools.

For those who favor shopping for recreation, El Cid offers as much variety as you'll find anywhere in Mazatlán. If dancing into the night is more your idea of exercise, there's a multimillion-dollar disco with the latest in sound, lights, and video.

The eight restaurants run the gamut in atmosphere from bare-foot basics to evening glitter, and the food ranges from prime rib to pasta. Our favorite dining choice, of the places we've tried, is La Cascada, where Mexican food is often dished up with imagination and flair. Even breakfasts emphasize the unusual, with tasty *tipico* dishes like *puntas* (beef tips) in chipotle sauce, and *machaca*, spicy dried beef in scrambled eggs.

Named after Spain's 11th-century epic hero, El Cid aspires to legendary stature itself. That seems unlikely to happen, but when you're in the mood for crowds and activity, the mega resort can offer a big time at a modest price.

El Quijote Inn

Apartado Postal 934-966
Mazatlán, Sinaloa
(69) 14-11-34 and 14-36-09
Fax: (69) 14-33-44

> **A small, quiet beachfront hotel**

Accommodations: 67 suites and studios. **High-season rates:** Back studios $70, front studios $95, junior suites $140, master suites $195. **Low-season rates:** Back studios $55, front studios $66, junior suites $100, master suites $135. **Payment:** Major credit cards. **Recreation:** Beach, swimming pool.

➤   **El Marinero (Paseo Claussen, 81-34-90) is a Mazatlán institution. It has always served up shrimp and seafood parrilladas with local flair to the accompaniment of mariachi music, and now it has added an oceanside location to this memorable mix at La Costa Marinera (Camarón Sábalo next to the Oceano Palace, 14-19-28).**

Built in the late 1980s, El Quijote is one of the brightest small hotels in Mazatlán, much more attractive and inviting than most of the monotonous and sometimes garish competitors in its price range.

Owned and operated by Spanish expatriates, the mid-rise inn boasts a Moorish style, with undulating stucco walls, prominent arches, and mosaic tiled domes. Two five-story wings, just steps from the sea, surround a handsome beachfront pool and Jacuzzi. The sand just beyond is a fine stretch shaded by a few *palapas*.

Both the Sancho Panza Bar and the Rocinante Restaurant sit on the edge of the beach, looking out to the islands in Mazatlán's bay. The Sancho Panza, a quiet, enclosed piano bar, offers Spanish atmosphere. Rocinante is tropical in flavor, featuring casual meals all day in a carefree, open-air setting.

Except for the back studios, which we would avoid, the rooms enjoy an ample terrace with a direct or angled view of the sea. The furnishings vary a little from room to room, but you can count on a pleasant contemporary decor. The studios provide a spacious sitting area that you turn into a bedroom by pulling down one or both Murphy beds from a side wall. A built-in kitchenette includes a mini-fridge, a two-burner stovetop, a sink, and an assortment of appliances for juicing, blending, or brewing your way to life each morning.

The junior and master suites also have Murphy beds in their living rooms as well as complete kitchens. The refrigerator is full size, the stove is complemented by an oven, and there's a dishwasher, too. All the quarters give you satellite TV, central air conditioning, a ceiling fan, and a phone.

El Quijote should shame some of Mazatlán's big resort hotels. It's as pretty and affordable as any place in the city, and more intimate and relaxed than any spot in its class.

Las Palmas

Apartado Postal 135
Mazatlán, Sinaloa
(69) 16-5664
Fax: (69) 16-5666
Reservations:
Jarvinen Worldwide Hotels
800-876-5278
Fax: 213-461-7559

> A pleasant, low-key hotel a
> block from the sea

Accommodations: 176 rooms and 12 suites. **High-season rates:** Standard rooms $55, deluxe rooms $65, suites $75, 2-bedroom suites $127. **Payment:** Major credit cards. **Children:** Under 12, free in room with parents. **Recreation:** 2 swimming pools.

➤ **At Las Palmas and elsewhere in Mazatlán, the beer of choice is Pacifico, which is brewed in the city.**

At Las Palmas, the fresh accommodations, playful courtyard pools, central Zona Dorada location, and reasonable rates compensate for a short walk to the sand and sea. The beach is a block away, across the busy Avenida Camarón Sabalo, though you can't see it from any of the rooms.

The hotel is larger than it appears from the streetfront office. One three-story motel block encircles the visible front courtyard, which contains a moderate-size swimming pool sprouting a peculiar mushroom-shaped fountain. Behind this area is a second, larger courtyard with a slide, another plaster mushroom, and a swimming pool that flows around it like a meandering river. Young children love the funny fungi, and a swing set and a playground are nearby for when they get waterlogged. Rooms line both sides of the water in wings that look as if they belong to a Sunbelt apartment complex.

All the rooms have *terrazas* overlooking one of the pools. The simple, bright quarters come with contemporary furnishings, two double beds, air conditioning, a TV, a phone, a mini-bar, and a tub-shower bath. The suites with kitchenettes are about twice the size of the regular rooms. A spacious downstairs sitting area enjoys its own balcony and a full bathroom. The bedroom and second, larger bath are upstairs, surrounded by windows that let in a lot of light and give you a courtyard view from the bed.

The two restaurants satisfy different moods. Crab's, beside the back courtyard, is an alfresco snack bar open from early morning to early evening. The Lobster Trap serves slightly fancier fare at breakfast, lunch, and dinner from a streetside perch overlooking the front pool. A felicitous bar terrace offers live music most nights. Plenty of additional options for eating and entertainment are nearby.

Most guests choose Las Palmas for its proximity to the sea. After a couple of days of the casual, comfortable ambience, many decide the only water they really need is in the courtyard right outside their door.

Pueblo Bonito

Avenida Camarón Sabalo 2121
Mazatlán, Sinoloa
(69) 14-37-00
Fax: (69) 14-17-23
Reservations:
Pueblo Bonito
800-442-5300

> **A value-minded all-suites beach hotel**

Accommodations: 247 suites. **High-season rates:** Junior suites $81, luxury suites $115. **Low-season rates:** Junior suites $70, luxury suites $100. **Payment:** Major credit cards. **Children:** Under 18, free in room with parents. **Recreation:** Beach, 2 swimming pools, fitness center, water sports center.

➤ **From Pueblo Bonito it's a short taxi trip to Mazatlán's baseball stadium. Maybe you'll see the next Fernando Valenzuela at the park where the famous pitcher got his start.**

Among the scads of beach hotels in Mazatlán, Pueblo Bonito is the only one designed in a Mexican style. The name means "pretty village," and the multihued architecture captures that feel. At the same time, the level of international luxury is as high as you get in the city, ensuring a copacetic combination of comfort and charm.

A long mid-rise wing of rooms lines an even longer beach near the western end of town. *Palapas* dot the shore and palms tower above the sand, where a water sports center arranges surfing, snorkeling, diving, and deep-sea fishing. A swimming pool sprawls inland, divided by a bridge into active and quiet sections, and accented with a waterfall and lush landscaping. Inside, a fitness center with a gym, massage rooms, and saunas keeps you in shape for the recreation.

A swim-up bar and a snack shop serve guests at the pool and beach, while two regular restaurants provide more complete meals. Las Palomas offers casual dining with a Mexican theme at three meals a day. On Sunday the breakfast buffet becomes an expansive and popular brunch. In the evening Angelo's Continental Restaurant features just what you'd expect from the name, plus live piano music.

The rooms are called suites, though the junior version isn't much more spacious than any large resort room. The appellation comes from the layout, which separates a small sitting area from a bedroom that holds little more than its two double beds. The luxury suites contain a similar bedroom, but a bigger living room with a sofa bed. All the quarters have a balcony, kitchenette, air conditioning, phone, and satellite TV.

The room design makes good use of the space, providing a lot of handsome functionality for the suite's size. Pueblo Bonito does something similar with its rates, giving you more for your dollar than almost any of the local competitors. For the accommodations, diversions, and radiance, it's one of the best overall values on the Mexican Riviera.

Rancho Las Moras

Avenida Camarón Sabalo 204, Suite 6
Mazatlán, Sinoloa
(69) 16-50-45
Fax: same as phone
Reservations:
800-400-3333

An enchanting inn in a historic hacienda

Accommodations: 31 rooms and *casitas.* **Rates:** $140 per person in a double. **Included:** Breakfast, lunch, dinner, all domestic drinks, tennis, horseback riding, airport transportation, taxes but not gratuities. **Payment:** Major credit cards. **Children:** Under 3, free in room with parents; children 4–12 $50 each. **Recreation:** 2 swimming pools, stables, 2 tennis courts, hiking trails.

➤   **Among the exotic and domestic animals and birds at Rancho Las Moras are miniature horses, giant draft horses, cows, lambs, rabbits, peacocks, guinea hens, ostriches, and pairs of both black and white swans.**

We sipped margaritas in the ranch's old granary, now converted to a classy cantina, as the moon rose slowly between two giant organ-pipe cacti on a nearby hill. At the crest of the hill, a small family chapel stood vigil over the scene, and down below near us, a white peacock scurried off to nest for the night. It may not have been a typical evening at Rancho Las Moras, but it was certainly in character.

A 150-year-old tequila ranch, abandoned until recently, Las Moras offers an experience of Mexico distinctively different from any other inn in the country. Though elegantly renovated, it retains the mood of yesteryear and all the sights, sounds, and smells of its farm heritage. More than a hundred species of birds and animals roam the range today, keeping you company wherever you go and making you feel at home in a way that no hotel staff can manage.

It's free to ride the fifty horses in the quaint old stables as often as you like, and they'll take you to all corners of the 3,000-acre estate situated in the foothills of the Sierra Madre about 20 minutes from Mazatlán. You can hike the trails, play tennis, swim in the Olympic pool, or, when you hear the call of the crowds, arrange for a driver to take you to town.

Eleven of the rooms, the first ones opened in 1992, are in the original ranch buildings, and 20 others are in separate *casitas* located a bit farther away from the pool and dining rooms. The architecture is Mexican in every detail and charmingly country too, at once robust, rustic, and refined. The air-conditioned quarters vary in decor, but you're likely to find a brick-and-beam ceiling, pottery lamps, antique furnishings, embroidered pillows on a king bed, a beautifully tiled bath, and a balcony or terrace. The *casitas* are larger than regular rooms and come with more lounging space, a kitchen, and a grand terrace.

All meals are included in the rate, which you'll appreciate since other restaurants are a fair drive away. The kitchen features classic Mexican preparations of steak and fresh seafood. The printed menu is limited, but you can order anything you wish as long as the ingredients are available.

Developed by Michael Ruiz and two partners (they named the Tres Amigos cantina after themselves), Las Moras is a flower-filled oasis of tranquillity on Mexico's bustling Pacific coast. We can't guarantee a stunning moonrise, but we know that you'll return home with special memories of your own.

Puerto Ángel and
Puerto Escondido

Best Romantic Hideaway

Best Bargain for Mexican Character

Best B&Bs or Budget Inns

Sister villages of the southwest coast, Puerto Ángel and Puerto
Escondido are an hour apart by rental car or micro bus but closer
together in earthy somnolence. Escondido is the perkier of the pair,
catering to the tourist market with a modern airport, a brick-paved
main street, and a number of shops and seafood and Italian restaurants. Those enhancements drove away some of its original fans
from the 1960s, sending them farther south to Ángel, where such
trappings are still not desired.

New town has resort hotels, Continental restaurants, recreation facilities, or a Ralph Lauren outlet. Escondido boasts a disco
now, but it attracts as many laughs as people. Backpacks are the
luggage of choice among many visitors.

In Ángel, a lovely bay is ringed by soaring hills dense with tropical luxuriance. More pigs than cars use the streets. Ángel is much
more down and out than Escondido. Though we suggest one simple retreat as a place to stay, most of the lodging is in small guest
houses. Escondido has many more hotels than Ángel, including
some charming choices and, in the summer peak season, is more
bustling with a striking combination of surfers from every continent and Mexican families.

Both Puertos remain fishing villages first and foremost. Still traditional in most ways, they are as far from the resorts as you can get on a good beach.

The Main Attraction

Long, Lonesome Beaches

There's enough sand on the shores of Ángel and Escondido to start a new Sahara. Each town has several major beaches and a scattering of others. A few require some effort to reach, but most are an easy walk from anywhere you stay. Despite the accessibility, they are never crowded and are often so big and wild that parts of them feel deserted.

Both towns have a Playa Principal spreading expansively around the bay and boat harbor. In Escondido, the area is lively in a low-key way, and palms, restaurants, and bars line part of the beachfront. Here you'll find two of the best seafood restaurants, Junto al Mar and Los Crotas. In Ángel, the *playa* of the same name is stark and sun-bleached. Swimmers and tanners head instead to Playa Panteón, on the north side of the bay. Named after the cemetery that sits above the sand, it's a small beach for this region, but it has friendly seafood cafés and is close to La Posada Cañon Devata, our recommended inn.

Beyond each town are long, windswept shores pounded by mighty waves. In Escondido you can walk on sand for miles in either direction, particularly on Playa Zicatela, beyond the Hotel Santa Fe. One of the world's best surfing sites that, with the big waves of summer, attracts many professionals and their movie-camera-wielding entourages, the vast beach is also great for running or lazy rambling even if its waters are too treacherous for swimming.

Playa Zipolite is a few miles west of Ángel, over a recently paved road. Although the sea here is murderously dangerous, the beach is as amazing as it is massive. A village built of adobe, thatch, and tin stretches under palm fronds on the fringe of the sand, offering occasional opportunities for "hammocks, food, cold beer, coffee, coconuts, and soft drinks," as one sign says. Nude sunbathing, rare in Mexico, is common all along the beach, though it is supposed to be limited to a secluded area beyond a boulder at the far end of the sand.

Puerto Ángel

La Posada Cañon Devata

Apartado Postal 10
Puerto Ángel, Oaxaca
(958)4-30-48
Reservations:
Fax: (958) 4-30-48

> **A pristine hideaway full of natural allure**

Accommodations: 20 rooms and bungalows, 17 with private bath. **Rates:** Rooms $16–$25, bungalows $35. **Payment:** No credit cards. **Recreation:** Massages.

➤   **At the Posada, you can greet the dawn with yoga classes and toast the sunset with cocktails from the roof terrace of the Casa Cielo, which enjoys majestic views of the Pacific.**

Mateo and Suzanne López started building "a place to rest from the world" in the 1970s, shortly after Suzanne moved to Puerto Ángel from the States. The couple gradually transformed a thatch-roofed two-story house in a denuded canyon into a garden wonderland with guest rooms. Their Posada Cañon Devata is a compelling creation, as colorful as Mateo's painting and as inviting as Suzanne's hospitality. In the past few years, it has been rejuvenated as well by Kali and Sarshan, their children, joining them in the running of the inn. In the fall of 1997, their paradise was damaged when the winds of Hurricane Pauline felled century-old trees, but with the help of their many friends, the inn was soon functioning for the winter season. This being the tropics, the garden should once again flourish as well.

The inn is a quick walk from the sands of Playa Panteón, but it's as far as you can get from beach resort styles. It's more of a tree-house than a hotel, an environmentally sensitve jungle retreat where flashlights are recommended to walk the dark paths at night and compost toilets contribute to the lushness of the garden. Some of the rooms share baths, and all of them share the few hand-hewn family-size tables in the open-air *palapa* dining room. A crafts shop, one of the best in the state of Oaxaca, is reached on a short wooden bridge from the dining room.

The breakfast and lunch menus include organic vegetables from a nearby farm, homemade breads, and tropical fruits and local fish. Meals revolve around such staples as granola with fresh fruits and yogurt, Mexican enchiladas and Italian sandwiches with *rajas* (mild cooked chilies). Dinner offers seafood and lots of vegetarian fare, such as cream of cilantro soup and Mexican *chayote* stuffed with cheese. Parrots provide the live entertainment.

The best lodging is up the canyon from the dining room at the end of a dirt and stone path that can get tricky on occasion. For just a few dollars extra you can stay at the top of the hill in one of the four colorfully contemporary rooms at Casa Cielo, which features grand views, or in two of the six bungalows perched just below. The smaller quarters, clustered together at the lower entrance level of the inn, hold little more than their twin or double beds. All the rooms are basic, but in a pleasant Mexican country fashion.

The Lópezes' Posada is an oasis in sun-bleached Puerto Ángel and a sheltered port of call on the tourist-teeming Pacific coast.

Puerto Escondido

Paraíso Escondido

Calle Unión 10
Puerto Escondido, Oaxaca
(9) 58-2-04-44
Reservations:
Tel/Fax: 415-680-2394 (in U.S.)

A Mexican inn above the Pacific

Accommodations: 18 rooms. **Rate:** $65. **Payment:** No credit cards. **Recreation:** Swimming pool.

➤ **For a traditional Mexican temascal "sauna" combined with a soothing massage, make an appointment at Temazcalli (582-10-23), a Japanese-style retreat in the hills above Zicatela beach.**

Several blocks uphill from Puerto Escondido's main beach, Paraíso Escondido monopolizes the Mexican charm in the center of town. A fancifully decorated inn with a lovely garden courtyard, it makes most of the surrounding businesses look like sun-bleached tokens to tourism.

A fountain graces the courtyard near the swimming pool, where a grass deck and a shaded sitting area serve as a gathering point for guests. Palms flutter above, and flowering shrubs encircle the realm. An inviting dining terrace and a bar are a few steps away under a *palapa* roof. Colorful native craft work and folk art decorate the public areas. There are painted animals on the walls, brimming *nichos*, even a chapel on a landing dedicated to San Antonio.

The rooms rise above the tranquil scene in a two-story building facing the pool and the Pacific. Each of the chambers differs from the others in some respects, but they all have tile floors, brick walls, a double bed and a twin, a shower in the bathroom, individual air conditioning units, and a cozy balcony or patio. Request the second floor to see the sea.

Paraíso Escondido is a small gem, a semiprecious reminder you're in Mexico after all, even if most of the people on the beach and in the streets are from elsewhere. It keeps your compass pointing south.

Santa Fe Hotel

Apartado Postal 96
Puerto Escondido, Oaxaca
(9) 58-2-01-70
Fax: (9) 58-2-02-60

Escondido's most sophisticated beachfront inn

Accommodations: 55 rooms. **High-season rates:** Rooms $82–$102, suites $204, Santa Cruz bungalows $96. **Low-season rates:** Rooms $57–$72, suites $170, Santa Cruz bungalows $67. **Payment:** MasterCard, Visa. **Recreation:** Beach, 3 swimming pools.

➤ **Playa Zicatela, the beach in front of the Hotel Santa Fe, is world famous for surfing but isn't safe for swimming. Safer swimming is on the adjacent Playa Marinero, only a few steps away, and an even calmer spot is Puerto Angelito, a lovely bay accessible by boat or car.**

Ten minutes along the beach from central Puerto Escondido, the Marinero rock formation divides the town beach from Playa Zicatela. Like a sentinel standing watch over the divide and the great

Zicatela beach beyond, the Hotel Santa Fe commands the best location in Escondido. Set just high enough above the beach to guarantee the privacy of its guests while at the same time mesmerizing them with the nearby crashing surf, the hotel exploits its location well. The inn is a delightful hideaway, an intimate world of its own that just happens to be an easy walk from Escondido center when you want a change of pace.

But that probably won't be often. The Santa Fe has one of the best restaurants on the Oaxacan coast, astonishingly good for a Mexican beach hotel, if a bit too bland in its flavoring. The extensive menu wanders through a range of starters from soups to salads, a variety of red snapper dishes, and a wealth of vegetarian preparations. Try the red snapper à la veracruzana, a moist, flavorful fish with a sauce of tomatoes, olives, and mild peppers (*rajas*), or the *chile relleno* platter — a huge *poblano* chile stuffed with tasty cheese, raisins, and almonds, then topped with spicy tomato sauce and served with brown rice, black beans, and salad. Fresh salsa and locally baked whole wheat bread accompany most of the selections.

The thatched-roof dining room matches the cooking in attention to detail, and it is without doubt one of the breeziest, most delightful spots in Escondido. The decor is simple, like the kitchen's ingredients, but in both cases inspiration has been applied. The terra cotta floors and *equipale* furniture blend into the environment, focusing your gaze on the surf and miles of sand.

We spend as much time in the restaurant as our stomachs will allow, relaxing to the sounds of the surf, but the swimming pools are also alluring spots. The palm-shaded courtyard around the main pool is the Santa Fe's social center during the day, a lovely oasis for sunning. The ocean views from the *palapa* of the newer adults-only pool provide a pleasing and often quieter alternative.

Most of the accommodations are up winding tiled stairways from the palm-tree-filled courtyards in attractive, well-constructed, colonial-style buildings that ramble like an old hacienda. The rooms vary in size; some have one double bed, some two double beds, and some one king-size bed. Most rooms are quite spacious — we recently stayed in a standard room that measured about 12 feet by 20 feet — and have a tiny balcony or terrace. All rooms are tastefully and comfortably furnished with *equipales*, the handsome chairs and tables made from Mexican leather and wood, as well as sturdy wooden desks and chests of drawers, and hand-woven bedspreads that are complemented by tiled floors and handsome tiled baths. A few rooms on the second floor of the new section have decent sea views; most rooms overlook the pools. All quarters come with air conditioning, ceiling fan, phone, and TV — and in late 2000, all will have cable TV. Currently there are only two master suites, consisting of a large bedroom and spacious living room. They have the best location, perched at the edge of the property with great sea views. In the Bungalows Santa Cruz adjacent to the hotel there are eight air-conditioned suites, a bit worn, but a good deal because of the kitchen facilities for families interested in long stays. These suites have a living room/kitchen combination and a separate bedroom with two double beds. The second-story suites are preferred for their better views of the sea. The bungalows even have their own pool.

The Santa Fe is a most comfortable and charming hotel, a place to linger surrounded by palm trees and gardens by one of the pools, or to pass hours in the open-air restaurant gazing at the sea, or to stroll a few hundred feet to the nearby beach. Those lures will always make us yearn to return.

Tabachín del Puerto

Apartado Postal 210
Puerto Escondido, Oaxaca
(9) 58-2-11-79
Fax: same as phone
Reservations:
info@tabachin.com.mx

A tiny hideaway with the best rooms in town

Accommodations: 6 suites. **High-season rates:** $45–$75. **Low-season or long-term rates:** Flexible. **Included:** Breakfast. **Payment:** No credit cards.

➤ **If you can relinquish your penthouse terrace at Tabachín del Puerto for a day, consider exploring the countryside with a visit to Posada Nopala, Paul Cleaver's restored hacienda and inn in the foothills about an hour and a half from Escondido. Day tours cost $35 a person and include lunch. Overnight stays at Posada Nopala include three meals for $85 for two people.**

Paul Cleaver, the original manager of the Santa Fe, has started his own inn on the sandy lane behind it, bringing with him his warmth and good humor as well as considerable savvy about laid-back beach comforts and good food.

Just a short block from Zicatela and Marinero beaches, the Tabachín del Puerto is tucked to the side of a quiet lane. Walking through the gated wall of the inn is like walking into a private garden, shaded by the spreading branches of a flame tree (the *tabachín* the inn is named for). The garden patio, with its fountain and umbrella-shaded tables, is the social center of the inn. Paul Cleaver often presides here during breakfast and late lunch, greeting his guests, advising them about local attractions, and enticing them to sit down and enjoy the daily specials from the kitchen. Escondido regulars stop by for a chat over breakfast.

Two cheerfully painted buildings enclose the sides of the garden; one has a sunning terrace on top with a fabulous panoramic view of Escondido and its beaches. The six suites are all large, some are enormous, and all have both air conditioners and ceiling fans, kitchenettes with a dining area, ample marble-tiled baths, and furnished terraces. The number of beds can be arranged according to your needs, but while the suites are furnished simply in a casual beach style, they also display Paul Cleaver's good taste, from the original art on the walls to the good books on the shelves. The very best and priciest suites are the three with panoramic views and wraparound terraces.

Although the vegetarian restaurant is open only through the late afternoon *comida*, its food is among the best in Escondido. All vegetables come from the owner's organic farm, and even the tortillas are brought in from the countryside. The whole wheat bread is made here, the terrific breakfasts are hearty and modestly priced. The choice for the *comida* is limited, but always tasty, whether pasta, a Spanish bean soup, or pizza. You can often put in an order for your favorite dish; green salads and the irresistible homemade lime ice cream are nearly always available.

Good rooms, good food, and good company make the Tabachín del Puerto a personal favorite.

Puerto Vallarta

Best Romantic Hideaway

Casa Tres Vidas, 198

Best Hotels for Stylish Sophistication

Sierra Plaza Golf & Spa, 210
Camino Real Puerto Vallarta, 193

Best Recreational Resort or Spa

Westin Regina Resort Puerto Vallarta, 212

Best Comfort Choices for All-American Abundance

Fiesta Americana Puerto Vallarta, 201
Presidente Inter-Continental Puerto Vallarta, 207

Best Beachfront Buys

Playa Los Arcos, 205

Quinta María Cortés, 209

Best Bargains for Mexican Character

Los Cuatro Vientos, 202
Condominio y Hotel Playa Conchas Chinas, 200

Best B&Bs and Budget Inns

Casa Corazón, 195
Casa Kimberley, 196
Posada de Roger, 206

Best Adventure Retreat

Lagunita Yelapa, 215

Best Place to Combine Business and Pleasure

Marriott CasaMagna Puerto Vallarta, 203

Tennessee Williams arrived in Puerto Vallarta the way everyone did in 1963, bouncing across a grass airstrip in a DC-6. Film director John Huston wanted the playwright's opinion on the small fishing village as a locale for the movie version of *The Night of the Iguana*, set originally in Acapulco when it was a sleepy Mexican beach town. Williams was elated. "This is precisely what I meant. This is Acapulco twenty years ago."

At the time, the airport doubled as a cow pasture. No roads or phone lines connected the village with the modern world. Pigs were as common as tourists on the streets, and burros provided most of the transportation.

Those were glamour days in Vallarta. The movie wasn't destined to be one of Huston's best, but it lured half of Hollywood to the shooting. Richard Burton, the male lead, brought his new friend, Elizabeth Taylor. Femme fatale Ava Gardner abandoned early retirement to join the cast, and Sue Lyon came fresh from her success in *Lolita*, still looking like the fictional vixen "who had misunderstood the axiom about early to bed," as one reporter put it.

The combination of sexy stars, torrid romance, and an undiscovered tropical paradise attracted a gaggle of journalists to the scene. They kept Americans informed about Burton and Taylor's growing passion and the pair's new homes near Río Cuale in Gringo Gulch. *Life* and *Time* joined the gossip columnists in portraying Vallarta as the ideal love nest. Even the *Saturday Review* gave its grudging agreement while pointing out how the primitive conditions made the town "the most unlikely resort this side of the Hindu Kush."

Ironically, as the media extolled the unspoiled enchantment, the reporters were aware they were creating a boom, and they fretted publicly about the advent of another Acapulco. Luck more than planning ultimately saved the town from that fate. Resort development has been concentrated outside the original village, leaving its cobblestone charisma remarkably intact. Vallarta does get as crowded as Acapulco these days, but the old section retains its native charm more fully than any other comparably developed destination in the tropics.

For people who want a good-time environment along with a good measure of romantic aura, Puerto Vallarta offers a copacetic blend of enticements. Despite the area's growth and new glitz, and even with today's abundant nightlife and recreation, Tennessee Williams still wouldn't mistake it for Acapulco.

The Main Attractions

The Cobblestone Village

Puerto Vallarta was founded in the mid-19th century along Río Cuale, a river that spills from nearby mountains into Banderas Bay. The Cuale is still the heart of Vallarta and the best place to get your bearings. The market is on the banks, and a tranquil island in the center is a popular spot for strolling, eating, and souvenir shopping.

Most of the town sprawls north of the river, confined by a hillside to a swath of land near the shore. Tourist businesses line the streets closest to the water, particularly along the Malecón, while residents live up the steep side streets that climb the hill. If you ignore the congestion and the T-shirt shops, the area retains much of its village feel.

Many of Vallarta's arts and crafts galleries, and a full range of restaurants and bars, are on this side of the river. Don't limit your exploration to the usual tourist stops, though. Venture up the hill and wander through the residential section, where life has a kind of vibrant simplicity few Americans know. The late afternoon is the best time for the trek, partly because kids are home from school and partly because you can stop for a sunset cocktail at the rooftop bar of Los Cuatro Vientos, which has a stunning view of the village, the crown-rimmed Church of Guadalupe, and out to the sea.

A less exerting way to savor the local flavor is to join the Sunday night promenade along the Malecón. Families gather around the main plaza, as they do in most of Mexico, to celebrate and socialize. Mariachis perform on the bandstand, boys play soccer on the beach, teens eye each other wishfully, and their elders walk and talk. The crowds are larger than they were a few decades ago, but little else has changed.

A Bouncy Budget Beach

The smaller section of town on the south side of Río Cuale is rapidly changing from a quiet neighborhood of dusty streets to one of the more chic sections of Vallarta; elegant restaurants are becoming more plentiful than sidewalk taco vendors. Even so, the streets attract fewer hustlers and cars, contributing to a peaceful mood you seldom encounter in major resort destinations. The shops and restaurants here, which tend to be interspersed among homes, are some of the best in the city. The beach, Playa Los Muertos, refurbished with truckloads of sand and a long, sweeping promenade, is big, frolicsome, and more Mexican in character than the beaches outside town where the large luxury hotels tower above the shore.

Rates at the hotels in this area, including those directly on the Pacific, are inexpensive to moderate, making Los Muertos one of the world's rare budget beaches. Here you still wake to cocks crowing and fisherman pushing off into the bay. Children are scampering to an elementary school just a block from the sand. The neighborhood remains Mexican and low-key, despite the newer resort trappings found within the cobblestone boundaries of the community. Although development is changing even this neighborhood, it remains a good spot to experience some of Vallarta's old allure at prices that seem equally old-fashioned.

Beach-Hopping

There are at least a dozen beaches along the 25-mile sweep of Banderas Bay. The exact number depends on whether you divide some of the longer stretches into separate sections, as the hotels in front like to do, and whether you count all of the small patches. In any case, there's more diversity than almost anyone can handle in a week.

The major hotel beach is Playa de Oro, just north of town along the original resort strip built in the 1960s and 1970s. It's a bustling commercial zone, characterized by high-rise hotels and shopping malls anchored with businesses like Denny's. There's little Mexican charm or natural beauty either, but the beach is long and sandy, and the massive hotels offer the kind of all-American vacations that many visitors seek.

The sand runs for several miles to the marina, where cruise ships dock and boats depart for the villages on the opposite shore. Between there and the airport, a couple of miles farther, is a huge new development called Marina Vallarta. Like Playa de Oro, the beach here is long and attractive but moderately quiet on most days because guests in the seaside hotels tend to congregate around their elaborate swimming pools instead of on the shore.

Playa Los Muertos, just south of the river, got its name ("Beach of the Dead") because it was the site of a battle between pirates and Indians a couple of centuries ago. The tourist authorities have been trying for years to get people to call it Playa del Sol or Olas Altas, but the old designation has stuck, though it's the liveliest shore in the area.

The main road south of town wanders along the coast under undulating slopes. The five-mile drive to Mismaloya Beach has always been pretty, though the landscape is increasingly blighted with ungainly, out-of-scale structures that dwarf a string of small beaches. Mismaloya, where *The Night of the Iguana* was filmed, used to be the most beguiling of these sands, but the cove has now been swallowed alive by a condo hotel.

Cruising to Yelapa

The primitive charms that stirred ardor in Burton and Taylor can still be experienced in Vallarta, but only by leaving the city. You have to visit Yelapa, Quimixto, or Las Animas, all on the southwest shore of the bay and reachable only by boat. These tiny beach villages are unspoiled gems, thriving happily without cars and other modern "necessities."

The easiest and cheapest way to go is on a day cruise from the main marina or the pier on Playa Los Muertos. A variety of boats depart for secluded southern and northern beaches daily between 9:00 and 10:00, returning in the mid- to late afternoon. In addition to their destinations, they differ in the amount of food and drink included, type of vessel, and number of passengers — the main factors in price. Your hotel should have the details on the current options.

Most people choose to visit Yelapa, at least on their first cruise. We prefer the boats that don't serve lunch on board, allowing us to sample the more flavorful fare at the *palapa* cafés on the beach where the boats land. The town greets the day-trippers en masse, selling beer, horseback rides to a beautiful waterfall, and guided tours of the quaint village. While the boats are in port, from about 11 A.M. until 2 P.M., Yelapa bustles like a miniature tropical theme park.

Some tourists probably think it's always that way, but the transformation after they leave is startling. With unbelievable suddenness, the town abandons all commercial commotion and reverts to a centuries-old pattern of calm. That's the best time to be here, staying overnight at Lagunita Yelapa (described below) and catching the boat back to Vallarta another day. If you do that, you'll probably encounter some of the North American expatriates who call the village home, dropouts from the 20th century returning to the elemental life. You may not want to take your fantasies of paradise that far, but a few days in Yelapa will make you think about it.

Savvy Shopping

Shopping can consume days in Vallarta if you're devoted to browsing and buying. Everyone should at least take a look. The range of distinctive shops and handmade items is greater than in any other beach destination in Mexico.

Finding the quality isn't easy, though. The modern malls north of town offer American convenience, but most of their businesses cater to touristy tastes. The ubiquitous beach vendors and the Mexican marketplaces with a concentration of stalls — such as the Mercado Central on the river and the nearby strip on Isla Río Cuale — are interesting primarily for local color, bargaining, and souvenirs. Most of the special places to shop are scattered around the old town, mixed in with a plethora of T-shirt and trinket emporiums. To see the best that Vallarta offers, you have to plan to do a fair amount of footwork.

The standard guidebooks usually list some prominent shops, and we mention a few, too, later in the chapter, but don't limit yourself to anyone's specific recommendations. Businesses come and go with regularity, and even the ones that stay for many years fluctuate in merchandise from one season to another. Besides, half the fun is stumbling onto a great discovery on your own. Pick a street

— perhaps Corona — and start poking around. The shops are generally open from 10 A.M. to 8 P.M., except on Sundays and during the midafternoon from 2:00 until 4:00 or 5:00.

Party Bars and Earthy Discos

Partying is the theme of the night in Vallarta, and the most popular bars compete actively with each other to attract the liveliest crowd. You can find a serene spot for a drink if you wish, but the music and dancing is so pervasive it becomes persuasive.

The biggest concentration of parties is along the northern half of the Malecón, a half-mile strip of hangouts thinly disguised as restaurants. The long-reigning king of this realm is Carlos O'Brian's (Diaz Ordaz 786), a member of the famous Carlos Anderson chain, which has learned how to make funky into splashy. Loud and uninhibited, it starts rocking early and doesn't close until the last Fish Smellington is sold. When the line outside is too long, try the Hard Rock Café (Diaz Ordaz 652), or any other door in the area that's erupting with music.

If you want to start your party early, go to El Dorado, directly on Los Muertos beach. Mariachis are usually around in the afternoon, playing for tips, and the thatched-roof restaurant fills up with tipplers who've had their share of the midday heat. Some of the crowd wanders later to Andale (Olas Altas 425), a couple of blocks away, for a spirited continuation of the festivities.

The discos open after dinner and really get moving in the hour or two before midnight. Forget the imitations of Acapulco discos in the hotels. Clubs like Christine at the Krystal and Sixties at the Marriott are fancier than the other choices, but they lack Vallarta vitality. The best places to get down in this town are south of the river, particularly Cactus (Ignacio Vallarta 399) and Sundance (Lazaro Cardenas 329).

Puerto Vallarta

Camino Real Puerto Vallarta

Playa de Las Estacas
Puerto Vallarta, Jalisco
(322) 1-50-00
(322) 1-60-00
Reservations:
Camino Real Hotels and Resorts
800-7-CAMINO (800-722-6466)

> **A Vallarta classic on a fine,
> almost private beach**

Accommodations: 337 rooms and suites. **High-season rates:** Deluxe rooms $180, lanai rooms $200, Camino Real Club rooms $230, deluxe Camino Real Club rooms with Jacuzzis $275, suites $600–$1,200. **Low-season rates:** Deluxe rooms $155, lanai rooms $175, Camino Real Club rooms $200, deluxe Camino Real Club rooms with Jacuzzis $245, suites $400–$750. **Payment:** Major credit cards. **Children:** Under 18, free in room with parents. **Recreation:** Beach, 2 swimming pools, 2 tennis courts, water sports center, small exercise room.

➤ **Most of the newer hotels in Puerto Vallarta are oriented toward their huge pools rather than the beach. The Camino Real has an attractive pool, but it's one of the few resorts in town where the beach is beautiful and calm enough to lure large numbers of sunbathers.**

Puerto Vallarta's Camino Real is tucked away south of town on Playa de Las Estacas, a long sandy shore bounded by rocky points that create a secluded estate. The grounds are big enough for everyone in your group to spread out, but contained enough so that you can still keep an eye on the younger ones. Extensively refurbished for the nineties, the hotel shines anew as a resort hideaway for families and couples.

The site is prime, selected back in 1965 when Puerto Vallarta was just awakening to its tourism potential. At the time the area was accessible only by boat. That had changed by the time the hotel opened its doors in 1969, but back then the phones in every room connected guests only with each other and the front desk.

While the road out of town is now rimmed with condos, time-share properties, and other hotels, the Camino Real has retained a sense of isolation. The two eleven-story towers screen the cove from the highway and, along with the contour of the coast, give you a sense of being in a private, walled world. Except for a low spot in the sand that catches the mountain runoff in the rainy season, the beach is one of the best in the area. Just a few vendors wander by, enough to be interesting without being overwhelming. Palm-thatched *palapas* and lounge chairs line the shore, and full refreshment services are available without leaving your chair or sandcastle. The water is usually calm and good for swimming, sailing, water skiing, snorkeling, and other sports.

The main pool is divided into two sections connected by a bridge. Water volleyball dominates one end, a swim-up bar the other. Energetic landlubbers can try the pair of lighted tennis courts or ask the staff to arrange golf, horseback riding, deep-sea fishing, scuba diving, and other diversions off the grounds. For children, an activities program is generally offered in peak periods.

The lush, attractive landscaping doesn't obstruct the direct ocean views common to the rooms in both towers. The quarters feature satellite TVs, air conditioning, phones, mini-bars, and two double beds or a king. Hand-crafted Mexican furnishings and reproductions of charming Manuel Lepe paintings mix comfortably with more conventional appointments.

The deluxe and lanai rooms, in the older wing, are similar except that the deluxes lack balconies. The Camino Real Club rooms in the newer tower provide more space and extra amenities such as robes, ceiling fans, a Continental breakfast, and complimentary afternoon cocktails and hors d'oeuvres. The deluxe Club rooms on the upper floors get a Jacuzzi on the private balcony and the duplex Fiesta and Virreyes suites have private plunge pools.

The restaurants offer a choice of cuisines and ambience. The elegant option is La Perla, open only for dinner. A transplanted French chef prepares a reasonable version of nouvelle dishes. If that's a little rich for you, La Brisa serves seafood by the beach at lunch and Finestra offers Italian cooking in the evening. The all-day eatery is Azulejos, a beachside café where you can get salads, soups, and a full range of entrées. For fast sandwiches, try the day-time Snack Shack. There are numerous bars, too, from swim-up to evening elegance.

The Vallarta Camino Real is expansive in activities and attractions, but contained in a realm of its own. It's an ideal combination of alluring options for many travelers.

Casa Corazón

Amapas 326
Puerto Vallarta, Jalisco
(322) 2-13-71
Fax: Same as phone
Reservations:
P.O. Box 937
Las Cruces, NM 88004
505-523-4666

A delightful blend of bed, breakfast, and beach

Accommodations: 13 rooms. **High-season rates:** $40–$76. **Low-season rates:** $35–$61. **Included:** Tax and breakfast. **Payment:** No credit cards. **Recreation:** Beach.

➤ **Casa Corazón is a short walk from Basilio Badillo, the street that has become known as the restaurant row of Puerto Vallarta. For authentic Mexican tamales and spicy fish soup, try the modestly priced Café de Olla (Basilio Badillo 62, 3-16-26); for nouvelle Mexican, don't miss the elegant Adobe Café (Basilio Badillo 252, 2-67-20).**

The name means House of Hearts, and it's as fitting as a quiver on Cupid. Originally a four-level villa, Casa Corazón is now a cuddly bed-and-breakfast inn, one of the few in Mexico and one of the best on a beach anywhere in the world.

Built into a hillside that tumbles down to Playa Los Muertos on the southern end of the sand, the Casa gives you a fine location, a distinctive room, a large sunset terrace, and a full breakfast for little more than the crowded resort hotels are charging for the meal alone. If you need more heart than that, you'd better check into a hospital for a transplant.

You enter the inn from the top, on Amapas Street, two blocks or so beyond the blocky Tropicana Hotel. A brick walkway wanders from there down the various tiers, past rooms, patios, and tropical gardens, ending at a gate that leads to the Looney Tunes Beach Club, the sand, and a wealth of water sports. A basic beach snack bar operated by the B&B, the Club provides a good spot to hang out in the sun during the day.

The guest rooms up the hill vary in size and price. Some are small and dirt cheap, others are enormous and still inexpensive. Each has tile floors, very simple furnishings, a ceiling fan, bath with shower, a double bed, and a twin; the more expensive rooms have an expansive shared terrace. Our favorites are the large rooms on the upper level, which enjoy the broadest ocean views, terraces, and the fullest breezes.

Casa Corazón calls itself a quaint inn on the beach. It's a modest claim for such immodest value.

Casa Kimberley

445 Calle Zaragosa
Puerto Vallarta, Jalisco
(322) 2-13-36
Fax: Same as phone
Reservations:
800-780-8595 access code 95

A B&B with a celebrated past

Accommodations: 8 rooms. **High-season rates:** Rooms $100, Cleopatra $175. **Low-season rates:** Rooms $70, Cleopatra $125, but August 15 to November 15, rooms $65, Cleopatra $100. **Included:** Full breakfast. **Payment:** No credit cards. **Recreation:** Swimming pool.

➤ **Puerto Vallarta has the best shopping of any resort. Exceptional Mexican folk art can be purchased at Nebaj (Morelos at Libertad), Arte Huichol (Corona 164) and Olinalá (Cárdenas 274), to name only a few.**

Once the love nest of Richard Burton and Elizabeth Taylor, who brought fame to Puerto Vallarta decades ago, Casa Kimberley allows you to relive the celebrated romance in its original setting. Named for a daughter of the man who sold the property to Burton, the B&B wouldn't make it as a Hollywood hangout today, but it retains some of the old amorous allure and attracts a fair number of sightseers for its five-peso house tour.

The new owner, Carolyn "Toy" Holstein, established the inn in the early 1990s out of the lovers' two homes, directly across the street from each other and linked by a "love bridge." She refurbished the houses in vintage style, decorated them throughout with photos of the actor and actress, and named the rooms after the couple's movies.

The pair lived in Vallarta when it was a tiny village, in the area called Gringo Gulch, now near the center of town in the modern city. Casa Kimberley is a few blocks uphill from Banderas Bay, a five-minute walk to shops and restaurants but a fair hike from the beach.

In the main house — a birthday gift from Burton to Taylor in 1964 — guests enjoy a stunning view of the bay and sunset from the couple's living room, atmospheric bar, and dining area, where the complimentary breakfast is served. The four bedrooms open to an interior courtyard. Once occupied by children, they are now basic B&B quarters. They offer double, queen, or king beds, white tile floors, beam ceilings, fans, and private bathrooms with showers. Toy's personal Cleopatra penthouse, rented for a minimum stay of five nights, comes with a king bed, air conditioning, a huge terrace with wonderful views of downtown and the ocean, and a passionately pink bathroom boasting Taylor's heart-shaped tub.

The three rooms at Burton's house, near the sizable swimming pool, used to accommodate Taylor's hairdresser and Burton's secretary. Now called Night of the Iguana, Boom, and the Sandpiper, they are similar to the kids' chambers across the street but are preferred in the summer for their air conditioning (for an extra fee).

Casa Kimberley is made of memories and could be a place to make your own. Certainly no one will forget a week with Cleopatra. Whether you end up with her or another epic adventure, you can count on a hot-blooded past to fan a few flames in the present.

Casa Tres Vidas

Conchas Chinas
Puerto Vallarta, Jalisco
(322) 2-18-15
Reservations:
Casa Tres Vidas
281-293-8670; 800-580-2243
Fax: 281-293-8970

> **Enchanting villas with
> private pools**

Accommodations: 3 three-bedroom, three-bath villas. **High-season rate:** $485–
$510 per villa, except Christmas season $650–$675. **Low-season rate:** $385–
$410 per villa and, available upon request, special rates for one or two
bedrooms. **Minimum stay:** 3 nights. **Included:** Services of a cook, maid, and
English-speaking house man. **Added:** Staff tip suggested for good service.
Payment: No credit cards; personal checks accepted. **Recreation:** Beach,
private swimming pool, Jacuzzi.

➤   **Fine dining coupled with sophisticated ambience is a Vallarta specialty. The best in nouvelle cuisine and elegantly prepared seafood can be
enjoyed in the chic in-town mansion of Café des Artistes (Guadalupe San-
chez at Vicario, 2-32-28), on the river terrace at Cuiza (Isla Cuale near Vallarta, 2- 56-46), and beachside at Daiquiri Dick's (Playa Los Muertos at Olas
Altas, 2-05-66).**

Casa Tres Vidas definitely isn't for everyone, but somehow we end
up recommending it frequently to friends. It offers an ideal blend of
pampering and privacy, of scenic solitude and proximity to pleni-
tude, of Mexican grandeur and homey ease. People who need to be
entertained won't like it, but those who entertain themselves will
be rhapsodizing with the muses.

Sally Sinclair bought Tres Vidas as a leisure retreat in the early
1980s. Later in the decade she expanded the house, divided it into
three separate dwellings, added a resident staff, gained the management assistance of her daughter, Laura, and created one of the
most unusual abodes in the tropics, a cross between an intimate
inn and a standard vacation villa. In the Conchas Chinas residential neighborhood, just south of downtown Vallarta, it's near many
other condos, homes, and other short-term rentals, but nothing
else comes close to matching the Sinclair hacienda in magnetism.

Terraced on a hillside directly above the ocean, the property
spreads over seven distinct levels, at least two per villa. Each of the

three realms is a world of its own, a 3,000-square-foot kingdom encompassing a private swimming pool, Jacuzzi or whirlpool, three spacious bedrooms with baths, a living room, a kitchen, and a heart-halting sunset view over a hidden beach splashing with Pacific surf. Each villa has its own cook who makes breakfast and dinner to your order from an extensive menu every day except Sunday. You pay for the groceries and make your own lunch, but those are hardly taxing demands in such a regal roost.

The penthouse villa, Vida Alta, is our favorite. You may gasp in awe on arrival, though all you see at first is one of the three floors. By the time you've reached the rooftop pool, you are certain to be smiling at your good fortune, and as you survey the panorama, your knees are bound to wobble a bit. If someone were to bring us food, we would accept permanent exile on the roof alone, content with the vista, half-bath, outdoor shower, and wet bar.

We thought of sleeping under the stars on the sun deck lounge chairs, but ultimately the bedrooms were too enticing. The two on the middle level, both as large as any junior suite in the country, are completely open to the sea breezes circulated by ceiling fans. Each has a king-size bed with a mosquito net, a comfortable sitting area, and a lovely tiled bath.

The third bedroom is downstairs, tucked behind an expansive living room furnished in a casually stylish Mexican manner. A kitchen is in one corner, and a large dining table stretches from the kitchen to the airy ocean views. You can indulge yourself in the bubbling Jacuzzi across the room while the cook makes meals — perhaps omelets, fresh juice, and a fruit platter for breakfast, and in the evening, maybe a savory chicken with honey and soy glaze.

The two other villas are down the steep hillside closer to the secluded shore. Both are tempting hideaways, but we would opt first for Vida Mar, at the bottom. The blue tile pool is the largest of the three and it, along with the living room, looks directly over the small, picturesque beach. One of the spacious bedrooms is on the same level and two more are upstairs, opening onto a stone sun terrace. Vida Sol is similar in configuration except that the 18-foot-high domed living room with fireplace is above the main bedroom level and slightly more formal in style.

If the villas were separate rentals, all three would be among the top accommodations in the country. By putting them together in one place with common management, Tres Vidas offers a potent package of delights. When you have an intimate occasion to celebrate — from a honeymoon to a family reunion — you won't find a better spot. We just invent occasions to stay here.

Condominio y Hotel Playa Conchas Chinas

Apartado Postal 346
Puerto Vallarta, Jalisco
(322) 1-52-30
Fax: (322) 1-57-63

**A quaint Mexican inn with
motel prices**

Accommodations: 30 rooms and suites. **Rates:** Rooms $86, two and three bedroom suites $110–$210. **Included:** 17 % tax. **Payment:** Major credit cards. **Recreation:** Beach, swimming pool.

➤ **One of the most popular bars and restaurants in town, El Set is
perched at the top of the hill above Playa Conchas Chinas. The major draw
is, as the T-shirts say, "another lousy sunset in paradise" rather than the
routine cooking.**

The *playa* at Playa Conchas Chinas is small and a little gravelly, but it's picturesque and tucked away from the resort crowds. Spilling down a steep, secluded hillside, the hotel underwent extensive renovation in 1997 and is expanding with a new wing of quite luxurious condominiums. The renovated rooms here are some of the best buys in Vallarta.

Colorful brick and tile walkways wind throughout the property. Designs are hand-painted on the walls and doors. *Palapas* shade the balconies, and palm trees shade the beach cove. The beachfront restaurant, open all day, is a tropical idyll, a guileless medley of greenery, bright tablecloths, and fresh sea breezes.

The fourteen rooms are quite fresh, with two double beds, Mexican-tiled bathrooms, a hot plate for making tea and snacks, and a sea-view terrace furnished with a table and chairs. The newly renovated suites with two to three bedrooms have full kitchens, Mexican-tiled bathrooms, and terraces with sea views; the three-bedroom, three-bath suite is attractively arranged on a huge terrace with a private Jacuzzi. All the rooms have air conditioning, ceiling fans, and phones.

Owned and operated by the Resendiz family, Playa Conchas Chinas is personable and soulful. Even if the rest of Puerto Vallarta succeeds someday in its mad quest to eliminate the area's original Mexican charm, you can count on finding it here.

Fiesta Americana Puerto Vallarta

Playa de Oro
Apartado 270
Puerto Vallarta
(322) 4-20-10
Fax: (322) 4-21-08
Reservations:
800-343-7821

> **A friendly chain hotel with
> first-class amenities**

Accommodations: 290 rooms. **High-season rates:** Rooms $131. **Low-season rates:** Rooms $86–$95. **Children:** 12 and under free, kids' programs winter and summer. **Payment:** Major credit cards. **Recreation:** Beach, 2 swimming pools, water sports, access to fitness center and spa.

➤ **Not too far from the Fiesta Americana, you can enjoy a lively Mexican evening at Cueto I (Brazilia 475, 3-03-63). A favorite with Mexicans and gringo ex-pats alike, the hacienda-style restaurant offers good seafood to the accompaniment of live mariachi music.**

When Puerto Vallarta began to take off in the 1970s, a number of first-class resort hotels opened along the Playa de Oro. The Fiesta Americana was one of the most fetching of the lot with its soaring thatch-roofed lobby open to the refreshing breezes of the sea. Well-maintained and well-managed, it remains one the most pleasant hotels along this beachfront strip. Smaller than the newer mega hotels, the Fiesta Americana is easier to navigate from hotel room to beach; less glitzy, it is also is more relaxed and its efficient service comes with Mexican warmth. The rates, especially the package variety, are very competitive for the quality.

The hotel is wider than it is tall. Its ten stories stretch and curve to enclose the palm-shaded terrace around the pools (one pool has a swim-up bar). The tawny beach is wide here, with lots of space for sunning and enjoying the sea; it's long, too, allowing for surfside walks and morning jogs. Water sports are arranged by the hotel, but for aerobics and a good gym, you need only walk next door and pay for a pass to the fully equipped Qualton Spa.

All the ample rooms, furnished in blond rattan with a little sitting area as well two good beds, have ocean views and balconies. The more limited views from the second-floor rooms are compensated for by extra large terraces. Our favorite rooms, on the top floor, have sloping wood-beamed ceilings and impressive views. All rooms have air conditioning, safes, mini-bars, phones, and satellite TV.

There eight bars and restaurants, enough to keep everyone happy. We especially appreciated the juice bar alternative to the breakfast buffet. Instead of starting our day seated under the pool-side *palapa*, we carried our coffee, juice, and sweet roll to the quiet of the beach. Live music fills the lobby bar in the evening and the Friday Lopez disco, set away from the hotel rooms, opens later at night.

The Fiesta Americana offers beachfront comfort and services at a price to make most travelers happy.

Los Cuatro Vientos

Matamoros 520
Puerto Vallarta, Jalisco
(322) 2-01-61
(322) 2-28-31

| **A small inn with big views** |

Accommodations: 14 rooms and suites. **Rates:** Rooms $57, suites $77. **Included:** Continental breakfast six days a week. **Payment:** Visa and MasterCard accepted with a 5% surcharge. **Recreation:** Swimming pool, sun deck.

➤ **Two places to look in town for the work of Rufino Tamayo are Galería Pacifico (Insurgentes 109) and Galería Uno (Morelos 561). Both galleries feature less well-established local artists, but they also carry works by Mexican masters, when they are available.**

Rufino Tamayo, the famous painter, once called Los Cuatro Vientos the "prettiest hotel in Mexico." The artist may have been a little blurry with tequila at the time, but he wasn't balmy. "The Four Winds" takes the prize for prettiest hotel in downtown Puerto Vallarta at least.

On the steep hillside above the center of town, a fair hike to the beach, the inn overlooks Banderas Bay from a glorious perch in the midst of a residential neighborhood. The rooftop bar, El Nido (the Nest), enjoys a grand panorama unexcelled anywhere on the Mexican coast, encompassing the sweep of the bay, most of the city, and brilliant sunsets.

The upper floor rooms and suites get good portions of the view, especially the corner Romantica suite, but avoid the Suite Wisconsin, which has no view at all. All the accommodations are decorated in a festive native fashion, with prints by local artists, tin mirrors in the bath, beaded curtains on the closets, and trim of Mexican design drawn on the white brick walls. The beds are doubles or two twins, amply cooled at night by a fan and the sea breezes coming through the louvered glass windows. Baths are small.

A Spanish colonial motif graces the public areas, from the wrought-iron entrance gate on Matamoros Street to the tiled sunning terrace by the small courtyard swimming pool and waterfall. The theme carries into Chez Elena, one of Puerto Vallarta's best-known dinner restaurants, where the menu features Mexican specialties. Though the kitchen prepares full meals only at night, the staff serves a complimentary juice and pastry breakfast each morning by the pool.

The owner, Gloria Whiting, and the manager, Lola Bravo, have made Los Cuatro Vientos into one of the most gracious and hospitable inns in Mexico. It may not be the prettiest hotel in the entire country, but you won't fault Tamayo for his enthusiasm.

Marriott CasaMagna Puerto Vallarta

Paseo de la Marina 5, Marina Vallarta
Puerto Vallarta, Jalisco
(322) 1-00-04
Fax: (322) 1-07-60
Reservations:
Marriott Reservations
800-223-6388

All-American allure at a middle-of-the-road rate

Accommodations: 433 rooms and suites. **High-season rates:** Garden-view rooms $159, partial ocean-view rooms $179, deluxe ocean-view rooms $199, suites $310–$600. **Low-season rates:** Garden-view rooms $99, partial ocean-view rooms $109, deluxe ocean-view rooms $119, suites $200–$245. **Included:** Breakfast. **Payment:** Major credit cards. **Children:** Under 15, free in room with parents. **Recreation:** Beach, swimming pool, golf (18 holes), 3 tennis courts, fitness center, water sports center.

➤ **If the Marriott is a bit of North America in Mexico, so is the baseball played by Puerto Vallarta's pro team, based at a stadium just north of downtown. Be prepared for Latin enthusiasm in the stands.**

For people looking for no surprises and middle-class comfort, Marriott's return to Mexico after a thirteen-year hiatus is good news. Like many of the chain's resort properties, the CasaMagna in Marina Vallarta specializes in convention and meeting business, but it also offers good package possibilities for individual vacationers. When the rate is right and you match the mood, the hotel shines.

You enter a lobby designed to be grandly contemporary, sparkling with marble, blond furniture, and peach-colored fabrics. The rooms are upstairs in a wing that fronts the ocean from a good distance back and in another wing that stretches toward the shore. All the quarters face the sea over the pool courtyard, but some have full views and others get a partial perspective, and this is the essential difference in what you pay. Spacious and upscale in a conventional way, the rooms feature a balcony, a king-size bed or two doubles, cable TV, a phone, air conditioning, and a mini-bar. More exceptional are the corner master suites with terrace Jacuzzi and wrap-around sea views.

The Marriott's pool, which appears to flow into the sea, is one of the largest in Vallarta, but the gray sand beach below is neither the biggest nor the best in town. A Jacuzzi roomy enough for a family reunion sits near the pool, and the surrounding stone deck and lounge chairs could seat a class reunion, probably with space to spare.

The hotel offers a variety of water sports, from windsurfing to jet skiing. Other ways to get your exercise include a fitness center, three lighted tennis courts, and the Marina Vallarta 18-hole golf course just outside the front door.

The poolside Las Casitas restaurant plies snacks and drinks to swimmers and sunbathers. La Estancia provides bigger meals during the day, with American and mild Mexican flavors, and adopts a Continental tone in the evening. Another option for dinner, Mikado, cooks steaks and fajitas teppan-yaki style. The Sixties disco serves burgers at night along with tunes from that era.

You can sample Mexico by leaving the property, but it never intrudes very much on life inside the Marriott. If that approach appeals to you, the hotel could be a comfy choice.

Playa Los Arcos

Olas Atlas 380
Puerto Vallarta, Jalisco
(322) 2-05-83
Fax: (322) 2-24-18
Reservations:
800-648-2403

> **Our version of the suite life
> on Playa Los Muertos**

Accommodations: 135 rooms and 10 suites. **High-season rates:** Standard rooms $65, superior rooms $85, oceanfront suites $105; in peak season minimum stay of three nights. **Low-season rates:** Standard rooms $40, superior rooms $50, oceanfront suites $70. **Payment:** Major credit cards. **Children:** 2 children under 12, free in room with parents. **Recreation:** Beach, swimming pool.

➤ **Enjoy the mariachis at Tequila's (Malecón at Mina) and the jazz at Club Roxy (Vallarta near Madero). The zaniest event in town, though, is the fiesta at La Iguana, held Sunday and Thursday (Lazaro Cárdenas, 2-01-05).**

We've known travelers who have spent more nights at Playa Los Arcos than at any other hotel in Mexico. Even when they can afford more in luxury and recreational facilities, they're still tempted by its Mexican exuberance, great beach location on lively Playa Los Muertos, and sunny ocean-view suites.

The suites are not fancy in any respect. The appointments are the same as those in the more numerous standard and superior rooms, a merry mélange of Mexican wood furniture and a hodgepodge of accents — tin, wrought iron, vinyl, and plastic. The kitchenettes in the suites aren't equipped for much more than chilling and opening a few *cervezas*. The reason travelers return is the huge oceanfront terrace, an ideal spot to sun, sip, sleep, and watch the setting sun. Directly below you on the sand, fishermen set out to sea, children romp after school, and visitors parade all day. The sights are particularly good from the suites on the top floors of the north wing of the U-shaped, five-story building because their balconies wrap around the corner and also overlook the hotel's luxuriant interior courtyard.

That's the view many guests get in the regular rooms, down to a pretty pool bordered by bougainvillea, hibiscus, and palms. We would avoid the standard rooms — cramped quarters without balconies. The terraces in the substantially larger superior rooms face either the courtyard (the perspective to request) or the sides of the property. All the chambers come with air conditioning, two double beds or a king, phones, tile floors, and small bathrooms.

Among the restaurants, Maximilian strives for elegance at its street location, while the cozier La Misión has a splendid beach-front site and a standard Mexican and international menu. At the weekly evening fiesta, the cooking takes a back seat to the setting, but the food is abundant and the atmosphere fun. Many nights there is live music at the poolside *palapa* bar, which serves up cool concoctions from early morning until midnight.

Los Arcos manages a carefree intimacy characteristic of places a third of its size. Though the staff occasionally get harried with crowds of package tourists, usually they are friendly and helpful. The hotel is not the most polished place in Puerto Vallarta, but from the balconies of the moderately priced suites, it may be the most enjoyable.

Posada de Roger

Basilio Badillo 237
Puerto Vallarta, Jalisco
(322) 2-06-39 and 2-08-36
Fax: (322) 3-04-82

An established favorite among budget travelers

Accommodations: 48 rooms. **High-season rates:** $48. **Low-season rates:** $35. **Payment:** MasterCard, Visa. **Recreation:** Swimming pool.

➤ **For a budget meal to match your accommodations at Posada de Roger, head up the cobblestone street to the tiny storefront bakery of Pays Catalina (Basilio Badillo 317). Around lunchtime, deliciously flaky empanadas are served hot from the oven.**

Roger's *posada* has been a fixture in Puerto Vallarta for many years. Comely for the price and always cheerful, it has a guileless blend of Mexican character and youthful American animation.

A block from Playa Los Muertos, the inn has become a bit over-whelmed by the tourist development on this street, now known as "restaurant row." Once you enter through a small gate onto a handsome tile and stone patio blooming brightly with flowers, most of the bustle is left behind. The office is to your right, and beyond that is a second courtyard and a swimming pool. The rooms rim the interior terraces up to the red tile roof above the second and third stories of the brick and stucco building. It's the kind of place that instantly makes you feel at home.

The air-conditioned rooms vary in size and furnishings. Some contain two doubles, some two twins, and some a combination of beds. A few enjoy a narrow balcony overlooking the lazy promenade outside. The only features shared by all the rooms are a phone, a shower in the bath, and a pleasantly rustic native air.

Posada de Roger is a top-notch budget inn. You won't find a surer sense of hospitality.

Presidente Inter-Continental Puerto Vallarta

Apartado Postal 448
Puerto Vallarta, Jalisco
(322) 8-05-07
Fax: (322) 8-05-09
Reservations:
Inter-Continental Reservations
800-327-0200

A classy all-inclusive resort with ocean views from all rooms

Accommodations: 120 rooms and suites. **High-season rates:** Superior rooms $235, deluxe rooms $320, deluxe rooms with Jacuzzis $350, junior suites with Jacuzzis $420, 2-bedroom master suites with Jacuzzis $650. **Low-season rates:** Superior rooms, $180, deluxe rooms $250, deluxe rooms with Jacuzzis $290, suites with Jacuzzis $360–$510. **Included:** All meals and domestic drinks, all recreational activities listed below, including tennis clinics and 2-per-room greens fees at the Marina golf club. **Payment:** Major credit cards. **Children:** Under 6, free in room with parents, 6–12 $20 extra per day for food; kids' club year-round ages 6–12. **Recreation:** Beach, swimming pool, 1 tennis court, fitness center with aerobics, golf (18 holes), cooking and bartending classes.

➤ **Try a jungle lunch in Vallarta, the polar opposite of a power lunch in Manhattan. Of the several places that offer the adventure, the oldest and most popular is Chico's Paradise (no phone), south of the city in a lush tropical setting with a waterfall and a river that rushes over huge rocks.**

The Presidente Inter-Continental became an instant favorite of ours as soon as it opened in the late 1980s under a different name. Puerto Vallarta needed a place like this — moderate in size, modern in accommodations, and most important, located on an almost private beach free of crowds and vendors. The hotel shares the shore with two condominiums, but rocky points on the ends of the calm cove assure that few other people will stumble onto your piece of paradise.

Inter-Continental saw the potential, too, and took over the property in 1994. With only 120 rooms, the hotel is tiny for a major chain resort, and that provides a rare, precious intimacy with the sea from all the quarters. Even people staying near the top of the small tower can hear the gentle surf from their balconies and their beds.

In the most expensive rooms and in most of the suites, you can make your own waves in the giant ocean-view Jacuzzi just inside the terrace, a few steps from the king-size bed, which is also positioned for the vista outside. The least expensive quarters lack the wonderful tub and come with two double beds, but they are similar in other respects. Each has a comfy sitting area, satellite TV, a mini-bar, phone, air conditioning, and a balcony peering directly over the water.

Between the tower and beach is an inviting free-form pool with a swim-up bar for drinks and snacks. There are a few palms around the pool, though none shading the beach just below. The thick sand is delightful for sunning, and swimming and snorkeling are usually good. For landlubber recreation, the Inter-Continental offers one tennis court and a beachfront fitness center with a gym, steam room, and aerobics.

The dining opportunities spill beyond set meal times with 24-hour room service, an all-day snack bar, and two à la carte restaurants. There are several bars and live music and entertainment.

The Presidente Inter-Continental is a worthy addition to the Vallarta shore. No hotel in town can top it for cozy seclusion and bedroom beguilement.

Quinta María Cortés

Calle Sagitario 132
Playa Conchas Chinas
Puerto Vallarta, Mexico
(322) 1-53-17
Reservations: 888-640-8100
Fax: 801-531-1633

An unconventional retreat off the resort beat

Accommodations: 5 suites. **High-season rates:** $100–$235. **Low-season rates:** $75–$175. **Payment:** No credit cards. **Recreation:** Beach, swimming pool.

➤ **If you want a private villa in the same neighborhood as Quinta María Cortés and Casa Tres Vidas, Puerto Vallarta offers a number of possibilities. One experienced source of help is Villa Leisure, 800-526-4244.**

Clinging to a hillside next door to Casa Tres Vidas, the Quinta María Cortés is the eccentric sister of the neighboring inn, less polished in a number of ways but a less expensive way to enjoy the same splendid setting. The Texan proprietor, known as Silver, came to Vallarta in the early years of its fame, bought the property, and spent a couple of decades embellishing it in her own personal style, producing a nine-level lodge that's a cross between a time-worn Italian villa and a rococo refuge.

The entry-level suite, Ana Gabriel, can be rented with or without its huge living room. The red bedroom has a brass double bed draped with mosquito netting, a fireplace, a large desk arrayed with books and old magazines, potted plants, and an intriguing collection of religious art. Folding French doors lead to an ocean-view terrace covered by a black and white striped awning. The black and yellow bathroom, also equipped with a fireplace, has a deep, black tile tub and other black fixtures, including a bidet. It overlooks the swimming pool and the Pacific through floor-to-ceiling windows.

The living room enjoys a third fireplace and lots of *banco* seating. An *equipale* table with chairs for eight is covered by *palapa* thatch but is open to the breezes. The kitchen could be handy, though the oven wasn't working during our visit.

The suite just upstairs, María, was Silver's apartment until she moved off property several years ago, a spot where she used to throw parties for visiting jet setters and guests. It has a piano, a clever fireplace that reveals a view of the small beach directly below the inn, a domed ceiling painted by well-known Vallarta artist

Manuel Lepe, and antlers displayed above the double bed in the large bedroom.

The bedroom is less elaborate in the penthouse Maximillian suite above, where the bed rests under a *palapa* roof but is otherwise exposed to the elements. An intricate wooden bar divides the living room from the kitchen and a fireplace painted to look like marble. The private sunroof provides glorious vistas of Banderas Bay. The two suites below street level, Alejandro and Guadalupe, are smaller and less desirable than the others, but are decorated in the same eclectic style, always expressive even when some features are a little dated, frayed, or soiled.

The Quinta María Cortés isn't refined, but it is radiant in its own individual way. Anyone who appreciates uncommon personality may relish a stay.

Sierra Plaza Golf & Spa

Pelícanos 311, Marina Vallarta
Puerto Vallarta, Jalisco
(322) 1-08-00
800-362-9170
Fax: (322) 1-08-01
Reservations:
Small Luxury Hotels of the World
800-525-4800

An elegant inn for country club recreation

Accommodations: 42 suites and 25 villas. **High-season rates:** Junior suites $225, superior suites $275, deluxe suites $285, villas $375–$420, Presidential Suite $1,500. **Low-season rates:** Junior suites $165, superior suites $215, deluxe suites $275, villas $315–$400, Presidential Suite $650. **Payment:** Major credit cards. **Children:** Under 12, free in room with parents. **Recreation:** Swimming pool, golf (18 holes), 2 tennis courts, fitness center, Jacuzzi.

➤ **Obstacles on the Marina Vallarta golf course, which wraps around the hotel, include waterfalls guarding greens and a lagoon filled with wildlife. You're likely to encounter ducks, herons, and sand cranes, and a really errant shot could anger an alligator.**

You're greeted warmly at the tiled porte-cochere of the elegant pink mansion, registered at a hand-crafted desk, and given a welcoming glass of champagne. The Sierra Plaza quickly teaches you the meaning of *Mi casa es su casa.* The phrase isn't just a cliché here, and the house you're staying in is easily the prettiest in the city, even if it is a short walk from the beach.

Originally a Quinta Real hotel, the hotel was built by the same architectural team that conceived the small chain's quintessential Mexican inns in Guadalajara and Zacatecas. The facade radiates elegantly with arches, columns, *nichos*, and *terrazas*. The interior design blends tropical greenery, marble and tile, classy antiques, and handmade furniture from Michoacán's finest artisans. A small pond meanders through the center of the lobby, encircling an intimate sitting area graced by a pair of ancient wooden camels from Goa. Another pond flows around the lobby bar, outside on a terrace, where you can sip champagne again in the early evening.

The restaurant, on several terraces leading down to a poolside patio, is a model of refinement. More of the striking hand-crafted furnishings, with animal motifs, are combined with floral upholstery and towering plants. A stencil design, inspired by paper cut-out folk art, rims the ceiling, and a series of skillfully done ceramic portraits fills the upper wall. Crowning all this is one of the most delightful chandeliers anywhere, a masterpiece of whimsy that includes swinging monkeys, mynah birds, cheetahs, and palms, all made from straw.

The food is some of the best served at a resort hotel in Mexico. At dinner the menu emphasizes Mexican and Continental specialties, though it also allows you to dine lightly. At one recent meal, a trio of tamales made a first-rate appetizer and the tortilla soup finished a strong second. Our entrée was an interesting surf and turf variation, a tender beef fillet and a succulent shrimp mole.

Breakfast offers pleasing additions to standard bacon and eggs. Good Mexican dishes like *chilaquiles* share the menu with unusual juices and hearty cereals. Fluffy omelets might be filled with shrimp or *huitlacoche*, a corn fungus much tastier than its literal description implies.

All the rooms are spacious and well designed, but the superior and deluxe suites enjoy Jacuzzis or tiny wading pools lacking in the junior suites, as well as more expansive views out over the golf course, sometimes with the ocean on the horizon. Each has a sunken sitting area that opens to a terrace, and handsome marble floors with inlaid terra cotta near the beds in the form of an area rug. Often the king or two double beds sit below molded ceramic masks and animals, the original creations of Sergio Bustamante, one of Mexico's most prolific contemporary artists. The giant armoire, another of the hand-crafted pieces from Michoacán, boasts a bright but tastefully painted tropical scene.

The Presidential Suite is the only one that's substantially more opulent than the others. With three full bedrooms, a studio office, enormous living room, massive dining table, and private pool, it's big enough to host a political convention. Satellite TV, a phone, air conditioning, and a capacious marble bathroom are common to all the quarters.

Separate buildings to one side of the main wing house four styles of villas, named after flowers. They range in size from studios to three-bedroom apartments, and all have Jacuzzis or private pools of modest proportions, kitchenettes, indoor and outdoor dining areas, and decor similar to that of the suites.

Many of the guests come for golf. Joe Fingers designed the 6,500-yard, par 71 course that surrounds the hotel. The Sierra Plaza's competitively priced golf packages include greens fees, a cart, and a caddy. Tennis is another option for recreation, and the fitness center another venue for exercise. The beach is just a fairway away, but most swimmers and tanners are content with the beautiful pool, a dreamy oasis with sapphire blue tile, a palm-thatched bar, and Arabian Nights cabañas.

If you're convinced you need a hotel directly on a beach, go ahead and book one. Then come by and take a look at the Sierra Plaza. Ask to see a room and stay around for a meal. We'll give you big odds you don't make the same mistake again.

Westin Regina Resort Puerto Vallarta

Paseo de la Marina Sur 205
Puerto Vallarta, Jalisco
(322) 1-11-00
Fax: (322) 1-11-21
Reservations:
Westin Hotels and Resorts
800-228-3000

A fresh beachfront resort with all the trappings

Accommodations: 280 rooms and suites. **High-season rates:** Garden rooms $155, resort rooms $185, deluxe ocean-view rooms $205, Royal Beach Club rooms $260, junior suites $395, master suites $495–$795. **Low-season rates:** Garden rooms $115, resort rooms $155, deluxe rooms $170, Royal Beach Club rooms $225, junior suites $340, master suites $395–$670. **Payment:** Major credit cards. **Children:** Under 18, free in room with parents; supervised playroom. **Recreation:** Beach; 4 swimming pools; golf (18 holes); 3 tennis courts; fitness center with aerobics, sauna, steam, Jacuzzi, and massage; water sports center with windsurfing and diving; horseback riding.

➤   **Puerto Vallarta offers a staggering number of designer boutiques. All the usual resort brands are available, along with fine Mexican labels at Sucesos (Libertad 232) and María de Guadalajara (Morelos at Corona and other locations).**

Once the site of a coconut plantation, the Westin Regina in Marina Vallarta shows its heritage. Hundreds of palms grace the grounds, lining the long, somewhat pebbly beach, supporting hammocks, and shading parts of a huge courtyard, where intricate stone paths lead around four meandering swimming pools.

The hotel is striking for its airy interior spaces decorated with contemporary art and contrasting materials of stone and tropical woods. Three intelligently designed wings rise directly above the old coconut grove, forming a V that steps up in stages from the sand to over a dozen stories high. The floors scale back slightly as they climb, enhancing the privacy on the balcony that each room enjoys. Except for the suites, the rooms differ primarily in their views, which are better from the sixth level and above in the deluxe and Royal Beach Club quarters. All the spacious accommodations have comfortable hand-crafted furniture, air conditioning, ceiling fans, direct-dial phones, mini-bars, safes, and satellite TV.

The Royal Beach Club rooms provide special complimentary services, including access to a private lounge that serves a Continental breakfast in the morning and hors d'oeuvres with cocktails in the afternoon. The expansive junior suites offer so much extra lounging space that there is even a separate foyer and the bathroom has two sinks, a marble bath and separate glass-enclosed shower stall with its own skylight, and, as if more were necessary, a whirlpool on the ample terrace. The master suites range from two-floor duplex models to a super-plush Presidential chamber, all with private Jacuzzis.

The Westin's restaurants and lounges are as diverse as the rooms. During the day two pool bars supply sunbathers and swimmers with drinks, burgers, *ceviche*, and pizza, and in the evening La Cascada serves cocktails and snacks in a colorful indoor galleria with a five-tiered waterfall. El Palmar gets you going in the morning with a lavish and tasty buffet of American and Mexican favorites and stays open for casual lunches and dinners.

The featured dinner restaurant, Garibaldi's, sprawls under a thatched *palapa* roof at one end of the beach. Named for the plaza in Mexico City where mariachi musicians perform, it specializes in seafood, steaks, and a fiesta spirit.

The hotel isn't on the fairways of Marina Vallarta's 18-hole Joe Fingers golf course, but it's in walking distance of the clubhouse and guests enjoy playing privileges. Three tennis courts are closer at hand, on the 21-acre grounds, and so is a children's playground and a state-of-the-art fitness center with a weight room, exercise equipment, aerobics classes, and gender-segregated sauna, steam, and massage areas. If you're more oriented to the ocean, the staff will arrange boating, diving, windsurfing, and other water diversions, though the beach in front of the property isn't a prime spot for water sports.

Opened in 1992, the Westin Regina is a fresh, invigorating addition to the local lodging scene. The palm trees may be gracefully mature, but the rest of the hotel flaunts a bright and youthful bounty.

Yelapa

Lagunita Yelapa

Yelapa, Jalisco
(329) 8-05-14 and (322) 2-47-99

An escapist fantasy for adventuresome travelers

Accommodations: 32 *cabañas.* **High-season rates:** $35–$45. **Low-season rates:** $23–$30. **Payment:** MasterCard, Visa. **Recreation:** Beach, swimming pool.

➤ **On the way to Yelapa, the boats pass by Los Arcos, the distinctive rock formations near Mismaloya. It's the best snorkeling and scuba site in the Vallarta area; Chico's Dive Shop, on Diaz Ordaz, has all the equipment and information you need.**

Most of Yelapa's scores of day visitors from Puerto Vallarta never realize the isolated village has a hotel. They cruise right by it in their boats, and they may even have lunch at its beachfront restaurant, but Lagunita Yelapa blends into the bucolic environment so well that it's virtually invisible.

From the bay and the beach the inn's scattered, bluff-top cottage rooms look like homes, particularly the original *palapa cabañas* characteristic of the rest of town. With conical thatched roofs and thatch shutters above short stone walls, they bear no resemblance at all to resort lodgings. Many people still prefer to stay in these native huts, but there are now some larger, more expensive bungalows with less rustic bathrooms. In either case, the water in the shower is usually warmed only by the sun's heat on exposed outdoor pipes, and the generator-powered electricity, such as it is, comes on for just a few hours in the evening.

The charm of the *cabañas* and their ocean vistas vary considerably. For unobstructed views close to the water, ask for numbers 6, 7, 8, or 9, which line the shore. Room 19 also enjoys a prime perch, overlooking the saltwater swimming pool as well as the sea. One of the most requested quarters, number 24 comes with two double beds instead of the usual double and twin, and it features an inviting bathroom built around a big boulder. Most of the rooms open onto a rock porch or sand terrace facing out to the bay.

Stone pathways connect the cottages to each other and to the Yelapa beach, where Lagunita's bar and restaurant serve as a social center for guests. You can eat either in the shade in a covered open-air dining room or at tables sunk securely in the deep sand. The cooking is often quite good, particularly if you stick with simple dishes and the freshest ingredients.

You don't have many fancy options anyway at Lagunita, in food, lodging, or the rest of life. This is a sanctuary for simple pleasures, a refuge at once luscious in natural radiance and unadorned in primitive plainness.

The
Extraordinary
Interior

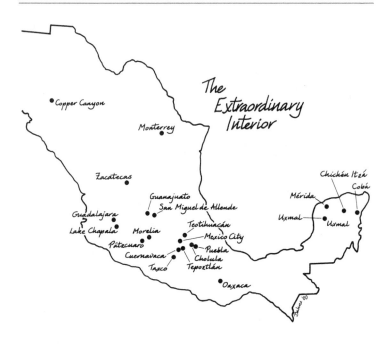

Archaeological
Treasures

Best Intimate and Affordable Inns

Best Bargain for Mexican Character

Best Adventure Retreats

Mexico has one of the most dramatic and enigmatic collections of ancient ruins in the world. The Indian civilizations that flourished in much of the country before the Spanish arrived left magnificent ruined cities that are stunning to see and puzzling to ponder. We review the most impressive of the accessible sites in a suggestive rather than detailed manner. Go to the experts for more information. Your neighborhood library should have a few books on the various civilizations, and university libraries are loaded with them. Guided tours are available at all the major ruins, and short guidebooks in English are sold there and throughout Mexico.

The Valley of Mexico

Modern Mexico City stands on the drained bottom of a massive lake that dominated the vast central valley of Mexico from the Pleistocene age to recent times. For the first settlers in the Mesoamerican region, who arrived at least 11,000 years ago, the lake provided a level of natural abundance found in few other places on the whole continent. Hunters and gatherers in the prehistoric period trapped animals for meat when they came to the lake to drink, and picked wild fruit, seeds, and vegetables flourishing along the banks. Since those early years, the valley has remained a major center of population, perhaps destined from the beginning to become Mexico's political center as well.

By 2000 B.C., most of the nomadic groups in the valley and elsewhere in Mexico were learning agriculture and forming permanent settlements, the first, critical steps toward development of the great civilizations. In the preclassic period, which lasted from 1200 B.C. until about 150 B.C., life reached new levels of complexity in social organization, ceremonial practices, and artistic sophistication. The Olmecs, who lived east of the valley on the Gulf of Mexico, were early leaders in these areas, though little remains of their ancient cities, built mostly of earth instead of stone. They left artistic artifacts mainly — often amazingly advanced — including anthropomorphic ceramics, jade carvings, and colossal basalt sculptures.

Olmec culture waned, for reasons unknown, toward the end of the preclassic, when Teotihuacán emerged as the monumental capital of the valley and much of central Mexico. The large city, encompassing 22 square kilometers, demonstrated remarkable sophistication in urban planning and architecture, still extraordinary today in ruins. Teotihuacán's ceremonial center was burnt and abandoned around 600 A.D., but its achievements in construction, stonemasonry, and the provision of public services continued to influence the design of subsequent pre-Hispanic cities.

Through the rest of the classic period and up to about 1000 A.D., power in the valley was dispersed among several cities, including Cholula, Cacaxtla, Xochicalco and Tula. Other city states continued to function through the early postclassic. None of them was as mighty as Teotihuacán until the arrival of the Aztecs.

The Aztecs came to the valley in the 12th century and gradually established an empire that extended far beyond. They founded their capital, Tenochtitlán, on an island in the lake. When the Spanish saw it, they were awed by its grandeur, which made European cities of the time seem petty and poor by comparison. Despite superior weapons, the Spanish needed considerable luck to subdue Tenochtitlán, which they then razed in religious zeal, using some of the stone to erect Mexico City over the old pyramids and plazas.

A scholar could spend weeks — even years — exploring the physical remains of the valley civilizations, but curious dabblers can cover the most impressive sights in a few days. Most people use Mexico City as a base, visiting the Aztec's Great Temple complex next to the Cathedral and taking day trips to Tula, Cholula, and Teotihuacán. Your hotel can arrange tours to these sites. For more leisurely sightseeing, consider staying overnight at Teotihuacán and Cholula (or better yet, in Puebla). To visit Xochicalco, plan a stay in Cuernavaca or Tepoztlán. Hotel listings for all these areas are listed in this chapter.

The Main Attractions

Mexico City

The National Museum of Anthropology is an indispensable starting point for amateur archaeologists. Allow a full day for your visit. The Templo Mayor ruins and its companion museum near the Zócalo can be covered in a couple of hours. Both are described briefly in the chapter on Mexico City.

Teotihuacán

An hour from Mexico City, Teotihuacán is the most impressive of the valley ruins. If you have time for only one excursion, it's the top choice. Climb the Pyramid of the Moon, at the north end of the city, to get an idea of the city's scale. Stretching south is a broad avenue — 130 feet wide — named the Street of the Dead. Lined with architecturally harmonious structures that were once vividly painted temples and palaces, the boulevard today runs a mile and a half to the enormous Ciudadela complex, originally the center of the metropolis. The Street of the Dead continued two miles farther south. A similar intersecting street ran east and west the same distance, into areas that have not yet been excavated.

The most memorable building is the Pyramid of the Sun. Though it's only half as high as the Great Pyramid in Egypt, it covers the same area. It's difficult — perhaps impossible — to fathom the human effort required for the construction. Without the wheel, draft animals, or metal tools, laborers transported, assembled, and carved three and a half million tons of stone. They raised their edifice to a height of over 200 feet, capping it with a temple now long gone. The earliest extant structure in Teotihuacán, the pyramid is built over a cave that ancient Mexicans seem to have regarded as the birthplace of the sun, the moon, and human life.

Tula

Judging by the few remains, Tula in its heyday probably was a fiercely haughty warrior city. Unfortunately, enemies burned and sacked the buildings before the Spanish conquest, leaving little to see except the Pyramid of Quetzalcoatl and the gigantic carved columns on top that originally supported the roof of a temple. The ruins are an hour and a half from Mexico City, a mile from the modern town of Tula.

Cholula

The pyramid at Cholula, once the main center for the worship of the feathered serpent god, Quetzalcoatl, is the largest on earth in total volume, with a base of almost 50 acres. It looks more like a hill today, though, overgrown with vegetation and unrestored. Its temple was one of 400 in the city when the Spanish arrived, but they destroyed many of the buildings, and most of those remaining have not been excavated. You can walk inside the pyramid, through tunnels excavated by archaeologists, and enter the only plaza area that has been restored. You have to use your imagination a lot at Cholula, about ten miles west of Puebla and two or three hours from Mexico City, depending on traffic.

Oaxaca

The archaeological treasures of Oaxaca are less famous than those to the north and the south but no less compelling. Easily the most important place to visit is Monte Albán, one of the earliest of the great Mesoamerican capitals, founded in 500 B.C. Zapotec laborers leveled an entire mountaintop to build the 15-square-mile city, which overlooked the three expansive valleys their ancestors had settled millennia before. The almost vertical road to the ruins will convince you instantly of the feat involved in the construction. A modern contractor with heavy equipment would call the job impossible, but the Zapotecs somehow managed it without wheels or animal labor.

Monte Albán thrived as a residential, administrative, and ceremonial center for over a thousand years, going into decline about the same time as Teotihuacán, possibly for similar or related reasons. The ruins visible today are from the last building phase, the classic period. They are concentrated around the Great Plaza, an expansive area that's contained enough for easy exploring. The low pyramid platforms formerly held temples and palaces, making them more imposing than they look today.

In the few centuries immediately preceding Spanish colonization, Mixtecs and then Aztecs invaded the Oaxacan valleys, primarily to exact tribute and control trade. Monte Albán was completely abandoned, but the Mixtecs used it as a cemetery, burying their leaders with a fortune in gold and other precious objects. Some of the fabulous pieces found in one tomb are on display in the Museo de las Culturas de Oaxaca.

The most significant Mixtec site excavated so far is Mitla, about 25 miles southeast of Oaxaca city. Though it was inhabited originally by the Zapotecs, the residential buildings exposed today are known for the intricate, skillful stonework of the Mixtec mosaics.

Neither Monte Albán nor Mitla offers visitor lodging since they are both easy excursions from Oaxaca. See the chapter on the city for hotel recommendations.

Mayan Mysteries

The Mayan culture extended through a vast region that encompasses much of southern Mexico, Guatemala, and Belize as well as parts of Honduras and El Salvador. While the highland peoples to the north, contained by mountains, tended to centralize authority in one or a few dominant cities, the Maya spread themselves over a greater area and erected many more religious and residential centers. Archaeologists have identified around 300 sites, though many remain unexcavated, buried today under dense vegetation in inaccessible jungles.

Maya civilization is renowned for its intellectual achievements in astronomy, writing, and mathematics. These ancient people conceived the mathematical concept of zero and developed a positional numbering system long before the Arabs brought something similar to Europe. They created a written, hieroglyphic language to preserve their knowledge and history and discovered how to use a false arch to increase the interior spaces and enhance the beauty of their colossal buildings. The art of the classic period, 250–900 A.D., is remarkable for intricacy and organic vitality.

After that epoch, Mayan culture declined. Descendants of the founders still inhabit the lands, but a combination of internal conflicts and outside invasions decimated the society centuries before

Cortés landed. Gradually the grand cities, where noble dynasties had held sway, fell into disuse. The ruins remain impressive, though, monuments to a civilization that in its prime was as advanced as any in the world.

We cover below the four major ancient sites that are easiest to reach. All are in the Yucatán peninsula, within driving distance of Mérida, Cancún, and other regional destinations, and each offers good overnight accommodations.

The Main Attractions

Chichén Itzá

The most famous of the ruins in Mexico, Chichén Itzá is also the most puzzling. Many of the features are Mayan, but others seem directly related to Toltec motifs at Tula. Archaeologists used to assume that there were two phases of construction, the latter following a Toltec invasion in the postclassic period. This thesis has come under attack recently, but it has not been displaced by another widely accepted explanation. Be skeptical of dates and theories offered by official signs and guides and focus instead on the august ruins themselves.

The north section of Chichén Itzá is the most controversial and the most striking. El Castillo, also known as the Temple of Kukulcán, towers above an enormous plaza. The ceremonial ball court, where losers were decapitated, is to the west of the pyramid and nearby is the Wall of Skulls. The Sacred Cenote, a sacrificial well, is to the north, and the Temple of the Warriors occupies the east side of the quadrangle.

The sights are amazing at any time, but particularly during the spring and autumn equinoxes, when the setting sun casts shadows on the balustrade of El Castillo in the dramatic image of a serpent descending the stairs of the pyramid. The figure, whose head shines with the lingering rays of the sun, represents the god Kukulcán, as the Maya called Quetzalcoatl. Try that priestly magic at home with modern science and technology.

The observatory the Mayas used for some of their astronomical research is in the south section of Chichén Itzá. The circular tower is called the Caracol (snail) because of its interior staircase. The so-called High Priest's Grave pyramid in this portion of the city was actually built not over a grave, but over a cave. Even so, it is impressive and, with its own cenote complex, a kind of miniature Castillo.

The most extensive ruins in the Yucatán, Chichén Itzá requires a full day to cover well in the intense heat. The bus excursions from the beach resorts, several hours away, seem too rushed to us. Consider flying in from Cancún or Cozumel to gain time or come by rental car and stay overnight. Most travelers will find the extra time and cost amply rewarding.

Cobá

The mysteries at Cobá are different from those at Chichén Itzá, though they are equally baffling. The city seems to have been the hub of a network of stone-rubble roads, usually broad, straight boulevards running as far as 60 miles. The numerous *sacbes* were formidable engineering feats, but their purpose is unknown. They hardly seem necessary for transportation since the Maya didn't have draft animals or wheeled vehicles.

The design of the city also raises questions. Cobá is closer in style to Tikal, hundreds of miles away in Guatemala, than to other places in the Yucatán. The relationship is particularly strong in the many stelae, or carved pillars, found in the ruins. Often depicting male and female rulers standing on captives, the stelae are the most compelling feature of the site. The ones in the Grupo Macanxoc, found down a jungle trail, are among the best preserved.

Cobá was a large city in the late classic period (600–900 A.D.), but most of it is still buried in the lush jungle. Though you can see the excavated portions in a few hours, you might want to spend the night and explore in the morning, when temperatures are the most bearable. Cobá is 30 miles inland from Tulum, which is 80 miles south of Cancún.

Tulum

Tulum is fun to visit, but more for its sensational clifftop perch on the Caribbean than for the magnitude or finesse of the architecture. Constructed centuries after the zenith of Mayan artistry and power, the city has a few buildings of moderate interest and a beautiful beach with rough surf. Underwater enthusiasts may be fascinated with the many depictions of the Diving God, though the peculiar figure has nothing to do with scuba diving. A small site, Tulum can be seen in an hour or two.

Uxmal

The most harmonious of the Yucatán cities architecturally, Uxmal thrived in the late classic period in a region with a paucity of natural water resources. The rain god, Chac, was important to all the Maya, but especially to the ones in this area, where there are no *cenotes* (natural wells). Chac's face, characterized by an elephantine snout, pops up throughout the city, accenting the graceful buildings like a gargoyle on a medieval cathedral.

The tiered pyramid just inside the entrance of the site is one of the most handsome in Mexico, though not as large as some. The geometric proportions are best admired from the ground because if you climb it, the descent is terrifyingly steep. The most striking structures are the nearby Nunnery, named by the Spanish after perceived resemblances to a convent, and the Governor's Palace, beyond the ball court. The intricate friezes of both buildings are Mayan masterpieces.

Plan to stop overnight in Uxmal to catch the evening sound-and-light show, also done at Chichén Itzá. Another plus of a stay here is the opportunity to visit some of the largely unexcavated ruins in the Puuc region. Kabah and Sayil are particularly worthwhile and easy to add to a rental-car itinerary.

Chichén Itzá, Cholula, Cobá, Teotihuacán, Uxmal

Villas Arqueológica

Chichén Itzá, Cholula, Cobá, Teotihuacán, and Uxmal
Reservations:
Club Med
800-CLUB MED

> **A collection of inns at major archaeological sites**

Accommodations: 40 rooms at each inn. **Rates:** $76. **Payment:** Major credit cards. **Children:** Under 12, free in room with parents. **Recreation:** Swimming pool, 1 tennis court at each inn.

➤ **Club Med management of the Villas Arqueológicas influences what kind of guests stay at the inns, but not in the way you might imagine. The**

organization's worldwide network ensures a mix of visitors from all corners of the earth.

In the late 1970s, the Mexican government invested millions of dollars in stimulating tourism at some of its major archaeological sites. Instead of putting the money into advertising or trade shows, the authorities opted for a long-term investment in facilities, erecting similar colonial-style inns at two ruins outside Mexico City — Cholula and Teotihuacán — and at three in the Yucatán — at Chichén Itzá, Cobá, and Uxmal. With the exception of the other recommended inns at Chichén Itzá, Uxmal, and Puebla (near Cholula) the Villas Arqueológicas remain the top places to stay near each city.

Club Med manages the inns, but not in the usual Club Med manner. Guests don't have to join the organization or deal with any of the customary resort rituals. Instead of focusing on recreation, the Villas emphasize archaeology, offering only a swimming pool and a tennis court for the playful. They present an audio-visual show daily about the adjacent site and provide a decently stocked library on all of Mexico's pre-Hispanic civilizations.

The two-story inns are built around a courtyard containing the pool. The small rooms have regional Mexican decor and usually a pair of twin beds. They are air-conditioned in the Yucatán and heated at Cholula and Teotihuacán.

The spirit of the villas is more international than local. Conversations in the bar are as likely to be in German as in Spanish. By the time you're ready for dinner or a drink after a day of sightseeing, the mood may feel just right. It's easy to overdose on the Mexican grandeur a short walk away.

Chichén Itzá

Hacienda Chichén

Chichén Itzá, Yucatán
(985) 1-00-45
Reservations:
Maya-Caribe Travel
914-738-8254
800-223-4084
Fax: 914-738-8257

> **An eccentric inn with a past of its own**

Accommodations: 18 rooms and suite. **Rate:** Standard rooms $85, suite $120. **Payment:** Major credit cards. **Recreation:** Swimming pool.

➤ **The Sacred Cenote, or "well of sacrifices," was used for human sacrifice, but the stories of drugged virgin victims are largely myth. The Maya seem to have offered men, women, and children to the rain god Chac in times of drought At the height of the ancient city, gold disks and carved jades were also sacrificed to the cenote.**

The Hacienda Chichén offers accommodations with a history almost as intriguing as the Mayan ruins themselves. Just across the road from the Villa Arqueológica, the hotel goes back in time some 450 years earlier than its neighboring inn.

A Spanish conquistador started construction of the central *casa*, using stones from the fallen temples of the abandoned Mayan city. The Maya in the area, astonished at the sacrilege in his choice of materials, eventually drove him away.

The property stood abandoned when American consul Edward Thompson bought the house and the Chichén Itzá ruins for under $100 at the turn of the century just so he could explore the ruins. He made some daring dives into the cenote and set up a dredging operation to discover its secrets. The Mexican government became suspicious and accused him of hauling priceless treasures out of the site and sending them to the United States under protection of his diplomatic title — the government seized Thompson's holdings. Eventually, the Hacienda was turned over to Carnegie Institute when they began their archaeological investigations.

The rooms occupy cottages built for the Carnegie staff, for whom the pool was added as well. The quarters are simple but spacious and comfortable. Each has a shower-only bath and a covered terrace, and some come with small refrigerators. Except in the hottest and most humid period of the year, the ceiling fans usually do an adequate job of relieving the heat.

The meals are ample and can include some interesting Yucatecan specialties, but the food is generally standard tourist fare. Guests dine at the main *casa* on an outside terrace or in an interior dining room, depending on the weather. The public areas, which feature antiques, are more handsome than the rooms but nearly as modest.

The real attraction is beyond the Hacienda's botanical garden, where a gate provides quick access to the ruins. The history-filled Hacienda Chichén puts you in the midst of, and in the mood for, Mexico's most famous ancient city.

Mayaland

Chichén Itzá, Yucatán
(985) 1-01-28 or 1-00-70
Fax: (985) 1-01-29
Reservations:
800-235-4079

> **A bit of polish in the Yucatán jungle**

Accommodations: 55 rooms and 50 bungalows. **High-season rates:** Standard rooms $134, bungalows $184, junior suites $197, King Jacuzzi $215. **Low-season rates:** Standard rooms $108, bungalows $159, junior suites $181, King Jacuzzi $200. **Payment:** Major credit cards. **Children:** Up to 2 children under 12 free in room with parents. **Recreation:** Swimming pools.

➤ **In the nearby Balankanche Caves, sealed for almost a thousand years, you can see ancient offerings to the rain god in a domed throne room and at the edge of a pond populated by blind fish and shrimp.**

Mayaland is the most luxurious and pricey of the archaeological hotels in Chichén Itzá, full of colonial atmosphere inside and tropical splendor outside in the exotic gardens.

The spacious standard rooms in the main lodge have air conditioning and private balconies, but the more expensive rustic bungalows spread around the garden grounds outclass these quarters in character. These large, thatched *cabañas* in the oval shape of Mayan huts have Mayan glyphs carved on the wooden doors and window frames as well as on the chairs and tables. Tastefully decorated with handsome bedspreads, all are now air-conditioned and have TVs, mini-bars, and outside terraces. Some even come with bathtub Jacuzzis. The bungalows in the front area of the hotel, near the main pool and restaurants, have the advantage of being set in the lush tropical gardens, filled with the sounds of birds in the morning. The disadvantage is that tour buses park nearby, and during the day, they seem to run their motors endlessly. After 5 P.M., quiet returns. Recently we stayed in one of these very comfortable and commodious front bungalows, spent our days at the ruins, avoiding the running bus motors, and were perfectly content. The newer area behind the main pool and restaurants contains additional bungalows, with another pool. These tend to be quieter (except for some highway noise), but because of the more open setting, they lack the tropical flavor and bird life of the front bungalows.

From the main entrance of the Mayaland there is a dramatic view of the Caracol at the ruins of Chichén Itzá. The ruins themselves are easily accessible, only a few minutes' walk away. When you return from the grand site, relax by the large pool while you enjoy a drink or meal, or wander through the lovely gardens. The five restaurants offer plenty of variety but often without much verve. One notable exception is the Mexican buffet, offered in the evening in the main restaurant, with its selection of interesting and flavorful fare. This is a better area to feed the soul anyway, taking in the accomplishments of the sophisticated society that flourished a thousand years ago. The Mayaland allows you to do that in a most attractive setting with a good measure of modern comforts and abundance.

Uxmal

Hacienda Uxmal

Uxmal, Yucatán
(99) 28-08-40
Fax: (99) 25-00-87
Reservations:
800-235-4079

The class act in the land of the Maya

Accommodations: 80 rooms and suites. **Rates:** Rooms $134, suites $190. **Payment:** Major credit cards. **Recreation:** Swimming pool.

➤ **Archaeologists say Uxmal's magnificent architecture rivals the finest of ancient Greece and Rome. The Hacienda Uxmal isn't that grand, but you'll appreciate its tasteful comfort after a day of doing monuments.**

Of all the inns at archaeological sites, the Hacienda Uxmal is the most polished and pretty. If you're dedicated to the creature comforts, you might want to use it as your main base for exploring the Yucatán.

Formerly a baronial private estate, the Hacienda has been converted to a hotel over the last few decades. Very little character was lost in the transition. Spanish antiques grace the public areas, under high, beamed ceilings reflecting a stately but natural warmth. The dining room is elegantly casual, although the cooking is more of the latter than the former.

The 80 guest chambers are attractively decorated but simply furnished, in keeping with the spirit of the place. Each has a ceiling fan and many also enjoy air conditioning. All open onto a verandah overlooking a magnificent garden and a lovely swimming pool. The two suites are especially handsome and spacious.

The ruins are directly across the street, easily accessible in the early morning before the sun gets too hot and again in the evening for the dramatic sound-and-light show. In between, you can visit other Mayan sites or simply relax in the hospitable enchantment of the Hacienda Uxmal. Either way, you'll relish it as a classy headquarters.

Copper Canyon

Best Romantic Hideaway

Best Adventure Retreat

The five major *barrancas* of Copper Canyon are one and a half times deeper than the Grand Canyon at points, and if strung together, four times longer. It's a spectacular region — covering 25,000 square miles — but still largely undiscovered by American travelers. The total number of visitors in a year barely equals a summer week's tally at the Grand Canyon.

A part of the seclusion is due to access. Until 1961, mules provided the only way in and out. Now the Chihuahua-Pacifico Railroad handles the transportation in moderate comfort, hauling passengers eastward from the town of Los Mochis or westward from the city of Chihuahua. Conceived almost a hundred years before its completion and in construction half of that time, the rail line traverses the rugged Sierra Madres into the canyonlands, dropping from mountain pine forests into tropical valleys. An engineering marvel, it crosses 39 bridges and burrows through 86 tunnels, one of them almost 6,000 feet in length.

For some people, the 13-hour train trip provides an adequate introduction to the natural splendor. Generally, they fly from Tucson to Los Mochis and catch the train early the next morning, taking the eastward route to ensure they pass through the canyon during daylight hours. The rail journey is inexpensive and the views are breathtaking for a part of the long day, but you miss the opportunity to really explore what you've come so far to see. To absorb the scenery and appreciate the majestic spirit of the canyon country, you need to stop along the way and spend at least a few days.

If you do, you can hike incredible trails, enjoy dramatic van excursions, or go horseback riding along the ridge of the chasm. You can walk to a waterfall, take a strenuous trek to hot springs at the bottom of a gorge, or go birding. You can poke in abandoned silver mines or probe the "Lost Cathedral," a 400-year-old Jesuit mission.

Most important, you'll get a glimpse of the culture of the reclusive Tarahumara Indians, who live in caves and simple cabins in the canyons without electricity or other modern conveniences. Though wary of outsiders and their ways, they make and sell crafts to supplement a living earned from herding goats and sheep.

Whatever your interests, you won't be disappointed in a stayover as long as your hotel takes an organized approach to exploring the area. You can manage on your own at places that provide little more than lodging, food, and advice, but you probably won't make optimum use of your time and you may overlook some special experiences. The two hotels we recommend excel at guiding guests from the planning stage of a trip through their last night in Mexico.

Copper Canyon Riverside Lodge

Batopilas, Chihuahua
(145) 6-06-32
Reservations and information:
Copper Canyon Lodges
810-340-7230
800-776-3942
Fax: 810-340-7212

| A wildly enchanting hacienda inn at the canyon bottom |

Accommodations: 14 rooms. **High-season rates:** $2,250 for 8 days, per person, double occupancy; $2,525 for 11 days, per person, double occupancy; day rate $250 per person. **Low-season rates:** $970 for 8 days, per person, double occupancy; $1,219 for 11 days per person, double occupancy; day rate $125 per person. **Minimum stay:** 3 nights. **Included:** Breakfast, lunch, dinner, transportation from Chihuahua City and back, days spent at the Sierra Lodge (see below), all guided excursions, tax. Day rate does not include round-trip transportation from Chihuahua City. **Payment:** MasterCard, Visa. **Recreation:** Hiking. **Closed:** June.

➤ **The eleven-day package, covering train transportation from Chihuahua on both ends of the trip, costs little more than the standard eight-day itinerary, making this quite a bargain. Both packages usually split the time between the two lodges, but you can opt for just one. And if you only have a few days, there are day rates available, but on a limited basis.**

The dream of Detroit businessman Skip McWilliams, who loves Copper Canyon, the Riverside Lodge is an extravagant escape from everyday life. You spend your nights in an ornately restored 19th-century adobe hacienda, a showcase of Victorian opulence, and spend your days surrounded by the natural magnificence at the bottom of the canyon. The combination of environments — so completely different but both so separately compelling — leaves the senses reeling.

The excitement starts with the train trip to Creel and a couple of nights at the Sierra Lodge, a necessary part of the package, but it really picks up steam when you leave the canyon rim and head precipitously downward in a van. At a pace of less than a thousand feet per hour, you descend more than a mile along a narrow, rocky road full of spine-tingling vistas. The journey ends at Batopilas, a one-street tropical town that has lived at a lazy pace since its boom days as a silver-mining center a century ago.

Among many possible adventures in the canyon, you can poke around ruins from the village's glory years, but it may seem redundant since you're staying in the best of them. Behind the three-foot-thick walls, the Riverside Lodge wanders aimlessly through antique-filled parlors, a salon with a mural ceiling, private patios shaded by bougainvillea and mango trees, garden fountains, and tiled domes. The walls are hand-stenciled, and even some of the elegant old-fashioned bath fixtures are elaborately painted. You dwell in sumptuous style, but with only kerosene lamps for lighting in the guest rooms and no phones closer than eight hours away.

Candles provide illumination in the dining room in the evening, when the tables are set with fine linen and china. The kitchen can suffer from unavoidable supply problems, but it does an admirable job considering the situation.

Like the cooks, everyone at the Riverside Lodge strives to please. That adds to the allure, but the inn would remain a great hideaway even if the staff suddenly turned to stone. The hacienda and its setting are the essence of escape. One writer, who said the Riverside Lodge must have been inspired by "the bordellos of yesteryear," also claimed that "the cozy and alluring property might be the most enticing little inn in all of Mexico."

Copper Canyon Sierra Lodge

Creel, Chihuahua
Reservations and information:
Copper Canyon Lodges
810-340-7230
800-776-3942
Fax: 810-340-7212

A peaceful retreat in the woods

Accommodations: 18 rooms. **Rates:** Same as the Riverside Lodge. **Miminum stay:** One night. **Included:** Breakfast, lunch, dinner, transportation from the train station and back, all guided excursions, tax. **Payment:** MasterCard, Visa. **Recreation:** Hiking. **Closed:** June.

➤ **If Sierra Lodge is booked, the best alternatives are near Divisadero: The stylish new El Mirador Barrancas (681-5-70-46 in Los Mochis) and the older Cabañas Divisadero-Barrancas (14- 15-11-99 in Chihuahua).**

A country cousin of the Riverside Lodge, under the same owner-ship, the Sierra Lodge is more rustic in its appeal but also more convenient for travelers with limited time. The staff meets you at the train station in Creel, drives you a dozen miles out of town to a scenic spot on Tarahumara land, and spends the next couple of days escorting you around the area on hiking and van tours. It's an intensive immersion course in the Copper Canyon, conducted with a sure sense of place.

The inn's intimacy with its environment is reflected in the log-cabin architecture, a perfect fit with the pine scents in the air and the mountain creek that ambles by the front door. The hot-water plumbing is up-to-date in the private baths, but the lighting in the rooms comes from kerosene lamps and the heating from wood stoves. It's a return to nature in comfortably appropriate rather than primitive ways.

The cook prepares good tortillas and soups from scratch, and most of the Mexican home cooking is as simple as the family-style service. The hearty fare maintains your energy for exploring, its main function, and the pre-dinner margaritas provide plenty of spice for most people.

Skip McWilliams's Sierra Lodge introduces guests to the Copper Canyon with guileless authenticity. Combine it with a stay at the Riverside Lodge for an unforgettable, once-in-a-lifetime experience, or do it alone for a quicker but still quintessential getaway.

Cuernavaca and Tepoztlán

Best Romantic Hideaway

Best Recreational Resort or Spa

Best Intimate and Affordable Inns

An hour and a half from Mexico City, Cuernavaca has been a getaway for residents of the nearby metropolis since it was the Aztec capital of Tenochtitlán. Moctezuma I maintained a winter hideaway in the area a half-century before the Spanish arrived, and Cortés followed suit, building a palace that's now a museum. Maximilian fled here during his brief rule to elude the political intrigues of his subjects, and more recently, the Shah of Iran did the same, retreating here in exile. They came for escape and rest, still the primary lures of Cuernavaca. And half an hour away, tucked below craggy mountains and lush with vegetation, is the village of Tepoztlán, a retreat for the capital's artists and intelligentsia.

The Main Attractions

Tropical Ease

Cuernavaca is in a subtropical valley about 2,000 feet lower than Mexico City. Flowers and trees bloom year-round in the ideal climate, producing some of the most magnificent gardens in Mexico. You won't see much of the brilliant foliage today, though, if you are just passing through the increasingly industrial town. Except for the delightful nearby village of Tepoztlán, most of the beauty is hidden away behind the walls of hotels and private residences, places of secluded splendor for owners and guests only.

You have to stay at one of the hotels or dine at their restaurants to enjoy the radiant gardens. Both are enticing pleasures in Cuernavaca and Tepoztlán, where the accommodations and the cooking are on an elevated level for Mexico. You may not find much to do beyond relaxing at a pool and eating, but you won't find many prettier settings for either pastime.

Day Trips

Mexico City and Taxco, described in other chapters, are about equal distances in opposite directions, a little too far for a regular commute but an easy excursion for shopping or sightseeing. The ruins of the ancient city of Xochicalco are closer, about 30 miles through the scenic valley to a dramatic hilltop site. The excavated area, complemented by a fine museum, is intriguing because of the Mayan influences.

Cuernavaca

Clarion Cuernavaca Racquet Club

Francisco Villa 100
Rancho Cortés
Cuernavaca, Morelos
(73) 11-24-00
Fax: (73) 17-54-83
Reservations:
Clarion Reservations
800-CLARION

A small inn in a parklike setting

Accommodations: 50 rooms and suites. **Rates:** Rooms $109, suites $141. **Payment:** Major credit cards. **Children:** Under 12, free in room with parents. **Smoking:** Nonsmoking rooms available. **Recreation:** Swimming pool, 9 tennis courts.

➤ **Water problems sometimes plague groundskeepers at the Cuernavaca Racquet Club. If you don't get your fill of flowers there, visit the Borda Gardens downtown, one of the few public places to admire the city's delightful foliage.**

The Cuernavaca Racquet Club is the most intimate tennis resort in Mexico. Built as a private estate in 1943, the country home and playground of a Swedish industrialist, the inn retains a genteel, homey air.

In its early years, the hotel established a reputation as a retreat for the "beautiful people." The reality was much different by the 1980s, when the Calinda hotel organization acquired the property. Aware of both its shortcomings and its promise, the company is intent on orchestrating a comeback.

The estate occupies a hillock about three miles north of the *zócalo* in a quiet residential neighborhood and it serves as a tennis club for the local community. One of Calinda's first and most visible improvements was to move the reception area from a small gatehouse just inside the wrought-iron entryway up to the magnificent hillside hacienda. The centerpiece of the property, the old mansion provides a much warmer and more elegant introduction to the Racquet Club. The hacienda and its lovely central courtyard hold a restaurant, bar, and a few meeting rooms and suites, all surrounded by red tile terraces.

Nearby are nine well-maintained Laykold tennis courts — four of them lighted — where tennis whites are mandatory. The facilities include a clubhouse with a sauna and a bar, but no pro services. After a few sets on the courts, you may be ready for a dip in the heated pool. Just behind the hacienda, it's encircled by a stone deck and grassy areas for lounging.

Guests can choose between two restaurants that are more different in setting than in cuisine. Both serve solid Mexican and Continental fare, El Patio inside the hacienda and La Terraza from a terrace above the pool. Nearby, the aptly named La Cava bar has thick stone walls and a heavy-beamed ceiling that create a cozy grotto for pre-dinner cocktails.

The preferred quarters here are the 33 suites in a low-rise wing that runs from the hacienda area down the hill to the entrance. Overlooking the tennis courts and the grounds, the quarters are spacious and attractive, and for their comforts they are quite a bargain. Each suite has a full sitting area with a fireplace, a built-in *banco* day bed, satellite TV, phone, mini-bar, and an adjoining patio or balcony. The bedroom comes with a king-size bed or two twins, and the large bathroom brims with hand-painted Mexican tile.

The Cuernavaca Racquet Club is a serene retreat for those to whom tennis is truly a game of love.

Hacienda Cocoyoc

Apartado Postal 300
Cuautla, Morelos
(735) 6-22-11
Fax: (735) 6-12-12
Reservations:
800-537-8483

> **A historic estate restored to a resort**

Accommodations: 292 rooms and suites. **Rates:** Standard rooms $91, superior rooms $122, deluxe rooms $130, suites $165. **Children:** Up to two 12 and under, in room with parents. **Payment:** Major credit cards. **Recreation:** 3 swimming pools, golf (9 holes), 3 tennis courts, horseback riding.

➤ **In addition to its own moderately challenging 9-hole golf course, Hacienda Cocoyoc gives its guests access to an 18-hole championship course a shuttle ride away. If you're feeling less active, lounge around one of the three pools, each of which is designated in busy periods for adults, families, or children.**

The Hacienda Cocoyoc boasts a proud history, evident in various ways throughout the 22-acre grounds. According to legend, the area was the birthplace of Quetzalcoatl, the plumed serpent god. We know for sure that Cortés built a home on the site in 1520, a gift for the daughter of Aztec Emperor Montezuma II as a token of his love. One of the maiden's 17th-century descendents sold the property to a sugar cane baron, and for nearly 200 years it flourished as a plantation and sugar mill. Revolutionaries burned the estate in the early 20th century and it lay in ruins until 1957, when the late Paulino Rivera Torres turned it into one of Mexico's loveliest resort retreats.

A real "country" club, the Hacienda is about 30 minutes east of Cuernavaca by car. The recreational facilities aren't world class, but they will keep all but the most ardent enthusiasts entertained. Every weekend, droves of golfers, tennis players, equestrians, and their children descend on the resort from Mexico City, an hour and a half away. It can get a little chaotic then, but on weekdays during much of the year you may feel that you and the Aztec spirits are almost the only ones in residence.

The manicured grounds are memorable, mixing nature's bounty with stately architecture. Noble trees shade lawns sprinkled with bougainvillea, century plants, flame red poincianas, and vines. Stone, brick, and wrought iron accent restored archways, colonnades, plazas, courtyards, and majestic aqueducts built to water the sugar cane. At every turn you encounter intimate nooks, bubbling fountains, and brilliant blossoms. The most soothing spot is the 16th-century chapel courtyard behind the hacienda, where ancient gnarled trees have fused with the church's walls.

Accommodations are spread throughout the core of the estate in handsome buildings of assorted vintages. There are almost as many variations to the layout and furnishings as there are rooms. Most are pleasant Spanish colonial quarters, but they aren't as grand as the grounds.

Generally guests can expect tile floors, phones, simple Mexican furnishings of heavy, dark wood, and large bathrooms. Most rooms have ceiling fans, the only climate control even remotely desirable in the temperate mountain climate. If you're lucky, you might get a private *terraza*, a distinctive octagonal room, a canopied four-poster bed, or even a small private wading pool. The Hacienda Cocoyoc recently went high tech with the addition of some of the most up-to-date spa and fitness facilities in Mexico. The gym offers Nautilus equipment and a jogging track, but the spa facilities are the real attraction. Here you can indulge in steam, sauna, Jacuzzis, and several types of exotic showers and hydromassages, as well as Swedish massages, seaweed baths, and mud baths.

At least three restaurants are always open, expanding to six when the room count is up. There are a couple of all-day coffee shops, a grill, a Mexican café, and a Continental restaurant. During busy times, the most elegant dining room, La Chispa, is reserved for adults only. Bars almost outnumber the restaurants and provide a variety of moods ranging from mellow to the energetic weekend disco in a converted sugar mill.

The Hacienda Cocoyoc isn't a fully polished resort, and the addition of the spa facilities may soon transform it. But it remains a relaxing retreat steeped in Mexican history. Cortés would still enjoy it as an escape from Mexico City, and even Quetzalcoatl would be proud of its vibrant plumage.

Las Mañanitas

Ricardo Linares 107
Cuernavaca, Morelos
(73) 14-14-66 and 12-46-46
Fax: (73) 18-36-72

**A Relais & Châteaux inn
that wins all accolades**

Accommodations: 22 rooms and suites. **Rates:** Standard rooms $128, terrace suites $174, *cabaña* suites $180, patio suites $258, garden suites $296, Mañanitas Suite $404. **Payment:** American Express. **Recreation:** Swimming pool.

➤ **For breakfast, try the chilaquiles, a popular Mexican dish that combines bits of leftover tortillas with chicken, cheese, and a piquant red or green sauce. Las Mañanitas's version is superb, as good as we've ever had in 30 years of travel in the country.**

The main courtyard at Las Mañanitas is capable of casting a spell over the most jaded of travelers. An idyllic image of refined relaxation, it mixes emerald lawns with stately palms and lilting fountains with lyrical Zuniga sculptures. Peacocks strut and egrets preen, and bougainvillea splashes painterly swaths across walls and windows. Tables of convivial lunch patrons closing business deals and celebrating birthdays spill off the terraces of the pink hacienda onto the grass. Time seems to stand still.

The Continental food being served isn't quite as special as the setting, but it is some of the best you can find in a Mexican hotel. On weekend and holiday afternoons, fashionable couples and families from nearby Mexico City flock to the restaurant. Lunches become major social occasions that can run on merrily for hours.

A meal alone is enough to infatuate anyone with Las Mañanitas, but spending the night is an even greater treat. A second courtyard, equally enchanting, is the exclusive province of overnight guests. Once inside, you might be willing to accept permanent exile.

A heated swimming pool, often adorned with flamingos, sits near the rooms at one end of a rolling lawn. At the other end, a waterfall trickles into a quiet pond designed in the simple but dramatic fashion of the finest Japanese gardens. Cranes and swans dart with more egrets and peacocks, two of them albino. A bubbling fountain, sculpted topiaries, and more Zunigas grace the grounds.

Rooms — and even hallways — in the vintage hacienda are fashioned with the same tasteful flair. The second-floor standard rooms, the only ones that lack balconies or patios, are ample quarters, but the truly special suites are worth their premium in price.

An additional 16 rooms are being planned for the near future, along with a second pool, but all the current accommodations at least feature handsome Mexican furnishings, antiques in some cases dating back hundreds of years. The masonry and woodwork are exquisite on the glazed red tile floors, the hand-painted Mexican tiles, and hand-hewn doors, corbels, and *vigas*. While some of the architectural elements are massive, the large, airy spaces keep proportions balanced. Every room has a phone, thick pile rugs, twin beds often combined into a king under one carved headboard, and an attractive bath, usually with a tub and a shower. Patio and garden suites enjoy tile-trimmed fireplaces with carved mantels.

Garden suite baths are larger than some Manhattan hotel rooms. Topped by a light-filled cupola, they are actually three connected rooms — a closet and dressing area, an outer vanity and storage area, and another space holding the tub, shower, water closet, and second sink. At the opposite end of the suites, the flower-rimmed stone terraces could accommodate a chamber orchestra for cocktails. Furnished for dining as well as for lounging, the balconies look over the pool to the enclosed gardens.

Massive stone and brick walls surround Las Mañanitas, insulating the inn from the congestion of Cuernavaca. Occasionally the sound of cars and buses will remind you that there is a world beyond, but most of the time your private preserve engrosses your senses completely, transporting you to a world you won't want to leave.

Posada María Cristina

Calle Juárez 300
Cuernavaca, Morelos
(73) 18-57-67
Fax: (73) 12-91-26

A small, serene inn near the bustling center

Accommodations: 18 rooms and suites. **Rates:** Rooms $109, junior suites $176, *cabaña* suites $186. **Payment:** MasterCard and Visa accepted for an additional 5% surcharge. **Recreation:** Swimming pool.

➤ **Posada María Cristina is well located for sightseeing in Cuernavaca. A fine Diego Rivera mural is just a couple of blocks away in Cortés's old palace and the fabulous home and art museum of Robert Brady as well as the impressive 16th-century cathedral are within walking distance, too.**

The serene Posada María Cristina is just two blocks from the bustling center of urban Cuernavaca, but once you step inside the vine-covered walls of the compound you enter a different world. Great arches and a red tile roof crown the colonial-style hacienda that sits on the top of a slight hill, overlooking a courtyard brimming with flowers and greenery. While the garden is not up to the caliber of Las Mañanitas, you get a modest facsimile at a modest rate.

The small reception area and La Casona, the gardenfront restaurant, are in the hacienda, and the guest quarters are attached, in two compatible additions to the original building. The pretty regular rooms have high ceilings, tile floors, blond Mexican wood furniture, bright bedspreads and rugs, a phone, TV, and usually a double and a twin bed or two doubles. The large bathrooms are decorated with Mexican tile. The standard rooms are often discounted during the week.

The junior suites contain a small second room that holds an equally small double bed, but they are similar to the regular rooms otherwise. The cabaña suites enjoy more light than the other chambers and a fireplace, a terrace, and the best garden views — though the bathrooms are more conventional than in the less expensive quarters.

The large swimming pool is at the lower end of the sloping lawn, set apart behind its own walls, shaded by palms and rimmed by lush vegetation. The adjoining Las Palapas Restaurant looks more like Cancún than Cuernavaca, but it's a pleasant setting for a casual meal. The more traditional La Casona is a tranquil spot for dining.

The staff speak little English, but they welcome guests from the States warmly. While you're within the walls of the Posada, you'll find a friendly and lovely respite from the commotion of the city outside.

Tepoztlán

Posada del Tepozteco

Paraiso 3
Tepoztlán, Morelos
(739) 5-00-10
Fax: (739) 5-03-23

> **An intimate inn with grand views and real comfort**

Accommodations: 18 rooms and suites. **Rates:** Rooms $77–$90, junior suites $99, suites $120. **Included:** Breakfast and tax. **Reservations:** For weekends and holidays, reserve months in advance. **Payment:** Master Card and Visa. **Children:** 12 and under, free in room with parents. **Recreation:** 2 swimming pools, 1 paddle tennis court, playground with swings and trampoline.

➤   **The Saturday and Sunday markets, like everything else in this tiny village, seductively attract two very different communities — the traditional Nahuatl farmers and residents and the cosmopolitan weekenders. Stalls brim over with fruits and vegetables as well as a plentiful assortment of handcrafts, from hand-painted children's furniture to beautiful silver jewelry.**

The village of Tepoztlán is a wonderful place for a retreat. With just a few streets, the town quickly becomes familiar, an intriguing extension of your stay at the Posada. The residents, mostly farmers, have lived off this land for hundreds of years. Atop the imposing hill called El Tepozteco, on the edge of town, are the ruins of an Aztec temple, reminder of their ancestors who lived here before the Spanish conquest. In more recent decades others have joined them in this lovely corner of the world — artists, writers, and New Age meditators. Their arrival has brought sophisticated restaurants next to cafés with Mexican home cooking, galleries and granola shops next to feed stores, making the village a popular weekend destination with both Mexicans and foreigners. When the weekend excitement is over, there is little to do except climb El Tepozteco or go horseback riding. You might visit the sights in Cuernavaca, but better yet, take a yoga class and relax.

On a hillside overlooking the village and the rugged hills encircling it, the Posada del Tepozteco takes full advantage of its setting. Cascading garden terraces, shaded by orange and plum trees and scented by jasmine, offer a full view of the mesmerizing scenery.

Many windows share parts of these views, smaller ones may simply frame the 16th-century church dome while balconies open to the daily miracle of the sun rising over the hills. Add the considerable comforts of the Posada to its setting and you'll never want to leave, although the main square and market are only a few blocks down a cobblestone lane.

The Posada del Tepozteco started out as a family retreat in the 1940s. Owned by the same family today, the original vine-covered stone villa houses the reception area, bar, and restaurant for the inn. Its cozy decor is enhanced by wooden beams, fireplaces in the bar and restaurant and, above all, by watercolors of local scenes by Señora Marta Villaseñor. Her English-speaking son, Alejandro Camarena Villaseñor, is the welcoming manager of the inn as well as the architect of its newer additions.

The standard rooms are found in the original villa and its earliest additions; these rooms vary quite a bit, although all are simply decorated and only a few have their own terraces. The oldest rooms, with their wooden floors, paneled doors, barrel vaulted ceilings, and hand-painted tile baths, are among the most expensive of these rooms. Our favorites are the junior suites and suites in the new wings, separated from the villa by patios and garden terraces. These large and airy quarters have good views, especially those above the garden level, and each has some distinctive architectural feature, whether a brick vaulted ceiling, an archway or molded adobe wall, or two balconies. The bedrooms have wooden beams, a desk area, thickly-loomed bedspreads and curtains, and a fine balcony. All the bathrooms have wood-beamed ceilings and a skylight or special window to let in the sunshine; suites with king-size beds also have Jacuzzi tubs. All rooms have a phone and TV.

The two garden pools, one heated, are joined by a snack bar in the warmer spring and summer seasons, but in other seasons you can order drinks and snacks from the staff to be served poolside. A new addition in 2000 is a *temazcal,* or Mexican sweat lodge, along with an area set aside for massages. The restaurant is next to a fountain and terrace brilliant with bougainvillea. Although there are a few tables for dining on the terrace, the windows in the handsome restaurant afford views good enough to make you linger over your meal. And the traditional Mexican food, from a *huitlacoche* omelette at breakfast to the homemade mushroom soup and chicken *mole* later in the day, is worth lingering over.

The Posada del Tepozteco offers a lovely Mexican retreat from urban bustle and megaresort glitz.

Guadalajara and Lake Chapala

Best Hotel for Stylish Sophistication

Quinta Real Guadalajara, 262

Best Intimate and Affordable Inns

La Nueva Posada, 264
La Villa del Ensueño, 260
Quinta Quetzalcoatl, 267

Best Bargain for Mexican Character

Frances Hotel, 259

Best B&B or Budget Inn

Nido Hotel, 266

Best Places to Combine Business and Pleasure

Camino Real Guadalajara, 256
De Mendoza Hotel, 258

Guadalajara, Mexico's second largest city, is modern and middle class, as close to Phoenix, Arizona, in its style as to Mexico City. For Americans it's primarily a business and retirement destination, but the frequent air service also makes it accessible for a weekend break and a good spot to consider for a stopover on the way to other places.

The Main Attractions

The Metropolitan Plaza

In truth a series of plazas rather than one, this expansive pedestrian promenade is Guadalajara's clever and contemporary answer to downtown preservation. Cars use a tunnel below the broad boulevard, which is dressed with fountains and gardens and lined with the city's most important sights.

The arts take top billing among the attractions. Attend a performance at the Teatro Degollado or at least try to see the ornate interior, highlighted by a painting on the ceiling vault depicting passages from Dante's *Divine Comedy*. Even more extraordinary are the murals of José Clemente Orozco in the nearby Governor's Palace and Hospicio Cabañas. An internationally known artist dedicated to the values and aspirations of Mexico's 1910 revolution, Orozco did some of his most expressive work in Guadalajara, at the university as well as at the two sites along the Metropolitan Plaza.

Shopping

The variety of ways to shop in Guadalajara may be more impressive than any items you can buy. The immense traditional market, Mercado Libertad, is just a block off the Metropolitan Plaza. It's worth exploring, though the medium is definitely the message here.

For higher quality crafts and boutiques, head to Tlaquepaque, about half an hour south of downtown. Once a separate village, now absorbed by the city, it's famous for hand-painted pottery and hand-blown glass, usually well made despite designs that tend toward the cute and commonplace. The best time to visit is late afternoon, around 3:00 to 6:00, after the mariachi music has started on the central plaza, El Parian, and when the many boutiques ae open. Craft shops, art galleries, and fashionable boutiques extend for blocks in all directions from El Parian.

Some of the pottery you'll see in Tlaquepaque is from the nearby village of Tonalá, seven miles east, where you are likely to see the potters at work. Closer to downtown, at the entrance to Agua Azul Park, Instituto de la Artesania Jalisciense features a broad range of traditional crafts. The government-sponsored outlet displays work in museum fashion, but most of it is for sale.

If you prefer stateside shopping styles, go to the Plaza del Sol, the biggest mall in Latin America, on Avenida López Mateos at Mariano Otero. You may not be tempted to purchase much, but you'll find it a good introduction to the sociology of modern Mexico.

Lake Chapala

The shores of Lake Chapala, an hour south of Guadalajara's city limits, are a major retirement center for Americans and Canadians. Golf courses, bridge clubs, and even an American Legion chapter have been established, but the old fishing villages of Chapala and Ajijic retain a great deal of Mexican spunk.

Chapala is a pleasant town of tree-lined boulevards and scattered Victorian buildings. Quiet during the week, it gets lively on weekends, when Guadalajara residents stream in for an afternoon of boating or a leisurely lunch.

The upscale retirement communities of Chula Vista and La Floresta are just west of Chapala, on the road to Ajijic, a hamlet that has developed an unusual brand of rustic chic. Although limited in number, Ajijic's shops, restaurants, and inns are often imaginative and always fun.

Guadalajara

Camino Real Guadalajara

Avenida Vallarta 5005
Guadalajara, Jalisco
(3) 647-8000
Fax: (3) 6-47-67-81
Reservations:
Camino Real Hotels and Resorts
800-7-CAMINO (800-722-6466)

> **A business and family hotel in a secluded setting**

Accommodations: 205 rooms and suites. **Rates:** Deluxe rooms $200, Camino Real Club rooms $230, Camino Real Club executive rooms $320, 1-bedroom suites $350–$400, 2-bedroom suites $450–$650. **Included:** Continental breakfast and one hour of tennis. **Payment:** Major credit cards. **Children:** Under 18, free in room with parents. **Recreation:** 4 swimming pools, 1 tennis court.

➤ **Other than the four pools, recreation at the Camino Real is limited to a single lighted tennis court and a putting green. Golf courses and exercise facilities are a short drive away, however.**

The Camino Real enjoys an enviable parklike setting and acres of well-tended gardens, unusual for a city hotel. But this is Guadalajara, after all, where flowers and fountains abound even along the busiest thoroughfares. The hotel is on one of those bustling avenues, about a mile out from Minerva Circle, oriented toward its grounds.

The Camino Real chain is generally associated with artful midrise hotels. In this case, the architecture is low-rise and less dramatic. One- and two-story blocks of rooms sprawl around the property in an upscale motel fashion, often overlooking one of the four swimming pools. Lawns and stately old trees separate the buildings from each other but don't screen the room terraces for privacy.

All the accommodations are decorated in contemporary international style with a few Mexican touches. They come with two double beds or a king, air conditioning, carpeting, a telephone, satellite TV, a mini-bar, and a tub shower in the bath. The Real (Royal) Suite is truly named, having hosted the king and queen of Spain.

The restaurants and bars are grouped together near the entrance and the biggest of the pools. A breezy and bright café, La Huerta, serves casual fare all day and a big buffet brunch on Sunday. Crystal and leaded glass abound in Aquellos Tiempos, an elegant setting for Mexican and international specialties.

The Camino Real is an unpretentious and uncommon amalgam of city style and casual ease. It offers plenty, whether your vocation or your vacation brings you here.

De Mendoza Hotel

Venustiano Carranza 16
Guadalajara, Jalisco
(3) 613-4646
Fax: (3) 613-7310
Reservations:
Jarvinen Worldwide Hotels
800-876-5278
Fax: 213-461-7559

**A rejuvenated downtown
hotel close to the sights
and shops**

Accommodations: 110 rooms and junior suites. **Rates:** Rooms $90, suites $98.
Payment: Major credit cards. **Children:** Under 12, free in room with parents.
Recreation: Swimming pool.

➤   **The De Mendoza is a short walk from the Guadalajara Cathedral, the
city's main landmark. Begun in the 16th century and finished in the 17th, it
features an unusual but successful amalgam of architectural styles, including Gothic, Moorish, and even Byzantine.**

When we entered the De Mendoza Hotel on our last visit, we were
temporarily disoriented and then delighted. We had spent a night
here a number of years ago and remembered it as a modest place
with a fine downtown location. A recent renovation had transformed everything to match the locale.

The hotel's immediate neighborhood remains remarkably devoid
of inner-city chaos. It's an easy stroll to the Plaza Tapatia and Guadalajara's historic attractions. The heroic facade of the De Mendoza
looks similar to the colonial buildings nearby, but the hotel was
built only a couple of decades ago, on the site of a former convent.

The property's face-lift begins right inside the door. The elegant
appointments, colonial in inspiration, mix paintings from the past,
stone colonnaded windows, chandeliers, marble floors, and contemporary wood furnishings. The expanded lobby now holds a
comfortable sitting area, a reception desk, a concierge alcove, and
the all-day La Forja restaurant.

The dining area is separated from everything else by only a low
railing, keeping the whole space open and airy. The menu is international, mostly Continental with a few Mexican choices. For a
drink or a snack, the top-floor bar has good views of the city and
live dance music many nights.

A new heated swimming pool and waterfall fill most of the courtyard behind the lobby. Many of the rooms in the five-story building overlook the pool area, some from a small balcony. The regular doubles are standard in layout, but they are ample in size for two double beds and, like all the quarters, they come with air conditioning, mini-bars, and phones.

The junior suites were always spacious, but now they are as tasteful as they are large. A wooden screen divides them into sitting and sleeping areas, with a sofa, a table, and chairs on one side and two queen-size beds on the other. A large color TV sits on a central turntable so that it can be viewed easily from anywhere in the room. The bathrooms have been refitted with marble floors, big vanities, a large mirror, a tub, and a shower framed by an attractive wood arch.

We are often sad to see good budget hotels go upscale because they sometimes lose sight of what made them special in the first place. With the De Mendoza, just the opposite is occurring. The management identified the hotel's strengths and set out to reinforce them. It's a case in which gentrification is everyone's gain.

Frances Hotel

Maestranza 35
Guadalajara, Jalisco
(3) 613-1190
Fax: (3) 658-2831

> **The building dates from 1610, but everything else is slightly more modern**

Accommodations: 60 rooms. **Rates:** Rooms $49, suites $55. **Payment:** Major credit cards.

➤   **The colonnaded lobby of the Frances has a stained glass ceiling, marble floors, and a brass and crystal chandelier. A birdcage elevator carries guests at a most deliberate pace.**

The promotional literature calls the Frances Hotel "an elegant lady with a distinguished past." Indeed, the lady is within a couple of decades of her 400th birthday, so you need to forgive the fact that her elegance is somewhat faded.

She holds court from a prime downtown corner in Guadalajara, across from the 18th-century Governor's Palace and an easy walk from the city's other historic sights. The three-story atrium lobby with its crystal chandelier and gilded antique elevator is a jewel. The addition of a discreet bar and quiet music has made the lobby a wonderful place to linger. In a separate courtyard to one side of the lobby, reached through a wrought iron gate, is El Molino Rojo, the hotel's Mexican restaurant. Down the street, in an annex but, unfortunately, under some of the rooms, is Maxim's Disco Club.

No two accommodations are alike, their sizes and shapes varying with the old contours of the four-story building; those near the disco should definitely be avoided. The TV and the phone are usually the only contemporary appointments, though the simple wood furniture has a semimodern look. Some of the suites above the lobby wing come with rich blue velvet drapes, etched glass windows, and hardwood floors. The beds are always doubles or twins.

While the true elegance is limited, the Frances Hotel is definitely dignified for its rates. The old girl has a kind of stately character you'll never find at home.

La Villa del Ensueño

Florida 305
San Pedro Tlaquepaque, Jalisco
(3) 635-8792
Fax: (3) 659-6152
Reservations:
800-220-8689
Fax: 818-597-0637

| **Guadalajara's best new inn** |

Accommodations: 10 rooms and suites. **Rates:** Standard rooms $55–$65, deluxe rooms $75, 2-bedroom suites $90. **Included:** Breakfast. **Payment:** Major credit cards. **Smoking:** Permitted only in outside areas. **Recreation:** Swimming pool.

➤   **Near the inn are Tlaquepaque's many patio restaurants. The best is Sin Nombre (Madero 80, 635-4520), the restaurant "without name," but with considerable fame for its handsome garden setting, live traditional music, and upscale Mexican cuisine.**

Until this attractive bed-and-breakfast recently opened, there were no good places to stay in Tlaquepaque itself. Yet there are lots of reasons to be in Tlaquepaque, especially if you like to shop. Connected to busy downtown Guadalajara by bus and collective taxi, the restored historic center of town has a quieter, village ambience; a few of its streets are even closed to traffic and lined with outdoor cafés. A stay here enables you to explore Tlaquepaque and relax from the more rigorous sightseeing of Guadalajara.

In a renovated 150-year-old mansion, La Villa del Ensueño is an intimate inn with lots of Mexican character. An enclosing wall enhances the feeling of privacy within the mansion and patios; fountains and sculptures provide tranquil spots for reading. There's a pool, a bar for guest use, and a most helpful staff that can make sightseeing arrangements for you.

The rooms are smartly decorated with Mexican crafts and furnishings. The baths have hand-painted tiles. Most of the rooms overlook the garden and pool area, some have private patios and terraces. The accompanying breakfast includes fresh fruit and cereals as well as the usual coffee and pastries.

Quinta Real Guadalajara

Avenida México 2727
Guadalajara, Jalisco
(3) 615-0000
Fax: (3) 630-1797
Reservations:
Quinta Real
800-445-4565

One of the finest hotels in Mexico

Accommodations: 78 suites. **Rates:** Master suites $220, grand class suites $240, Presidential Suite $860. **Payment:** Major credit cards. **Children:** Under 16, free in room with parents. **Recreation:** Swimming pool.

➤ **The Quinta Real prides itself on personalized service. Many of the staff have a better command of English than the average American high school student.**

A handful of Mexican hotels achieve international elegance. Even fewer have the confidence to attain it with indigenous architecture, decor, cuisine, and character. The Quinta Real's visionary Mexican owners have taken their country's finest features, sprinkled in a healthy dose of worldly savvy, and created a hotel that sings with sophistication.

The food is some of the best overall in the nation and is certainly a model for Mexican hotels. Like much of the superior cooking throughout the world today, the fare at the Quinta Real is inspired by traditional regional dishes and fresh ingredients, but is prepared with classic techniques and talent.

The *alta cucina* (high cooking) menu items are as different from a fast-food taco as *foie gras* is from french fries. Even breakfast, a culinary wasteland in most hotels, is good cause to roll out of bed. Fresh juices might include mango and papaya as well as orange. Eggs come in a range of tantalizing combinations — layered with spinach in a *torta*, scrambled with peas, chiles, and Gruyère, or poached with anchovies and watercress.

Lunch and dinner are equally inventive. For an appetizer, try the creamy cilantro soup sprinkled with walnuts and *nopalitos rellenos* — small cactus pads stuffed with shrimp. The entrées might include a superb chicken *mole* that pairs a complex version of Mexico's famous chile-chocolate sauce with a tender boneless chicken breast. Several preparations of fresh fish are always offered. For an unusual variation, when it's available, try the grilled fillet served chilled with more *nopalitos* and cilantro.

The bread, breadsticks, and crackers, all baked fresh, are so tempting it would be easy to fill up on them alone. Even usually mundane side dishes are standouts. French chef Joel Robuchon gained fame for deifying the lowly mashed potato. The Quinta Real kitchen is well on its way to doing the same thing with refried beans, subtly perfect in texture and flavor.

Patrons can sit in the handsome interior dining rooms or on a more casual terrace. The terrace is in an intimate courtyard, a soothing oasis in bustling Guadalajara, replete with a trickling waterfall, a small pool, and a goldfish pond.

The courtyard divides two wings of guest suites. The low- and mid-rise buildings are meticulously inlaid with multihued stone and accented with small wrought-iron balconies, brick trim, and a tangle of clinging ivy. Although the structures look centuries old, they date only from 1986.

All of the suites are minor masterpieces, generally unusual in layout, with a sitting area and fireplace separated from the bedroom by a columned stone arch and a couple of steps. As in the public areas, the decor emphasizes stellar craftsmanship. Supple leather couches and chairs are combined with hand-painted *trasteros* from Michoacán and glass-topped desks with hefty carved stone bases. The beds are kings or two doubles, and a TV, a phone, plush robes, and carpeting are standard. The bathrooms invite lingering. Finished in marble, brass, and stone, the oversize chambers have an equally oversize soaking tub, shower, and vanity. Grand class suites come with a Jacuzzi tub.

If you are traveling with a group or just have an urge to splurge, the three-bedroom, two-level Presidential Suite shames the White House. It faces the courtyard, as the most desirable rooms do. Try to avoid the ones on the outside, where the views are less tranquil.

Business travelers account for a high percentage of the guests at the Quinta Real. The hotel is well located for getting around Guadalajara, just west of downtown a little beyond the Minerva Circle, at the edge of an upscale residential neighborhood.

This was the first of several Quinta Reals now operating in Mexico, and it remains the overall standard setter in the elite collection. It's a joy to experience, thoroughly Mexican and graciously worldly at the same time.

Lake Chapala

La Nueva Posada

Donato Guerra 9
Apartado Postal 30
Ajijic, Jalisco
(376) 6-14-44
Fax: (376) 6-20-49

| A budget inn with elegance |

Accommodations: 17 junior suites. **Rates:** $45–$65. **Included:** Full breakfast. **Payment:** MasterCard, Visa. **Recreation:** Swimming pool, access to horseback riding and nearby golf and tennis.

➤ **The Eager family's Mexican in-laws often provide the evening entertainment. From mariachi to norteño, you can count on lively dance music, but the crowd is more sedate than at the old Posada, where evenings got a little raucous.**

From 1977 to 1990, the picturesque Posada Ajijic was a fixture in the center of the quiet lakefront village of Ajijic. The hotel and bar were the liveliest spots in town, attracting a fascinating mix of young residents, American retirees, expatriate artists, budget tourists, and knowledgeable travelers looking for earthy local character. All were welcomed warmly by Morley and Judy Eager, the Canadian hosts, and by their sons, Mike and Mark.

After one too many hassles with the landlord, the Eagers decided it was time to move to their own property, which they named La Nueva Posada, on the edge of the village. The organic funkiness of the original has been replaced with classy comfort, and the cramped camaraderie has given way to expansive ebullience. Guests still get the same down-home hospitality and reasonable rates, but their digs have gone uptown.

The new Posada sits on the shore of Lake Chapala, about a hundred yards back from the water. If we hadn't seen it under construction, we wouldn't have guessed that the three-story stucco building was vintage 1990. Designed mostly by son Mike, the hotel has an antique look reinforced by stone accents, airy cupolas, and colonial brick arches and trim.

In contrast with the original Posada's tiny anteroom reception area, the new lobby is large, full of light, and crowned by a dramatic winding stone stairway. Everywhere you look, the interior is awash in color, with pink stucco walls and arches, floral arrangements, and potted plants.

The bar and restaurant are just beyond the lobby, facing the lovely garden and lake. La Corona serves up plenty of *cerveza* in a casual *equipale*-filled space; at night it features live mariachi music. The restaurant, La Rusa, offers an atmosphere of informal elegance and a Continental and Mexican menu to match, but for the popular Sunday brunch or a leisurely afternoon lunch, the garden terrace is the place to dine. A hearty breakfast is included in the rates.

Though the rooms are priced much the same, they vary in size and situation. Our first choices would be any of the third-floor rooms that enjoy lake views. Our second choices would be the second-floor rooms with views. All these rooms have balconies. Those on the second-floor are especially narrow, but the sitting area is arranged so that it becomes an extension of the terrace when the sliding glass doors are open wide. If these quarters are taken, the ones by the pool are another good option. Most of the rooms come with two double beds and all feature large marble bathrooms.

Though the Posada is *nueva*, its character is not. With the Eagers in charge, it should continue to be one of the friendliest and most delightful spots in Mexico to rest and refuel.

Nido Hotel

Avenida Madero 202
Chapala, Jalisco
(376) 5-21-16
Fax: same as phone

> **A budget hotel with a lot of local character**

Accommodations: 31 rooms. **Rates:** $24–$26. **Payment:** MasterCard, Visa. **Recreation:** Swimming pool.

➤ **If you're eating out in Chapala, try Cazadores; in a former mansion, it overlooks the lake. Mariachi music enlivens the mood on most weekends.**

If easygoing Chapala had any activity, the Nido would be in the middle of it. The vaguely colonial red brick building sits on the broad main avenue about a block from both the lake and the *zócalo.* Attractively low-key and a little frayed at the edges, the Nido mirrors the spirit of the village.

One of Chapala's favorite restaurants is found in the Nido's skylighted lobby, which rises two stories to the top of the building. It's a basic but perky spot with a red tile floor, potted plants, and plain wood furnishings. The hotel kitchen serves simple, ample fare all day to natives and the many American retirees in the area. The bar, decorated with only a fishing net, faces out from the lobby, toward the street.

The rock-bottom rates include the use of a modest-size swimming pool surrounded by a concrete deck and a few lounge chairs. Many of the rooms have a view of this courtyard area, while others overlook the street from wrought-iron balconies. The rooms vary in size and the degree of wear, but all are clean and have private baths. Rooms with a TV are slightly more expensive than those without.

While the Nido is a little down on its heels, bargain hunters in the Lake Chapala area will kick up their heels at this find.

Quinta Quetzalcoatl

Zaragosa 307
Chapala, Jalisco
(376) 5-36-53
Fax: (376) 5-34-44
Reservations:
800-577-2555

A truly unconventional inn

Accommodations: 8 rooms. **Rates:** $150, El Castillo $185 (up to 4 people). **Included:** Breakfast (except Sundays). **Minimum stay:** 3 nights. **Payment:** No credit cards. **Children:** Not permitted. **Open:** Alternate weeks, year-round. **Recreation:** Swimming pool, guided tours.

➤   **D. H. Lawrence landed in Chapala in 1923 during an exhaustive search for a "suitable place to settle down and write my Mexican novel." The day he arrived, he wired his wife with characteristic hyperbole: "Chapala paradise. Take evening train."**

D. H. Lawrence once lived in the main villa at Quinta Quetzalcoatl and wrote *The Plumed Serpent* while he was in residence. The current American owners, Barbi and Dick Henderson, lovingly restored the turn-of-the-century home and converted it into the centerpiece of the most unusual inn in Mexico, a place that's as delightful as Lawrence's prose and as romantic as his soul.

The largest suite in the villa is named after the writer. You enter it through a book-lined foyer that leads to a brightly decorated living room with a fireplace. A second small fireplace graces the rattan-furnished bedroom, which also has a king bed, a sitting area, and a collection of fine prints. The yellow tiled bathroom contains a double-sink vanity, a tub, and a separate shower. Just off the living room, a balcony overlooks the inn's beautiful one-acre garden, swimming pool, and Jacuzzi.

You can also stay in the room called the Plumed Serpent, full of Mexican crafts, or in Lady Chatterley's Lover, a pink and blue Victorian bedroom attached to two terraces and two bathrooms, one a huge haven with a sunken tub and elaborate tile work. Birds, Beasts, and Flowers is a sun worshipper's dream, with an expansive private balcony, colorful flowers, and a vine-covered pergola.

The Carriage House, next to the main villa, is a studio apartment with a kitchenette built into a brick dining alcove. The nearby El Castillo, or "castle," is exactly that, a two-story stone house consisting of twin towers joined by a slate-floored living room with a fireplace. Each tower has a bedroom, one with a full bath and the other with a half bath. There's also a complete kitchen, wet bar, library, and a pair of terraces.

The secluded Gamekeeper's Cottage contains a couple of striking chambers. The Secret Love has peach walls with black floral wallpaper, a high double canopy bed draped with yards of lace, a corner fireplace, and a private patio outside a large picture window. Our favorite accommodation is the Gamekeeper's Suite, combining English and Mexican countryside in a radiantly rustic blend of stone walls, hand-hewn wood furnishings, a brick fireplace, and a bucolic kitchenette. The Jacuzzi tub in the bath is shaped like a heart and covered with tiny red tiles, and the separate shower comes with his-and-hers showerheads and a window wall that faces a hidden garden.

The Quinta Quetzalcoatl is set up for seven-night stays, though the inn will accept guests for shorter periods when it has vacancies, but not longer ones because it is open one week and closed the next. The rates include breakfast every day but Sunday. On Sundays and one other day of the week your hosts take everyone north to explore colonial Guadalajara and go shopping in the local markets and villages of Tonala and Tlaquepaque. The fully stocked bar also is included in the rate, available to guests 24 hours a day.

On a quiet street near the shore of Lake Chapala, a couple of blocks from the center of town, Quinta Quetzalcoatl is a singular hideaway, unlike any other on earth. That's the kind of allure D. H. Lawrence loved, and the chances are strong that you will too.

Guanajuato

Best Intimate and Affordable Inn

Best Bargain for Mexican Character

Best B&B

The Spanish came to Mexico looking for gold, but they found silver in much greater abundance. Cortés himself opened the New World's first silver mines in Taxco shortly after subduing the Aztecs, and within a few decades, frontier friars discovered the precious metal in the arid northern reaches of Mexico's central valley. Cities such as Guanajuato, San Miguel de Allende, and Zacatecas developed around the mines as opulent, ornate centers of wealth, surpassing Mexico City in prosperity and rivaling it in population. The silver cities declined in economic importance during the 19th century, but they remain lovely examples of Spanish colonial luxuriance.

Of them all, Guanajuato is the most captivating but also the least devoted to tourism. While San Miguel de Allende and Taxco cater to visitors — and colonies of English-speaking expatriates — with commercial diligence, Guanajuato remains adamantly and wholesomely Mexican in its way of life. Two institutions, the huge Hidalgo market and the 18th-century university, dominate the downtown, creating a cheerful chaos where outsiders are observers rather than a focus of attention.

True travelers will love the atmosphere, but the restless among them may be ready to move on after a couple of days if they aren't enrolling in one of the Spanish-language programs. If you are in that camp, consider a short stay in Guanajuato after a longer stop in San Miguel de Allende, just an hour away. The proximity of the two cities to each other makes them naturals for a combined visit, similar in allure though quite different in mood.

The Main Attractions

The Picturesque Setting

The 16th-century colonists built the city into the bottom of a narrow canyon along the meandering path of the Río Guanajuato. The river has been diverted — and the old drainage tunnel converted to a subterranean street — but the town still winds around with the flow of the water and moves up and down the walls of the canyon in a confusing, quaint maze of alleys, stairways, and small plazas. Forget an orderly exploration of the guidebook sights, which won't compel you for long anyway, and just wander about the two-mile-long town in its own directionless manner. You'll encounter everything on your list of places to see and a good deal more.

Old World Ambience

Guanajuato is like a European university town lost in Mexico. The baroque churches, the Moorish facades of buildings, the palatial Juárez Theater, and the range of cultural activities converge to convey a courtly Renaissance air. The spell is strongest off the busy main streets, particularly in the tree-shaded plaza called Jardín Union, complete with sidewalk cafés, vintage lampposts, and wrought-iron benches.

International Cervantes Festival

In late fall, usually in October, Guanajuato stages the International Cervantes Festival, the most significant annual performing arts festival in Mexico. The roster of featured orchestras, theater companies, and dance groups changes each year, but it's generally a stellar collection of talent from around the world. Two things never vary: the need to make reservations months in advance and the repetition of the entertaining Cervantes *Entremeses*, short comic pieces written for intermission amusement and now performed together as a special evening event. For a schedule and additional information, write the Oficina de Turismo, Plaza de la Paz, Guanajuato, Gto. 36000.

La Casa d'Espiritus Alegres

Ex-Hacienda La Trinidad 1
Marfil, Guanajuato
(473) 3-10-13
Fax: same as phone

| **An exuberantly decorated B&B** |

Accommodations: 8 rooms and suites. **Rates:** Rooms $95, suites $115. **Included:** Full breakfast. **Payment:** No credit cards. **Children:** Not permitted. **Smoking:** Permitted only in garden.

➤   **Since Spanish colonial times, Guanajuato has been recognized as a major center for Talavera pottery. Boutiques in town sell traditional examples of these hand-painted vases, tiles, and plates, but your hosts can direct you to the workshops of two artists, Gorky Gonzalez and Capelo, who have created their own distinctive styles.**

Marfil is about two miles and a 10-minute bus ride from downtown Guanajuato, but it is a world apart. In the 18th century many haciendas were located here along the Marfil River, but most of them were destroyed in a flood in 1906. A few decades ago the area was revived by the Italian sculptor Georgio Belloli, who created gorgeous homes out of the ruins, incorporating old columns and stone carvings into the new architecture. The result is a fascinating and artsy neighborhood on the edge of Guanajuato.

La Casa d'Espiritus Alegres, "The House of Good Spirits," occupies a house in one of these refurbished haciendas. Two California artists, Joan and Carol Summers, modernized it, added terraces and a wonderful garden to its already considerable beauty, and converted their home and studio into a bed-and-breakfast. Joan recently passed away, and La Casa d'Espiritus Alegres is now managed by Betsy McNair, who had been running it with Joan for several years.

The Summers were devotees of Mexican folk art and they joyfully decorated their B&B with objects from all over Mexico. Their own folkloric touches are often painted on the walls; hand-painted tiles cover the walls of bathrooms and kitchen alike. The glass-covered interior courtyard and the garden are wonderful places for lounging, and on a cool evening there is no place better than the cozy living room with its carved stone fireplace. Breakfast is served on a glass-enclosed terrace overlooking the parklike garden, where, tucked off under a colorful tent, is the bar.

There are five rooms and three suites, including a separate *casita* in the garden with its own kitchen. Each room has its own decorating theme but all are colorfully folkloric and have a patio or balcony with garden views, a fireplace, private bath, and robes to wear while lounging around the house.

The House of Good Spirits is a good place for a leisurely Guanajuato sojourn.

Parador San Javier

Plaza Aldama 92 (on Route 110)
Guanajuato, Guanajuato
(473) 2-06-26
Fax: (473) 2-31-14

> **A converted colonial estate just outside town**

Accommodations: 115 rooms and suites. **Rates:** Rooms $86, junior suites $125, senior suites $155. **Payment:** Major credit cards. **Recreation:** Swimming pool.

➤ **One of the richest silver mines in history, the Valenciana, is a short drive down Route 110 from the Parador San Javier. You can poke around the site and visit a fabulous church built with mining profits.**

The Parador San Javier sits on the edge of one of the original silver mines in Guanajuato, which produced more than a third of the world's silver at the turn of the 18th century. After the vein was tapped out, the property was converted into a private home and garden estate. When it opened as an inn in 1955, the architects retained the hacienda feel and gracefully enhanced the old features, making the hotel one of the most charming spots in a city that specializes in charm.

The mine's ramparts now enclose manicured lawns canopied by giant laurel and jacaranda trees and a profusion of flowering shrubs and plants. The rooms and public areas sprawl around the vibrant grounds, oriented to two major courtyards. Except for one modern six-story wing at the back of the property, the buildings exude colonial character.

The grand but comfortable lobby boasts huge arched windows, wooden chandeliers, old paintings, and stone columns supporting massive beams. The reception staff don't speak much English, but they are efficient and helpful.

The restaurant, spread through several rooms, is even more beautiful than the lobby. Its copper fireplace, tile floors, domed brick ceiling, and chapel alcove compensate well for any deficiencies in the cooking.

San Javier opened originally with 12 rooms, and those are still the best of the regular doubles, particularly the ones with a *terraza* and a pool view. Each has a fireplace and well-crafted woodwork, masonry, and tile. Our favorite is number 10, featuring a domed brick ceiling and matching brick mantel, and two double beds. A small stone stairwell leads down one floor to the moderate-size swimming pool and the back courtyard.

Among the suites, the top values are numbers 5, 6, and 7, on the front courtyard. A dome ceiling tops the sitting and sleeping areas, both with fireplaces and country-style wood pieces. The bathrooms are wonderful, with blue-gray tile made in Guanajuato, a tub and a shower, and a dressing alcove with a small skylighted brick dome. The senior suites with two bedrooms contain many of the same appointments.

Other than the pool, San Javier's diversions are limited to a disco and a streetfront bar. You'll want to spend most of your time in town, within walking distance, but buses and taxis ply the route as well. You'll love returning to your alluring abode.

Posada Santa Fe

Plaza Principal
Guanajuato, Guanajuato
(473) 2-00-84
Fax: (473) 2-46-53

A historic hotel in a lively location

Accommodations: 50 rooms and suites. **High-season rates:** Rooms $72–$94, suites $127–$140. **Low-season rates:** Rooms $58–$73, suites $81–$95. **Payment:** Major credit cards.

➤   **The Posada Santa Fe's sidewalk café serves some of the best traditional Mexican cooking in town. The atmosphere is particularly spirited on weekend afternoons, when you can count on appetizing specials and fresh tortillas.**

The Jardín Unión, or Plaza Principal, in Guanajuato feels more European than any spot in Mexico. The shaded pedestrian mall attracts a cosmopolitan mix of students from the nearby university, romantic couples, business people, and the few tourists who venture into town. Many meet at the sidewalk café of the venerable Hotel Museo Posada Santa Fe, where you may have to shake the notion of murmuring *"bonjour"* to the waiter and ordering a croissant with your coffee.

Founded in 1862 and recognized as a national monument, the hotel is steeped in the kind of elegance characteristic of the belle époque. Its grand flamboyant lobby also serves as a museum for the work of artist Manuel Leal, who painted scenes from Guanajuato's rich traditions, culture, and history. The adjoining formal dining room shares the decor, mixing magnificent heavy beams with delicate chandeliers.

An ornate staircase winds from the lobby to several floors of rooms. The hallways maintain the turn-of-the-century mood, but it dissipates considerably inside the guest chambers. All are different, but expect a simple room with a phone, a TV, a built-in minibar, a shower-only bath, and plain wood furniture except for an occasional brass bed. Though the suites are grander than the regular rooms, the price is too. A few of the quarters have small wrought-iron balconies, some overlooking the plaza from the second or third floor.

Even if you don't stay here, take a few minutes to wander

through the lobby and soak up the insouciant atmosphere in the alfresco café. It's an authentic but perhaps unexpected side of Mexico.

Mérida

Best Place to Combine Business and Pleasure

Best Romantic Hideaway

Best Comfort Choice for All-American Abundance

Best Bargain for Mexican Character

Best B&B or Budget Inn

Mérida's *zócalo* is an enchanting spot today, but underneath the lovely landscaping lies a long and bloody history. This was the site of the Mayan city of Tiho, conquered in 1541 by the Spaniards. As the European seat of government here expanded, the stones from the Mayan city were used in its construction. Up until the early part of this century, traces of Mayan pyramids still could be seen around the main square. But the modern city has finally swallowed up almost every trace of its ancient past.

Ironically, most Mérida visitors today use the Spanish capital as a base for exploring the remains of other Mayan cities. It makes a gracious place to stay, hospitable and colorful, and offers some rewarding sights of its own in addition to the ruins down the road.

The Main Attractions

City Scenes

The *zocálo* is a wonderful spot to absorb the mood of Mérida, particularly in the late afternoon and on Sundays. The cathedral on the east side of the plaza dates to the 16th century, as does the more interesting Casa de Montejo, now a bank and open to the public during business hours.

Two other places definitely worth a visit are the delightful market, a few blocks south of the *zócalo*, and the Archaeology Museum, a longer walk or short ride in the opposite direction. The museum is in one of the most impressive mansions on Paseo de Montejo, a beautiful boulevard of elegant turn-of-the-century homes.

Convenience to Chichén Itzá and Uxmal

Mérida sits almost equidistant from the two most impressive Mayan cities in the Yucatán. Chichén Itzá is 80 miles to the east and Uxmal is an even quicker 60 miles south. You can rent a car easily through your hotel or directly with international agencies, or take guided day-long tours, also offered at the hotels. See the chapter "Archaeological Treasures" for an overview of the ancient ruins.

Caribe Hotel

Calle 59 #500
Mérida, Yucatán
(99) 24-90-22
Fax: (99) 24-87-33

Authentic Mexican mood at budget rates

Accommodations: 52 rooms and suites. **Rates:** Standard rooms with fan $39, standard rooms with air conditioning $44, superior rooms $48. **Payment:** Major credit cards. **Recreation:** Swimming pool.

➤ **Yucatecan hammocks are made to sleep in. Just stretch horizontally across, opening the web of cotton or nylon threads into a comfortable sup-**

port for the back, and swing yourself to sleep. In the area of the daily market, La Poblana (Calle 65 #492) has an immense selection. Remember to ask for the matrimonial size — and bargain!

The Caribe Hotel bills itself as "the real colonial atmosphere in the Yucatán." The converted convent fulfills that promise and even gives you a little more in cheery radiance.

The hotel faces the Parque Hidalgo, a pedestrian plaza just north of the cathedral and a pleasant corner of the city. The hotel has smartly opened an informal sidewalk restaurant and café here, the popular El Mesón. You enter the hotel through a lobby of black and white tile and stone arches. In an interior courtyard, sunlight floods a lovely garden and spills into El Rincon restaurant and bar, where you can enjoy Yucatecan specialties at moderate prices from early morning until late at night. Upstairs on the top floor of the three-story hotel, a small swimming pool and lounging area provide good views of church spires.

The standard rooms line the first two floors of the quadrangle building. They are simply furnished with a variety of double and twin beds, a phone, a black and white TV, and either a fan or air conditioning. The superior rooms on the third floor all come with air conditioning as well as two double beds and a color TV and the baths are more recently renovated.

The Caribe is a pretty place in a pretty city, offering the right kind of atmosphere for Mérida at very reasonable rates.

Casa Mexilio

Calle 68, #495
(between Calles 57 and 59)
Mérida, Yucatán
(99) 28-25-05
Reservations:
Turquoise Reef Group
303-674-9615
800-538-6802
Fax: 303-674-8735

A homey and tasteful B&B

Accommodations: 8 rooms. **Rates:** $47–$67. **Included:** Breakfast and tax. **Minimum stay:** 3 nights in high season. **Payment:** No credit cards. **Children:** Minimum age is 16. **Recreation:** Swimming pool.

➤ **For a true taste of the Yucatán, plan at least one meal at the famed Los Almendros restaurant. The original location on Calle 50 between Calles 57 and 59 is a quick taxi trip from Casa Mexilio.**

Mexico doesn't have many bed-and-breakfast inns, but the ones that exist are often wonderful places to stay. That's certainly the case with Casa Mexilio in Mérida, a lovely 150-year-old home that proprietor Roger Lynn preserved and remodeled in a quiet residential neighborhood just west of downtown. An amiable host who knows the Yucatán intimately, Roger provides a cozy and apropos environment for anyone exploring the land of the Maya.

Each room is different, but they all contain private baths with showers, ceiling fans for cooling (only one room, without much ventilation, has air conditioning), and a wealth of beautiful local tiles in a myriad of rich colors. Regional art and artifacts intensify the Yucatecan flavor. Our favorite room is the one on the top floor, which enjoys good cross-ventilation as well as a pleasant view of the town across a roof garden. Downstairs there's satellite TV in a shared parlor and access to a phone and refrigerator.

The breakfast included in the rate consists mainly of fruit, juice, and pastries, with eggs on request. When Roger is not leading excursions in southern Mexico and Guatemala for Vagabond Tours, he sometimes cooks seafood dinners for interested guests. Either meal is a good occasion to meet fellow travelers, who are likely to share many of your interests.

When you return home from a day of Mayan sightseeing or wandering around Mérida, you can take a refreshing dip in Casa Mexilio's small pool. It's a nice way to end the day in an inn that makes you glad you came to stay.

Hacienda Katanchel

Km 26 Carretera 180 (Mérida-Cancún)
(99) 23-40-20
Fax: (99) 23-40-00
Reservations:
800-223-6510
Fax: 888-882-9470
Small Luxury Hotels of the World
800-525-4800

A beautifully restored colonial retreat in the heart of the Yucatán

Accommodations: 39 pavilions and suites. **High-season rates:** Pavilions $250, suites $300, honeymoon suite $300, Presidential suite $350. **Low-season rates:** Pavilions $220, suites $220, honeymoon suite $250, Presidential suite $300. **Added:** 10% service plus tax. **Payment:** Major credit cards. **Children:** Up to 2 children under 13 free in room with parents. **Recreation:** Swimming pool, nature walks, massages, facials.

➤ **From the Hacienda Katanchel you can make one-day excursions to the great Mayan sites of Chichén Itzá or Uxmal, to the beautiful colonial town of Izamal, or to the beach at Progreso.**

Situated on 740 acres, the Hacienda Katanchel's main buildings appear after a two-and-a-half-mile drive on a narrow path off the main highway that runs from Mérida to Cancún. Just 15 miles from Mérida, this wonderful retreat takes you to another world. Dating to the 17th century, the Hacienda was established as a cattle ranch. In the 19th century, it joined a good deal of the rest of Yucatán in the very profitable production of *henequén*, or sisal, the fiber used to make rope, bags, sacks, and mats. Recently purchased by architect Anibal Gonzalez and his art-restorer wife, Monica Hernandez, the Hacienda has been renovated — and, indeed, restored — and in the process was found to have been built on an ancient Mayan site. This is a hotel imbued with history.

The setting is soothing and grand, filled with trees and old lanes, brightened by gorgeous tropical flowers, and punctuated with flame trees. After the 10-minute trip from the highway on the narrow path, a clearing leads to the Hacienda's principal building, which houses the reception area, lobby, chapel, and Presidential suite. The Hacienda's restaurant has an even more impressive setting. It is in the former *Casa de Maquinas*, or machine house, where the *henequén* was processed. The dramatic setting for the dining room features ceilings that must be about 25 feet high and incorporates materials and designs from the original factory. Adjacent to the restaurant is a lovely lounge area and game room with a handsome veranda that is a perfect spot to relax with a drink.

Throughout the Hacienda's common areas you find tasteful antiques and tapestries, hand-painted ceramics and wicker furniture, and wonderful old ceiling fans. The old narrow-gauge railroad that brought in the *henequén* has been preserved, and with the help of a horse is used to take guests to their rooms. Walls and wells, and little ruins and *cenotes*, give added romantic definition to this glorious estate, as do the many trails lined with lighting in the shape of Mayan huts. A huge, chemical-free, naturally fed swimming pool is an added source of enjoyment for the Hacienda's guests, as are the many species of birds whose chatter greets you in the early morning. Near the entrance to the Hacienda is a huge vegetable garden, which supplies the restaurant. Spanish-speaking guests will find the head gardener full of enthusiasm and eager to talk about what he is growing for your eating enjoyment.

Most of the accommodations are in individual air-conditioned *casitas*, or pavilions, that formerly were workers' homes. These *casitas* are spread out throughout the immense grounds of the Hacienda, and each comes with an outdoor dipping pool. Most have front and rear terraces, and all feature Yucatecan hammocks for relaxing. The ample rooms have antique wardrobes, rocking chairs, and iron bedstands decorated with medieval pennants.

Several air-conditioned suites add variety to the available accommodations. Recently we stayed in Suite #37, an impressive and imposing room with 14-foot ceilings and a bedroom/living room about 18 by 27 feet. Bright yellow walls, a four-poster iron bedstand, high-back armchairs, and an antique wardrobe make for attractive and comfortable quarters. A covered patio about the size of many hotel rooms and a huge bathroom with swinging doors and a double sink complete the suite's interior. A screened archway leads to an outdoor terrace and private dipping pool surrounded by gardens. If it weren't for the many other attractions at the Hacienda, we would have been content never to leave our own suite.

The Hacienda Katanchel has become a very popular stop for tour groups, which come to view the architecture and grounds and often to dine in the restaurant. The appearance of these groups can be jarring; the serenity of the Hacienda suddenly ceases. But calm returns when the tours leave. You can then savor once again this special, tasteful retreat in the heart of the Yucatán.

Holiday Inn Mérida

Avenida Colon 498
Mérida, Yucatán
(99) 25-68-77
Fax: (99) 25-77-55
Reservations:
Holiday Inn Reservations
800-HOLIDAY

A dependable choice for familiar comforts

Accommodations: 213 rooms and suites. **Rates:** Rooms $90–$97, Mérida Club deluxe rooms $102–$109. **Payment:** Major credit cards. **Children:** Under 12, free in room with parents. **Recreation:** Swimming pool, 1 tennis court, fitness center.

➤ **A sizable Lebanese community established itself in Mérida during the 19th century. A happy result for travelers are the numerous Middle Eastern restaurants. The place to sample Lebanese-Mexican tabouli and kafta is in the lovely Alberto's Continental Patio (Calle 64 at 57, 285-367).**

In a city of old colonial buildings, Mérida's Holiday Inn stands in stark contrast to its surroundings, a modern block and stone structure that reminds you that this is the 20th century after all. The hotel gives you up-to-date comfort for enjoying a region of ancient wonders.

A sunny courtyard graces the interior, greeting you with a bubbling fountain and tropical greenery. The Mil Flores restaurant faces the patio, providing service alfresco or inside in an airy dining room full of light, ceiling fans, and white furniture. The name, meaning "a thousand flowers," is reflected in bright chair cushions and wall fabrics. Both buffets and à la carte menus are offered at all meals, with occasional mild versions of Yucatecan specialties among an assortment of international dishes. The breakfast buffet is particularly ample, with fresh fruit, juices, pastries, cereals, and several appetizing entrées such as *huevos motuleños.*

Most of the rooms are upstairs in the mid-rise building and overlook a large swimming pool. The least expensive quarters have two double beds under rattan headboards, carpeted floors, satellite TVs, phones, air conditioning, mini-bars, and plain motel-like bathrooms with tub-showers. Pretty floral bedspreads and radiant prints on the wall add splashes of color. The Mérida Club rooms are newer and more sumptuous and have pool or fountain views, safes, and hair dryers.

For many people the Yucatán is a daunting area — a sweltering and timeworn land despite the glories of its past. The Holiday Inn allows you to savor the magnificence of the region without enduring all of its possible trials.

Hyatt Regency Mérida

Avenida Colón esq. Calle 60
Mérida, Yucatán
42-02-02
Fax: (99) 25-70-02
Reservations:
800-400-3319

The most sophisticated spot in town

Accommodations: 300 rooms and suites. **Rates:** Standard rooms $115, Regency rooms $140, Regency executive suites $290, Presidential Suite $1,000. **Payment:** Major credit cards. **Recreation:** Swimming pool, 2 tennis courts, Jacuzzi, fitness center with sauna and massage, jogging track.

➤   **The city sponsors free outdoor concerts many nights of the week. Thursday night, when traditional *serenata* music is performed in Plaza Santa Lucia, is our favorite.**

When the Hyatt Regency opened in 1994, it heralded a new level of sophisticated accommodations for travelers to this very traditional city. An 18-story contemporary tower, the Hyatt must be the highest building in the entire Yucatán Peninsula. Its glass and concrete facade certainly contrasts with the nearby Belle Epoque elegance of the Paseo de Montejo, and its sheer monumentality overshadows the neighboring Holiday Inn, long considered the city's best hotel. No hotel, not even the new Fiesta Americana across the street, has quite caught up with the Hyatt.

The sophistication is most apparent in the gleaming lobby. The centerpiece is the fountain, but just as eye-catching are the contemporary paintings and witty architectural accents. The lobby boutiques are some of the finest shops in Mérida. Two attractive restaurants and a lobby bar with music add to the liveliness of this inviting area.

The 300 rooms have air conditioning, of course, and satellite TV, mini-bars and the like. The Regency rooms and one-bedroom suites, with their complementary robes, breakfasts, and snacks as well as a business center, are the quarters to opt for. Located on the top floors, these rooms have the most exceptional views over the city and are decorated with fine furnishings, fabrics, and bath fixtures that give them a European feel. The standard rooms on the lower floors are definitely a step down: adequate, but nothing special.

The hotel has taken advantage of its rooftop views by placing most of the recreational activities there. The swimming pool, sun deck, and hammock terrace are complemented by a bar and restaurant. Nearby are the Jacuzzi and the cardiovascular machines of the fitness center.

The Hyatt has brought a welcome level of luxury to Mérida.

Mexico City

Mexico City

Best Hotels for Stylish Sophistication

Best Comfort Choices for All-American Abundance

Best Bargains for Mexican Character

Best Places to Combine Business and Pleasure

Best Intimate and Affordable Inn

Mexico City is one part disaster, one part delight. The oldest urban center in the Americas and one of the largest in the world, it is growing at a pace that could send the population beyond 30 million by 2000. Only social scientists would want to spend an entire vacation in the bulging metropolis, but many people will enjoy a few days at the beginning or end of a trip.

You do need to be prepared for the urban conditions. The first thing you're likely to notice — particularly if you have a window seat on the plane — is the air pollution. The problem wasn't seriously addressed until the late 1980s, when all cars (including rentals) were assigned a regular day off during the week. That law, enforced with stiff fines, also had the secondary benefit of removing half a million cars daily from the routine traffic jams. Streets still get snarled, but not as badly as in the past.

A special caution unfortunately needs to be made about crime. People have been robbed and assaulted in taxis; one person was killed. The U.S. State Department recommends that you do not flag down cabs. Instead, have your hotel or restaurant arrange for an authorized taxi. The Mexican Ministry of Tourism provides information about safety in Mexico City and other Mexican cities at their toll-free number, 800-482-9832, and their Web site, www.safemexico.com.

The delightful side of the city is just as compelling. The long, proud history pervades the air as thickly as the smog. The people are vibrant and animated. Many of the museums are world class and some of the international restaurants really are international in flavor. Even natural beauty survives in the glorious parks.

Mexico City manages to thrive despite itself. It's been damaged by the phenomenal growth of recent decades, but not defeated.

The Main Attractions

The Historic Hub

The heart of Mexico City, the *zócalo* is also the heart of the country. From Aztec times forward, political and religious power has been concentrated around the immense plaza. The National Palace, built over the ruins of Moctezuma's mansion, spreads along the eastern edge. Colonial viceroys, 19th-century liberators and dictators, modern presidents, and even a couple of self-proclaimed emperors have ruled the land from here.

The imposing cathedral, the largest in Mexico, stands to the north, deliberately erected over Aztec ceremonial center to symbolize the triumph of Christianity in New Spain and, not incidentally, the vast authority of the Church.

Among the most striking parts of either structure are the Diego Rivera murals in the National Palace, depicting the Mexican heritage from ancient ages to the Revolution of 1910. Rivera also painted the courtyard walls at the Ministry of Public Education (Argentina 28), a few blocks north, and his colleague José Clemente Orozco did the graphic murals around the interior patio of the National Preparatory School (Justo Sierra 16).

Be sure to see the excavated remains of the Aztec Templo Mayor (Great Temple), the sacred center of the Indian capital, Tenochtitlán. Workers discovered the ruins accidentally in 1978 while digging underground across the street from the eastern side of the cathedral. The government tore down several blocks of colonial buildings to rescue this small but significant corner of the Aztec city buried long ago by Cortés. A museum adjacent to the site provides background on Tenochtitlán and explains the religious import of the main temple, dedicated to the gods of war and rain.

Museums Galore

Mexico City has a museum for every interest, covering topics ranging from foreign interventions to *charros* (gentlemen equestrians). Even many places that aren't actually museums seem to be, including the National Pawnshop just off the *zócalo*, the opulent Palace of Fine Arts (the concert hall across from Alameda Park, but with murals and painting galleries), and the House of Tiles (Madero 4), where Sanborn's operates a drugstore, gift shop, and decent moderately priced restaurant.

The National Museum of Anthropology is a must. A massive two-story structure built around a huge patio, it displays a wealth of archaeological treasures from Mexico's many ancient civilizations, plus ethnographic exhibits on contemporary Indian cultures throughout the country. Don't rush your visit. Get one of the catalogs in English and spend a day — or, better, two half days — engrossed in the magnificent collection.

Some of the numerous art museums are definitely worth a stop. The Rufino Tamayo Museum and the Museum of Modern Art, which focuses on 19th- and 20th-century Mexican work, are near the Museum of Anthropology in Chapultepec Park, a vast wooded playground that also contains a zoo, one of the world's highest roller coasters, and lovely pathways. The Center for Contemporary

Art is a short walk from both museums by the Hotel Presidente Inter-Continental on Avenida Campos Eliseos.

Don't overlook the Museo de la Alameda in the smaller, downtown Alameda Park, a half dozen blocks from the *zócalo*. It was constructed in the late 1980s to hold a mural that may be the most famous in Mexico, Diego Rivera's *A Dream of a Sunday Afternoon in Alameda Park*. The boy in the center of the painting, holding hands with a skeleton, is Rivera himself, and Frida Kahlo, his equally talented wife, stands behind him, touching his shoulder. Not too far away is the Museo Franz Mayer (Plaza de Santa Veracruz) with its exceptional collection of colonial art and crafts.

In attractive residential neighborhoods in the southern part of the city are the Frida Kahlo Museum (Allende and Londres in Coyoacán), her fascinating home, and the Museo Estudio Diego Rivera (Altavista and Diego Rivera),a short drive away in San Ángel, across from the San Ángel Inn.

For history buffs, Leon Trotsky's home in exile (Viena and Morelos), where he was assassinated in 1940, is also in Coyoacán, several blocks from Kahlo's house. The exhibits at the National Museum of History in Chapultepec Park can be a disappointment, but the setting in the 18th-century Chapultepec Castle redeems a stop.

The Zippity Zona Rosa & Elegant Polanco

Most American visitors stay at hotels in or near the Zona Rosa, a lively neighborhood packed into ten square blocks. A mix of tacky commercialism and refined elegance, it's the nucleus of modern middle-class Mexico City. Shops and restaurants line the main streets, selling everything from chic fashions to Big Macs. Young residents flock in at night, particularly on weekends, to drink at sidewalk cafés and dance until the wee hours. Although frayed on a few edges, the Zona Rosa accents the fresh and the frisky, the smart and the slick.

To avoid some of the slick and some of the pickpockets, the Polanco area has rapidly developed into the preferred destination for Mexico's beautiful people. Near Chapultepec Park, the neighborhood has witnessed the opening of many fine restaurants and hotels in recent years and they have been followed by art galleries and designer boutiques. Less compact and less central than the Zona Rosa, Polanco probably will attract you to at least one of its restaurants even if you haven't opted for one of it hotels.

Camino Real Mexico City

Mariano Escobedo 700
México, D.F
(5) 203-21-21
Fax: (5) 250-68-97
Reservations:
Camino Real Hotels and Resorts
800-7-CAMINO (800-722-6466)

> **A stunning hotel with the best art and swimming pool in the city**

Accommodations: 716 rooms and suites. **Rates:** Deluxe rooms $189, pool-view deluxe rooms $239, Camino Real Club rooms $269, master suites $350–$1,500. **Payment:** Major credit cards. **Children:** Under 18, free in room with parents. **Recreation:** 2 swimming pools, 4 tennis courts, fitness center.

➤ **Have cocktails in the opulent Fouquet's lounge, listen to piano tunes in the Lobby Bar, or enjoy the music and graze through the appetizers at the Tapas Bar**

You won't forget your arrival at the Camino Real. You enter the circular drive through an opening in a shocking pink honeycomb wall. In the center of the drive a large pond swishes and swirls in all directions, splashing water on the roadway with its fountain-driven simulation of Pacific surf. As you gaze across the spectacle from the entrance to the hotel, a bright yellow wall forms the background, creating a Day-Glo effect around the scene.

The dramatic porte-cochere comes from the fertile imagination of minimalist architect Ricardo Legorreta. The hotel was the first of his several Camino Real and Westin projects, built to open just in time for the 1968 Olympics. The design lacks the smooth flow of his work in Cancún and Ixtapa, but it captures much of the energy and formality of the urban environment, and the lobby and other public spaces are enlivened by pools and waterfalls as well as an array of contemporary art, including a huge mural by Rufino Tamayo and a stabile by Alexander Calder.

The only low-rise luxury hotel in Mexico City, the Camino Real is spread around landscaped grounds across from Chapultepec Park in the Polanco area, about a 20-minute walk from the center of the Zona Rosa. The larger of two swimming pool, heated against highland chill, is in a parklike garden that banishes all sense of the surrounding city with its calm. The rooftop tennis club provides four courts and pro services, plus steam baths and a weight room with some cardiovascular machines. If you're traveling for work instead of pleasure, the hotel's business center supplies secretarial, interpretive, fax, and other services. And there's efficient concierge service.

All except the least expensive rooms look out to the grassy patios and gardens from large private balconies. The original Legorreta decor was lost to the more anonymous hotel style of the eighties, but recently new fixtures and works of art designed by the architect have giving more character to the comfortable, if somewhat spare, rooms. The spacious quarters come with sitting areas and marble baths, air conditioning, phones, and satellite TVs.

The Camino Real's restaurants and bars are the best hotel collection in the city. For breakfast the coffee shop called La Huerta, open 24 hours, is a lively place with good food. Even better is Azulejos, which serves a fine morning buffet. You start with an extensive selection of fresh fruit and juices, and then have the option of ordering à la carte or sampling from a wide range of hot dishes. All the American standards are available as well as spicy meat stews, *chilaquiles*, eggs Méxicana, fried bananas, and much more.

Azulejos remains open for casual lunches and dinners, but you might want to try Fouquet's de Paris, one of the city's top French restaurants. The fare is not Parisian in refinement, and the setting is self-consciously ornate, but the kitchen can excel with the imported preparations. Save room for dessert.

The Camino Real is older than its prime competitors today, but it keeps up with the times in most respects and remains a pacesetter in some.

De Cortés Hotel

Avenida Hidalgo 85
Colonia Centro
México, D.F.
(5) 518-21-81
(5) 512-18-63
Reservations:
Best Western
800-528-1234

> **A baroque hospice still
> offering hospitality**

Accommodations: 21 rooms and 8 suites. **Rates:** Double rooms $70–$80, suites $130. **Payment:** Major credit cards. **Children:** Under 12, free in room with parents.

➤ **Two of the best places in the city to shop for Mexican crafts are across Alameda Park from the De Cortés. Start at the government-sponsored FONART at Juárez 89, and then check out the Museo Nacional de Artes e Industrias Populares, just down the street at Juárez 44.**

Colonial charm is easier to find in the provinces than in Mexico City. The historic areas of town between the *zócalo* and Alameda Park retain much of their old character, but most of the hotels went modern decades ago.

The changes left the Hotel de Cortés a semiprecious relic, a place where you can still experience the atmosphere of the past. An 18th-century building on the north end of Alameda Park, it once provided lodging for visiting friars. The facade shows its age clearly, making you wonder perhaps whether it's worth a stop. The charm is inside, around a lovely arcaded courtyard full of plants and personality.

The patio functions as a bar and restaurant for the hotel and is one of the most romantic places to eat in the inner city. The light orange walls of the two-story quadrangle, *equipale* chairs, stone tables, and sun umbrellas create a magical mood, far removed from the bustle beyond the doors. Mexican musicians provide entertainment at some meals, and the kitchen always prepares satisfying versions of native and international dishes.

The rooms lack the enchantment of the dining terrace, but they were renovated in 1994. The standard doubles are simple quarters sparsely furnished, usually with twin beds, a TV, and a phone. The suites, a better value, enjoy more space and sense of style.

The Hotel de Cortés is a fine spot for a meal and a good place to stay. The Majestic (see index) may have more overall historic appeal and a better location, but the Cortés certainly earns consideration for its courtyard coziness.

Four Seasons Hotel

Paseo de la Reforma 500
Colonia Juárez
México, D.F.
(5) 230-18-18
Fax: (5) 230-18-17
Reservations:
Four Seasons Hotels and Resorts
800-332-3442

**A worldly hotel with
sterling standards**

Accommodations: 240 rooms and suites. **Rates:** Standard rooms $260, superior rooms $310, deluxe rooms $330, executive suites $430, deluxe executive suites $480. **Payment:** Major credit cards. **Children:** Under 18, free in room with parents. **Recreation:** Swimming pool, fitness center.

➤ **The Four Seasons sits on the most prominent boulevard in Mexico, the Paseo de la Reforma, where diplomatic, corporate, and historic districts converge. The location provides quick access to both the Zona Rosa and Chapultepec Park.**

Shortly after the Four Seasons opened in 1994, we were discussing the new hotel with two of the most experienced and perceptive resort managers in Mexico. One said she thought the elegance was too understated for Mexico, a land of exuberance, after all. The other claimed that the design didn't matter because the hotel would soon surpass every other in the country in the true essentials — service, accommodations, and food. Both may be right.

The architecture seeks to blend Spanish colonial and French traditions, to create an air of stately permanence. The eight-story building, deftly set back from the busy Paseo de la Reforma, surrounds a huge courtyard modeled on ones typical of Mexican mansions. Most of the rooms overlook the central gardens, providing a lovely perspective as well as a sense of place. Inside, the hotel feels more like Paris than Mexico City. The interior speaks of subdued sophistication, projecting a spare, cool formality that follows you from the Old World lobby into your room.

In addition to the restrained European decor, the guest quarters boast a full array of contemporary conveniences, including remote control TV, a safe in the closet, a mini-bar, air conditioning, and an extra phone outlet for fax or computer needs. You get a choice of a king bed or two doubles, and always a large marble bath with a separate shower and soaking tub. The Four Seasons Executive Suites allow you to seal off the sleeping space with French doors, making the sitting area suitable for informal meetings or other work. For more of the same, upgrade to a master suite with a full parlor and one or two bedrooms.

Guest services range from a 24-hour concierge desk to one-hour pressing. A business center provides translation, secretarial, and courier services, plus copy, fax, and personal computers. When you're ready to relax, you can exercise in the fitness center, swim in a small rooftop pool, or simply melt into a massage.

The cooking excelled in both hotel dining rooms during a recent visit. The refined El Restaurante serves leisurely business breakfasts, copious lunches, and dinners featuring urbane dishes from around the world, including a selection of authentic Mexican delicacies. The casual El Café, also open all day, offers lighter and quicker meals without sacrificing quality. We particularly enjoyed a red snapper *veracruzano* one night, perfectly prepared. For a cocktail before dinner, head to the grand Lobby Lounge or the cozy, clubby El Salón, with dark wood walls and floors, bookcases, maps, and overstuffed wing chairs as well as service on a garden terrace.

The Four Seasons made an immediate impact in Mexico City, challenging all contenders to match its standards. It may be more tasteful than tantalizing, more European than Mexican, but the new hotel has set its sights as high as any in the country.

La Casona

Durango 280 at Cozumel
Colonia Roma, Mexico D.F.
(5) 286-30-01
Fax: (5) 211-08-71

| **A European inn just steps from the Zona Rosa**

Accommodations: 30 rooms. **Rates:** $157. **Included:** Taxes. **Payment:** American Express. **Recreation:** Gym.

➤ **This upscale residential neighborhood is rapidly becoming a favorite with artists and young sophisticates. Check out the contemporary Mexican paintings exhibited at Galería Pecanins (Durango 186) and OMR (Plaza Río de Janiro 54) and then enjoy nouvelle Mexican cuisine at Tecla (Durango 186, 525-4920), a popular restaurant with Greenwich Village–like ambience.**

La Casona opened in 1996 in this three-story pink mansion, a historic landmark dating to the 1920s. It is as stylish as it is homey. A Tiffany glass dome now crowns the elegant stairwell and almost-antique English clocks and prints give the inn an old-fashioned ambience. The presence of a doorman, though, should alert you to the attention to service here, which is like anything but an English B&B.

As you enter, you'll see a small reception area and sitting room decorated with antique musical instruments. Down a short flight of stairs is the dining room, decorated in Provençal patterns and rustic furnishings. French windows line one wall, giving onto a garden patio with a fountain where breakfast sometimes is served. To guarantee interesting cuisine, the dining room is open to the public as well as guests. The charming cellar bar, though, operates on the honor system and is exclusively for guests.

Each air-conditioned and tranquil room has a distinctive decor based on a musical theme. Some open to a little patio, others to the outside; some have a sitting area or desk, and some have wooden floors and Oriental carpets. Each room comes with bathrobes, a hair dryer, satellite TV, a safe, a basket of fruit, and a privacy pass-through window for room service.

The sunny top floor includes a small gym with cardiovascular equipment as well as weights and a steam bath. There's also a roof terrace with bar service. Other amenities certainly include the valet parking: just drive the car up and the doorman will whisk it away. There's a small business center, too.

La Casona manages to make you feel at home and pampered at the same time. It is an unusual urban inn, one that will make any visit to the capital all the more enjoyable.

Majestic Hotel

Avenida Madero 73
Colonia Centro
México, D.F.
(5) 521-86-00
Fax: (5) 512-62-62
Reservations:
Best Western
800-528-1234

An old favorite in the historic zone

Accommodations: 85 rooms and suites. **Rates:** Double rooms $88, suites $150–$200. **Restrictions:** 2-night minimum stay. **Payment:** Major credit cards.

➤ **A short walk from the Majestic is Los Girasoles (Calle Tacuba near #8, 510-0630), the favorite power lunch spot in the downtown area. Reserve a table, enjoy the scene, and dine on memorable haute Mexican cuisine.**

When it opened in 1937, the Hotel Majestic was an elegant downtown establishment. Directly on the *zócalo*, it was in the commercial and governmental hub of the city in those days, and the graceful colonial decor reflected the grandeur of the surroundings. Time has shifted the center of city life and eroded the hotel's prominence, but the Majestic has maintained much of its original allure, as well as rates barely higher than they were in the beginning.

The delightful lobby is a gem of craftsmanship, small by today's standards though as welcoming as any in Mexico. Every corner sparkles with color from handsome tiles, plants, pottery, a fountain, and flowers. The upstairs hallways in the seven-story building share the exuberance and get splashes of sun from skylights over an atrium.

The rooms are plainer in decor, but ample and comfortable. They come with double or twin beds — often both — tiled baths, dark wood furniture, a TV, a phone, wrought-iron accents, and incongruous carpeting.

The most desirable rooms face the *zócalo*, but if you don't have the view from your quarters, you can enjoy it from the top-floor bar and restaurant. The best perspective is from a pleasant outdoor dining terrace that surveys all of the huge plaza. The à la carte menu offers Mexican and international dishes, and breakfasts are buffet style.

Though the Majestic is not everything it used to be, it's still one of the cheeriest places to stay in Mexico City. Many people prefer to be closer to the Zona Rosa for its evening diversions, but if historic atmosphere is more important to you, this is the best stop in town.

Marco Polo

Amberes 27
México, D.F.
(5) 207-18-93
Fax: (5) 533-37-27
Reservations:
Utell International
800-44-UTELL

A boutique business hotel in the heart of the Zona Rosa

Accommodations: 64 rooms and suites. **Rates:** Deluxe rooms $125, executive suites $160, penthouse suites $208–$260. **Payment:** Major credit cards.

➤ **The San Ángel Inn (Diego Rivera 50 in San Ángel, 548-67-46), in an old hacienda half an hour by taxi from the Zona Rosa, may be the most beautiful restaurant in the country. The margaritas are famous, the Mexican and seafood dishes are quite fine, and the Bavarian cream with fresh berries, irresistible.**

Whenever we're inside the Marco Polo, we're always a little surprised to find Mexico City outside. The hotel feels as if it would be more at home in San Francisco, in uptown Manhattan, or other places where small, luxury establishments for business travelers are more common.

The Marco Polo goes straight up 13 compact floors in the center of the Zona Rosa. The design is simple yet classy, an effect carefully planned by the four Mexican owners, who are architects by trade. The narrow lobby is dressed in black and cream with gold accents. Just a few steps beyond, the intimate bar-restaurant has the ambience of a casually sophisticated European café and an Italian menu to match.

Only a handful of the spacious rooms can fit on each floor, reached by a dilatory elevator that could use a companion. The quarters are not opulent but pleasantly international in character and first class in decor. Each is a long rectangle with a sitting area at one end by a cleverly concealed kitchenette and mini-bar. The bathroom is at the opposite end, along with an executive desk in the suites. The beds sit in the center, usually two doubles. All the chambers come with air conditioning, phones, art on the walls, and satellite TV.

For the utmost in style and luxury, upgrade to one of the four penthouse suites. They feature a king-size bed, a private balcony overlooking the city, and a marble bathroom built for pampering, with dramatic sloping skylights and a Jacuzzi tub.

Opened in 1986, the Marco Polo established itself quickly as a first-rate boutique hotel. It lacks the diversions of its big competitors, but few places in town will treat you better. Whether you're in the city to buy a bank or to unload a bankroll in the shops, it's the address of choice in the Zona Rosa.

María Cristina

Río Lerma 31
Colonia Cuauhtémóc
México, D.F.
(5) 566-96-88
Fax: (5) 592-34-47

An economy hotel popular among foreign visitors

Accommodations: 150 rooms and suites. **Rates:** Double rooms $56–$62, junior suites $70–$74. **Payment:** MasterCard, Visa.

➤ **With the money you save at the María Cristina, splurge on dinner in one of the sophisticated restaurants blending French flair and Mexican verve. Among the best are Isadora (Moliere, 280-55-86), in Polanco, and Champs Elysees (Paseo de Reforma 316, 533-36-98), in the Zona Rosa.**

A short walk from the center of the Zona Rosa, the María Cristina presents a comfortably classy facade that attracts many *norteamericano* visitors. You enter into a Victorian-era Mexican parlor with marble floors, a grand winding staircase, iron and brass chandeliers, and a big fireplace adorned with a Spanish colonial painting. On one side is a brightly tiled interior courtyard with a fountain; on the other, a flower-splashed lawn with chirping birds and umbrella-shaded tables.

The rooms are less enticing, mostly utilitarian quarters for sleeping and showering. The standard rooms, moderate in size, contain double or twin beds, carpeting, basic wood furniture, a phone, and a TV. Many lack views outside. The suites are a better value for the extra space, and they usually get more light and upgraded appointments. The higher prices are for those rooms renovated in 1996.

The Río Nansa restaurant serves a broad range of American and Mexican dishes, though it's hard to imagine eating in the hotel when the Zona Rosa is so close. That proximity is the ultimate reason for the María Cristina's popularity, and it's an advantage worth pursuing.

Marquis Reforma

Paseo de la Reforma 465
Colonia Cuauhtémoc
México, D.F.
(5) 211-36-00
Fax: (5) 211-55-61
Reservations:
Small Luxury Hotels of the World
800-525-4800

> **Elegant design, plus fine food and service**

Accommodations: 125 rooms and 84 suites. **Rates:** Double rooms $265, executive suites $350, corporate suites $420, Reforma deluxe suite $480, Presidential suites $730–$1,590. **Payment:** Major credit cards. **Children:** Under 12, free in room with parents. **Recreation:** Fitness center with saunas, Jacuzzi, and massage.

➤ **Among Mexico City's many shopping opportunities, the one visitors usually enjoy the most is the Bazaar Sábado, held each Saturday in the San Ángel neighborhood (Plaza San Jacinto). Permanent stalls selling contemporary crafts occupy two floors of an 18th-century villa, and in adjacent parks individual painters and artisans show their work.**

The new Marquis Reforma is a visual knockout, a glitzy art deco monument that stands out in Mexico City like a cherry on a sundae. Massive glass tubes in hues of blue highlight the striking rose facade, composed of marble and granite blocks in an elaborate mosaic. While you're still trying to absorb the artistry of the architecture, your taxi pulls into a vaulted porte-cochere capped with highly polished metal. You alight and enter the lobby, where an Aztec couple greet you from a remarkable fountain, sculpted so that the water seems to reflect a mirror image of the scene. It's a stunning introduction to a hotel that is one of the most sophisticated in Mexico City.

Though the design is what impresses you first, the moderate-size Marquis Reforma strives to make sure your lasting impression is about great service. Staff training was a priority well before the hotel opened in 1991. All employees spent four to six weeks in workshops before interacting with guests, and they continue participating in professional development courses. Service started out as alert and attentive as we've ever seen in Mexico, and it continues to be so.

Whatever the level of success, it won't totally outshine the art deco opulence. Even the hallway leading to your room is a minor masterpiece, a blend of gleaming wood and geometrically patterned carpet. Inside you find a well-conceived layout, marble baths, a king or two double beds, and a full contingent of conveniences, including soundproofed windows, air conditioning, a mini-bar, and satellite TV.

The suites feature a spacious sitting area with a sofa, wing chairs, and more gorgeous woodwork. The TV spins on a lazy Susan, the two phone lines accommodate fax or computer hookups, and the bathrooms contain either a Jacuzzi or a shower separate from the tub. The four presidential suites come with private boardrooms. Both deluxe rooms and suites can be booked at special rates on the executive floors, where a comfortable lounge serves the primarily business clientele on weekdays.

The elegance of the design extends into the lobby's Bar Caviar and the two restaurants. The intimate La Jolla is particularly stylish, accented throughout with etched glass panels. You dine on Continental and nouvelle Mexican specialties, always good and sometimes grand. The Café Royal, open 24 hours, is more casual in atmosphere and menu.

A fitness center, the best hotel gym in the city, provides guests with weight and exercise rooms, massages, three outdoor Jacuzzis, a sauna, steam room (for men only), and juice bar. The business center offers an equal range of services, from bilingual secretaries to any kind of computing or communications equipment you're likely to need. For outside diversions, the Zona Rosa and Chapultepec Park are within walking distance.

The Marquis Reforma set a new standard for luxury in Mexico City, and has maintained a level of excellence over time in food and service. If it stays as adroit as it is artful, it's destined for a magnificent future.

Presidente Inter-Continental Hotel

Campos Elíseos 218
Colonia Polanco
México, D.F.
(5) 327-77-00
Fax: (5) 327-77-37
Reservations:
Inter-Continental Hotels
800-327-0200

A worldly hotel in stylish Polanco

Accommodations: 659 rooms and suites. **Rates:** Standard rooms $180, superior rooms $220, deluxe rooms $250, Club deluxe rooms $280, junior suites $450, master suites $500–$700. **Payment:** Major credit cards. **Children:** Under 12, free in room with parents. **Recreation:** Fitness center.

➤ **The many designer shops on fashionable Avenida Masaryk are nearby, but the hotel can launch your shopping splurge with its many exclusive boutiques. Next door, the museum shop in the Cultural Center for Contemporary Art is one of our favorite spots for Mexican crafts.**

From the moment you drive up to the entrance of this 42-floor modern tower you are assisted by the staff in the pleasantly efficient manner that is the hallmark of this fine hotel. From the bellhops to the concierge, the staff competently assists you. Small details, such as the urn of coffee in the lobby for early departures, make your stay here, whether for sightseeing or business, completely comfortable.

The dramatic five-story atrium lobby bustles with the lively conversation of guests. Dominated by a soaring yellow sculpture by Antonio Gutierrez Prieto, the lobby is a welcoming spot with comfortable sofas, parquet floor, gorgeous flower arrangements in Talavera vases, and bold paintings by contemporary Mexican artists.

Off to the side of the lobby are the many shops and restaurants surrounding the sunken living-room-style lobby bar. Different musicians, mostly pianists and jazz groups, perform here each evening to the delight of both locals and hotel guests. The exceptional array of seven dining spots range from the 24-hour informal mezzanine restaurant to the elegance of the Balmoral Salon de Thé, Maxim's of Paris, Alfredo di Roma, and the Palm, a branch of the U.S. steak house.

The rooms themselves, decorated in soothing lavenders and grays with a few bright Mexican accents, vary little in size and appointments. All have air conditioning, mini-bars, satellite TV, and a complementary newspaper each morning. It is the view through the large picture window that determines the differences in price: standard rooms are on the lowest floors, the superior rooms have city views, and the deluxe rooms enjoy panoramas over either the city or the much preferred view of Chapultepec Park. There are a variety of suites as well, from junior suites to two-bedroom master suites with marble dressing areas, VCRs, and multiple phone lines. The rooms and suites on the club-level floors are more luxuriously appointed and share an executive lounge and business center with computers and stenographic and translation services.

Another feature of the hotel is its gym, housed in two bright rooms with both weights and cardiovascular equipment.

Near Chapultepec Park, within walking distance of the National Museum of Anthropology, a few minutes from a subway stop, and a short cab ride from the Zona Rosa, the Presidente Inter-Continental is an urban hotel with lots of Mexican verve.

Westin Galería Plaza

Hamburgo 195
Colonia Juárez
México, D.F.
(5) 230-17-17
Fax: (5) 207-58-67
Reservations:
Westin Hotels and Resorts
800-228-3000

An excellent business hotel in the Zona Rosa

Accommodations: 439 rooms and suites. **Rates:** Deluxe rooms $190–$225, executive floor rooms $245, master suites $375. **Payment:** Major credit cards. **Children:** Under 18, free in room with parents. **Recreation:** Swimming pool, fitness center.

➤ **The Lobby Bar at the Westin Galería Plaza swings with live music every evening. That may be all the nightlife you need, but if not, you are just a short walk from the brightest lights in the city.**

The Westin Galería Plaza is on the quiet end of the Zona Rosa, an ideal location for business travelers and vacationers alike. It's a short walk to the most active area of Mexico City, but it's far enough away when you want to escape the noise and bustle.

The hotel specializes in convenience and solid comfort rather than glitzy affectations. There is a swimming pool as well as a small exercise room on the roof and a French restaurant, *de rigueur* in the city on its level of luxury, though the thrust is toward the basics — dependable service and accommodations.

The recently redecorated rooms feature light colors and handsome contemporary furnishings. The deluxe rooms are ample in all respects, but the most desirable quarters — and the best overall value — are the 10th- and 11th-floor executive rooms on the top of the building. Stylish in decor, they contain a range of special amenities, including robes and elevated city views. More important, guests enjoy free use of the executive lounge, where there's a Continental breakfast in the morning, canapés in the afternoon, newspapers, a concierge, and a desk for a personalized check-in and check-out. All the rooms and suites come with satellite TV, fax and computer jacks on the phone, a mini-bar, and a marble bath.

The Île de France restaurant is authentically French in elegance, menu, and chefs, if not always in the success of preparations. Try it for a leisurely late-afternoon lunch, when it's a popular gathering spot. The Plaza, a casual café, serves hearty American and Mexican breakfasts and later in the day, a variety of native and international dishes. For something different, head to Cava Baja, a Castillian-style bar with Spanish wines and *tapas*. Plenty of other fine restaurants are nearby, which isn't the case with all the hotels in a similar class.

The Galería Plaza isn't flashy or pretentious, just good at what it does. You won't go wrong at the Westin, whether it's business or pleasure that brings you here.

Monterrey

Monterrey

Best Places to Combine Business and Pleasure

The third largest city in Mexico, and a booming international industrial center, Monterrey attracts an increasing number of
norteamericano visitors. Most of them come on business, but
pleasure travelers are also discovering that the northern capital
makes an easy and unconventional weekend getaway.

Less than 150 miles from the Texas border on good highways,
Monterrey enjoys a scenic setting in a valley of the Sierra Madres,
under the shadow of Saddle Mountain. Though the city lacks the
colonial charm and intimacy of places farther south, it compensates with prosperity and modern urban style.

The Main Attractions

The Gran Plaza

One of the largest public squares in the world, almost 100 acres,
the Gran Plaza dominates downtown Monterrey. Graced by fountains and sculpture, and lined by monumental buildings, it's the
heart of the city in all ways.

The architecture along the plaza blends the ancient and the in-
novative, ushering you from a cathedral begun in 1601 to a spectacular contemporary theater. Among the many sights, don't miss
the Palacio de Gobierno (seat of the state government of Nuevo
León), the Dulces Nombres Chapel, the imposing facade of Monterrey's oldest bank, and the museums mentioned below.

Memorable Museums

Monterrey's Museum of Modern Art (MARCO), near the cathedral
on the Gran Plaza, is itself a work of art, designed by the renowned
Ricardo Legorreta. The 14 exhibition halls can hold several shows
at a time, usually featuring Mexican artists of recent centuries.

The Museo de Monterrey often takes a more contemporary bent, sometimes on the avant garde edge. The changing exhibits meander through a 19th-century brewery on the park-like grounds of the Cerveceria Cuauhtemoc, the company that makes Tecate, Carta Blanca, Bohemia, and other popular Mexican beers. After a tour of the museum and a mug or two in the beer garden, stop by the Mexican Baseball Hall of Fame, also on the grounds.

Back on the Gran Plaza, the Museo de Historia provides an overview of national and regional history, tracing the industrial and cultural development of the Monterrey area. Other local museums, scattered through the city, are devoted to astronomy, glass making, antique cars, and natural sciences.

Gran Hotel Ancira Sierra Radisson Plaza

Ocampo Oriente 443
Monterrey, Nuevo León
(8) 150-70-00
Fax: (8) 345-78-15
Reservations:
Radisson Worldwide
800-333-3333

A palatial Old World hotel that sets standards for service

Accommodations: 240 rooms and suites. **Rates:** Traditional rooms $177, Plaza Club rooms $190, junior suites $290, master suites $330, Presidential Suite $725. **Payment:** Major credit cards. **Recreation:** Swimming pool, fitness center.

➤ **Jazz musicians play in the lobby lounge at the Ancira Sierra Radisson, but the mood is even more mellow in the hotel's Bar 1900. A handsome amalgam of old wood, ornate booths, and French café murals, it's one of the most captivating cantinas in Mexico.**

The most elegant hotel in downtown Monterrey, the Ancira Sierra Radisson opened in 1912 flaunting the latest and fanciest in French architectural style. A finely detailed facade greets you from the street, inviting you inside to a magnificent marble lobby. Revolutionary hero Pancho Villa once hitched his horse in the grand foyer, according to legend at least, but you'll have trouble imagining the stately chamber as a stable.

Los Barandales dining room occupies one end of the lobby, facing a winding, balustraded stairway and looking up to the mirrored ceiling. The restaurant specializes in copious Mexican and international buffets, offered daily for breakfast, several times a week for lunch, and at brunch on Sunday with champagne.

The guest rooms vary considerably in size, but all provide a balanced blend of period decor and contemporary convenience. Each comes with a king bed or two doubles, TV, phone, mini-bar, and air conditioning. The most desirable quarters are on the executive club floor, which features a private lounge where you register and check out, enjoy a free Continental breakfast, and gain access to the hotel's well-equipped business center. A butler serves all these rooms, and all are furnished with their own exercise bikes. The junior suites are extra large and with a sitting area; the master suites have the luxury of an extra half-bath.

If you opt out of the executive amenities, you can use the hotel's small fitness center or relax at the petite pool. That's about it for recreation at the Ancira Sierra Radisson, but you shouldn't need more. An officially recognized cultural and historical landmark, the hotel lures you with lore and luxury.

Sheraton Ambassador

Hidalgo Oriente 310
Monterrey, Nuevo León
(8) 380-70-00
Fax: (8) 345-19-84
Reservations:
Sheraton Hotels
800-325-3535

> **A center of activity in
> downtown Monterrey**

Accommodations: 241 rooms and suites. **Rates:** Standard rooms $185, executive rooms $210, junior suites $265, suites $385–$750. **Payment:** Major credit cards. **Recreation:** Swimming pool, fitness center, 1 tennis court, 1 racquet ball court, sauna, Jacuzzi, massage.

➤ **Monterrey is famed for its *cabrito al pastor*, slow-roasted kid. Los Vitrales serves a good rendition, but for full local flavor, head to El Rey del Cabrito (Constitucion 817, 45-32-32), a downtown institution decorated in tribute to the area's long ranching tradition.**

Downtown Monterrey boasts two grand, vintage hotels that put you in the center of the city and its social life. Both the Sheraton Ambassador and the Ancira Sierra Radisson are conveniently located just off the Gran Plaza, and each offers an air of Old World elegance at reasonable rates, but they differ in diversions.

The Ambassador is the more playful of the pair, with a lighted tennis court, racquet ball court, and aerobics in addition to a swimming pool with sundeck, Jacuzzis, sauna and a full fitness center. Whether you're working off stress from a day of meetings or just in search of sun, the hotel caters much better than you expect from a downtown establishment.

The Sheraton also features an enticing choice of dining rooms, both adjoining the ornate lobby. The informal Los Vitrales serves solid *norteño* food 24 hours a day, with a bountiful breakfast buffet on Sundays, under a huge stained glass ceiling. Le Pavillón, one of the city's finest Continental restaurants, surrounds you with brass chandeliers, etched glass panels, and other elements of opulence. The lounges have live music.

The guest rooms are rather plainer than the public areas, though comfortable. They show their era in some respects, but not their age. Each has satellite TV, two phones, a writing desk, mini-bar, and air conditioning. Opt for the executive rooms to get the broadest array of amenities and services.

The Sheraton Ambassador combines the casual and the classy in an urbane way, just like Monterrey.

Morelia and Pátzcuaro

Best Romantic Hideaway

Villa Montaña, 319

Best Intimate and Affordable Inn

Fiesta Plaza, 322

Best Bargains for Mexican Character

Los Escudos Hotel, 323
Posada de la Soledad, 318
Posada La Basílica, 324
Villa Pátzcuaro Hotel, 325

Best Place to Combine Business and Pleasure

Virrey de Mendoza, 321

Many areas of Mexico are magical in different ways at different times, but none so consistently as the state of Michoacán and its enchanting cities of Morelia and Pátzcuaro. A strong Indian culture bursts through an overlay of Spanish colonial traditions, creating a regional personality that's a vibrant variation on Mexico's amalgam of peoples.

Michoacán has always stood apart from the rest of the country, despite a central location. The earliest inhabitants may have had as much contact by canoe with Pacific Coast Indians as far south as Peru as they did with the closer civilizations in the Valley of Mexico. Unlike their neighbors, they knew metallurgy, but they didn't build great cities or form powerful kingdoms until the Tarascans united the area politically a couple of centuries before the Spanish arrived. The streak of independence remains strong, manifesting itself in recent years in political protests against Mexico City.

Though Michoacán extends to the ocean, the heartland is concentrated within easy driving distance of Lake Pátzcuaro. The most remote villages worth visiting are a couple of hours west of the lake, and the state capital, Morelia, is an hour to the east. The opening of an airport outside the capital in the 1980s improved access substantially.

The best bases are Morelia and the town of Pátzcuaro, right on the lake. One is a large city, Spanish colonial in style, and the other is much smaller and more Indian in character. If you don't want to split your time between the two, as we prefer to do, you may want to make a choice on the basis of accommodations. Morelia features one of the very best places to stay in all of Mexico, while Pátzcuaro offers a collection of inexpensive inns brimming with local flavor.

The Main Attractions

Colonial Nobility

Downtown Morelia is an aristocratic grande dame, stately and restrained in contrast to many of her 17th- and 18th-century Mexican cousins. The center of the city is the flower-filled *zócalo,* a gathering spot any time but particularly on nights when free concerts are scheduled at the gazebo bandstand. The lofty cathedral, almost a hundred years in construction, soars above the plaza, showcasing the Old World harmony of the architecture.

Although Morelia is not loaded with singular sights, a regal colonial aura flows through the streets around the *zócalo.* We like to wander aimlessly and absorb the spirit, but if you need to have a destination, seek out the Michoacán Museum (Allende and Abasolo) and the home of Independence War hero José María Morelos (Morelos Sur and Aldama), both interesting history museums. The Colegio de San Nicolas (a block west of the plaza on Madero), now a preparatory school, is the second oldest college in the Americas. When you're ready for something more fanciful, head for the Mercado de Dulces, a popular sweets market. It's behind the tourist office (Nigromante near Madero), where you can get city maps and sightseeing information.

The architecture of Pátzcuaro is older than Morelia's and is therefore simpler. The village has changed little since the 16th century, when single-level adobe construction was more common than stone palaces. A patina of perpetuity spreads through the cobblestone streets, imparting an air of country dignity.

The hub of the town consists of a pair of hillside plazas above the shore of Lake Pátzcuaro. The smaller of the two is the site of the regular market, and the larger, the Plaza Vasco de Quiroga, hosts special fiesta markets. Both are wonderful spots for sitting and observing the lulling rhythms of life in the region.

Village Crafts

Most of the Indian villages of Michoacán specialize in a particular traditional craft, a system fostered centuries ago by the respected early bishop Vasco de Quiroga. Lacquerware is the specialty in Pátzcuaro and Uruapan, copperware in Santa Clara del Cobre, guitars in Paracho, straw work in Tzintzuntzán, weavings and furniture in Erongaricuaro, masks in Tocuaro, ceramic tableware in Capula, and imaginatively bizarre pottery pieces in Ocumicho.

The most enjoyable way to see the work is to tour the villages. Most have a few shops featuring the local craft as well as artisan workshops open to visitors. If you have only a short time to spend in the area, at least get to Santa Clara del Cobre, a picturesque town only ten miles from Pátzcuaro. Tzintzuntzán and Erongaricuaro are also an easy drive.

Often you won't find the highest quality work in the villages because it's been shipped already to busier markets. A good portion goes to Morelia to the Casa de las Artesanías (Plaza Valladolid), one of the top craft stores in Mexico. The enormous range of items, displayed in museum fashion, covers the entire state. Pátzcuaro also has several notable shops, particularly the beautiful Casa de los Once Patios (a block southeast of Plaza Vasco de Quiroga), and a special regional museum, the Museo de Artes Populares (Quiroga and Arciga).

The best selection of all is at the fiesta market during the Day of the Dead week in Pátzcuaro, which falls during the last few days of October and the first few days of November. Artisans come from all the villages and sell their work at prices well below those in the shops. The celebratory atmosphere makes the browsing and buying an experience you'll never forget.

Purépecha Perseverance

The Day of the Dead is one of many Indian customs preserved by the Purépecha people, who populate most of Michoacán. Descendants of the Tarascans, they have absorbed many European influences without losing the vigor of their native culture. El Día de los Muertos is a joyous time for the Purépecha because it's a family reunion. The unusual part is that the dead are the special guests, and their gravesites are the gathering spot.

Living members of the family construct a beautiful altar full of marigolds and decorations that recall the deceased's favorite foods, friends, pets, and other passions. They bring the altar to the cemetery in the early hours of November 2, just after midnight, and commune with the soul of the dead until sunrise. Those who no longer conduct the vigil still clean and adorn graves at this time, making departed family members comfortable while decorating their cemeteries with more color than a Mardi Gras parade.

You have to be in Pátzcuaro at the right time for the Day of the Dead, but you can see the Dance of the Little Old Men, Danza de Los Viejitos, all year. The pre-Hispanic significance of the dance is uncertain, but it is definitely memorable entertainment today. Boys dress as stooped elders who can barely walk when they enter the room. The music gradually restores the youth of their step, and by the time they exit, their feet are moving at jitterbug speed.

Morelia

Posada de la Soledad

Ignacio Zaragoza 90
Morelia, Michoacán
(43) 12-18-88
Fax: (43) 12-21-11

| Once a religious sanctuary, still a harbor for the soul |

Accommodations: 58 rooms and suites. **Rates:** Rooms $58–$65, suites $75.
Payment: MasterCard, Visa.

➤ **If you're in Morelia on a Saturday, stop by the Posada de la Soledad for the traditional Mexican buffet, loaded with specialties of the area.**

Downtown Morelia bustles with modern activity, but the colonial buildings in the vicinity of the central plaza rise majestically above the commotion. The one housing the Posada de la Soledad, just a block from the *zócalo,* is the most tranquil of them all.

The calm spirit goes back to 1719, when the building was constructed as a convent. In a later period it became a carriage house, and though the property has been a hotel for three decades, it still retains many of the old carriages. They are unusual relics of the past, scattered around the handsome portal that rings the stone and grass courtyard.

The two-story quadrangle structure is small but heroic in proportions, with massive wood doors and beams, great arches, and stone walls accented by period paintings. A fountain in the center of the courtyard provides a soothing background, especially for diners. The restaurant extends outside from the rotunda dining room, which shares the colonial distinction of the other public areas. Open for three meals daily, La Capilla serves Mexican food along with some American and Continental dishes.

The rooms are less consistently charming. Avoid the least expensive ones that surround the back courtyard. Rooms around the main quadrangle feature domes, woodwork, and high ceilings along with mundane carpeting, TVs, and a few architectural oddities. Bedding runs from one king to two twins to three doubles. Bathrooms mix marble with Mexican tile, not always in the most pleasing combinations, but they are adequate in size and contain at least a shower and sometimes a tub as well.

The Posada's staff is eager to please. Their rooms aren't fancy, but the hotel offers as much character and calm as you can get anywhere at the price.

Villa Montaña

Patzimba 201
Morelia, Michoácan
(43) 14-02-31
Fax: (43) 14-71-60
Reservations:
Small Luxury Hotels of the World
800-525-4800

An inn that's a work of art

Accommodations: 40 rooms and suites. **Rates:** Rooms $130, junior suites $200, master suites $220–$330, Presidential Suite $330. **Included:** tax and service. **Payment:** Major credit cards. **Recreation:** Swimming pool, 1 tennis court.

➤ **Some people simply stay cloistered at Villa Montaña — relishing their room, the gardens, the pool, and maybe a game of tennis — but the staff encourage you to explore the area. They can arrange for a rental car or set up tours with English-speaking drivers.**

An opulent but understated retreat in the hills above Morelia, Villa Montaña reflects the international sophistication of its owners, Count and Countess de Reiset of France. Staying here is like spending a convivial country weekend as the houseguests of aristocratic friends.

The count scoured Mexico for years looking for ranch property, but turned his business interests from agriculture to accommodations after discovering Villa Montaña. He bought the hotel in 1973 from its American owner and set about enlarging the property and decreasing its number of rooms. The countess came as a guest, fell in love with the property and the count, and stayed on to become his wife. An engaging couple fluent in several languages, they split their time between the hotel, France, and the United States. While they do take an active interest in Villa Montaña and their guests, day-to-day management is handled very capably by Ana Compeán, one of Mexico's few female hotel managers.

The hillside site, behind Morelia's largest park, gives guests broad views over the city and surrounding environs. The vista is best from the bar terrace above the small reception area and from the pool deck and tennis court. Many of the rooms, set on a multitude of levels, share portions of the panorama.

The accommodations are in one- and two-story villas, clustered like a European village. Hedges, ferns, evergreens, orchids, and ivy-covered walls skirt the *casas* and line the walkways, where stone benches invite quiet contemplation of the lovely setting. Diminutive stone fish, *santos,* animal figures, and other sculptural accents dot the grounds.

The guest quarters are sumptuous chambers, individually decorated with extraordinary taste. Furnishings combine Mexican antiques with contemporary pieces, creating comfortable spaces of casual elegance. You may get a terrace, a domed brick ceiling, a fireplace, or in some suites, all three. Most rooms have king-size beds, and all have phones and TVs. The baths are usually enormous spaces with a shower, a bidet, a soaking tub, and Mexican tile and tin accents.

The hotel's dining room is a charming spot, filled with sunlight during the day and candlelight at night. Service matches it in warmth. Over the years food quality has been a few notches below that of the setting, but Villa Montaña has worked diligently to upgrade the cooking. A fresh commitment to searching out the finest ingredients and concentrating on a limited number of specialties bodes well.

The dinner menu includes an ample selection of Continental and Mexican dishes. Breakfast can include as much nourishment as you want. As in a private home, there is no set menu. Guests help themselves to the buffet of fruits and juices, and warm bread and rolls are brought with coffee to the tables. If you want a morning entrée, just let the waiter know what you have in mind.

Sipping a margarita on the bar terrace as the sun sets, you'll understand easily why Villa Montaña changed the direction of Count de Reiset's life. It's a noble hideaway, as comely and captivating as any in Mexico.

Virrey de Mendoza

Avenida Madero Pte. 310
Morelia, Michoácan
(43) 12-06-33
Fax: (43) 12-67-19

**A historic hotel with
character and class**

Accommodations: 55 rooms and suites. **Rates:** Double rooms $96, suites $100–$133. **Payment:** Major credit cards.

➤ **The Presidential Suite, the most expensive chamber, is a sumptuous salute to colonial grandeur. You sleep on a carved bed fit for royalty, store your clothes in an ornate antique armoire, and read by the light of a crystal chandelier.**

Built originally as a residence in 1565, enlarged in a gracious colonial style in 1744, and completely restored as a hotel in 1991, the Virrey de Mendoza has a history almost as long as Mexico's. You see the heritage everywhere, from the formal dining room to the antiques in the suites. If it doesn't put you in the mood for Morelia, you picked the wrong city to visit.

Leaded glass doors lead directly from the *zócalo* into an expansive, Old World lobby framed by stone columns and arches. Tile, hardwood, and a massive rug cover the floor, directly under an imposing stained glass ceiling. A piano graces one corner, providing part of the live music nightly in the lobby lounge, where you sit and sip in august style.

The rooms upstairs share much of the mood, particularly the suites. Even the regular double rooms are likely to offer beamed ceilings, polished wood floors, and carved Mexican furniture, in addition to modern conveniences such as TVs, phones, and large beds. The suites offer extra measures of elegance. Each is different, but you might find a Victorian parlor, oil paintings, a pair of pedestal sinks in the bath, lace curtains on the windows, or a Romeo-and-Juliet balcony overlooking the *zócalo*.

In the handsome restaurant, open all day, pink linen contrasts smartly with dark wood on the walls and ceiling. The tone is refined, but the menu is far from fussy, featuring local specialties and familiar international dishes.

The Virrey de Mendoza puts you in the heart of Morelia, geographically and spiritually. No other place in town is more in tune with the grand old times.

Pátzcuaro

Fiesta Plaza

Plaza Bocanegra 24
Pátzcuaro, Michoacán
(434) 2-25-15
Fax: Same as phone

| **A small modern hotel in the center of town** |

Accommodations: 60 rooms and suites. **Rates:** Standard rooms $60, junior suites $80. **Payment:** MasterCard, Visa.

➤ **Friday is the big market day in Pátzcuaro. The sprawling outdoor bazaar starts just steps from the Fiesta Plaza.**

For years, most of the lodging in Pátzcuaro has been a bit elemental — picturesque perhaps, but basic in many respects. The opening of the Fiesta Plaza in the spring of 1990 introduced a new dimension in design. Though the hotel takes its inspiration from the colonial character of its downtown environs, it combines the charms of yesteryear with the comforts of today.

The three-story facade blends with the other buildings on Pátzcuaro's colorful market plaza, but the interior is fresh and peaceful in comparison with the street. The "lobby" is a tiled central courtyard brimming with potted plants. A bubbling fountain glistens in the sun. Oversize wood columns support heavy corbels and beams designed to last for centuries.

The small rooms are contemporary in a simple way, with a few neocolonial touches. They come with wrought-iron light fixtures, carpeting, a tiny TV, and pleasant country pine furniture. Each room has a tiled shower-only bath, modest in size, and windows facing the courtyard.

The cheerful all-day restaurant is decked out in Mexican fiesta decor. Start with either the garlic or Tarascan soup, while you contemplate entrées featuring area trout and whitefish, seafood, and beef, prepared in Mexican and Continental styles.

The Fiesta Plaza is a refreshing change for Pátzcuaro, a place that's making the most of both the past and the present. That bodes well for its future.

Los Escudos Hotel

Portal Hidalgo 73
Pátzcuaro, Michoacán
(434) 2-01-38

A colonial gem, still full of life

Accommodations: 30 rooms. **Rates:** $33. **Payment:** MasterCard, Visa.

➤ **Room 231 at Los Escudos features a Romeo-and-Juliet balcony overlooking the Plaza Vasco de Quiroga, two double beds, handsome dark wood furniture, and a comfy sitting area, all for a rate lower than an interstate motel in Omaha.**

Hotel Los Escudos and the Posada La Basílica, described next, are as quaint and quirky as the town, if not quite as memorable. Either of them can be a delightful place to stay, depending on the room you get and the mood of the staff at the time, and each is an amazing bargain, providing more colonial character for the dollar than hotels anywhere else in Mexico.

Los Escudos occupies one of the 16th-century white stucco mansions that line the Plaza Vasco de Quiroga, a shady park crowned with a statue of the beloved bishop for whom the plaza is named. Entering through the old wood and glass doors from the main plaza, you follow a red tile vestibule toward the reception desk and a restaurant that is popular with residents as well as guests. Both spill into the space that once served as an open two-story courtyard atrium, now topped with hard plastic.

The restaurant serves ample Pátzcuaro dishes at breakfast, lunch, and dinner, but the best time to go is on Saturday nights, when the simple fare is accompanied by the Danza de Los Viejitos (Dance of the Little Old Men). You can see the regional *danza* elsewhere in town, but this is the most authentic local setting.

A few rooms are downstairs just behind the restaurant, an adequate location as long as you know about the Saturday evening performance, when a wrongly timed step out the door could put you onstage. Most of the rooms are upstairs, arranged around two quadrangles. The ones facing the quiet plaza — particularly number 231 — are easily the most desirable quarters, but not always easy to book.

The rooms differ in many ways, but most have TVs, double beds, and shower-only baths. Some come with fireplaces, murals of Michoacán scenes, and red velvet drapes. The furniture is simple wood, with occasional carved touches.

There are few spots in Mexico as serenely beautiful as Pátzcuaro's main plaza. Los Escudos puts you in its midst at a price that will hardly buy a parking space in most U.S. cities.

Posada La Basílica

Arciga 6
Pátzcuaro, Michoacán
(434) 2-11-08

**A quiet downtown hotel
near the Basilica**

Accommodations: 11 rooms. **Rate:** $45. **Payment:** MasterCard, Visa.

➤ **The highest body of water in Mexico, Lake Pátzcuaro used to be the main route between the towns that line the waterfront. You can still take a boat from the Pátzcuaro dock to the fishing village on the island of Janitzio, the most popular place to observe the Day of the Dead rituals.**

The first thing likely to attract your attention at the Posada La Basílica is the large straw *Cristo* hung behind the registration desk.

The image of Christ on the cross is one of the handsomest examples of work from the nearby village of Tzintzuntzán that you'll see outside a museum. Although the reception staff may not speak much English, they will welcome you warmly and humbly in the spirit of their icon.

The guest rooms are up a few steps from the simple lobby, around a small courtyard filled with greenery. Each chamber is different, but you can count on high, beamed ceilings, hand-carved furniture, bright Mexican tile in the bath, and exterior windows with wrought-iron grillwork and floral patterns painted around the border. The beds are twins and doubles, two or three per room in all possible combinations.

The chambers to request are numbers 10 through 13, which look out on the Pátzcuaro Basilica, built in the 16th century by the beloved bishop, Don Vasco. These four rooms also have functioning fireplaces, as do three others without the church view.

The Posada's restaurant serves only breakfast and lunch in a pleasant perch with vistas over the town's picturesque red tile roofs to Lake Pátzcuaro and the island of Janitzio. It's a good place to sit savoring your good fortune and the fortune you are saving at the Posada. That should keep you smiling the length of your stay.

Villa Pátzcuaro Hotel

Avenida Lázaro Cárdenas 506
Pátzcuaro, Michoacán
(434) 2-07-67
Fax: (434) 2-29-84

| **The warmest hospitality in town in a family-run inn** |

Accommodations: 12 rooms. **Rates:** Rooms $22–$27, tents $10, RV sites $11. **Payment:** MasterCard, Visa. **Children:** Discouraged. **Recreation:** Swimming pool, 2 tennis courts, hiking trails.

➤ **Villa Pátzcuaro recently added a communal kitchen for guests in a small building near the pool. The cooking facilities are a significant advantage if you're trying to save money or just like to fix some of your own meals.**

We first learned about the Villa Pátzcuaro from a friend, a seasoned Mexico traveler who has a reputation for stretching his pesos infinitely. At the time, in the mid-1980s, you could spend three nights here and still get change from a $20 bill.

We needed a last-minute reservation during the popular Day of the Dead fiesta, so we took a chance, assuming a hotel on the edge of town in this price range was going to give us little more than a roof. What we found was low-key but delightful country charm in an inn managed attentively by the owner, Arturo Pimentel. He and his family live on the property, and guests register in their living room. Señor Pimentel is the only one who speaks much English, but everyone is warm and helpful.

The hotel's entrance, set back a hundred feet from the main road through town, more often called Avenida de las Americas than Lázaro Cárdenas, is essentially the home's small front yard, maintained with care and personal pride. Jacaranda trees are the focal point, blooming in purple profusion in late spring. The Pimentels' house is on the left, and the guest rooms are on the right, in a single-story wing of white brick and red tile. To the rear of the property are sites for tents and recreational vehicles.

Hiking trails up nearby hills begin a the rear of the property. A swimming pool sits between the home and the small L-shaped hotel block. It's an inviting spot with umbrella tables and a grassy deck, but days in Pátzcuaro are seldom warm enough to get serious about a dip. You are more likely to use the corner fireplace found in each room. A basket of wood is delivered daily to take away the chill of cool evenings.

Most rooms face either the pool or the two tennis courts at the back of the property. The quarters are scrupulously clean and distinctively rustic, with log ceilings, simple Mexican wood furniture, terrazzo tile floors, brick and stucco walls painted white, double beds, and a closet that's bigger than the basic shower-only bath.

Most guests come in a rental car, useful for trips into the center of town, which is a long hike away. A number of restaurants are within easy walking distance, though, mainly clustered around Lake Pátzcuaro. The closest is directly across the street at a place that looks and feels like a typical motel. Most visitors from the States stay there, paying three times your rate. You may want to join them for breakfast, but you'll be happy afterward to return to the homey hospitality of the Villa Pátzcuaro.

Oaxaca

Best Hotels for Stylish Sophistication

Best Comfort Choice for All-American Abundance

Best Intimate and Affordable Inn

Best Bargain for Mexican Character

Best B&B

The prehistoric settlers of the Oaxaca valley, the Zapotecs, still dominate the population, thriving in the shadows of their majestic ancient city, Monte Albán. Mingling with them are the Mixtecs from the highest villages in the Sierra Madres. The Spanish erected a capital in their own image and converted the Indians to Christianity, but somehow they never left much of a mark on Oaxaca's soul. Underneath the elaborate colonial shell there's a heart of

Zapotec gaiety and quiet endurance, of earthiness and ethereal spirituality.

For a visitor the mingling of moods is akin to a space-time warp. In the old downtown, away from the shanty suburbs, the city often assumes the dimensions of a dream, a land of forever, full of small surprises and big memories.

The Main Attractions

The Spell of the *Zócalo*

The center of the city and its social life, the Oaxaca *zócalo* is the essence of Mexico, a microcosm of the national melting pot. Everyone, from affluent businessmen to indigent Indians, from playful children to vacationing visitors, gathers on the plaza. They come for a drink at the sidewalk cafés, to rest on the shaded benches, to buy a balloon, or to listen to the musicians who perform almost nightly at the lovely gazebo bandstand. The *zócalo* is the hub of most Mexican towns, but nowhere is it more magnetic and magical than in Oaxaca.

The cathedral stands serenely on one side of the plaza, a melancholy counterpart to the merriment beyond its baroque facade. It's one of Oaxaca's two dozen churches, the highest structures in the city. Seek out a couple of others particularly popular with residents, both a few blocks from the *zócalo*. The massive 16th-century Church of Santo Domingo is plain on the outside but exuberantly gilded inside. The Basílica de la Soledad houses a revered statue of Oaxaca's patron saint, the Virgin of Solitude.

Markets

Plan travels to Oaxaca to coincide with the Saturday market, held a short cab ride from downtown on the outskirts of the city. Both Zapotec and Mixtec Indians come from miles around for the enormous, sprawling bazaar, oriented much more to their daily needs than to tourist interests. Past and present dissolve in the tumult. Polyester dresses sit next to traditional cotton *rebozos,* and plastic pails adjoin pottery jugs. One vendor sells medicinal herbs for cures that existed before Hippocrates, while another watches TV. Fruits and vegetables are stacked in appealing mounds, an age-old sales technique, though purchases are packaged in plastic bags. It's an amazing spectacle, colorful and convivial, exhilarating and exhausting.

Other towns nearby have smaller rustic markets on different days. The one on Sundays in Tlacolula, 20 miles away, is the most primordial, as close as you can get to the way things were a millennium ago. On Wednesdays visit Etla, a cheese center, the next day head to the former Zapotec capital of Zaachila, and on Fridays, go to the pottery village of Ocotlán.

Craft Shopping

The villages around Oaxaca produce as fine a selection of folk crafts as any area on earth. Some of the work is extraordinary. The pottery — made without a wheel — ranges from the famous black bowls of San Bartolo Coyotepec to the fanciful figurines of the Aguilars in Ocotlán. The woodcarving is the most expressive in Mexico — sometimes amusing, sometimes sacred, always striking. Handwoven garments and rugs are vividly regional, whether it's a cotton *huipil* (blouse) or a wool *serape* from fascinating Teotitlán del Valle.

Little of the best work is sold in the markets. Look instead in Oaxaca's many craft shops or visit the villages, where you can enjoy the adventure of seeking out artisans in their homes and workshops. The top city stores are concentrated on two parallel streets north of the *zócalo*, García Vigil and M. Alcala. Don't overlook La Mano Mágica (M. Alcala 203), Corazón del Pueblo (M. Alcala 307-309), and Aripo (García Vigil 809).

December Festivities

Oaxaca approaches fiestas gleefully, whether it's the mid-summer Guelaguetza, featuring indigenous dances, music, and costumes, or the autumn Day of the Dead. The longest festival season is the second half of December, when you need hotel reservations far in advance. Events start on the 16th with an all-night parade honoring the town patroness, the Virgin of Solitude. Her fiesta, full of fireworks and music, continues over the next two evenings. *Posadas*, reenactments of Mary and Joseph's quest for lodging, begin at the same time and continue up to Christmas Eve. Meanwhile, around the *zócalo*, everyone is eating the crisp pastries called *buñuelos* and smashing their plates afterward for good luck in the New Year. On December 23 the central plaza becomes the scene of the Night of the Radishes. Hundreds of people display elaborately carved giant radishes, shaped like animals, mangers, and anything else imaginable. Christmas Day is ushered in with a midnight mass, announced by the simultaneous ringing of all the church bells in town. Oaxaca is quieter the next week, but the joyful atmosphere lingers until early January.

Monte Albán, Mitla, and the Regional Museum of Anthropology

See the chapter "Archaeological Treasures" for a brief introduction to the ancient aspect of Oaxaca, which shouldn't be missed.

Camino Real Oaxaca

Calle 5 de Mayo 300
Oaxaca, Oaxaca
(9) 51-6-06-11
Fax: (9) 51-6-07-32
Reservations:
Camino Real Hotels and Resorts
800-7-CAMINO (800-722-6466)

A revered favorite in Oaxaca

Accommodations: 91 rooms. **Rates:** Deluxe rooms $190–$210, Camino Real Club rooms $235–$260, junior suites $280. **Payment:** Major credit cards. **Children:** Under 12, free in room with parents. **Recreation:** Swimming pool.

➤ **The Camino Real has a heated pool, but you'll want to spend most of your time sightseeing, browsing, and lounging on the city zócalo, a few blocks away. Excursions to the many neighboring ruins, markets, and traditional craft-making villages can easily be arranged through tour groups or taxi drivers.**

In the city center, the Camino Real Oaxaca is a national treasure in Mexico, a historic convent carefully converted to a hotel in the 1970s. It's one of the most beautiful places to stay in the country and can be the most romantic when everything is flowing gracefully.

The Santa Catalina convent, founded in 1576, was the second nunnery established in Mexico. Construction of the current building started a couple of decades later. Like many colonial structures, it grew gradually over time until the government abolished all monasteries in the 1860s. By then the sprawling convent was one of the largest buildings in Oaxaca, but local authorities were puzzled by how to use it. They made it the city hall, then a jail, and finally a theater. Eventually the federal tourism agency, Fonatur, restored the property and transformed the nuns' cells into lovely hotel rooms.

The quarters vary considerably in size and serenity. A few face the street and can be noisy at night if you open the window or stuffy if you don't, although all rooms are air-conditioned. Most deluxe rooms open to a garden or courtyard and are more naturally quieter and cooler. The Club rooms are quite spacious, as are the junior suites, and both are more likely to be on the second floor, the best place to be. With the Club rooms you get a Continental breakfast and afternoon hors d'oeuvres.

You can count on loads of allure in any of the quarters. The thick walls feature sections of old frescoes and *nichos* containing prints and crafts. The floors are of terra cotta, furnishings are dark, heavy wood, and the ceilings have hefty beams. Although the historic character is well preserved, all modern conveniences are near at hand, including satellite TV and phones.

The rest of the hotel strives for the same balanced blend of the past and the present. The handsome formal dining room fuses colonial architecture with a stunning wall design of contemporary Oaxacan pottery, and the adjacent luxuriant courtyard restaurant, like the dining room, serves traditional Oaxacan cuisine but with *nouvelle* and international accents.

We've always enjoyed breakfast in the handsome dining room. The bountiful buffet covers a selection of fruit, juice, and cereal for starters, and for the main course there's an egg bar plus a variety of hot dishes such as *chilaquiles*, beans, Mexican stews, and potatoes with *chorizo*.

Two lovely lounges offer live music most evenings. Friday is the big evening of the week, though, when the hotel uses the beautiful chapel of the former convent to stage its Guelaguetza, a reenactment of a popular summer festival. The kitchen prepares a hearty buffet, and folkloric performers stage traditional dances from the seven regions of Oaxaca state. It's one of the most colorful hotel fiestas in the country.

The Camino Real combines contemporary standards with historic allure, assuring that your stay in Oaxaca will be both comfortable and memorable.

Casa Caruso

Calle Allende 11 (212)
Oaxaca, Oaxaca
(9) 51-6-11-26
Reservations:
315-696-8334

A rare blend of comfort and good taste

Accommodations: 4 rooms and suites. **Daily rates:** Rooms $92–$104, townhouse (for three people) $172, suite $138. **Weekly rate:** Rooms $618–$686, townhouse (for three people) $1,190, suite $939. **Monthly rate:** Entire house $3,500 May–June; $4,500 July–September; $6,800 October–April. Includes full staff and utilities. **Included:** Full breakfast, open refrigerator and pantry policy includes soda, beer, and wine. **Smoking policy:** In outdoor areas only. **Payment:** No credit cards.

➤ **For reliable Mexican cooking, including some Oaxacan specialties, try El Naranjo (Trujano 203, 51-418-78), set in a large covered courtyard and presided over by an attentive English-speaking owner. Several varieties of very good stuffed chiles are offered, as well as flavorful soups, salads, and other main dishes. Oaxacan cuisine is famous for its many rich and densely flavored *mole* sauces, including the well-known black version. Dining in one of the handsome patios at Los Pacos (Constitución 104; 51-6-17-04), you can sample several sauces with an order of chicken or grilled meats.**

The Casa Caruso is one of Oaxaca's special inns. Although a mere four blocks from the bustling main square, this colonial mansion is a tranquil world unto itself.

Nick Caruso, a retired architect from New York, has restored this mansion and decorated it with art and antiques. Tamayo lithographs, fabulous ceramic creations, Talavera dinner sets, and bright Navajo-style rugs combine to create a Mexican decor of uncommonly good taste and warmth. He has also created a home — a place to curl up in the library with a book or a video, to nap on the verandah in the afternoon sun, or to raid the refrigerator for a midnight snack. A most generous host, Nick (and his staff) is also extremely attentive. Not surprisingly, the Casa Caruso attracts an interesting group of guests.

With so few guest quarters, the extensive common areas really are yours to use, just like home. The front courtyard, with its stone arches, has two invitingly furnished verandas situated around a bright splash of bougainvillea. You might choose to look at something on the VCR in the comfortably large library/living room with high wood beam ceilings or to play the piano in the more formal and carpeted music room. The elegant dining room seats twenty, in case you plan to entertain. But you can also eat in the cheerful Mexican-style kitchen or on the back patio, with its fruit trees and fountain.

The fan-cooled rooms exhibit the same good taste and warmly inviting comforts as the rest of the inn. All have some special headboard or stucco wall treatment, lamps made from local ceramic pots, tin bathroom mirrors, bright throw rugs, and the like, but each is different despite having private baths, a small sitting area, and either a queen-size or two double beds. The handsome suite, which shares the second floor with the two standard rooms, looks over both patios, with a French door and tiny balcony opening over the rear garden. Set off by itself in the rear garden, the duplex townhouse has a tiny kitchen, bath, and master bedroom with French doors opening to the patio and, like a treehouse, a smaller bedroom upstairs.

Whether you rent the entire house or just a room, Casa Caruso gives you the luxury of feeling right at home. If it weren't for the many attractions of Oaxaca, you would never want to leave this very special inn.

Casa Conzatti

Gómez Farias 218
(9) 51-3-85-00
Fax: (9)-51-5-07-77

> **A modernized colonial-style hotel in an attractive area**

Accommodations: 45 rooms and suites. **Rates:** Standard rooms $90, junior suites $141, master suites $192.

➤ **Just a short walk from the Casa Conzatti is the magnificently restored 16th-century Centro Cultural Santo Domingo (Alcalá at Gurrion), which houses the stunning Burgoa Library, with its collection of books dating from 1484, and the Museo de Las Culturas de Oaxaca (formerly the Re-**

gional Museum), with its extraordinary collection of Mixtec art and jewelry found in Tomb 7 at Monte Albán, as well as other pre-Columbian and colonial art.

The attractive area around the Conzatti Park, home of the Casa Conzatti, was virtually unknown to tourists until just recently. About a 10-minute walk from the zócalo, it has now been discovered, and with good reason. The tranquil park is popular with locals, and on Fridays it bursts with life with the arrival of a vibrant outdoor market, with stalls of fruits, vegetables, meats, and household items for sale. Here, in the late morning, you can join the long line of locals at the taco stands, waiting patiently to purchase — and consume — vast quantities of some of the tastiest tacos in the city. Just two blocks away is the lovelier and larger Juárez Park, a real gem, known as El Llano ("The Plain") to Oaxaqueños, where children frolic, couples stroll, bands play, and in the summer months Oaxaqueños of all ages try out their best *danzon* steps. This is one of our favorite areas of this special city.

A number of the buildings surrounding Conzatti Park have been recently renovated and now house the most interesting wine store in the city, the tiny La Esquina Oaxaca (Gómez Farias 212B), one of the best boutiques, Beatriz Russek (Gómez Farias 212A), and the Casa Conzatti. (A short distance away is a new Holiday Inn Express, but you won't find us touting this place in this *Best Places to Stay* guide.) The colonial Casa Conzatti, which opened in 1999, is a modernized, serene hotel with a bright yellow façade and warm tones throughout the interior. The small reception area has high ceilings with *vigas*. To the right is the Conzatti's restaurant, Magnolias, with a handsome outdoor courtyard and indoor setting. The common areas are filled with quality art and folk art, including the work of some of Oaxaca's most prominent artists, such as Sergio Hernández, Rubén Leyva, and Felipe Morales. In addition, the common areas house changing exhibits of Oaxacan artists.

The 45 rooms and suites are located in three buildings of two floors each and are set around small courtyards and garden areas, where an occasional fountain flows quietly. Although the rooms are neither luxurious nor spacious, they are tastefully designed, warm, and cheerfully appointed with terra cotta floors, white and orange walls, two double beds, bright, attractive bedspreads and curtains, small modern baths, TVs, irons and ironing boards, and art and folk art. The junior and master suites have upholstered chairs and/or sofas, a coffeemaker, and a mini-bar, as well as a canopied shower curtain over the tub. Free parking is available next door. Because the Conzatti is a relatively new hotel, its owners eager to build up a clientele. Room rates are sometimes negotiable.

Warm and welcoming, the Casa Conzatti is a new face that deserves a following.

Casa Oaxaca

Calle Garcia Vigil 407
(9) 51-4-41-73
Fax: (9) 51-6-44-12

A stylish inn in the center of historic Oaxaca

Accommodations: 6 rooms and suites. **Rates:** Rooms $125–$150, suite $185, entire house $798. **Included:** Continental breakfast and tax. **Payment:** MasterCard, Visa. **Recreation:** Swimming pool.

➤ **For such a traditional city, Oaxaca has an unusually lively contemporary art scene. Casa Oaxaca exhibits paintings for Galería Quetzalli (Constitución 104), one of the city's several excellent art galleries specializing in works by local artists. Other galleries to seek out are Arte de Oaxaca (Murguia 105) and Galería Socuro (Plazuela Labastida 104). And don't miss the Museo de Arte Contemporaneo de Oaxaca (Alcalá 202).**

Walking a few blocks from the zócalo in the historic and bustling center of Oaxaca, you come to the cobalt blue facade of a former private mansion. Through its colonial doors you enter the serene ambience of this inn, with a small reception area, dining room, five rooms, and a stunning duplex suite all arranged around three courtyards. In the rear garden courtyard is a sparkling blue pool and a *temazcal* where arrangements can sometimes be made for a traditional Mexican steam bath and massage.

The inn preserves the beautiful spaces and high ceilings of the colonial mansion, but it has also created a minimalist contemporary environment. Stark, Mediterranean white walls prevail, enlivened by dramatic contemporary paintings and photographs by local artists. Windows open to interior courtyards and skylights brighten rooms (but they are thoughtfully provided with shades to accommodate late sleepers).

Nowhere is there clutter. Rather, the furnishings tend toward the essential, with each piece eye-catching: an antique wardrobe and red chair here, a built-in bedside table and copper sconce there. Bathrooms, too, have a spare elegance of skylight and marble. A few cozy chairs on the terraces, though, would add to the comfort of guests without diminishing the aesthetic, but maybe the right ones haven't been found yet — the inn just opened in 1997.

Casa Oaxaca functions like a private mansion with its own concierge and staff — indeed, you can rent the entire house, just as the president of Mexico recently did. You can have your breakfast in the dining room with its fireplace, on the courtyard terrace, or in the privacy of your room. The kitchen can prepare special requests beyond the Continent breakfast included in the price of the room; for other meals, you can arrange with Evelyn Carlton, the manager, to have food catered from one of the nearby restaurants.

All of the rooms are fan-cooled, more than adequate for Oaxaca's mountain air. Three of the double rooms are similar and have appealing writing alcoves with windows opening to the tranquil pool and garden area. A smaller room, with a sumptuous green marble bath, can be rented at the lowest rate for a double, but the inn encourages its use as a single (at a slightly lower rate). There is also one enormous double room with a king-size bed , a desk of weathered wood and stone, a dressing room, and that same sumptuous green marble for the bath. The duplex suite, well worth the higher price, is the piece de resistance. The first floor has a fireplace, its own terrace overlooking the pool, a bathroom, and a sitting room that can be converted into a sleeping alcove, if you prefer. A stone staircase sweeps up to the second floor, its windows overlooking the treetops. Here are the master bedroom, bath, and writing area.

European in character, Casa Oaxaca brings a new level of international sophistication to this beautiful city.

Las Bugambilias

Reforma 402
(9) 51-6-11-65
Fax: same as phone
Reservations:
904-738-0474

| A cozy bed-and-breakfast

Accommodations: 8 rooms. **Rates:** $65–$78. **Included:** Breakfast; tax. **Children:** Children under 11 years, not permitted. **Minimum stay:** 3 nights. **Smoking:** In garden only. **Payment:** No credit cards.

➤   **Oaxacan families love to celebrate holidays and special occasions by eating good traditional food in a rustic setting. Just on the edge of Oaxaca, La Escondida (Antigua Camino San Agustín) has succeeded in providing**

exactly that. Under a huge open-air *palapa,* **you can eat to your heart's content from vast buffet tables covered with casseroles and** *moles* **and from grills where fresh tortillas and meats are prepared — all for an inexpensive fixed price. There are usually live mariachis, too. Take a taxi and join in. For the best seafood in Oaxaca, continue half a kilometer up the road past La Escondida to Neptuno. The ceviche and whole fish here are especially good.**

On the edge of the central historic district and only a few minutes from Santo Domingo church, the Cabrera family runs a sweet café-style restaurant. Behind the restaurant and away from the street, the Cabreras have converted their home into a bed-and-breakfast inn.

The family has tried to give some Mexican charm to their basically modern home. The result is surely a one-of-a-kind decor, with linoleum flooring vying with folkloric altars. Yet this design approach does succeed in brightening the small, functional bathrooms and in creating a cozy and comfortable environment.

The inn is wedged between a small garden and a bright courtyard, with a separate wing in the back where the family can live with some privacy, apart from the guests. The small garden, if it were outfitted with some lounge furniture, could provide outdoor space for reading and enjoying Oaxaca's good weather, but there was only the beckoning grass on our visit. (You're sure to enjoy the outdoors, though, if you arrange for a traditional sweatbath and massage at this enterprising family's *temascal* complex in a lovely garden on the edge of Oaxaca).

The first floor includes the Victorian living room and formal dining room, with a chandelier hanging from the low ceiling. Our favorite area is the large kitchen, where cooking lessons can be arranged. Off to the side are the three best rooms for privacy, although the two largest ones share a small patio. As with all the rooms, they are fan-cooled, have hand-painted "headboards" on the wall, and a private bath. Upstairs is the coziest part of the house, the TV and reading room filled with books and magazines in English. Two rooms share a small terrace but, due to the lack of privacy and the fact that one bath is down the hall, this section is best used as a suite. On the other side of the TV room are another three rooms, including two sunny ones that overlook the lower patio.

Although the Cabreras don't actually live with guests in this bed-and-breakfast, Las Bugambilias satisfies those travelers looking for simple but homey accommodations.

Las Golondrinas

Calle Tinaco y Palacios 411
(9) 51-4-32-98
Fax: same as phone
Reservations:
lasgolon@prodigy.net.mx

> **The most enticing budget hotel in Oaxaca**

Accommodations: 29 rooms and suites. **Rates:** Standard rooms $36, "honeymoon" suites $45. **Included:** Tax. **Payment:** No credit cards.

➤ If you long for a mountain retreat in a village untouched by tourism, the owners of Las Golondrinas have a home for rent with a beautiful setting in the serene, flower-filled village of Calpulalpan in the Sierra de Juarez, about two hours from Oaxaca. This striking former friars' house features antique carved wooden doors, a huge living room/dining room with beamed ceilings, two bedrooms, two baths, and a very large kitchen. There's also a garden and veranda for reading and relaxing, with wonderful mountain and valley views. Arrangements can be made for a cook to shop and prepare your meals. The rental is for a minimum of one month. For rates and other information about this special place, contact the owners of Las Golondrinas.

The favorite budget hotel with travelers, Las Golondrinas becomes better every year. New flowers bloom among the already luxuriant array of potted plants; small private patios are created for a few more rooms; king-size beds are added to four large "honeymoon" quarters. A garage is purchased to help travelers arriving by car. A striking new piece of folk art makes one of the several patios all the more beckoning. Construction of a *temazcal*, a traditional sweat bath, is planned.

Fortunately, what doesn't change is the warm reception by the staff and the homey ambience created by the attentive owners, Guillermina and Jorge Velasco. Nowhere is their touch more evident than in the breakfast patio. Partially shaded by an arbor and brightened by the colorful tropical designs of the oil cloths covering the tables, the patio is the most convivial spot in Oaxaca. Over breakfast, guests share their travel experiences and advise each other on plans for the coming day. Jorge and Guillermina often join in, adding their considerable expertise. The good food — wonderful Mexican breakfast dishes, such as Guillermina's creation eggs Las Golondrinas — is fuel for further conversation. Like us, most guests find it hard to leave. If other meals were served, guests surely would never see Oaxaca.

The clean rooms with private baths are simply furnished and scattered around the several patios and plant-filled walks, but their similarities end there. Some have windows on the street, most open to the patios, and some open to small private terraces. The humorously nicknamed "honeymoon" suites are especially ample, with king-size beds; quite a few have attractive features like beamed ceilings. As varied as they are, all are comfortable and very well priced. We recently had a wonderful stay in the honeymoon suite A-2, a large room with white stucco walls, a cathedral ceiling, and brick details throughout. The extremely comfortable king-size platform bed had a lovely bedspread; tasteful fabrics covered the sofa and chair. A few well-chosen pieces of art and folk art were placed around the room, and a pine wardrobe and coffee table enhanced the rustic atmosphere. As an added treat there were very good reading lights next to the bed, an unusual feature in many Mexican hotels and virtually unheard of in a budget hotel.

About a six-block walk from the *zócalo*, Las Golondrinas is a special place, a budget inn that's full of Mexican welcome.

Victoria Hotel

Apartado Postal 248
Oaxaca, Oaxaca
(9) 51-5-26-33
Fax: (9) 51-5-24-11
Reservations:
800-44-UTELL (800-448-8355)

A restful aerie overlooking the city

Accommodations: 151 rooms and suites. **Rates:** Standard rooms $134, bungalow rooms $170, junior suites $208, Fiesta Suite $225. **Included:** Shuttle to and from the historic center; tax. **Payment:** Major credit cards. **Children:** Under 12, free in room with parents. **Recreation:** Swimming pool, 1 tennis court.

➤ **Most Oaxaca visitors take the half-hour trip to the rug-weaving village of Teotitlán del Valle. Have a traditional Oaxacan lunch at Restaurante Tlamanalli, which the *New York Times*, with considerable exaggeration, has called one of the top ten culinary destinations in the world.**

The Victoria sprawls serenely across a hillside overlooking downtown Oaxaca and the surrounding mountains. The hotel is the most tranquil spot in the bustling city, close to the sights and the shops but removed from the tumult.

The inviting, palm-lined pool area has the feel of a resort, with yellow and white umbrellas and lounge chairs. Activities are limited, however, to swimming, tennis on one hilltop court, and disco dancing in the late evening. The lobby bar and El Tule, the restaurant, sit above the pool, enjoying broad vistas over the tropically landscaped grounds and down to the church spires below. El Tule's menu offers something for everyone, from Mexican dishes to lasagna. The cooking is not exceptional, but the views from some of the tables are.

If you want the panorama from your room, too, opt for a junior suite, with big windows facing the scenery. In a motel-like three-story wing, they are spacious quarters with two double beds, a desk, a mini-bar, and ample baths. The Fiesta suite has panoramic views of the city and valley. The standard rooms and the more desirable bungalows are twin bed size and plainer, though most of them have a garden terrace. All the accommodations come with satellite TV and a phone.

This Victoria is not a queen among hotels, but she is a pretty lady and modestly playful for Oaxaca.

Puebla

Best Hotel for Stylish Sophistication

Best Bargain for Mexican Character

The Main Attractions

A World Heritage City

Puebla was founded in the sixteenth century by the conquering Spaniards. Straddling the route between the capital and the Gulf port of Veracruz, Puebla replaced the nearby pre-Columbian city of Cholula that was famous not only for its massive pyramid, but also for its pottery. Puebla, too, became famous for pottery, producing European-style hand-painted tiles, urns, and dishes called Talavera ware. Wealthy in clay and pots, colonial Puebla built mansions and churches exuberantly decorated with them — on mansion walls, public fountains, and shimmering church domes. These distinctive architectural works were responsible for the city's selection by the United Nations as a World Heritage site.

Musuems, Mansions, and Churches

Puebla is only a two-hour bus trip from Mexico City or its airport. Recently one U.S. airline began flying directly to the small local airport, making visits all the more feasible. And a visit is well rewarded. Walk through the town's historic center and visit some of the city's many museums — the Museo Amparo is one of Mexico's most exceptional museums of pre-Columbian and colonial-period art. There are mansions, such as the Casa de las Muñecas ("House of the Dolls"), and churches, such as the Chapel of the Rosary, with its ultra-baroque interior, and the lovely park gracing the main square. On the outskirts, visit the ruins of Cholula and the nearby tiled fantasy, the San Francisco Acatepec church.

Camino Real Puebla

7 Poniente 105
Puebla, Puebla
(22) 29-09-09
Fax: (22) 32-92-51
Reservations:
Camino Real Hotels & Resorts
800-722-6466

A 16th-century convent is now a luxurious inn

Accommodations: 83 rooms and suites. **High-season rates:** Standard rooms $145, junior suites $193, master suites $230. **Low-season rates:** Standard rooms $130, junior suites $176, master suites $209. **Payment:** Major credit cards. **Children:** Up to 2 children under 12 free in room with parent. **Services:** Business center, transportation from the Camino Real Hotel in Mexico City, garage.

➤ **Puebla is as famous for its cooking as for its Talavera ceramics. The Fonda de Santa Clara (Av. 3 Poniente 307, 42-26-59), just a few blocks from the hotel, is our favorite restaurant for sampling the intricacies of** *mole poblano* **and, in late summer,** *chiles en nogadas.*

Don Leonardo Ruiz de la Peña honored Our Lady of the Immaculate Conception, whom he believed had saved his life during a flood, by constructing the Convento de la Concepción in 1593. Judging from its present refurbishment, he spared no expense. True, the Camino Real has added the lace bed linens and Talavera tiled bathrooms, the soft illumination of the courtyard arcades, the antique light fixtures, and the brocaded textiles as well as the many other small touches that make this such a fine hotel.

Only a few blocks from the main square, the Camino Real is a world apart from the bustling city center that surrounds it. All the facilities face inward on the graceful courtyards of the old nunnery. The soothing sounds of the water tumbling in the fountains, the sparkling sun, and the thick stone walls combine to make the hotel hard to resist. And it appears no one can. The hotel is perfect for travelers, but it is also favored for small business meetings and loved by locals as a spot to sip a drink or celebrate with dancing in the gorgeous ballroom.

The Novicias lounge, with its armchairs and live music most evenings, has a stunning 12th-century stone balcony from India as its bar and centerpiece. The lounge extends into the first arcaded courtyard to join the terraces of the hotel's two restaurants. Azulejos serves meals and snacks throughout the day and offers very good Mexican dishes and snacks along with international ones. The El Convento restaurant, adorned with colonial paintings and Oriental rugs, serves roasted quail and Chateaubriand, duck and salmon in the most elegant setting in the city.

Most of the rooms open onto the two main courtyards, but a few have windows overlooking smaller patios. The standard rooms, found primarily on the third and fourth floors, have the textured walls and pastel washes of the better rooms. All are air-conditioned and have satellite TVs, a phone, a mini-bar, and an attractively tiled bath. Most of the spacious superior rooms and suites, with their 18-foot-high wooden beam ceilings and adobe walls with traces of frescoes, are located on the first two floors. Some have brass beds and Venetian glass chandeliers, one was the nunnery chapel. The second-floor suites have large furnished terraces while other master suites have a bath with Jacuzzi and views of the historic center.

The Camino Real has succeeded in creating the best inn in Puebla.

Colonial

Calle 4 Sur 105
(22) 46-46-12
Fax: (22) 46-08-18

| **A budget inn with everything** |

Accommodations: 70 rooms. **Rates:** $46. **Payment:** MasterCard, Visa. **Services:** Garage.

➤ **Talavera ceramics are still made in Puebla's *azulejerías*, some of which are open to visitors and buyers. La Trinidad (Avenida Poniente 305, 42-34-32; no credit cards) produces fine pieces but has only a small showroom and is not geared for international trade. Uriarte (Avenida 4 Poniente 911; 32-15-98) not only has an immense showroom but also offers guided tours of the workshops.**

The Colonial occupies an immense, rambling colonial building near the main square. The entire first floor has been left as public space, a lobby and reception area and a series of cozy sitting rooms. Off to the side is a cavernous restaurant, made welcoming by wood-paneled walls, arches, and medieval-style chandeliers. But no matter how many seats there are, they always seem to be full of people engaged in happy, animated conversation. Many small groups, especially European ones, check into the rooms here, confident that there is no more convenient and well-run spot for the money.

The hotel rooms are of various vintages, but they all are basically furnished. Some are larger than others, a few of the older ones have terraces or hand-painted tiles in the bath. The bathrooms are better in the more recently renovated rooms, though, and the interior rooms may have no view, but they are the quietest.

There's a roof terrace atop the six-story structure, an elevator for transporting your luggage, and a useful garage for travelers who have been on the road.

San Miguel de Allende

Best Romantic Hideaways

Best Intimate and Affordable Inn

Best B&Bs and Budget Inns

San Miguel de Allende resembles Santa Fe, New Mexico, a half-century ago, when it was a quiet adobe village with a small Anglo art colony. San Miguel is more worldly than Santa Fe was before the tourists came, but the guileless enchantment is the same, a blend of cobblestone streets and magical skies, of timeworn buildings and a timeless spirit.

Americans discovered San Miguel decades ago, shortly after the Second World War. Adventuresome veterans found they could spread their funds from the G.I. Bill almost to infinity at the Instituto Allende, an English-language college founded by an American-Mexican couple. Like the students who continue to flock to the Instituto, many visitors from north of the border come for extended stays, hoping to shed layers of stress in the slow, down-to-earth environment of a *simpático* village.

San Miguel offers that opportunity, plus a considerable measure of worldly sophistication, imported in many cases on the luxury express buses from Mexico City on weekends, when the hotels are full and the prices highest. Foreign affluence supports a small, active art colony, an English-language newspaper, and several fine hotels and restaurants that strive for Continental style and finesse.

For the most part, the outside influences are readily absorbed, broadening the community. The combination of indigenous serenity and international ease makes San Miguel a relaxing retreat of refreshing contrasts.

The Main Attractions

Cozy Colonial Charm

The cobblestone streets are almost as hilly as San Miguel itself, laid, you suspect, to keep cars moving at about the same pace as the pedestrians. As long as you have comfortable shoes, the town is wonderful for lazy strolls to nowhere in particular. You'll happen on a couple of churches and historic homes worth a peek, but it's the simple wandering that's the real reward. If you ignore the occasional intrusions of the 20th century, you feel you've stepped into an age preceding Mexican independence from Spain, a past more innocent and heroic than the present.

When you are ready to rest, take a bench on the *zócalo,* the central plaza shaded by trimmed trees and lined with 18th-century buildings. Get a spot facing La Parroquia, an old parish church with a pink stone Gothic facade added just a hundred years ago. A self-trained Indian architect designed the elaborate exterior from postcards of European cathedrals, drawing his plans in the sand as instructions for the workers.

Cosmopolitan Earthiness

Despite its grand colonial heritage, San Miguel has the earthy radiance of a country village. The produce market spills through the streets, particularly on Sundays, when young residents also gather on the *zócalo* in the evening for a traditional *paseo.* Interwoven in the rough, rural texture, though, are many threads of city sophistication.

Some of the most interesting places mix elements from both worlds. The best restaurant in town not in a hotel, Bugambilia (Hidalgo 42), gives refined resonance to regional cooking. Another popular spot, Mama Mía (Umaran 8), serves light meals with an Italian bent in a cheery garden courtyard. Two of the top crafts shops, Veryka (Zacateros 6A) and La Calaca (Mesones 93), sell excellent Mexican work, some from the vicinity.

To see the cosmopolitan side of colonial architecture, take the house and garden tour that leaves from the library most Sundays at noon. You will be amazed by the elegance behind some of the plain walls.

Artful Leisure

San Miguel has been an artists' hangout since American painter Stirling Dickinson helped found an art school in 1938. When it folded a decade later, the Instituto Allende rapidly took its place as the main cultural center. More recently, a branch of Mexico City's Instituto de Bellas Artes opened in town, attracting additional artists.

If you're looking for the artsy crowd, check at the Institutos about their activities. You can also ask around at the several galleries downtown, or go barhopping in the evening, particularly spots with entertainment, maybe Mama Mía and La Fragua (Cuna de Allende 3).

Casa Carmen

Correo 31
San Miguel de Allende, Guanajuato
2-08-44
Fax: same as phone
Reservations:
Contact Natalie Mooring at the inn
or write her at Box 152.

A downtown bargain with a cheerful spirit

Accommodations: 11 rooms. **Rates:** $50 for one person, $75 for two. **Included:** Breakfast and lunch. **Payment:** No credit cards.

➤ **The whole village of San Miguel de Allende is a national historic monument. The first part of the name comes from the Franciscan friars who established the town in 1542; the second honors native son Ignacio Allende, a hero of the 1810 War of Independence.**

Tourists wandering in downtown San Miguel de Allende often pass the city's most delightful budget inn without realizing it. In the commercial center of town, a quick walk from the central plaza, Casa Carmen is hidden behind wooden doors heavy enough to withstand another revolution. Inside, a small hacienda wraps around a pleasant patio with potted plants and a bubbling fountain.

Your English-speaking hosts, Horace and Natalie Mooring, are as warm as the congenial mood they create. At first glance their prices may seem a little high for the simple surroundings, but rates include breakfast and lunch in the cozy dining room, which overlooks the central patio.

Like the restaurant, the guest quarters open directly to the sunny courtyard. All are plain, though they are individually decorated with more charm than you find in most budget accommodations. Armoires and area rugs add homey touches, and high beamed ceilings and tile floors are common. The private baths are small but adequate, like the two twin beds.

Most of San Miguel's economy hotels are bleak and overpriced. Casa Carmen is a wonderful exception, a fine place to pinch pesos.

Casa de Sierra Nevada

Hospicio 35
San Miguel de Allende, Guanajuato
(415) 2-70-40, El Parque (415) 2-71-55
Fax: (415) 2-23-37,
El Parque (415) 2-71-52
Reservations:
Small Luxury Hotels of the World
800-525-4800

**An internationally
acclaimed gem of an inn**

Accommodations: 38 rooms and suites. **Rates:** Standard rooms $185, deluxe rooms $209, suites $250, master suites $295–$385. **Included:** Continental breakfast. **Payment:** Major credit cards. **Recreation:** Swimming pool, spa services, and riding packages.

➤ **Casa de Sierra Nevada's new owner also has a horse ranch in San Miguel. The hotel now has its own Equestrian Center, offering 15 miles of riding trails and instruction in a variety of special skills.**

Casa de Sierra Nevada may be Mexico's most cosmopolitan hotel. Under the guidance of former owner Peter Wirth, a fifth-generation Swiss hotelier, and new owner James J. Sprows, the inn has found an ideal blend of European finesse and Mexican beauty.

Housed in thirteen mansions whose origins date back as far as 1580, most of the Sierra Nevada sits on a narrow cobblestone street just a few blocks from San Miguel's *zócalo*. You enter the main hacienda into a plant-filled courtyard that serves as the alfresco terrace for the restaurant and the bar. The efficient staff greet and register you in a small office off the patio and escort you to your nearby quarters.

The other historic homes that make up the hotel are nearby but not contiguous. Most of the rooms and suites are across the small street, hidden behind plain stucco facades and heavy wood doors. All overlook tranquil courtyards, each a soothing mix of old stone and brick, climbing ivy, potted greenery, and folk art accents. Another mansion, Casa de Sierra Nevada el Parque (Sta. Elena 2), opened in 1997 with five new luxurious suites on the lovely Juárez Park, several blocks away but with its own resident manager to insure that every service is at hand for the guests.

Every room celebrates the spirit of Mexico, but each does it in a different way. It's worth spending as much at the inn as your budget will allow. The Spanish colonial–style suites are especially charming and many enjoy fireplaces and terraces, especially the new luxurious master suites at the Sierra Nevada el Parque.

Among our favorite suites are the intimate El Nido and the grander Bella Vista, both aptly named. "The Nest," up two steep flights of stairs, comes with a king-size bed, a tiny balcony, and a distinctive plaster fireplace mantel. As in all the rooms, a spread woven in San Miguel tops the bed. The big second-floor terrace of "Beautiful View" overlooks the spires of the ornate La Parroquia and beyond to the rest of the town. The suite contains two twin beds combined as a king and an enormous bathroom.

Primavera is also lovely, a vision of springtime in green and cream. On the ground floor, it has no patio, but you can peer out through large windows and doors to a bubbling courtyard fountain. A pair of twin beds sit behind a king-size wrought-iron headboard painted grass green. Other features include a fireplace adorned with a whimsical plaster flower vase, stunning bathroom tiles from the nearby village of Dolores Hidalgo, and a glass brick wall that fills the bath with light.

Casa de Sierra Nevada's restaurant is one of the top hotel dining rooms in Mexico, perhaps the best with an international menu. The wine list, predominantly French, matches the menu in refinement, as does the chandeliered indoor dining room, where men are requested to wear coats and ties. Classical guitar music accompanies dinner most evenings.

The menu changes frequently, but it is usually ambitious. You might find among the appetizers a sashimi of sea bass — a tasty mélange that draws on Japanese, Mexican, and Continental traditions. Tender pastas are homemade and combined with varied toppings. The steak entrées are excellent, whether you choose one with a béarnaise, Roquefort, or green peppercorn sauce. Several kinds of fresh fish are cooked in a range of ways, including a simply savory meuniére style with pine nuts. A light meal can be made of the house salad, which changes according to the ingredients available but on our last visit consisted of tiny shrimp, asparagus, broccoli, tomatoes, Roquefort, and crisp greens.

Casa de Sierra Nevada's newest features are a swimming pool and a Health and Beauty Center that offers oriental massages, facials, body wraps, and other spa treatments. If you prefer golf or tennis, the hotel can arrange them at a nearby private country club. If you would rather shop, the inn's Primavera boutique is steps down the street, and San Miguel's shops and galleries are an easy walk.

Few if any hotels in the country can match the breadth and depth of the Casa's amenities and services. The blend of colonial Mexican enchantment and international refinement produce an experience you'll savor for years to come.

La Puertecita Boutique'otel

Santo Domingo 75
San Miguel de Allende, Guanajuato
(415) 2-50-11
Fax: (415) 2-55-05
Reservations:
800-447-7462

An artfully designed hideaway overlooking town

Accommodations: 36 rooms and suites. **Rates:** Rooms $165, junior suites $190, 2-bedroom suites $350. **Included:** Breakfast. **Payment:** Major credit cards. **Smoking:** Not permitted. **Recreation:** 2 swimming pools, Jacuzzi, fitness area.

➤ **A Conference Park in the woods nearby has meeting space, an acoustically tuned chamber music room, and a learning center. The latter**

specializes in fun but intensive Spanish-language programs, among the educational and cultural packages the inn offers.

After years of experience in the hotel business in Hawaii, John Kay moved to San Miguel de Allende to get away from the tourism industry and become a professional sculptor. He achieved both goals, paradoxically, by opening an all-suites inn, a handcrafted masterpiece of a boutique hotel far removed from the commercial crassness of Waikiki.

As Kay says, La Puertecita emphasizes "service, service, service." With a high ratio of staff to guests, the owner tries to make you feel as if you're staying in the home of a close and caring friend. There's always someone to shuttle you to the center of town, suggest shops to seek out, or help you with your Spanish. If the swimming pools and fitness center don't provide enough exercise opportunities for you, the inn has a corporate membership in a nearby country club that offers golf and tennis.

The inn even resembles a home, an elegant villa that's as worldly as it is authentically Mexican. Just a 20-minute walk from town, you enter the hacienda down a curving staircase that wraps around a tiled fountain, leading you to a dining room terrace overlooking the heated pool. Inside the restaurant a parquet floor gleams up at a handsome domed brick ceiling, a feature shared by many of the rooms. Nearby, guests lounge cozily in a music room and library with a grand piano, fireplace, and views of manicured gardens. Across the lane, nestled in a parklike setting with one of the swimming pools, are villa complexes with many of the handsomely appointed double rooms.

The suites differ in decor, but each partakes of the delightful architecture in its own special way, perhaps with round windows of carved stone, rock walls, or hand-painted tiles from Dolores Hidalgo. Most of the chambers have two queen-size beds, and all enjoy large, luxurious baths, cable TV, a phone, and electric blankets, and, for a few rooms, private fireplaces for San Miguel's cool evenings. The aptly named Jardin suite is filled with plants, two others come with private Jacuzzis, and one has its own wine cellar and wet bar. Smoking is not permitted in any of the quarters.

In contrast with the Continental tone at most of San Miguel's hotel dining rooms, La Puertecita focuses on fine Mexican food supplemented by an international selection of salads and soups. We had an excellent dinner recently of seafood soup, spinach salad, chicken mole, and enchiladas. The Arboleda restaurant provides an abbreviated version of its menu 24 hours a day for room or pool service.

John Kay has sculpted a monument to good taste at his boutique hotel. He doesn't miss the madding crowds of the tourism business one bit, and neither will you.

Villa Jacaranda

Aldama 53
San Miguel de Allende, Guanajuato
(415) 2-10-15
Fax: (415) 2-08-83
Reservations:
800-310-9688

A quiet, pretty, tasteful inn

Accommodations: 16 rooms and suites. **Rates:** Rooms $135, suites $148–$178. **Included:** 17% tax. **Children:** Not suitable. **Recreation:** Swimming pool, Jacuzzi, gym.

➤ **The inn is named for a jacaranda tree near the entrance. In spring it blooms in violet profusion, making the usually warm welcome even more special.**

On an old colonial street between downtown and Juárez Park, Villa Jacaranda is a compact compound featuring an elegant hacienda, meandering stone paths, garden terraces, and ivy-covered walls. It exudes an unassuming classiness that reflects the tastes of the creators — Don Fenton, an American, and his Mexican wife, Gloria.

A small, formal plunge pool and a Jacuzzi overseen by a parrot occupy the center of the inn. The water separates the casual daytime gazebo restaurant, El Kiosco, from the more urbane evening dining room. Dinners are tasteful events featuring traditional Continental dishes such as chicken Kiev, coquilles St. Jacques, and trout amandine. Though the preparations tend to be heavy on salt and butter in our experience, the cooking and the service are skilled.

Most of the guest rooms are suites, and most enjoy flower-filled *terrazas* or patios. Though each chamber is different, they vary in the standard way, with the size of the sitting area in particular expanding in proportion to price. Many have fireplaces, fabrics woven in San Miguel, and a bath filled with Mexican tile. The beds are usually doubles or twins with attractive headboards, often carved wood or wrought iron. Phones are limited to the lobby, but each room has a TV.

Villa Jacaranda successfully blends a decorous, worldly formality and comfortable Mexican character. It's not as sophisticated as some places in San Miguel de Allende, but it's in the same league with the best in most respects except price.

Villa Mirasol

Pila Seca 35
San Miguel de Allende, Guanajuato
(415) 2-66-85
Fax: (415) 2-15-64

A homey B&B with down-to-earth rates

Accommodations: 9 rooms. **Rates:** $75–$85. **Included:** Breakfast. **Payment:** MasterCard, Visa.

➤ **Carmen Avery serves a hearty breakfast at her B&B inn, perhaps French toast or *huevos mexicanos,* and she also offers sweet snacks at teatime in the afternoon.**

Hidden behind a high wall in a residential neighborhood, about equidistant from downtown and the Instituto Allende, Villa Mirasol is a comfy bed-and-breakfast inn. The sign out front is small, but the welcome is big, thanks to hostess Carmen Avery, who creates a warm, hospitable environment.

The rooms are spread around the upper and lower floors of a large hacienda. Each of the nine quarters is different in size and decor, but all have private bathrooms with hand-painted Mexican tile, sunny patios, and a cheerful spirit. Guests share use of the living room, a cozy spot with a fireplace, TV, and laden bookcases.

The least expensive rooms, Orchard and Escondido, are downstairs near the kitchen. They are the smallest chambers, with two twin beds, and they look out on an inner courtyard. La Casita and La Paloma, in the middle of the price range, are upstairs and share a tile *terraza.* La Paloma enjoys lots of light and a distinctive *boveda* (domed) ceiling. Across the way, La Casita has windows facing a profusion of bougainvillea.

Bellavista is true to its name, with views over the gardens. Also in the mid-range of rates, it comes with two twin beds, a stone floor, and a fireplace. Bugambilia, with another of the handsome *boveda* ceilings, overlooks the quiet front street. If you're traveling with a child or just want to spread out, Rosa María features a second small bedroom or dressing area with a single bed. Though it's the most expensive chamber, it's hardly costly for what you get. Discounts for weekly and monthly stays provide even greater value.

Taxco

Best Recreational Resort or Spa

Best Intimate and Affordable Inn

Best Bargains for Mexican Character

Among Mexico's colonial silver cities, Taxco remains the most faithful to its original source of wealth and attracts the most visitors. Tourists arrive daily on bus excursions from Acapulco and Mexico City — several hours by toll road in opposite directions — and many others in rental cars stop for a night or two on journeys between the capital and the beach. In years past, this route was a favorite of American tourists, so much so that many lingered and created a small expatriate community. Acapulco is most often reached by air these days, bypassing Taxco. It remains popular, though, especially with silver merchants and Mexican travelers. At times the small, pretty downtown area swarms with commerce, but Taxco absorbs it with friendly goodwill and an abiding sense of self.

Modern businesses line the road into the city, but once you start up the cobblestone streets into the center, especially when it isn't rush hour, you go back in time to the 18th century, when silver baron José de la Borda struck a rich vein and Taxco peaked in prosperity. The mines played out after a number of decades, and silver dwindled in importance until American author William Spratling came to town in 1929 to write a book. When his publisher went bankrupt, Spratling took up silver craftsmanship and serendipitously started a major new industry. Taxco thrives again on the silver legacy.

The Main Attractions

Up, Down, and Around the Hill

The heart of Taxco is on a steep hill rimmed with narrow, winding streets, orange tile roofs, flowers, and fountains. The *zócalo* sits at the top under the restful spell of the Santa Prisca Church, one of the loveliest in Mexico. José de la Borda gave a fortune to refurbish the 16th-century church in a baroque manner. The architect did a magnificent job, adding a blue tile dome and two elaborately carved towers that soar above the city.

Other spots to seek out in town are nearby and down the hill. Just behind Santa Prisca, the Museo Guillermo Spratling exhibits the silversmith's collection of pre-Columbian art. You can glance into Borda's former home on the *zócalo*, now the city hall, but a couple of other historic buildings may be more fascinating. Borda's friend Count Cadena lived in Casa Figueroa (Guadalupe 2), also known as the House of Tears because of the conscripted Indian labor used in its construction. The Moorish Casa Humboldt (Ruiz de Alarcón 6), originally an inn, is interesting on its own and also as a museum of colonial art.

Silver Shopping

Taxco silver pieces, shipped around the world, aren't any cheaper at the source than elsewhere in Mexico, unless you are buying in large enough quantities for wholesale prices. But the selection is certainly enormous at the hundred or so shops. Before you buy anything, visit some of best-established dealers to get a sense of quality standards. Try Pineda's (on the *zócalo*) perhaps, and Los Castillo (Plazuela de Bernal 10), where you can tour the workshop. If you can't afford anything from these shops, at least know you what you're giving up to get a lower price.

Hacienda del Solar

Apartado Postal 96
Taxco, Guerrero
(762) 2-03-23

A stylish inn on the
outskirts of town

Accommodations: 30 rooms and junior suites. **High-season rates:** Deluxe rooms $110, junior suites $150. **Low-season rates:** Deluxe rooms $85, junior suites $120. **Payment:** Major credit cards. **Children:** Under 12, not permitted. **Recreation:** Swimming pool, 1 tennis court.

➤ **Guests at Hacienda del Sol congregate on warm days at the pool then move inside in the evening to a lounge with a fireplace and a meal in La Venta de Taxco restaurant. Some spend more time at these pursuits than in hiking around Taxco.**

Spread organically around 80 acres just south of Taxco, off Highway 95, the rustic but refined Hacienda del Solar is the top hotel in town. It's not as polished as it likes to pretend, but it offers grand vistas and the grandest accommodations around.

In the main hacienda, the 22 guest quarters are divided almost equally into deluxe rooms and junior suites, all captivating despite occasional signs of wear. The space increases as you climb the rate scale, as does the likelihood of domed brick ceilings, a fireplace, Mexican tile, Taxco wood and *equipale* furniture, and stone walls. Many of the quarters have terraces, sometimes with a spectacular view of Taxco. Scattered around the many acres are *casitas* containing the remaining junior suites, two in each handsome villa.

The view at the hacienda is featured at the aptly named restaurant, La Ventana de Taxco, the city's most attractive spot for fine dining. *Ventana* is Spanish for window, where your eyes are drawn immediately for a vista that's particularly stunning at night. The menu is primarily Italian with a sprinkling of Mexican dishes.

In 1997 the Hacienda del Solar advertised for investors in the hotel or in a residential development planned for the estate. We can only hope the country setting and lovely hacienda will not be lost in the years to come.

Los Arcos

Juan Ruiz de Alarcón 2
Taxco, Guerrero
(762) 2-18-36
Fax: (762) 2-32-11

**A historic hotel with
bargain rates**

Accommodations: 25 rooms. **Rates:** $27. **Payment:** MasterCard, Visa.

➤ **Just up the hill from Los Arcos, Paco's Bar enjoys an enviable perch
on the *zócalo*, peering directly across the plaza at the Santa Prisca Church.
The food is often as good as the drinks, and the people-watching is superb.**

In Taxco, a city resplendent with colonial character, there are few
places we enjoy more for the local flavor than the Hotel Los Arcos,
just a block below the *zócalo*. A converted 17th-century monas-
tery, the small inn personifies the town's architecture, an enchanting mix of red tiles, stately columns, organic arches, and walkways
of brick and stone.

These features are particularly striking in the entrance courtyard
of the three-story hotel. It's a lovely spot, with an ancient tree
growing toward the sky overhead, a fountain, and decorative folk
art accents. Take a chair in the open-air lobby and absorb the atmosphere while you relax with a drink or a book.

The rooms are less alluring, but all are a good value and some are
wonderful for the price. Our favorite is number 12, a split-level
chamber with a sitting area and a tiled bathroom on the first floor
and a loft above with a double bed and a twin. The stone floors,
heavy wood furnishings, and a Mexican tree of life make it a special spot. Most of the other rooms are more conventional in style,
but they are clean and generally spacious.

A rooftop terrace where plants grow in bathtubs has pretty views
of the city, but it may not tempt you away from the courtyard too
often. Once you're inside Los Arcos, the sights outside seem a little
less compelling.

MonteTaxco

Fraccionamiento Lomas de Taxco
Taxco, Guerrero
(762) 2-13-00
Fax: (762) 2-14-28

A country resort with lofty vistas

Accommodations: 170 rooms and suites. **Rates:** Rooms $103–$120, suites $174. **Payment:** Major credit cards. **Recreation:** 2 swimming pools, golf (9 holes), 3 tennis courts, fitness center, horseback riding.

➤ **The whole town of Taxco is a designated historical monument, a fact that will be etched in your memory after you survey the sights from the lofty perspective of the cable car up to MonteTaxco.**

A mountaintop aerie, the MonteTaxco is perched in the clouds high above Taxco at the summit of a steep, winding cobblestone road. The breathtaking views of the colonial city are worth a stop alone, and the convivial atmosphere makes the visit a double delight.

A popular weekend getaway for Mexico City residents, the hotel offers an abundance of activities. You can go horseback riding, play tennis, laze by your choice of pools, or dance the night away in the disco. The nine-hole golf course shows off the spectacular setting, which requires caddies instead of carts because of the terrain you cross. If you need more thrills, take the long, almost perpendicular tramway into town, a cable car ride guaranteed to keep you alert.

Renovated extensively in recent years, the MonteTaxco feels fresh and brightly Mexican. The lobby announces the mood with a wealth of hand-painted fluorescent plants and animals. The drawings, done by a well-known local artist, continue down the hallways, around door jambs and elevators, and into the guest rooms.

An all-day restaurant, Taxqueño, shares the main building with the lobby, serving Mexican and Continental dishes either à la carte or buffet style. Toni's, open only for dinner, features prime rib and lobster, and for lunch a poolside *palapa* café offers *horno*-baked pizzas, grilled chicken, and sandwiches. There are two bars, one with live music nightly and other planned entertainments as well as a rollicking fiesta on Saturday nights with a bountiful Mexican buffet and fireworks.

The exuberant personality of the public areas spills into the peach and white rooms. They come with a king bed or two doubles, a floral bedspread, TV, phone, and tiled bathroom. Most have a balcony with a stunning view of Taxco, but some rooms in the main building overlook only a parking lot.

The best way to arrive is on the *teléferico*, or cable car, found on the entrance road into Taxco. Or you can drive up the spiraling road from town. However you arrive, you'll relish the sights and the Mexican sparkle. The refurbished resort is bound to lift your spirits.

Posada de los Castillo

Juan Ruiz de Alarcón 3
Taxco, Guerrero
(762) 2-13-96
Fax: (762) 2-29-35

> **A colonial hacienda converted into a budget hotel**

Accommodations: 15 rooms. **Rates:** $23. **Payment:** MasterCard, Visa.

➤ **If silver is your reason for visiting Taxco, schedule your visit to coincide with the week-long National Silver Fair in late November or early December. Judges award prizes that bring recognition and maybe fame to aspiring artisans.**

The Posada de los Castillo combines friendly management and the quaint architectural character of Taxco with a handy location near the *zócalo* and Santa Prisca church. It has a less colonial atmosphere than the neighboring Hotel Los Arcos, but it's more convivial in spirit and even less expensive.

The lobby you enter from a serpentine downtown street is shared with a silver shop, allowing you to start your browsing while you register. The rooms are upstairs, encircling a tiny four-story atrium. They are simple quarters, featuring pleasant touches such as hand-painted Mexican tile in the bath, tin mirrors, red tile floors, and nicely crafted furnishings. The beds, all with attractive headboards, vary between doubles and twins.

The hotel has no restaurant or bar, but we know from experience that the English-speaking manager, Teo Contreras, offers solid recommendations about places to try. That eagerness to please makes the Posada de los Castillo a budget gem in the silver city.

Santa Prisca

Plazuela San Juan
Taxco, Guerrero
(762) 2-00-80
Fax: Same as phone

A relaxing spot with a sunny garden

Accommodations: 38 rooms and suites. **Rates:** Rooms $40, junior suites $55. **Included:** Breakfast. **Payment:** Major credit cards. **Children:** Under 12, free in room with parents.

➤ **The pageantry of Holy Week in Taxco is famed throughout Mexico. Processions start on Palm Sunday and continue until Easter, culminating in reenactments of the Last Supper and the Resurrection.**

Up a cobblestone drive from Plazuela San Juan, the Santa Prisca is a quiet refuge in the heart of Taxco, only two blocks from the main plaza and directly across from the entrance to the market. All the shopping you want is immediately at hand, but you can also withdraw readily into serenity.

The three-story inn is a picture-perfect example of local architecture, a colonial-style building with white stucco walls and a red-tile roof. It wraps around a beautiful central courtyard replete with orange trees, bougainvillea, palms, and a bubbling fountain. Upstairs, you can read in a cozy second-floor library or scan the city from a rooftop terrace.

The rooms are plain but clean, guileless quarters with basic wood furniture, red tile floors, a shower in the bath, and not much more. Usually you get a double and a twin bed. Junior suites are no fancier, although they are larger and worth the minimal extra expense. Be sure to request a room overlooking the courtyard, easily the most desirable view.

Breakfast, included in the rate, is served in an airy dining room between the bustling street and the peaceful interior garden. Also open for lunch and dinner, the restaurant is a bright spot with a fireplace, mobiles of doves, yellow wood chairs, blue and white tablecloths, and white Mexican pottery bearing the Santa Prisca name in blue. The kitchen makes a good, piquant version of *huevos rancheros.*

Nothing gets much more complicated than that dish at the Santa Prisca. The hotel is a simple but tranquil haven in the Taxco tumult.

Zacatecas

Best Romantic Hideaway

Best Bargain for Mexican Character

Best Place to Combine Business and Pleasure

Mexico still leads the world in silver production, and the old silver city of Zacatecas leads the country. The industry is one of the factors behind a recent boom in the city that is stimulating modern development everywhere except in the colonial downtown, as tranquil today as in its 18th-century prime. Surrounded by desert scrub, Zacatecas lacks the setting of such sister cities as Guanajuato and San Miguel, but it concentrates similar architectural allure in the walkable central area and is the only one of the towns directly accessible by air.

The Main Attractions

Baroque Bewitchment

The spirit of downtown is dominated by the cathedral, directly on the *zócalo.* Completed in 1752 after decades of decorating, it's the most exuberantly Mexican church anywhere. Covered completely by sculpture and elaborate designs, the facade is a mind-boggling profusion of ornate detail. One legend explains the extravagance by claiming that an artist, given a reprieve on a death sentence to work on the cathedral, kept embellishing the exterior until he died of natural causes.

A stroll south or west from the *zócalo* takes you up and down narrow, hilly streets to small plazas and pleasant parks. Don't miss the three art museums. The Museo Pedro Coronel (Calle del Correo, near the cathedral) houses the personal collection of Zacatecan artist Pedro Coronel. It's an eclectic collection, like a mini Metropolitan Museum of Art, with Chinese bronzes, African masks, and Picasso lithographs. His own paintings and the work of other Zacatecan artists are displayed at the Museo de Francisco Goitia (Enrique Estrada 102). Coronel's brother's fabulous collection of Mexican masks can be seen at the Museo Rafael Coronel (Plaza San Francisco).

The Tramway and the Mine

At an elevation of 8,000 feet, Zacatecas is in a high valley surrounded by mountains. Two hills, Cerro Grillo and Cerro La Bufa, rise above the center on opposite sides of the *zócalo*, the peaks connected by an aerial tramway. The views are spectacular, particularly starting from the lower Cerro Grillo and going to the top of La Bufa, where a small history museum and a venerable church supplement the sights below.

Before or after the trip, visit the Eden Mine, near the tram terminal on Cerro Grillo. Closed for ore operations centuries ago, it's open today as an example of an early mine. You can see the interior of the shaft and learn about the wretched conditions, conducted mainly by Indian slaves. At night, it's a disco!

Aristos

Loma de la Soledad S/N
Zacatecas, Zacatecas
(492) 2-17-88
Fax: (492) 2-69-08
Reservations:
Aristos Hotels
512-631-2000
800-5-ARISTO
Fax: 512-631-8416

A modest hotel with moderate rates and a grand perch

Accommodations: 100 rooms. **Rates:** Rooms start at $48. **Payment:** Major credit cards. **Children:** Under 12, free with parents. **Recreation:** Swimming pool.

➤ **The former 19th-century market, El Mercado (near the cathedral), has been turned into a stylish mall stocked with Zacatecan products: tooled leather saddles and belts, wine, mineral stones, and antiques. Here, too, cluster some of the tourist restaurants, like the handsome La Cuija (Tacuba 5, 2-82-75).**

A chain property that resembles a motel, the Aristos offers more quirky quaintness than you expect, affordable rates, and most important, a prime hillside view over one of Mexico's loveliest downtowns.

The two-story hotel tries to reflect its colonial surroundings with columns, red tile, and other features, but the overall effect is definitely of the 20th century. The rooms contain two double beds or a king, color TV, a telephone, fully modern baths, and furnishings that are occasionally a little worn and dated in style. Every room has a balcony or a patio, but vantage points vary. The best views are from the second floor.

The staff don't speak much English, but they strive to be helpful. They will arrange sightseeing tours, as well as golf at a nearby club. On-site recreation includes a skylighted indoor swimming pool and a sauna. A walk into town provides a pleasant 15 minutes of exercise, but you'll probably want a cab for the uphill return.

In many respects the Aristos is a typical chain hotel, but its casual ambience is local in flavor, and locations like this can't be franchised.

Continental Plaza Zacatecas

Miguel Hidalgo 703
Zacatecas, Zacatecas
(492) 2-61-83
Fax: (492) 2-62-45
Reservations:
Continental Plaza
800-882-6684

**Centrally located for
business or pleasure**

Accommodations: 115 rooms and suites. **Rates:** Standard rooms $100. **Payment:** Major credit cards. **Children:** Under 12, free in room with parents.

➤   **The nearby colonial village of Guadalupe played a role in American history as the base for Franciscan missions established in the Southwest when the region was the northern frontier of New Spain. The gilded Capilla de Napoles in Guadalupe's church and convent is a monument to the age of the silver baron.**

Located across from the cathedral, the Continental Plaza couldn't be more central to the sights. The pink 18th-century mansion has been refurbished inside with a modicum of colonial charm and a business-oriented environment, but the hotel is a lively meeting spot for Mexicans. From the fifth-floor terrace you can survey the whole of the city and the surrounding hills.

Dark hallways lead to rooms that are modern but small. The quarters come with a king bed or two doubles, a phone, satellite TV, air conditioning, a mini-bar, and a few pleasant design touches such as hand-woven rugs, tin lamps, and tile bathrooms. The very best rooms are on the fourth and fifth floors and have terraces with views of the cathedral. The slightly larger junior suites and suites are reserved for time-sharing rather than hotel use.

Downstairs on the ground floor, the bar features live music and Los Candiles serves Mexican and international dishes in a cafeteria-like setting. That's it for dining and diversions at the hotel, but you have the rest of Zacatecas at your feet.

The Continental Plaza keeps you comfortable and also close to the reasons why you came.

Quinta Real Zacatecas

Avenida Rayón 434
Zacatecas, Zacatecas
(492) 2-91-04/7
Fax: (492) 2-84-40
Reservations:
Quinta Real
800-445-4565

> **A breathtaking hotel with first-class food and service**

Accommodations: 49 suites. **Rates:** Master suites $170, grand class suites $180, Presidential Suite $440. **Payment:** Major credit cards. **Children:** Under 12, free with parents.

➤ **One of our favorite spots in the Quinta Real is the grotto-like El Botarel bar, where you can sip cocktails in front of a brick fireplace surrounded by handsome stonework.**

In the midst of the historic splendor of downtown Zacatecas, Quinta Real created a new, late-20th-century landmark that imaginatively incorporates the ruins of the Americas' second-oldest bullring and a portion of an equally ancient aqueduct. The inn blends harmoniously with its environment in one of most remarkable achievements of recent hotel architecture anywhere in the world.

Driving under and through the aqueduct, guests arrive near the top of the multilevel circular hotel, a picture of colonial grandeur in cream stone and ocher stucco. New colonnaded arches, emulating the originals, surround the property majestically. Inside, the antiques and the art maintain the mood, exuding a sense of classic repose.

The enormous suites have walls of stone and pastel stucco coordinated with the floral bedspreads and drapes, and oriental rugs. The king-size or two double beds are usually crowned by a lighted triptych painting, and two heroic stone lions hold up the glass top of a writing desk. All the quarters come with cable TV, a direct-dial phone, air conditioning, and views of fountains and gardens. The large bathrooms feature spacious vanities, excellent lighting, and a hefty tub-shower framed in a handsome arch. Grand class suites enjoy Jacuzzi tubs.

The restaurant, La Plaza, is one of the country's best for sophisticated dining. The menu updates traditional Mexican fare and adds good renditions of international dishes, usually accented with local flavors. For dinner on our last visit we had chicken with *nopalitos* and a stuffed pork chop in a *pulque* sauce. Both were superbly prepared and presented, masterful examples of Mexican *alta cucina* (high cooking).

As with the sister hotels in the small Quinta Real collection, the management takes pride in high service standards meant to appeal to Zacatecas's business travelers as well as to tourists. There are excellent meeting facilities, though the staff are careful to discourage large groups that would diminish the feel of quiet sophistication.

Mexico has long needed more small luxury hotels that reflect the country's endearing spirit, cultural wealth, and complex cuisine. The Quinta Real in Zacatecas blazes new trails in those ways and more.

Baja California

Ensenada, Rosarito, and Tecate

Best Recreational Resorts and Spas

Best Beachfront Buy

Best Intimate and Affordable Inn

As the primary access point to the Mexican borderlands just south of San Diego, Tijuana attracts more American visitors than any other foreign city in the world. Most people come just for the day, but an increasing number take the short toll expressway over to northern Baja's Pacific coast to spend a few nights by the beach. It's an easy, quick, and inexpensive getaway, not only for southern Californians but for anyone traveling in the area.

The two main destinations, Rosarito and Ensenada, are a cross between a touristy border town and a Mexican village. Neither offers the breadth of culture and character found in the interior, and the beaches won't inspire many toasts, but you do get a slice of Mexico and plenty of sand and sun.

Thirty minutes from Tijuana, Rosarito is known for its seafood, especially the lobster that has made the neighboring village of Pueblo Nuevo famous. The truth is that the lobster here has been depleted, and this Pacific crustacean must be trapped farther south. But the tradition of dining on it here continues. It's served in most of the local restaurants, including the two at the Rosarito Beach Hotel, described below. Artisans in the town specialize in hand-crafted home furnishings, particularly *equipale* chairs.

Another hour south, Ensenada is bigger, busier, and more popular. The action ranges from deep-sea fishing, at a peak in the summer yellowtail season, to the nightlife at the colorful Hussong's Cantina. The center of Baja's emerging wine industry, the city also features a winery tour and several cosmopolitan restaurants where you can sample the area's *vino.*

East of Tijuana, away from the ocean, Tecate gets far fewer visitors than Rosarito and Ensenada, but the ones who come are more serious about their mission. The only major attraction is the well-known health resort, Rancho La Puerta, a great place to go when you want to shape up.

Northern Baja may not give you an in-depth experience of Mexico, but it does have its lures, more than any of the other entry points along the extended U.S. border. It's an introduction to the country and usually a fun one.

Ensenada

Coral Hotel & Marina

Carretera Tijuana-Ensenada Km 103, Zona Playitas
(617) 5-00-01
Fax: (617) 5-00-05
Reservations:
619-523-0064
800-946-2742

A grand hotel with superb recreational facilities

Accommodations: 150 rooms and suites. **High-season rates:** Standard double suite $135, junior suite $150, deluxe suite $220, master suite $285, Presidential suite $600. **Low-season rates:** Sunday–Thursday, 40% off high-season rate, Friday–Saturday, 20% off high-season rate. **Payment:** Major credit cards. **Children:** 12 and under, free in room with parents; playground, game room. **Recreation:** 2 swimming pools (1 indoor lap pool, 1 outdoor pool); 3 indoor and outdoor Jacuzzis; 2 tennis courts; spa with massage, facials, saunas and steam rooms; gym with cardiovascular and weight machines; 600-slip marina.

➤ Downtown Ensenada is only a few miles from the hotel and offers lots of shops and restaurants. Two elegant spots for dinner are El Rey Sol (López Mateos 1000, 8-17-33), which offers French cuisine and ambience,

and La Embotelladora Vieja (Avenida Miramar at Calle 7, 4-08-07), owned by the Santo Tomas winery, which features its wines with the Continental cuisine.

The Coral Hotel & Marina opened at this coastal location just north of Ensenada in 1995, presenting a new level of luxury for the port city and, for boaters, the first marina on northern Baja's Pacific shore.

Everything at the hotel was designed with an eye to spaciousness. The monumentality of the gleaming lobby has a European elegance, with parquet floors and leather armchairs, original works of art and a concert grand piano. Even the service has a hint of Continental polish. Two six-story wings embrace the pool and sunning terraces and provide a frame for the magnificent view over the marina, the sea, and rocky promontories of the bay. The view is a soothing presence from all over the hotel and its facilities.

The rooms are extremely generous in size and appointments. All have a sitting area and furnished terrace with a view, but what is remarkable is that every room, except the few standard ones, has a sitting room that is larger than most living rooms as well as a separate bedroom. Each room has satellite TV and at least one phone and the bathrooms are very well appointed. The best rooms for views and large terraces are in the center building. Some suites have wet bars, others two or more bedrooms.

Dining facilities are limited, probably because the hotel is less than a three-mile ride into downtown Ensenada. Most guests don't move from the outdoor terraces of the hotel during the day, when light meals can be ordered from the poolside bar. We had trouble moving from our terrace in the central tower and made considerable use of room service. The restaurant is informal, but the food is far from relaxed. The breakfast pastries are made on the premises and other meals show a very competent hand in the kitchen, from the Mexican dishes such as *sopa poblana* and César salad (yes, it was invented in Tijuana) to international ones such as pork loin in mustard sauce. And although the hotel has a captive audience, the prices are reasonable. On weekends, when all Baja hotels are their busiest, there is piano music in the lobby lounge.

The recreational facilities at the hotel are exceptionally good. The two large swimming pools make up for the lack of ocean swimming (because of the marina), and the marina promenade, though not as satisfying as a beach, did provide an opportunity for a moonlight stroll. The gym has quality equipment in sunny, glass-enclosed rooms. The marina itself has 24-hour security and includes use of hotel facilities and all utilities in the cost of a slip.

The Coral Hotel & Marina offers one of the finest vacation opportunities in Baja Norte.

Las Rosas Hotel and Spa

Apartado Postal 316
Ensenada, Baja California Norte
(617) 4-43-10
Fax: (617) 4-45-95

> **A small seaside inn with a rosy disposition**

Accommodations: 51 rooms. **High-season rates:** Double rooms $126–$137, honeymoon and junior suites $154, master suites $170. **Low-season rates:** Double rooms $116–$127, honeymoon and junior suites $139, master suites $150. **Payment:** MasterCard, Visa. **Recreation:** Swimming pool, small gym and spa with massage and sauna, indoor tennis and racquetball center.

➤ **Baja's vineyards lie in the valleys outside Ensenada, but most of the winemaking is done in Ensenada, where you might want to visit the facilities and tasting rooms. Monte Xanic (behind the Plaza Civica, 3-31-46), is Baja's premier boutique wine; tastings can be arranged by appointment only. The Santo Tomás facility (Avenida Miramar 666; 8-25-09) is more extensive; tours and wine tastings are available several times daily.**

About four miles north of Ensenada, right after the end of the expressway, Las Rosas extends a rosy welcome in all ways. The entrance glows in soft pink tones, inviting you inside to a lobby blushing with the same color. You spot the ocean immediately, framed through rear windows, and see it reflected around you in seafoam accents. Beyond the reception desk, a fountain leads you down a few steps to a cozy piano bar and an elegantly dressed restaurant, both peering out to the Pacific.

The hotel sits directly on the water, atop a rocky coast splashed with surf. The swimming pool is so close to the scene that it appears to flow into the sea. A Jacuzzi enjoys a prime perch too, on a sunset observation deck, and so does a massage *palapa* overlooking the waves. There is no beach.

All the rooms face the same view and have balconies for savoring it. The smallest and least expensive quarters are snug, but the honeymoon suites (with a fireplace) and the junior suites are ample, with a sitting area that opens into the bedroom. Each is pleasantly decorated in a contemporary tropical style and comes with a TV, phone, air conditioning, and a ceiling fan.

The restaurant offers an enticing breakfast menu, featuring a range of Mexican and American dishes plus such house specialties as eggs Georgette, chopped lobster and Hollandaise sauce on an artichoke base. Lunch is mainly local in flavor and dinner is more international, with an emphasis on fresh seafood. The kitchen takes particular pride in its squid steak with crab sauce. The next day you can work off the calories playing tennis or simply pamper yourself further with a facial or other spa treatment.

Las Rosas exudes a sunny Southern California air. You won't mistake Ensenada for Malibu, but at home in your hotel you won't feel far away.

Rosarito

Rosarito Beach Hotel

Rosarito, Baja California Norte
(661) 2-01-44
Fax: (661) 2-11-76
Reservations:
Rosarito Beach Hotel
619-498-8230
800-343-8582

**An old-timer with a
fascinating past**

Accommodations: 235 rooms and suites. **High-season rates:** Main building rooms $119, oceanfront rooms $179, oceanfront suites $199, apartments $259, 2-bedroom master suites. **Low-season rates:** Main building rooms $79–$99, oceanfront rooms $89–$139, oceanfront suites $100–$149, apartments $139–$179, 2-bedroom master suites $179–$209. **Included:** Dinner. **Payment:** Master-Card, Visa. **Children:** Under 12, free in room with parents. **Recreation:** Beach, 2 swimming pools, 1 tennis court, gym.

➤ **Just down the road from the Rosarito Beach Hotel, the fishing village of Puerto Nuevo looks like one giant restaurant. Every building seems to house a café, and all of them specialize in the local lobster, which gives some indication of how tasty it can be.**

In the freewheeling 1920s, Rosarito became the glamour destination in Mexico for American visitors. While prohibition reigned in the States, booze flowed legally and liberally in Baja, and casinos and racetracks flourished until the Mexican government outlawed gambling in 1935. Southern Californians, including many Hollywood celebrities, flocked across the border in search of forbidden pleasures, heading as often as not to the Rosarito Beach Hotel. Orson Welles came, and Vincent Price, and even King Farouk.

Remnants of that era pervade the older sections of the hotel to-day. The entrance flaunts a stained glass portrait of a smiling *señorita*, a guitar by her side, one knee raised provocatively and a hiked skirt exposing lots of thigh. The lavish lobby is a museum of Mexican art and craftsmanship, boasting elaborately decorated ceiling beams, vibrant tile work, and dramatic murals painted by Matías Santoyo.

The classy Continental restaurant, Chabert's, dates to the same period, when the owner built it as an Italianate mansion for his wife. You dine surrounded by Old World heirlooms, including mirrors shaped like dragons, a marble fireplace, and a 17th-century tapestry. In another part of the home, now a spa featuring beauty treatments, is Spanish tile that tells the story of Don Quijote.

Compared to these delightful touches from the past, the rest of Rosarito Beach is a little mundane. The hotel shows its age in dispirited as well as spirited ways, and newer parts of the big property may remind you of an interstate motel. The video game room and prominently placed Ping-Pong tables seem out of place, and the lackadaisical landscaping and untended beach *palapas* won't inspire any rhapsodies about paradise, but the pool is beautifully tiled.

The rooms are comfortably contemporary and spacious for their price, except for the least expensive quarters. All come with cable TV and a phone, and most have small balconies, two double beds, and marble baths. Be sure to get an ocean view, the most attractive trait in any of the various styles of rooms. In the off-season, the rates peak on weekends, just like the crowds.

Plan on a dinner in Chabert's, for the atmosphere if not the food, but Azteca is the main restaurant, open all day and overlooking the beach The menu emphasizes Mexican dishes, particularly Baja lobster, at moderate prices. For sunset cocktails, head to the Beach-comber Bar.

The beach just beyond the bar is wide and long, but the grayish sand attracts far fewer sunbathers than horseback riders and walkers. Despite the name, the Rosarito Beach Hotel isn't heavily oriented to the shore. It's more a precious relic than a resort, a treasure trove of Mexican magnificence. Appreciate the heritage and you'll have a grand old time.

Tecate

Rancho La Puerta

Apartado Postal 69
Tecate, Baja California Norte
(66) 54-11-55
Reservations:
Rancho La Puerta
619-744-4222
800-443-7565
Fax: 619-744-5007

**A beautiful and famous spa
with reasonable prices**

Accommodations: 83 rooms and suites; total capacity 150 people a week. **High-season rates** (per person per week double occupancy): Ranchera rooms $1,727; hacienda $1,906; villa studios $2,158; villa suites $2,588 double occupancy, $2,037 each for 3 or 4 occupants. **Low-season rates** (per person per week double occupancy): Ranchera rooms $1,502; hacienda $1,670; villa studios $1,895; villa suites $2,226 double occupancy, $1,785 for 3 or 4 occupants. **Included:** 3 modified vegetarian meals daily, exercise classes, use of all equipment and facilities; in summer, rates also include a free massage and herbal wrap. **Added:** Charges for massages, facials, and other beauty treatments; some personal expenses, but not 6.93% tax and service. **Minimum stay:** 7 nights. **Payment:** MasterCard, Visa. **Smoking:** Not permitted. **Recreation:** 8 fitness centers, 4 swimming pools, 6 tennis courts.

➤ Years after opening Rancho La Puerta, the Szekelys also founded the famous Golden Door spa in Escondido, California. The two health resorts differ in a number of ways, including price, but they pursue a common philosophy.

Everyone from William F. Buckley to *Harper's* writes about Rancho La Puerta as one of the top fitness and health resorts in North America. The publicity hasn't led to pretension, though. The luxury coed spa remains relaxed and moderately priced, substantially less expensive than its big-name competitors in the States.

Despite a secluded setting in dramatic high-desert country, the Rancho is easy to reach. Guests fly to the San Diego airport and are met by buses that take them an hour southeast to the Mexican border and three miles beyond it. Everyone arrives on the same day and spends the week, so guests usually become well acquainted with at least some of their peers.

For over 50 years, Rancho La Puerta has espoused a philosophy of long-term health and fitness that only recently became fashionable. Established by Edmond and Deborah Szekely, it's sometimes called "the spa that started it all," and the staff today maintains the original inspiration. The focus is on mental and physical rejuvenation — eating well, getting regular exercise, reducing stress. The resort isn't dedicated to quick weight loss, though that is a goal of many clients.

The food must have seemed strange in the early years, before the rest of the world realized the nutritional benefits of organically grown vegetables, fresh fish (served two nights during a week), and complex carbohydrates such as beans, whole grain breads, and pasta. Lunch can be the most tempting meal because the buffet includes, along with hearty salads, a few no-no's — treats to keep you from getting desperate and going into Tecate for beer and nachos. Dinner is a set menu, beautifully presented, with extra side dishes available on request. Guests dine communally in a handsome hall with a soaring ceiling and a massive fireplace often filled with crackling logs. On Fridays, wine and beer are served.

Nothing in the extensive regimen is required, allowing you to unwind as much as you wish by one of the four pools. Most people leap eagerly into the meadow and mountain hikes, tennis matches, or classes such as "backs and bellies," "the bottom line," and "absolutely abdominals." Each day you can work on cardiovascular conditioning, strengthening and toning, flexibility, coordination and balance, and more. Men and women use separate facilities most of the time, and the activities for each are tailored to various levels of fitness. The large staff helps you plan as much or as little as you like and will try to keep you inspired without being pushy.

When you are ready to stumble into bed, it may be in a *ranchera* studio with a bedroom and a bath, a bigger hacienda with a living room and kitchenette, or a newer villa studio with kitchenette and bedroom alcove, or a villa suite with living room, kitchen and dining room, and two bedrooms and two baths. The charming Mexican-style accommodations, accented with native arts and crafts, are far from spartan. Each has a patio or garden and is equipped with a refrigerator, hair dryer, and alarm clock. If you are traveling alone but willing to share a room with up to three people, you pay the same as the Ranchera but might get upgraded.

Rancho La Puerta lies in rugged terrain at the foot of Mount Kuchumaa, a peak the Kumeyaay people regarded as sacred. For centuries only shamans climbed the heights. Today most of the guests make the trek and return with strengthened spirits. Whether it's the spell of the mountain or the spa itself that works the wonders, after a week you're almost certain to feel renewed.

Los Cabos

Best Hotel for Stylish Sophistication

Best Recreational Resorts and Spas

Best Comfort Choices for All-American Abundance

Best Bargain for Mexican Character

Longer than the state of California, Mexico's Baja peninsula stretches south from the U.S. border through scantily populated wilderness until it collides with the sea in Los Cabos, "The Capes." The towns of San José del Cabo and Cabo San Lucas, along with the coast between them, have been retreats for the adventure-some since the 1950s. Some intrepid explorers made the trek south in four-wheel-drive vehicles. Others came in private planes and yachts, often for a few days of deep-sea fishing. No one else both-ered much with the tip of Baja until recently.

Mexico didn't even accord statehood to the peninsula's southern territory, Baja California Sur, until 1974, a year after the Transpeninsular Highway connected Los Cabos with Tijuana far to the north. A decade later the government tourism agency that created Cancún and Ixtapa targeted Los Cabos for similar development. The authorities built an international airport, now among Mexico's most pleasant points of arrival, and made the area much easier to visit. That inaugurated a period of growth and development that is continuing at a feverish pace.

Today, Los Cabos is Mexico's fourth most popular tourist destination, but it is still removed from the rest of the country, physically and spiritually. You find less of traditional Mexico — in arts, architecture, cuisine, and culture — than in any other region. What does exist is concentrated in San José del Cabo, the oldest town in the vicinity. Built around a pleasant plaza, it's worth a brief stroll, as is the Paseo del Estero, a lush tropical walk where the San Juan River meets the sea, but most visitors end up at the less traditional San Lucas.

Cabo San Lucas is a brash, partying youngster in comparison with San José. Lively joints like the Cabo Wabo Cantina, owned by rockers Van Halen, seem to be the wave of the future. Most of the town is a little schlocky, but the shore is dramatically beautiful at points, particularly around the rock arches at Land's End.

Twenty miles of coastal road connects the sibling cities, feeding off at various points to some of the most swimmable beaches in the area and to some of the most distinctive, self contained resorts including the Hotel Cabo San Lucas, Palmilla, Twin Dolphin, and the Westin Regina. They are easily the best places to stay in Los Cabos, but if you are looking for more people and action, we also recommend a couple of alternatives in Cabo San Lucas.

The Main Attractions

Rugged Natural Beauty

The convergence of desert, mountains, and churning sea in Los Cabos makes for a stunning natural landscape. As in areas of the American Southwest, the beauty is unconventional and surreal. Craggy boulders rise primordially among more species of cactus than are found anywhere else in the world. Statuesque saguaros tower over the rocks and sand. Out in the water, the Pacific Ocean and the Sea of Cortés come together in a crash of waves. The sunlight is dazzling.

The climate is arid all year except during the brief fall rainy season. Midsummer can be extremely hot, but the lack of humidity makes the temperatures more tolerable than in much of the United States. Midwinter days get a little cool, and some nights are downright cold.

The World's Biggest Fish Trap

The Sea of Cortés is a 1,000-mile long ocean trench between the Sierra Madres in the Mexican interior and the highlands of Baja. It teems with marine life, making the sea a world-famous fishing haven. Yellowtail, bonito, snapper, sea bass, and other medium-size fish are abundant, but marlin is the big prize. Striped marlin ply these seas year-round. Runs of black and blue marlin are seasonal, from late summer until the winter.

Some of the recommended hotels have their own fishing fleets, and any of them can help you arrange a charter. The usual policy is to release the fish unless the catch is intended for food or is of record size, which can mean close to 1,000 pounds.

Whale Watching

Schools of California gray whales migrate to the warm Baja waters from January to March, leaping and cavorting through their mating ritual. Thousands of whales make the trek annually from Alaska's icy Bering Sea. Almost extinct from overhunting as late as the 1940s, the gentle mammals have made a remarkable comeback. Humpback, blue, and killer whales can be seen as well. Although the action is often visible from shore, excursion boats take visitors to the prime viewing areas. Be sure to bring binoculars.

Great Golf

Until recently, few Mexican resorts featured golf. When they offered the sport, it was usually a secondary attraction. That has begun to change, and Los Cabos is leading the way.

In the last few years, courses have begun to bloom everywhere across the coastal desert, mainly connected with real estate projects geared to American buyers. Jack Nicklaus alone added 45 holes in about as many months in the early 1990s. His Palmilla course appeals to players of all abilities, while his Cabo del Sol course provides serious challenges and an exciting finish. Roy Dye designed the links at the Cabo San Lucas Country Club, and Robert Trent Jones was the architect at the Cabo Real development.

Los Cabos

Cabo San Lucas Hotel

Apartado Postal 22
Cabo San Lucas, Baja California Sur
(114) 4-00-14
Fax: (114) 4-00-15
Reservations:
Hotel Services Corporation
213-655-2323
800-733-2226
Fax: 213-655-3243

A casual beach hotel on an expansive estate

Accommodations: 103 studios, suites, and villas. **High-season rates:** Standard rooms $110, studios $130, junior suites $200, master suites $230, 2-bedroom suites $265 for up to 4 people, villas from $475. **Low-season rates:** approximately 20% discount. **Added:** 17% tax and 10% service charge. **Payment:** Major credit cards. **Children:** Under 5, free in room with parents; special kids' programs. **Recreation:** Beach, swimming pools, 3 tennis courts, horseback riding, skeet shooting, sport fishing, water sports center, nature walks.

➤ **The Cabo Acuadeportes water sports operation serves both the Cabo San Lucas and the Hacienda Hotel, providing instruction and equipment for almost all ocean activities. Scuba diving is a specialty at the PADI and NAUI facility.**

If you portioned out Hotel Cabo San Lucas's extensive grounds, guests in each room would have over 35 acres and 240 palm trees to call their own. It's a princely plot for everyone, and the resort gives you a multitude of ways to enjoy it.

The hotel is the dream hideaway of Bud Parr, the pioneer who brought tourism to Baja's southern tip a generation ago. When he started the construction along azure Chileno Bay, on one of the coast's few safe swimming beaches, there were no roads, no electricity, and none of the 18,000 palms that now grace the grounds. What he couldn't find nearby — almost everything other than rock and cactus — he brought in. Tools, building materials, plants, and people were imported by plane or boat. When the hotel was completed in 1961, it was a stunning testament to Parr's tenacity and vision.

Little has changed since. Parr and his son Mitch, who now manages the property, continue to update facilities, but they maintain the laid-back tropical spirit that has been a hallmark from the beginning. The hotel's only hard and fast rules remain the same: no swimming naked until after 10 P.M., no mermaids in the room because they tear up the sheets, and you pay for anything you break. We can live with that, and so do legions of return guests.

Though the low-rise residential buildings look a little motelish on the outside, the interiors are well designed, except perhaps in the smallish standard rooms. Traveling as a couple, we probably would opt for a studio room, only average in size inside but enhanced by an enormous terrace overlooking the sea. The tile or wood floors, hand-hewn woodwork, simple furnishings crafted at the hotel's mill, and baths with onyx accents contribute to casual ease, as does the refrigerator in each room, though phones and TVs keep you in touch with the world. Families and larger groups have a choice of spacious suites with a stone wall fireplace and terrace overlooking the sea in the distance. There are luxurious villas that contain three to seven bedrooms, sleeping up to 14 people in one mansion with a private swimming pool.

The resort has a peaceful air, but it specializes in recreation and other activity. The renowned game fishing of the area starts directly off the coast and the hotel offers packages in conjunction with its sister hotel, La Hacienda. If you prefer just looking at the fish, snorkeling is excellent in Chileno Bay, and plenty of deeper-water sights are accessible with the help of the dive shop. Other ocean sports include Sunfish sailing, windsurfing, and water skiing. Landlubbers can enjoy tennis and nature walks. For a change of scene, shuttle buses take you to La Hacienda's beach and recreations, not far from downtown Cabo San Lucas.

The hotel dining room sits on a breezy bluff overlooking the sea and a splashy, cascading swimming pool. The stone walls and hefty fireplace may remind you more of Taos than the tropics, but on winter evenings you'll likely appreciate the warmth. The kitchen serves both Mexican and American dishes, which seldom rise much above average. Stout margaritas may help the flavor.

Los Cabos is destined for major growth in the decade ahead. That's a big change from the days when Bud Parr bought his 2,500-acre estate, but it won't affect much at the Cabo San Lucas Hotel.

This will remain an original, a secluded principality of palms and play.

Hacienda Beach Resort

Cabo San Lucas, Baja California Sur
(114) 3-01-23
Fax: (114) 3-06-06
Reservations:
Hotel Services Corporation
213-655-2323
800-733-2226
Fax: 213-655-3243

**A convivial beachfront inn
with a wide range of rooms**

Accommodations: 115 rooms, suites, and townhouses. **Rates:** Garden patio rooms $162, colonial rooms $209, deluxe studios $209, *cabaña* rooms $246, deluxe suites $288, 1-bedroom townhouses $330, 2-bedroom townhouses $372. **Added:** 17% tax and 10% service charge. **Payment:** Major credit cards. **Children:** Under 5, free in room with parents. **Recreation:** Beach, swimming pool, 2 tennis courts, water sports center, sport fishing fleet, Wellness Institute with massage.

➤ **The restored colonial village of Todos Santos has the best folk art and clothing boutiques in all of Baja. It also boasts the Peninsula's loveliest Italian restaurant, the Café Santa Fe (Calle Centenario 4, 114-5-03-40). Just an hour away from Cabo San Lucas, Todos Santos is an appealing diversion from the beach.**

Owned and managed by the same family as the Hotel Cabo San Lucas and connected to all its facilities by a shuttle service, the Hacienda is a low-key, in-town alternative to the bigger resort. A long walk or an easy cab ride from the center of Cabo San Lucas, the Spanish mission-style hotel enjoys a prime location pretty much to itself on a peninsula jutting into a lovely bay.

The most prominent feature is the beach that grabbed Bud Parr's attention almost a generation ago. Wide, long, and still uncrowded, it borders the area's calmest water, safe for swimming. The Hacienda offers plenty of ocean activity, including scuba diving, sailing, windsurfing, and snorkeling. The area's renowned sport fishing begins close to the shore, and the staff arrange charters. Just inland from the beach, guests lounge at an ocean-view pool and play tennis on a couple of courts, one regulation size and one for paddle games. You can even while away your time having a facelift at the Plastic Surgery Institute here.

The Bougainvillea restaurant, back from the water, is handsomely colonial in decor. Stick with simple preparations of fish, abalone, and other fresh seafood for the best meals. The Azteca bar next door has an expansive stone terrace with a sea view, a good spot for enjoying the mariachi music presented some evenings. Other restaurants and bars are conveniently located by the beach.

All the air-conditioned rooms have simple Mexican wood and wrought-iron furnishings, phones, TVs, and tile floors, either terrazzo or glazed terra cotta. The least expensive quarters are too plain for us, with a pair of twin beds and no views of note. The other rooms have ocean vistas and a patio or a balcony. The deluxe studios and the older colonial rooms, which both come with two double beds, are spacious enough for some families, but the suites and townhouses really allow you to spread out. A deluxe suite gives you a separate bedroom, generally with a king-size bed, plus a wet bar and two daybeds in a large sitting area. The split-level townhouses have full kitchens as well.

Our favorite chambers are the *cabañas*, individual bunkers built into beachside dunes and surrounded by desert and tropical landscaping. They feature a king bed or two twins in the sleeping nook, a sitting area with a sofa, and a private terrace — the very best ones overlook the sea.

Lounging on your terrace and surrounded by the magnificent gardens of this hotel, make a toast to Bud Parr's foresight in securing this spit of land long ago. You'll find it a fine place to relax and romp.

Las Ventanas al Paraiso

Km. 19.5, Carretera Transpeninsular
Cabo San Lucas, San José del Cabo
Baja California Sur
(114) 4-03-00
Fax: (114) 4-03-01
Reservations:
Rosewood Hotels
888-767-3966

The newest luxury resort in Los Cabos

Accommodations: 61 suites. **High-season rates:** Garden-view junior suites $525, ocean-view junior suites $625, roof-top terrace junior suites $750, 1-bedroom luxury suites $2,000, 3-bedroom luxury suites $3,500. **Low-season rates:** Garden-view junior suites $325, ocean-view junior suites $425, roof-top terrace junior suites $550, 1-bedroom luxury suites $1,200, 3-bedroom luxury suites $3,000. **Added:** 12% tax and 15% service; meal plan packages available. 15% gratuity added to all food and beverage checks. **Minimum stay:** 4–7 nights during certain periods in the high season. **Payment:** Major credit cards. **Recreation:** Beach, pool, golf, 2 tennis courts, spa and fitness center, deep-sea fishing, water sports.

➤ **For the ultimate in indulgence, Las Ventanas al Paraiso now offers massages and other therapies right on the beach in its specially designed Spa Pavilion, where guests can view the ocean but outsiders can't peek in. In the evening you can even have a massage in the Pavilion by torchlight, while savoring the soothing sounds of the surf.**

Located in the Cabo Real development, Las Ventanas al Paraiso is the newest and arguably the most luxurious resort in the area, with prices that reflect the amenities. The rooms are huge. Even the "least expensive" garden-view junior suites are about 1,000 square feet and feature tile floors, fireplaces, and marble baths, and are well appointed with Mexican crafts. If you opt for an ocean-view junior suite, you'll be able to enjoy the sea from your 300-square-foot terrace. The rooftop terrace suites add another level of luxury — a second terrace with a dramatic setting for sky and sea views, a telescope for sky watching, and a private Jacuzzi on the lower terrace. With the one-bedroom suites you get an amazing 1,600 square feet of oceanfront space, along with your own private pool. All of the air-conditioned suites come with satellite TV as well as a VCR.

No matter what level of luxury you choose, you'll have more than enough space to savor the many delights of this ambitious resort.

If you can pull yourself away from your suite, a number of choices await you. There's a lovely beach area and a sinuous swimming pool, with a handsome *palapa* bar nearby to help quench your thirst. Las Ventanas recently introduced an interesting tequila and *ceviche* bar that offers a sampling of a variety of tequilas as well as an intriguing array of *ceviches* that are sometimes made with abalone or tuna rather than the more usual sierra or red snapper. If you are feeling energetic, there are two lighted tennis courts, and, in keeping with Las Ventanas's aim to coddle you, ball boys are provided so that you don't have to move too much. Golf enthusiasts surely win out here. Next door is the beautiful 18-hole Cabo Real golf course designed by Robert Trent Jones II. For fishing fans, Las Ventanas has two yachts. The larger 80-foot model is used for packages that combine nights at the hotel with nights at sea. While on board you'll be able to soak in the Jacuzzi. The smaller 55-foot yacht takes you on half- or full-day sea voyages. After a day of golf or tennis or at sea you can head for the popular spa, which has eight treatment rooms, where you have a choice of a variety of massages and other therapies.

You'll certainly be pampered at Las Ventanas al Paraiso. For many travelers, this resort will truly be the windows to paradise.

Mar de Cortez

Calle Lázaro Cárdenas at Guerrero
Cabo San Lucas, Baja California Sur
(114) 3-00-32
Fax: (114) 3-02-32
Reservations:
800-347-8821
Fax: 408-663-1904

A small hotel with the feel of old Baja

Accommodations: 72 rooms and suites. **Rates:** Old section rooms $41, new section rooms $51, suites $58. **Payment:** MasterCard, Visa. **Recreation:** Swimming pool, fishing arrangements.

➤ **Near the Mar de Cortez are the curio market and many shops of Cabo San Lucas. For something special, look for the native Baja baskets and pottery at El Rancho (Calle Guerrero, a half block from Madero) and the**

Mexican folkart at Casas Mexicanas (Avenida Cabo San Lucas at Mi Casita Restaurant).

When Cabo was a fishing village rather than a megadevelopment, the Mar de Cortez was one of the three hotels in town providing accommodations and deep-sea fishing to adventure travelers. A 1995 renovation and expansion has brought the hotel up to standard without any loss of its simple charms.

The colonial-style hotel wraps around a considerable lawn and garden with a nice pool in the center. Along the street, acting as a buffer for the rooms and garden, is a cheerful restaurant with good, hearty food and a bar opening to the garden. Concerned with the comfort of their guests, the friendly owners and staff close the bar at 10 P.M. They also make arrangements for sports fishing and will provide a freezer for your catch — or the restaurant will cook it on request.

All the rooms are ample and well maintained, with air conditioning, private baths, and furnished terraces. The older rooms have tiled floors and wood beam ceilings; the newer rooms have slightly upgraded bathrooms and larger terraces, all with pool views. The suites are nothing more than two rooms sharing a bath, but without the terrace.

Mar de Cortez is a surprisingly pleasing bargain in the heart of Cabo.

Melia San Lucas

Playa El Medano S/N
Cabo San Lucas, Baja California Sur
(114) 3-44-44
Fax: (114) 3-04-22
Reservations:
Meliá Hotels
713-820-9500
800-336-3542
Fax: 713-999-7373

> **An upbeat, upscale hotel on a broad beach**

Accommodations: 142 rooms and suites. **High-season rates:** Double rooms $240, superior rooms $275, junior suites $435, 1-bedroom suites $500. **Low-season rates:** Double rooms $210, superior rooms $240, junior suites $325, 1-bedroom suites $375. **Added:** 17% tax and 10 % service. **Payment:** Major credit cards. **Children:** Under 12, free in room with parents. **Recreation:** Beach, swimming pool, 2 tennis courts, horseback riding, water sports center with windsurfing and deep-sea fishing.

▶ **The tourism boom in Cabos San Lucas has swelled the ranks of restaurants in town. They compete with each other mainly in catchy names: besides Carlos 'n' Charlie's there is Señor Sushi and Tai Won On Bar, El Squid Roe, and the Giggling Marlin.**

Opened just ten years ago, the Meliá San Lucas ushered in a new lodging style for Los Cabos — flashier, fancier, and bouncier than anything seen before. Even newer places in the same mode are going up throughout the area, including a bigger and brassier Meliá, but the first of the breed may remain the best.

Poised above a wide sweep of beach on the calm bay in Cabo San Lucas, a short cab ride from the center of the town, the hotel extends a breezy and inviting welcome. As you enter the lobby, Cabo's rocky point at Land's End is perfectly framed out expansive windows. After you're able to pull your eyes away from the dazzling sight, you find yourself in a second-floor atrium overlooking a large courtyard that sweeps out to the sea.

A giant bi-level pool, ringed by an attractive brick and stone deck, dominates the courtyard. A small water slide connects the two swimming areas, one set up for water volleyball and the other featuring a shady swim-up *palapa* bar. The landscaping around the pool and contained grounds is a well-planned mix of desert and tropical greenery.

The long, wide beach is a few steps farther, stretching around the bay to a scattered selection of restaurants and night spots. The water is usually good for swimming and for sports such as windsurfing and parasailing, though the most popular recreation among guests is deep-sea fishing.

The rooms are in a mid-rise horseshoe structure designed to create the feel of a village. All the quarters peer over the pool to the sea, but the view from the terrace is usually from an angle and can be a little restricted in some of the least expensive rooms. The contemporary Mexican decor mixes wicker furnishings with an array of colorful accents. The rooms all come with satellite TV, a phone, air conditioning, a mini-bar, a safe, and a king-size bed or two doubles. The junior suites enjoy a sitting area, which is fully separated from the sleeping space in the one-bedroom suites.

The Meliá San Lucas has a casual, all-purpose restaurant, El Jardín, that offers bountiful morning buffets and features a different cuisine nightly, but we wouldn't count on anything more than variety. We got canned vegetables at our one meal, an overpriced lunch at the beachfront La Palapa.

The hotel overall is fresher than the food, a cheery, new-wave youngster on the block. If you want to be lively in Los Cabos, it's the spot to stop.

Palmilla

San José del Cabo,
Baja California Sur
(114) 4-50-00
Fax: (114) 4-51-00
Reservations:
714-833-3033
800-637-2226
Fax: 714-935-2030

A dreamy village for golfers

Accommodations: 114 rooms, suites, and villas. **High-season rates:** Ocean-view rooms, $395, oceanfront junior suites $595, beachfront junior suites $690, oceanfront 1-and 2-bedroom suites $950–$1,100, beachfront deluxe suites $1,210. **Low-season rates:** Ocean-view rooms, $225–$350, oceanfront junior suites $345–$525, beachfront junior suites $435–$605, oceanfront 1- and 2-bedroom suites $600–$990, beachfront deluxe suites $825–$1,100. **Added:** 17% tax and 15% service charge. **Minimum stay:** 3 nights on weekends. **Payment:** Major credit cards. **Children:** Under 14, free in room with parents. **Recreation:** 2 beaches, swimming pool, golf (18 holes), 2 tennis courts, fitness center, water sports center.

➤ **Vacation villas and condos are another lodging option in Los Cabos, especially when you need more space. Vacation Villas Los Cabos (800-621-**

5539) books a variety of private homes and might even help you find a chef to make your stay all the more relaxing.

On the rugged coast between the towns of San José del Cabo and Cabo San Lucas, the Palmilla was built as a fishing resort, but it's far more fetching than anglers alone deserve. The pretty Spanish mission–style hotel is intimately inviting for anyone, once you pass through the new adjacent residential resort community that has marred the Palmilla's previous isolation.

The original building and rooms date back to 1956, when the Palmilla opened as a club for sport fishermen who flew in on the private air strip. Conceived by Abelardo Rodríguez, son of a former Mexican president, the hotel hosted a heady array of the day's celebrities — Bing Crosby, John Wayne, Desi Arnaz, even President Eisenhower.

Over time the hotel declined in glamour and cachet. It was coasting on its past glories by 1984, when Koll International purchased it and set out to rebuild its reputation and expand its appeal to golfers, lovers, and other contemporary vacationers. The 18-hole, Jack Nicklaus–designed course covers mountain and arroyo terrain, almost always with view of the sea. A second 18-hole Jack Nicklaus course opened nearby at Cabo del Sol and the hotel offers a shuttle for its guests to play there.

In 1997 the Palmilla completed a $13 million overhaul of all its facilities, nearly doubling the number of its guest quarters in the process and renovating all the older ones, providing each with a private terrace, usually with an ocean view, and more modern appointments. The increase in the hotel's facilities as well as the development of an adjacent resort community have marred the previous desert isolation of the Palmilla. But the groomed ambience of the hotel has been retained and the accommodations are more private and wonderful than ever.

The Palmilla is justly proud of its two beaches — one in a protected cove for snorkeling and swimming. Above the beaches, the original inn sits on a rocky point accented by large sandstone formations growing from the shore like oversize sandcastles. Accommodations are scattered in a village of *casas* strung along the gardens here and along the shore; the new *playa* suites are a few steps from the beach.

The quarters are more relaxed than refined, comfortably Mexican rather than international. Maintenance is sometimes spotty, but in all the rooms you're compensated with ocean views, handcrafted furniture, and folk art accents. All the rooms have a king-size bed or two doubles, a sitting area — the size of which expands into a living room/dining room in the case of the two-bedroom primera suites — tiled shower, a mini-bar, air conditioning, phones and satellite TV and VCR.

The hacienda rooms have the most limited views, either of the pool or partial ocean views. Among the bougainvillea quarters, we like number 10 in Casa Angelica and the second-floor rooms in Casa Bougainvillea for their perspectives on the sea. A slight step up in price, the air-conditioned vista suites enjoy a little more of everything, from better ocean views to extra space in the sitting area and bathroom. The most spacious of the junior suites are the 62 new *bahía* and *playa* units, provided with sunken sitting areas, fancier baths, and terraces with full sea views. The *playa* units, the only beachfront quarters at the Palmilla, are the best. Families and friends traveling together may prefer the grand *bahía* and *playa* suites, each an ample 1,000 square feet, or the two-bedroom *primera* suites.

Light meals can be enjoyed at the poolside El Jardín and a Continental breakfast is delivered to your room each morning, upon request. La Paloma Restaurant is for more formal dining, such as it is at a resort. Although there is a large, cheerful air-conditioned dining area with an exhibition kitchen, usually everyone prefers dining on the adjoining terraces, the prime setting on balmy days or warm candlelit evenings. Lunches and dinners are prepared on a mesquite grill and rotisserie. Like the convivial cocktail lounge nearby, the terraces overlook the swimming pool, one of the beaches, and the stunning coastline.

Those are just a few of the principal attractions when you're ready to play. If the ocean tempts you, a water sports center will arrange fishing or diving. The dramatic 18-hole Jack Nicklaus golf course wraps around the property, and another of the master's links is just 15 minutes away at an affiliated real estate development. Many guests simply unwind at the pool with its swim-up bar and perhaps take a break in their lounging for a game of tennis or a workout in the fitness center, where you will also be treated to ocean views.

A wedding could be another possibility. The hotel provides a small, charming chapel for that purpose. Perched on a hilltop in a forest of palms, the white stucco church has just eight pews and grand ocean views. Whether or not you come to tie the knot, Palmilla may make you feel as if you're on your honeymoon. The old fishing lures are still around, and golf has become the new game of the day, but the beachfront suites have kept romance at the Palmilla.

Twin Dolphin

Cabo San Lucas, Baja California Sur
(114) 3-25-90
Fax: (114) 3-48-11
Reservations:
Hotel Twin Dolphin
Small Luxury Hotels of the World
800-525-4800

A small and exclusive hideaway of striking design

Accommodations: 44 rooms and 6 suites. **High-season rates:** Deluxe rooms $285; suites $485. **Low-season rates:** Deluxe rooms $195, suites $350. **Added:** 17% tax and 15% service; meal plan packages available. **Payment:** Major credit cards. **Children:** Under 3, free in room with parents. **Recreation:** Beach, swimming pool, deep-sea fishing fleet, fitness center, putting green, 2 tennis courts, 2-mile desert path, shuttle vans to golf courses and downtown Cabo San Lucas.

➤ **The best place to dine in downtown Cabo San Lucas is Mi Casa (Avenida Cabo San Lucas near Madero, 3-19-33), where authentic and elegantly prepared Mexican dishes are served on a colorful patio.**

If Georgia O'Keeffe had designed a beach hotel, it might have looked a lot like the Twin Dolphin. The hotel's dramatic simplicity parallels aspects of the famous painter's work and produces an aesthetic triumph in resort design that's unique in Mexico and the world.

The architecture of the open-air reception area is minimalist in mood, fashioned to frame a view of the sea past a soothing pond and a stunning pool, a sight that offers a magnificent welcome. The buildings, pool umbrellas, and Japanese-style raked gravel beds are stark white counterpoints to the indigo pool, sky, and sea. A few strategically placed pots of bougainvillea add splashes of color, but your eye will more likely be drawn to the cacti and other desert plants. Statuesque organ-pipes and squatty barrel cacti share the grounds with aloe veras, yuccas, ocotillos, and a scattering of fan palms. Nothing mars the omnipresence of the desert and sea.

The pool and its *palapa* bar are the gathering points during the day for most guests, at least for those who aren't fishing along the Baja coast or basking on the beach. The pool shares the highest point on the property with the reception building, giving it broader vistas than any of the rooms. Instead of lounge chairs, the hotel provides white modular pillows and mattresses for sunning and reading. The surrounding cacti, punctuated by giant boulders, make for a serene and scenic setting.

The spacious rooms and suites, all of which enjoy ocean views, are down the hill in a couple of rows of single-story cottages. Those in the lower tier are closest to the water, but the ones farther back have an elevated perspective, albeit over some of the other *casitas*. The decor is deliberately simple, featuring glazed red tile floors, almost bare white stucco walls, a pair of platform double beds or a king, a plain dresser, a small table with a pair of chairs, a compact refrigerator, and a narrow patio. The bathrooms provide the only hint of extravagance. Larger than some Manhattan hotel rooms, they have stone showers, large vanities, good lighting, and comfy robes. There are no TVs or phones to mar the mood.

The suites are similar but more attractive, we think, with tiled wet bars, fireplaces, and large terraces. Each comes with a big second bath and two daybeds or a sofa bed in the sitting area to complement the king or two queen beds in the sleeping room. The individual air conditioning units in all the quarters can be a bit noisy and usually aren't necessary at night except in the summer. Telephones and televisions are banned, thankfully.

The kitchen at the Twin Dolphin has some of the highest quality ingredients we've come across in Mexico — succulent shrimp, tender chicken, and fresh greens and vegetables raised on the hotel's own nearby farm. They are skillfully cooked, but many of the dinner dishes tend to be in the heavy Continental style that peaked when we all liked Ike. Most guests enjoy the richness, at least on vacation. The dining room opens onto the pool deck on three sides, providing fine views by day or by night from most of the tables. The lounge, with its huge stone fireplace and armchairs, is a comfortable spot for evening music and drinks.

For recreation, the hotel specializes in deep-sea fishing, a strong interest of about a third of the guests. Snorkeling and diving can be enjoyed in the cove at the foot of the estate, swimming and snorkeling are quite fine at the neighboring Santa Maria beach. Tennis, exercising on fitness equipment, and playing an 18-hole putting course are other possibilities on the grounds, and close at hand you can find scuba diving, horseback riding, and a Jack Nicklaus golf course. You may want to spend part of a day in Cabo San Lucas or in San José del Cabo, about equidistant in opposite directions.

We usually pass on the activities, preferring to lie indolently on a poolside mattress and absorb the sublime setting. You feel as if you're inside a painting, and indeed you are a temporary prop in a masterpiece of design. It may not be an O'Keeffe canvas, but it's as close as you can get with a pool and an ocean view.

Westin Regina Resort Los Cabos

San José del Cabo, Baja California Sur
(114) 2-90-00
Fax: (114) 2-90-11
Reservations:
Westin Hotels and Resorts
800-228-3000

> **A dashing and daring beachfront resort**

Accommodations: 305 rooms and suites. **High-season rates:** Resort rooms $310, deluxe ocean-view rooms $330, Royal Beach Club rooms $435, junior suites $460, master suites $975–$1,750. **Low-season rates:** Resort rooms $245, deluxe ocean-view rooms $265, Royal Beach Club rooms $249, junior suites $410, master suites $865–$1,350. **Added:** 17% tax. **Payment:** Major credit cards. **Children:** Under 18, free in room with parents. **Recreation:** Beach, 5 swimming pools, fitness center with aerobics, saunas, steam baths, Jacuzzi, and massage, 24-hour tennis on 2 courts.

➤   **A marina in the center of Cabo San Lucas offers slips for hundreds of boats. A contemporary shopping mall, a sprawling hotel, and several condos wrap around the huge harbor.**

The new Westin Regina is a dazzler, an architectural gem that makes most other hotels look as inviting as a Los Angeles freeway. As you approach the lobby, you are met by an audacious canary yellow wall and led into an open-air reception area ablaze with fuchsia and the desert glow coming from potted cacti and a cactus sculpture. The staff welcomes you with a blue margarita about the time your eyes drift toward the beckoning blue ocean and horizon, which splash into sight through a six-story "window to the sea" that opens like a parted stage curtain between the Westin's beachfront wings.

The red stone building on the shore sweeps in a grand arc along the contour of the cove, disappearing gracefully at both ends into hills that are as ruddy as the walls. A group of time-share villas in a similar style sit to the side of the hotel, but nothing else intrudes on the peaceful seclusion. In the words of the Westin's master Mexican architect, Javier Sordo Madaleno, the structure "speaks softly, allowing the environment to sing."

The centerpiece of that natural endowment is the wide beach just below the guest rooms, an unadorned, almost wild expanse of white sand peppered with craggy rocks. Rough conditions restrict water sports and sometimes prevent swimming in the sea, but five pools cascading down to the beach keep most active vacationers content. If you need more recreation, the Westin offers a pair of tennis courts and a well-equipped fitness center. The staff will also book tee times on two fine golf courses, both nearby, or send you out to sea on a fishing or diving adventure.

A juice bar caters to athletes, La Playa offers drinks and snacks to sunbathers, Margarita's serves swimmers from inside the pool, and La Cantina attracts almost everyone at cocktail hour. Adjacent to the evening bar, La Cascada features Mexican and American meals all day, starting with a bountiful buffet breakfast. Arrecifes, a dinner-only restaurant, stands apart from the rest of the hotel on a bluff overlooking the surf. The menu focuses on Mediterraean specialties but touches on other cuisines as well.

The Westin's spacious rooms share the bold colors of the lobby and the sea. Folk art enhances the walls and unpolished marble adorns the floors. A triangular balcony provides both privacy and ocean views, though the perspective is a little limited in the least expensive rooms. The Royal Beach Club chambers come with upgraded amenities and access to a member's lounge that lays out a complimentary Continental breakfast in the morning and hors d'oeuvres with drinks in the afternoon. The huge junior suites enjoy a full sitting and dining room, as well as a Jacuzzi on the oversize lanai. All the air-conditioned quarters have satellite TVs, direct-dial phones, safes, ceiling fans, mini-bars, two double beds or a king, and a luxury bathroom with a marble shower and separate tub.

When you need something in your room, whether it's towels or tea, you dial one number for express service. A desk in the bowels of the hotel then dispatches the proper person and assumes responsibility for action. It's part of the management's commitment to guests, the linchpin of a policy on quality that's as ambitious as the architecture. If it succeeds over time to the same degree as Sordo Madaleno's inspired design, the Westin Regina could set new standards for all of Mexico.

What's What

Best Romantic Hideaways

Mexico is instinctively and passionately romantic. These places capture that spirit in a variety of wonderful ways and offer it to guests with experienced élan. Ranging from exclusive resorts to a "camptel," they vary in price but not in escapist allure. Though each speaks of romance in a separate tongue, each is sublime when the language is your own.

The Mayan Riviera

Cancún South
  Maroma, 70

The Mexican Riviera

Acapulco
  Las Brisas, 109
Huatulco
  Casa del Mar, 123
Ixtapa and Zihuatanejo
  Villa del Sol, 143
Manzanillo and the Gold Coast
  The Careyes, 149
  Villa Polinesia, 159
Puerto Ángel and Puerto Escondido
  Santa Fe Hotel, 181
Puerto Vallarta
  Casa Tres Vidas, 198

The Extraordinary Interior

Copper Canyon
  Copper Canyon Riverside Lodge, 237

Best Hotels for Stylish Sophistication

Creating a standard luxury hotel today is simple. Formulas abound. These resort and urban establishments go beyond the formulas, providing frills with deft finesse. Their combination of elegance and overall excellence earns them international distinction.

The Mayan Riviera

The Mexican Riviera

The Extraordinary Interior

Guadalajara and Lake Chapala
Mexico City
Oaxaca
Puebla

Baja California

Los Cabos

Best Recreational Resorts and Spas

If you travel for play or pampering, Mexico satisfies in multiple ways. These recommendations vary considerably in style — from polished resort hotels beside golf courses to lively Club Meds — but each features extensive sports or spa facilities and each caters well to its own crowd.

The Mayan Riviera

Cancún

The Mexican Riviera

Acapulco
Huatulco
Ixtapa and Zihuatanejo

Manzanillo and the Gold Coast
Puerto Vallarta

The Extraordinary Interior

Cuernavaca
Taxco

Baja California

Ensenada, Rosarito, and Tecate
Los Cabos

Best Comfort Choices for All-American Abundance

The most popular resort hotels in Mexico are large, luxurious in a familiar fashion, and full of energy. They specialize in the kind of all-American abundance that has a broad appeal for *norteamericano* visitors, from singles to families. Among the multitude of such places, our recommendations stand out in a variety of different ways. Pick your pleasures appropriately and you'll enjoy a spirited getaway.

The Mayan Riviera

Cancún
Cozumel

The Mexican Riviera

The Extraordinary Interior

Baja California

Best Beachfront Buys

When you want a lot for a little on a beach, these hotels are likely to delight. Usually smaller and more Mexican in character than the pricey all-American resorts that share the shore, they approach a similar level of comfort and fun at a moderate rate. None of the choices is cheap in any sense of the term, but each provides a combination of beachfront location and value that's hard to top — in Mexico or anywhere else.

The Mayan Riviera

Cancún
Calinda Beach & Spa, 27
Na Balam (Isla Mujeres), 48
Villas Tacul, 48
Cancún South
La Posada del Capitán Lafitte, 64
Las Casitas Akumal, 58
Shangri-La Caribe, 68
Vista del Mar, 59
Cozumel
La Ceiba, 81
Scuba Club Dive Resort, 86
Sol Cabañas del Caribe, 87

The Mexican Riviera

Acapulco
Boca Chica, 102
Elcano, 105
Ixtapa and Zihuatanejo
Las Urracas, 140
Sotavento-Catalina, 142
Manzanillo and the Gold Coast
La Posada, 178
Villa Polinesia, 159
Mazatlan
El Quijote Inn, 168
Puerto Vallarta
Playa Los Arcos, 205
Quinta María Cortés, 209

Baja California

Ensenada, Rosarito, and Tecate
Rosarito Beach Hotel, 387

Best Intimate and Affordable Inns

For cozy charm and casual elegance, these small hotels and inns are some of the most enchanting places to stay in Mexico. Generally in the interior, they feature polish without pretension at a reasonable price. All offer some qualities that should shame the large resorts.

The Extraordinary Interior

Archaeological Treasures
  Hacienda Uxmal, 233
  Mayaland, 232
Cuernavaca and Tepoztlán
  Clarion Cuernavaca Racquet Club, 243
  Posada del Tepozteco, 250
Guadalajara and Lake Chapala
  La Nueva Posada, 264
  La Villa del Ensueño, 260
  Quinta Quetzalcoatl, 267
Guanajuato
  Parador San Javier, 273
  Mexico City, 292
  La Casona, 297
Morelia and Pátzcuaro
  Fiesta Plaza, 322
Oaxaca
  Casa Caruso, 333
San Miguel de Allende
  Villa Jacaranda, 357
Taxco
  Hacienda del Solar, 364

Baja California

Ensenada, Rosarito, and Tecate
  Las Rosas Hotel and Spa, 385

Best Bargains for Mexican Character

These small hotels and inns hark back to the days before mass tourism. Although they vary in price from dirt cheap to moderate, each is a bargain for authentic Mexican allure. In some cases quaintness may border on eccentricity, but you can always count on a special sense of local character.

The Mayan Riviera

Cancún
  Novotel, 44

The Mexican Riviera

The Extraordinary Interior

Baja California

Los Cabos

Best B&Bs and Budget Inns

B&Bs are less common in Mexico than in the United States, but the ones that exist usually exude charm, personality, and good value. The same is true of the inns we include here, *posadas simpáticas* with a homey feeling. Many of the recommendations are on or near a fabulous beach, and the others enjoy choice locations in the interior.

The Mayan Riviera

Cancún South

The Mexican Riviera

Ixtapa and Zihuatanejo
Puerto Ángel and Puerto Escondido
Puerto Vallarta

The Extraordinary Interior

Guadalajara and Lake Chapala
Guanajuato
Mérida
Oaxaca
San Miguel de Allende

Best Adventure Retreats

Mexico brims with natural and archaeological adventures, from hiking in Copper Canyon to probing Mayan mysteries. These hideaway havens, secluded in the splendor, allow you to take full advantage of the opportunities.

The Mayan Riviera

Cancún South
Cabañas Ana y José, 72
Costa de Cocos, 75
Maya Tulum, 74

The Mexican Riviera

Manzanillo and the Gold Coast
El Tamarindo, 151
Puerto Vallarta
Lagunita Yelapa, 215

The Extraordinary Interior

Archaeological Treasures
Villas Arqueológicas Chichén Itzá, Cholula, Cobá, Teotihuacán, and Uxmal, 229
Copper Canyon
Copper Canyon Sierra Lodge, 239

Best Places to Combine Business and Pleasure

All major cities and resort areas in Mexico have some hotels that cater equally well to business and pleasure travelers. Our selections offer a range of leisure diversions, a convenient location, and an array of business services from fax machines to meeting space. Each has a professional and helpful staff, including people who speak English well.

The Mayan Riviera

Cancún
Marriott CasaMagna Cancún, 41
Omni Cancún, 45

The Mexican Riviera

The Extraordinary Interior

Best of the Best

Friends frequently ask us which is the best Mexican hotel. There isn't a single answer for everyone; your favorite will depend on the kind of experience you are seeking. At any given time, however, several hotels or inns are likely to have a perceptible edge over the others in quality standards. The leaders shift over the years, but currently these seem to us to stand out in overall excellence.

The Mayan Riviera

The Mexican Riviera

The Extraordinary Interior

Baja California

Best Beaches

Mexico is rimmed by thousands of miles of sandy shoreline, but the beaches are not equal in appeal and neither are the seaside hotels. Beach lovers generally want a beautiful stretch of fluffy sand along calm water and accommodations that are intimate with the setting. They want an oceanfront balcony with a good view of the shore and would like to be able to awake to the sounds of the surf. The following places, which vary considerably in style and price, do the best job in Mexico of satisfying these desires.

The Mayan Riviera

Cancún
  Casa Turquesa, 30
  Camino Real Cancún, 28
  Club Med Cancún, 33
Cancún South
  Cabañas Ana y José, 72
  La Posada del Capitán Lafitte, 64
  Las Casitas Akumal, 58
  Maroma, 70
Cozumel
  Presidente Inter-Continental, 84

The Mexican Riviera

Ixtapa and Zihuatanejo
  Westin Brisas Resort Ixtapa, 136
Manzanillo and the Gold Coast
  Las Alamandas, 153
  Villa Polinesia, 159
Puerto Vallarta
  Camino Real Puerto Vallarta, 193
  Lagunita Yelapa, 215
  Presidente Inter-Continental Puerto Vallarta, 207

Baja California

Los Cabos
  Hacienda Beach Resort, 399

Best Places Under $70 a Day

Even some expensive hotels in Mexico provide good value, but the following manage to do it at budget rates without sacrificing comfort and character. While we cover and recommend other places with similar prices throughout the book, these provide the most for your money in the whole country.

The cost calculation is based on a room for two people without meals. In some cases the criterion applies only to the least expensive rooms and only in the low season, and in other cases the inclusion of meals in the official hotel price makes it appear higher than it is for our purposes.

The Mayan Riviera

Cancún South
Cabañas Ana y José, 72
Quinta Mija, 65
Maya Tulum, 74
Vista del Mar, 59

The Mexican Riviera

Ixtapa and Zihuatanejo
Las Urracas, 140
Raúl Tres Marías, 141
Manzanillo and the Gold Coast
Villa Polinesia, 159
Puerto Ángel and Puerto Escondido
La Posada Cañon Devata, 178
Tabachín del Puerto, 183
Puerto Vallarta
Casa Corazón, 195
Lagunita Yelapa, 215

The Extraordinary Interior

Guadalajara and Lake Chapala
La Nueva Posada, 264
La Villa del Ensueño, 260
Mérida
Casa Mexilio, 280
Morelia and Pátzcuaro
Los Escudos Hotel, 323
Posada La Basílica, 324
Villa Pátzcuaro Hotel, 325
Oaxaca
Las Golondrinas, 339
San Miguel de Allende
Casa Carmen, 352
Villa Mirasol, 358
Taxco
Los Arcos, 365
Posada de los Castillo, 367

Recommended Books

Since this book focuses on making critical planning decisions before leaving for Mexico, many people will want to supplement it with a standard guidebook to use after their arrival. When we first traveled to Mexico, we didn't find any of the guidebooks especially helpful for understanding the country, its people, and its numerous attractions, or for informing us about quality accommodations, food, art, or crafts. To fill this gap, we eventually wrote our own general guidebook to Mexico, but after fifteen editions, it no longer is in print. Of the current general guidebooks, *Lonely Planet Mexico* seems to be the most popular. It can be very helpful for practical information, but not for leading you to quality places. The *Michelin Green Guide* (Michelin) is informative for its emphasis on history, art, and archaeology in a guidebook format.

If fine arts are your interest, the most comprehensive study is *Splendors of Thirty Centuries* (Metropolitan Museum), which was released at the 1990 opening of the blockbuster exhibition of the same name at New York's Metropolitan Museum of Art. For insight into many of the most important archaeological sites of ancient Mexico, you should consult John Pohl's *Exploring Mesoamerica* (Oxford University Press).

For understanding the fascinating and turbulent history of Mexico, *A Brief History of Mexico* (Facts on File), written by Lynn V. Foster (coauthor of *Best Places to Stay in Mexico*) is up-to-date, informative, and eminently readable. The sections of this book on pre-Columbian and colonial Mexico are especially useful. Alan Riding's *Distant Neighbors* (Vintage) is harsh in its judgments about Mexico and a bit out of date, but it is full of details about the country's complex politics, economics, and psychology. Bernal Diaz del Castillo's *The Discovery and Conquest of Mexico 1517–1521* (Da Capo Press) is the well-known account of the conquest written by a conquistador who traveled with Cortés. The very different Aztec view of the conquest can be found in *The Broken Spears* (Beacon Press), edited by Miguel Leon-Portilla. For a literary and philosophical perspective, check out the powerful novels of Carlos Fuentes, or Octavio Paz's epic probe of the Mexican psyche, *Labyrinth of Solitude* (Grove Press).

A growing number of books deal with the remarkable cuisines of Mexico. The best-known authors are Diana Kennedy, who has lived much of her life in Mexico and at an advanced age still travels to remote villages in search of new recipes and ingredients, and Patricia Quintana, a native from the Veracruz area. Kennedy's *Cuisines of Mexico* (Harper and Row) is the classic Mexican cookbook that looks at the distinctly different specialties of Mexico's many regions. Quintana's lushly photographed *Mexico's Feasts of Life* (Council Oak Books) has recipes for traditional dishes to accompany ceremonies marking traditional passages, from a christening feast to meals for the Day of the Dead.

Index

Best Places Report

Authors of the Best Places to Stay series travel extensively in their research to find the best places for all budgets, styles, and interests. However, if we've missed an establishment that you find worthy, please write to us with your suggestion. Detailed information about the service, food, setting, and nearby activities or sights is most important. Finally, let us know how you heard about the place and how long you've been going there.

Send suggestions to:

> The Harvard Common Press
> Best Places to Stay Suggestions
> 535 Albany Street
> Boston, Massachusetts 02118

NAME OF HOTEL_____

TELEPHONE_____

ADDRESS_____

_____ ZIP _____

DESCRIPTION_____

_____

_____

_____

_____

_____

_____

YOUR NAME_____

TELEPHONE_____

ADDRESS_____

_____ ZIP _____

Best Places Report

Authors of the Best Places to Stay series travel extensively in their research to find the best places for all budgets, styles, and interests. However, if we've missed an establishment that you find worthy, please write to us with your suggestion. Detailed information about the service, food, setting, and nearby activities or sights is most important. Finally, let us know how you heard about the place and how long you've been going there.

Send suggestions to:

> The Harvard Common Press
> Best Places to Stay Suggestions
> 535 Albany Street
> Boston, Massachusetts 02118

NAME OF HOTEL_____

TELEPHONE_____

ADDRESS_____

_____ ZIP _____

DESCRIPTION_____

_____

_____

_____

_____

_____

_____

YOUR NAME_____

TELEPHONE_____

ADDRESS_____

_____ ZIP _____

Best Places Report

Authors of the Best Places to Stay series travel extensively in their research to find the best places for all budgets, styles, and interests. However, if we've missed an establishment that you find worthy, please write to us with your suggestion. Detailed information about the service, food, setting, and nearby activities or sights is most important. Finally, let us know how you heard about the place and how long you've been going there.

Send suggestions to:

> The Harvard Common Press
> Best Places to Stay Suggestions
> 535 Albany Street
> Boston, Massachusetts 02118

NAME OF HOTEL _____

TELEPHONE _____

ADDRESS _____

_____ ZIP _____

DESCRIPTION _____

_____

_____

_____

_____

_____

_____

YOUR NAME _____

TELEPHONE _____

ADDRESS _____

_____ ZIP _____